WYOMING RANCH GIRL

A JOURNEY SEEKING RESPECT, SECURITY, AND SOLACE

———

CYNTHIA GALEY PECK

Illustrations by David Kinker

VALLEY PRESS
PUBLISHING

WYOMING RANCH GIRL

A JOURNEY SEEKING RESPECT, SECURITY, AND SOLACE

—•—

CYNTHIA GALEY PECK

Illustrations by David Kinker

Will James drawing commissioned by White Grass Ranch for their brochure.

Wyoming Ranch Girl: A Journey Seeking Respect, Security, and Solace, revised edition

Copyright © 2022, 2024 Cynthia Galey Peck

Valley Press, 2024
Young, Arizona
valleypressaz.com

Printed in the United States of America

Illustrations: David Kinker
Cover design: Beth Ellen Nagle
Typesetting: Matthew P. Hicks

Library of Congress Cataloging-in-Publication Data pending

Wyoming Ranch Girl: A Journey Seeking Respect,
Security, and Solace
    Includes bibliographical references
    ISBN: 979-8-9898295-5-2 (pbk.)
    ISBN: 979-8-9898295-6-9(e-book)
1. Western 2. History 3. Memoir 4. Introspective Memoir 5. Wildlife I. Title

Wyoming Ranch Girl: A Journey Seeking Respect, Security, and Solace,
revised edition

Copyright © 2022, 2024 Cynthia Galey Peck

Valley Press, 2024
Young, Arizona
valleypressaz.com

Printed in the United States of America

Illustrations: David Kinker
Cover design: Beth Ellen Nagle
Typesetting: Matthew P. Hicks

Library of Congress Cataloging-in-Publication Data pending

Wyoming Ranch Girl: A Journey Seeking Respect,
Security, and Solace
    Includes bibliographical references
    ISBN: 979-8-9898295-5-2 (pbk.)
    ISBN: 979-8-9898295-6-9(e-book)
1. Western 2. History 3. Memoir 4. Introspective Memoir 5.
Wildlife I. Title

CONTENTS

FOREWORD

THIS MEMOIR IS AN EXAMPLE OF NOT HAVING TO SUCCUMB TO bitterness or fall prey to anger and resentment when faced with deep emotional pain and less-than-helpful relationships with one's peers or parents. Cindy's stories exemplify moving around, through, and above disappointment to find first some solace, then peace, and then joy, components of the life journey for most humans.

Embedded in the intricacies of a personal journey, this memoir speaks of the three months each year when prominent families came from the East to experience the freedom of western culture while living as dudes in rustic log cabins with few amenities. Where in contrast, Cindy, a ranch child with no sisters or brothers, was sent to boarding school in Salt Lake City starting in sixth grade and then to Massachusetts as a teenager. She struggled to learn Eastern culture with the social skills taught to her mostly by her animal companions. Early married life with two children brought difficulties as her husband gave up a stable job, including family housing, to try to make it as a summer fishing guide. They and their two children lived in a tent at White Grass and cooked over a campfire and in log cabins without plumbing. Winters brought unusual hardships for Cindy on the ranch as a child and in other Western settings as an adult. This memoir also introduces the reader to the lives of Forest Service Wilderness rangers in Montana and Arizona, where Cindy worked, typically alone on horseback, leading a mule loaded with tools and supplies for several days in the backcountry. The last chapter of the book tells the story of Cindy's reuniting with her family of origin when she was in her seventies.

Cynthia Galey Peck was the only child of Frank and Inge Galey. Frank was being discharged from the US Army as a pilot at the conclusion of World War II. He returned to White Grass Ranch to reunite with his mother and assist with the ranch operations. White Grass became Cindy's childhood home, and she readily adapted, as it presented her with many fulfilling learning experiences. Her prominent childhood teachers were the animals on the ranch and in the surrounding mountains. Animals became her companions and consolers when she needed affirmation and support. She believed animals were honest and always told the truth. Her horse, Eva, provided her transportation to travel deep into the mountains, where she believed God must live.

Hopefully, this memoir can be a great teacher about the triumph of the human spirit in unimaginable ways. Cindy had many triumphs in parenting her children into adulthood, leaving one marriage for the support of another that gave her permission to be who she needed to be and returning to school in her fifties as preparation for her lifelong pursuit (i.e., having a career that could support her independently). She found profound affirmation as a woman and a person when her biological siblings, aunts, uncles, and cousins invited her in as family after she wrote letters of inquiry to find possible family matches.

Cindy continues to maintain loving relationships with her two adult children. Tami has a physical disability as a result of a not-her-fault vehicle accident and endured a tragic end to her marriage. She has since carved out a successful career working for the federal government in the West. David fought his way through dyslexia and, as a teenager, endured a tough summer of working for his grandfather and his grandfather's second wife at White Grass Ranch. David is now a successful river guide in the Northwest, a college art teacher, and a successful working artist. His illustrations appear throughout his mother's memoir.

I encourage all to come to know Cynthia Galey Peck in the chapters that follow; you may become wiser, and your personal journey may become richer. My journey certainly has.

So, to Cindy, I say thank you. To the reader, I say ready yourself to find joy, laughter, tears, the thrill of triumph amid heartbreak, and the rewards of being a decent human while listening, as best as one can, guidance from a spirit guide.

Roger Butterbaugh, Ph.D.
Marriage and family therapist, retired Caretaker at White Grass Ranch 2011–2018
Coordinator of the White Grass Heritage Project

For more about Cynthia Galey Peck and the White Grass Ranch, visit *www.whitegrass.org*, Jackson Hole History Museum website. Cynthia's website, *www.wyomingranchgirlcynthiap.com*

PREFACE

I DID NOT THINK MY LIFE WAS INTERESTING AND CERTAINLY NEVER thought of writing about it until talking to friends. Questions came up, "How did you know how to pack a mule?" "How are you comfortable going into the forest by yourself for days?"

Pat and Gordon Sabine were particularly encouraging; both had spent a lifetime in the publishing industry and were amazed at my going alone to Montana for a job, with only a horse and mule, living in the Wilderness for days at a time. "Aren't you afraid?" they asked. "Your life is so interesting; you must write about it. You must journal." I started to write. Pat taught me about using active rather than passing verbs; show, describe rather than tell. Without Pat, I would never have had the courage to write my story.

I feel especially blessed to have lived in spectacular mountains, Jackson Hole, Wyoming against the Teton Mountains. White Grass Ranch was the only home I remember as a child. It is nestled under Buck Mountain. For me, it was a magical spot within an easy horseback ride to sparkling glaciated lakes and wildlife habitat. The ranch, homesteaded by my grandfather starting in 1913, was in a natural sagebrush meadow surrounded by lodgepole pine forest sprinkled with a few Douglas. In 1990, it was listed in the National Register of Historic Places, and in 2005, it became the Western Center for Historic Preservation training facility.

I was honored with the freedom to have friends among the ranch animals - horses, cows, chickens, cats, and dogs.

The horses became my siblings as I had no others. Many Days I explored as far as my horse and I could go and still be back at the barn before four pm when the horses were turned loose. I climbed to the cirque between Static Peak and Buck Mountain, followed Park trails to the lakes, or followed game trails throughout the foothills, watching elk and moose, occasionally coming close to black or grizzly bears. I felt especially at home in the forest with the wild animals, though I always respected their space.

I feel fortunate that I grew up in a state that respected women as they were an essential part of settling it. Wyoming Territory was the first to vote for women's suffrage and appoint and vote women into public office. Jackson, the nearest town to the ranch, was the first to vote in an all-women-town council. Not only were these women in public view, but many were so strong that they held ranches and families together through Wild West times; their example influenced me. I only knew strong women, and I wanted to be one.

Writing has been a trek with many stops and starts, stumbles and falls, as my life also has had many stumbles and falls. I determinedly picked myself up and found a way to continue towards finding life's rewards and joy.

My wish is that my readers find something helpful to their life's journey, in the following pages, to find rewards and joys of their own.

Cynthia Galey Peck

MAPS
Hand drawn by Cynthia

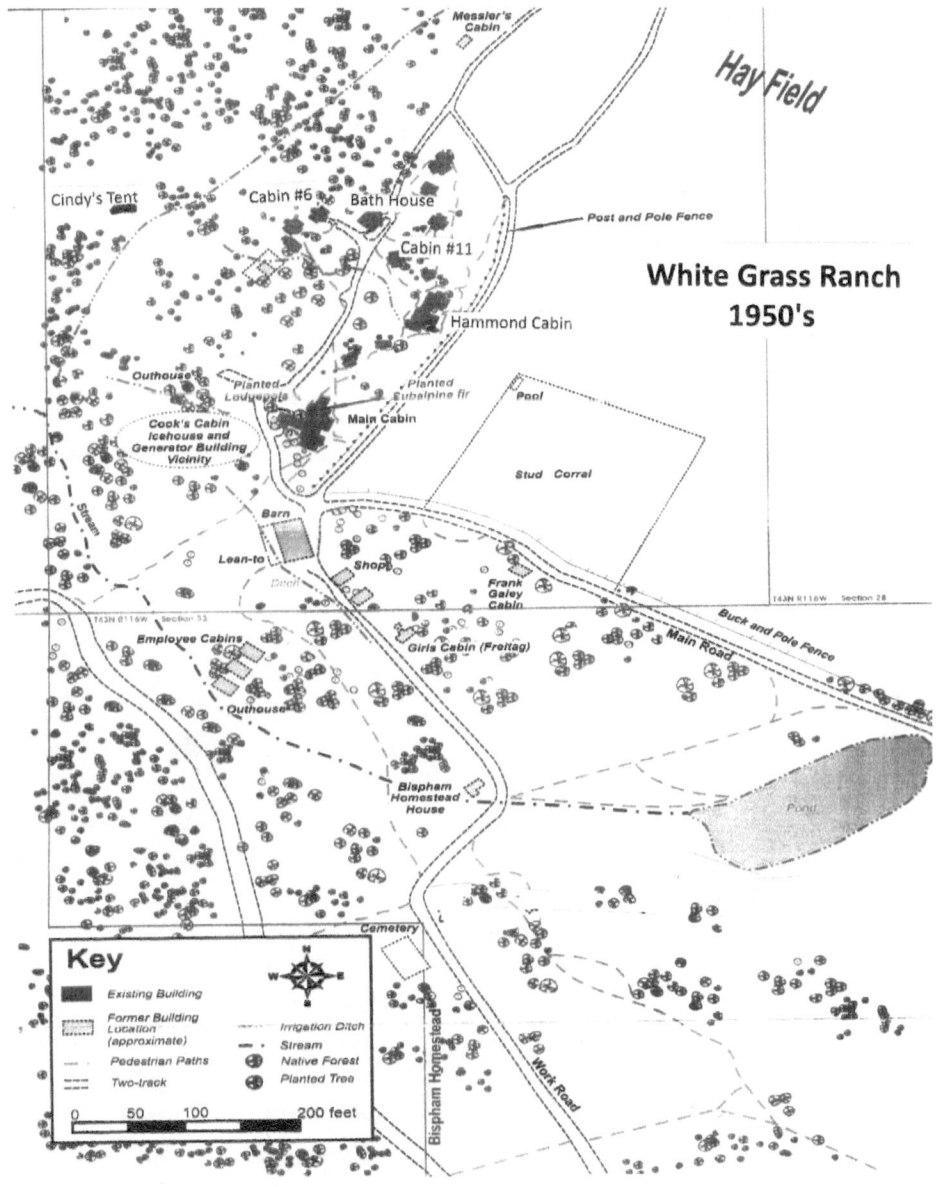

White Grass Ranch, Teton County, Moose, Wyoming

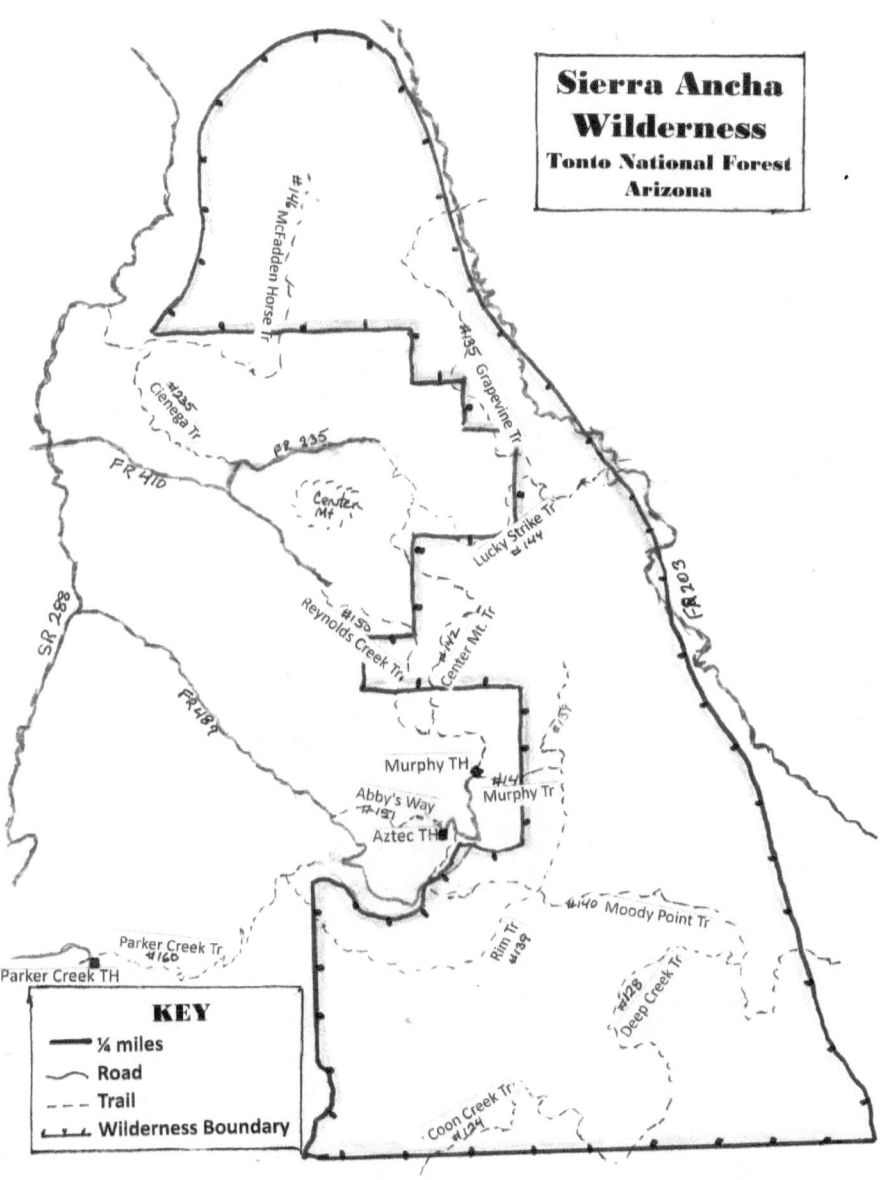

Sierra Ancha Wilderness, Tonto National Forest, Gila County, Arizona

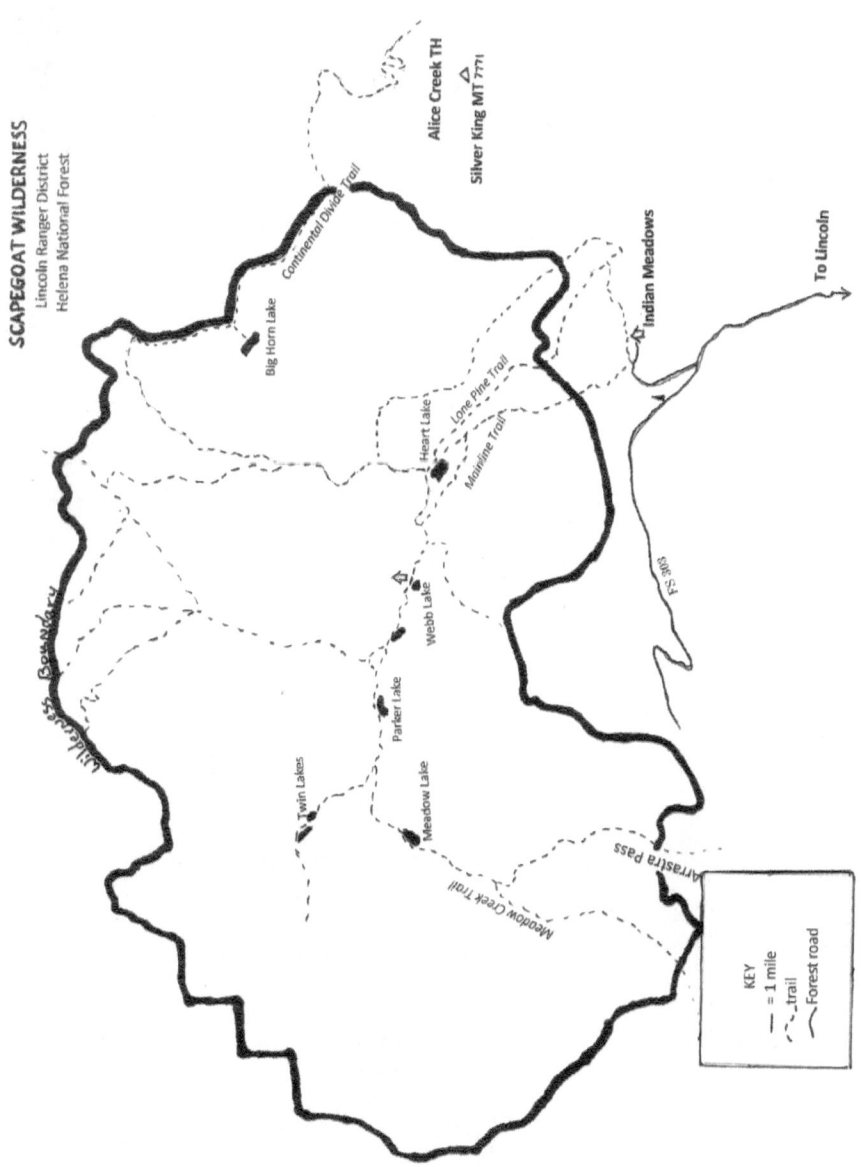

SCAPEGOAT WILDERNESS
Lincoln Ranger District
Helena National Forest

Continental Divide Trail

Big Horn Lake

Alice Creek TH

Silver King MT 7771

Heart Lake

Lone Pine Trail

Mainline Trail

Indian Meadows

To Lincoln

Webb Lake

Parker Lake

F.S. 3905

Wilderness Boundary

Twin Lakes

Meadow Lake

Arrastra Pass

Meadow Creek Trail

KEY
— = 1 mile
trail
Forest road

Scapegoat Wilderness, Lincoln Ranger District, Helena National Forest, Montana.

LIST OF CHARACTERS

CYNTHIA'S FAMILY

Aunt Nati	Renate Keller, Inge's sister, Cynthia's aunt
Bill	William King Peck MD, Cynthia's second husband
David	David Kinker, Cynthia's son, illustrator of this book
Fran	Francis Fox, Cynthia's cousin
Frank Holt Galey	Cynthia's father, White Grass Ranch owner
George	George Clover, White Grass foreman and friend
Harold Hammond	Frank Galey's stepfather and homesteader
Inge	Inge Freitag Galey, Cynthia's mother, Frank's wife
Jim	James Kinker, Cynthia's first husband
Marmie	Marian Chandler Galey Hammond, Frank's mother
Nona	Frank Galey's second wife
Oma & Opa	Wanda & Ottmar Freitag, Inge's parents
Tami	Tamara Densmore, Cynthia's daughter

WYOMING CHARACTERS

Doc McLeod...................... A much-loved, long-time MD in Jackson, skied to patients

George Tucker Bispham ... Co-homesteader of White Grass Ranch w. Harold Hammond

Jack Dennis........................ Jim's rafting partner & Sporting Goods entrepreneur

Jack Crenshaw.................... Jack Crenshaw MD, family friend, Cynthia's obstetrician

Jack Dornan....................... Owner of Dornan's Chuckwagon & Bar at Moose, WY

Judy.................................... Judith Schmitt, co-kid wrangler w. Cynthia & dear friend

Rachel................................. Rachel Trahern, manager with Inge & dear friend

Roger Butterbaugh .... Grand Teton NP's Ranch caretaker, Cynthia's writing mentor

ARIZONA CHARACTERS

Tommy Jones...................... Wilderness Ranger & Friend

Ranger Jordy...................... Forest Service District Ranger

THE LINCOLN DISTRICT, MONTANA CHARACTERS

Charley............................... Recreation Staff Officer, Jerry's supervisor

Jerry................................... Cynthia's supervisor, Lincoln RD, Helena NF

Tim, Keith, Carol, Race .... Scapegoat Wilderness Trail Crew

Will.................................... Will Vigen, mule packer, supporter of Wilderness crews

CHAPTER 1

White Grass Ranch, 1945–1950

IN OCTOBER 1945, AT AGE THREE, MY PARENTS, FRANK AND INGE GALEY, and I arrived at the base of the Teton Mountains, a place of outstanding beauty in Jackson Hole, Wyoming, a place that was frequented by elk, black bears, grizzlies, coyotes, and wolves. The cold weather had already arrived when we came home to Dad's family ranch, White Grass Ranch.

In the log cabin's living room, my playpen was the big pole couch. I stayed on its twin-mattress seat with back-rest cushions in front of the river-rock fireplace which emanated the only heat in the room. The cabin, couch, and fireplace were all built by Grandpa Hammond. Since Mom thought getting cold would make me sick, she would get angry if I was on the freezing floor.

I remember Dad carrying me on his hip, supported by his strong arm, into the dark barn, which was filled with new and interesting odors and animals. He held me up to meet Molly and Queenie, the huge sorrel workhorses. Molly's shiny brown eyes with long black lashes fascinated me. In exploration, I put my finger in one of her eyes. She threw her head and scared me, but Dad told me to speak gently, be calm, and move with slow purpose around the horses. Soon,

I was introduced not only to the horses but to dogs, cows, calves, and barn cats that became my playmates and friends. The four-legged ones became my siblings.

Our second winter on the ranch, we were in the Hammond cabin, a log cabin Grandpa Hammond built for himself and my grandmother, Marmie. Since it was built for year-round living, unlike the dude cabins, it had a kitchen, a living room, and three bedrooms. It also had a large covered porch facing south, overlooking the field, to the edge of the forest and the Gros Ventre mountains in the distance. Our pigs, Porgy and Bess—Dad named them after Gershwin's 1935 opera—enjoyed the food scraps Mom threw out the kitchen window to them. Porgy and Bess were free-roaming and clean, never smelled. They would follow us with the dogs to the barn to feed the stock or to the wood pile to fetch firewood.

From the window, I watched the raucous scrub jays come to fight over the small scraps of food Porgy and Bess left behind.

The spacious living room had another river-stone fireplace, which Grandfather Hammond had also built. Mom and Dad used the

White Grass Ranch barn built in 1913, the hub of the dude's activities.

bedroom next to the living room, which acted as a hallway. I had the corner room, the coldest one, past the bathroom which had ugly pea-soup-green fixtures but had no water during the freezing winter. The room past mine was Grandma Hammond's sitting room, which was shut in winter to conserve heat as Northwest Wyoming winters were bitterly cold. The cabins were made of thick logs, but there was no insulation in the floors or ceilings. All the windows were single panes; they collected a rim of ice on the inside.

On bathing day, Mom would put hot water from the stove into the round galvanized wash tub in front of the fireplace. I was washed first and put to bed. Mom would use the same water. Dad received fresh hot water.

One January, I became extremely sick. The daytime temperatures were below zero. When Dad went outside, he had to wrap a scarf over his nose to prevent his nose hairs from freezing. Mom was afraid to take me by sleigh to see Doc McLeod. So, Dad took the team and sleigh to Moose to call the doctor. Doc McLeod skied the six miles to the ranch. He listened to my chest and gave me a penicillin shot. Doc McLeod often went on house calls, though maybe not often on skis. On another snowy day, Dad decided to make bathtub gin. He had a hot concoction on top of the propane kitchen stove. After a time, it boiled over, causing a kitchen fire. With jet speed, Dad dumped a bucket of water onto the stove. Mom cleaned the mess. That was the last time Dad tried to make gin. I think Mom made the decision.

When the three months of summer arrived, Mom and Dad focused on the clientele that come to the ranch as dudes. Dudes were paying guests who arrived with reservations and were assigned a cabin, served meals, and introduced to the freedoms of Western culture, which was filled with horses, wild animals, and leisurely living. Dudes tended to stay for weeks or sometimes a month and returned year after year. Dad said that dudes paid better and wintered easier than cattle and horses.

Dad was always busy managing cowboys, animals, and maintenance of the buildings while Mom was busy managing reservations, billing, payroll, the cabin and the kitchen staff. She also planned menus with Ellen, the cook, each week and ordered staple supplies. The perishables she would pick up in Jackson. With little time for a child, Mom and Dad hired a nanny to care for me. At the end of the dude season, Nanny went to Mom. She said she could not keep up with the rambunctious towheaded four-year-old anymore and would not be coming back.

Eva, My First True Friend

The following summer, I had a new sitter. She had beautiful, big brown eyes. Her hair shone like gold in the morning sunlight. Eva was a rotund elderly mare who had a flaxen mane and tail. She was chosen because she was calm and reliable. Dad thought if I rode with a saddle, I might tangle my foot in the stirrup and be dragged. Dad lifted me onto Eva's bareback. I do not remember being led.

"Pull the reins against her neck like so," Dad said as he demonstrated from the ground. "Stop her by pulling on the reins. That's right. Now take her in a circle here," he pointed.

I rode Eva in a circle to the left and another to the right. "Good girl," he said.

That was my riding lesson. At age five, I was turned loose to explore what I thought was the expanse of the whole world on Eva. However, my earliest riding was around the 320 ranch acres. I rode to the front gate, to the dump, and back to the barn. Soon I was allowed to go on the dude rides into the mountains.

The following year, I was allowed to explore the trails and woods beyond the ranch fence by myself. Eva always came back to the barn for food. This behavior, called barn sour, served the purpose of bringing me home with her. If she came back alone, Dad knew to start searching, but that never happened. She was my best friend and always treated me the same no matter my mood. I would go to the barn to see her when the wranglers brought the horses in from the mountain each morning. I would stay with her until she was turned loose in the evening to graze. Everywhere I went, I went with Eva: picnicking at Phelps Lake or Taggart Lake, lazing around the ranch, or taking naps on her as she grazed. I draped myself over her back with my legs and arms dangling on each side and my face nestled in her mane. I loved the feel of her solid, warm body and her smell of hay, grass, and horse. I did not fall off while sleeping on her. I would have brought her into the house, but Mom would have thrown a fit. As it was, I tried to stay in the barn to sleep, which was not acceptable either. I spent all my waking hours with Eva. I would brush her, take her swimming, and try to go on every dude ride.

We explored the forest that surrounded the ranch by ourselves. We followed the riding trails toward Moose, climbed the Teton foothills, following game trails. We were often gone all day. I knew the woods were filled with game, elk, deer, moose, bears, coyotes, and sometimes wolves. Dad told me to watch out for them and never to get between a mother and her young was dangerous because mothers were fiercely protective of their young. But the forest made me feel protected by its tall pine trees. I did not need to share my discoveries with anyone. The woods or barn became more my home than the cabin. I was at peace surrounded by the forest.

It was a time when I began spreading my wings and felt confident enough to investigate beyond ranch boundaries. I awoke each morning excited to be on my horse and enjoy the exploration of the mountainside, which satisfied my curiosity. When I saw elk, I would stop and watch, seemingly undetected by them. Like the horses, they communicated with body language and showed no mean-spirited actions; they were peaceful but alert to danger. When they detected danger, they ran, often with the bull protecting the back of the herd. They showed me I did not have to confront mean- spirited people; instead, I could avoid them.

Hammond and Bispham

As I grew older, I learned that the White Grass Ranch had its beginning in 1913 in Jackson Hole, Wyoming, before Grand Teton National Park was established. My grandfather Harold Hammond was a cowboy from Blackfoot, Idaho, and was well versed in ranch life, hunting, and guiding. George Tucker Bispham was a Rhodes scholar from Philadelphia who came as a dude to Bar BC Ranch to visit his friend Struthers Burt. Hammond and Bispham met at Bar BC Ranch, which was a well-known place where intellectuals, writers, and actors vacationed.

As partners, Hammond and Bispham filed adjoining claims of 160 acres each under the Homestead Act, which was designed to encourage people to move west. Many homesteaders failed because of poor soil or lack of water. But Hammond and Bispham chose well. Their claims included a large natural meadow surrounded by lodgepole pine forests located on a bench under Buck Mountain with

Steward Creek nearby and a mountainside spring was even nearer. The land had good soil covered with sagebrush.

The Homestead Act required the claimant to live on the property and prove it up, so over the next several years, the sagebrush was cleared, and ditches were dug to direct water from Steward Creek for irrigation. Fields were planted, harvested, and grazed by cattle. The log barn and cabins were built. In 1923, Hammond and Bispham were awarded ownership. Eventually, Grandfather bought Bispham's acres. Everywhere I looked, I could see the results of their hard labor. The place filled my chest with joy.

Myth says the area was named White Grass by the Indians who came to hunt in Jackson Hole. It was their meeting place and looked white because of the sage-covered opening that was easily spotted from the valley below. A Clovis point was found near the town of Jackson that confirmed early humans had used Jackson Hole even before the Indians.

Hammond and Bispham's initial plan was to establish a cattle ranch. They chose a brand, H quarter-circle B, to mark their cattle and horses. Because of the many friends visiting from the East, the ranch evolved into a dude operation. Hammond and Bispham built additional cabins to accommodate visitors. A central lodge was built with a big kitchen and dining room in which to feed the guests. White Grass became a well-known and respected dude ranch.

White Grass became a widely spaced cluster of rental cabins with the added advantage of all meals at the lodge; optional horseback-riding lessons; rides with a wrangler guide; and a beautiful, peaceful, leisurely western setting included in the base price. Nestled in the trees, there was a good distance between the cabins for privacy, and had wonderful views, often with wildlife grazing in the field. The lodge, called the Main Cabin, exuded Western atmosphere; the sitting room had pine-pole couches covered with hides, pole side tables, and taxidermy heads of elk, deer, and buffalo made by Hammond. The buffalo head hung above the fireplace, which scorched his beard, making him look sad. However, the dudes had an opportunity to see what the native wild animals looked like. The dining room had a large T-shaped table able to seat all the dudes and had miniature Conestoga-wagon lights. Reading books from Bispham's extensive collection in the library was a favorite pastime. Horses were available for half-day rides or all-day picnic rides. The ranch offered an amazing amount of freedom to the dudes and to me. As days passed, I might only see my parents at a distance; however, I think the employees were directed to watch for my safety.

In the early 1930s, the widowed Marian Chandler Galey met Harold Hammond, the dashing cowboy on the Bar BC dude ranch. They were married in 1936 and lived on White Grass. Grandfather Hammond raised silver foxes during World War I. He said the income from the silver foxes helped him keep the ranch. Only three years after they married, Harold died and bequeathed White Grass Ranch to Marion. Marion's son, Frank Galey, left Princeton to come west to help manage the ranch in Hammond's place.

Frank joined the US Army as war was threatening. Marion Hammond, my grandmother, whom I called Marmie, hired Ollie and Twila Van Winkle to manage the ranch in Frank's absence. I knew Ollie and Twila when I was very young. As far as I know, Marmie never spent a winter on the ranch; instead, she returned to her home in Philadelphia.

Shortly after Frank Galey was discharged from the army in the autumn of 1945, he bought the ranch from his mother for $15,000 and took over the $22,000 mortgage, which in part was the remaining

1920's Harold Hammond with the resident antelope herd
in front of the White Grass Ranch Main Cabin.

mortgage from when Hammond had purchased White Grass from Bispham. The buildings were in poor repair, and materials were hard to come by after World War II. Dad did the best he could to prepare for the dude season. He continued to raise horses, chickens, cattle, and pigs, but the primary business was the dude operation. At its closing, in 1985, White Grass Ranch was one of the oldest, continually operated ranches in Wyoming.

Besides the ranch culture of freedom and communion with the great outdoors, Wyoming's culture molded my character. In Wyoming, a person's worth is measured by the individual's actions. It became known as the Suffrage State since the 1869 Territorial Legislature was the first to vote to give women suffrage rights. It was the first state to appoint a female judge. In those early days, the ratio of men to women was six to one. The women were valued because a man was often gone to find employment or herd cattle, leaving a lone woman with children guarding the homestead.

The territory of Wyoming became the forty-fourth state on July 7, 1890. Even though Wyoming was forward- thinking about the rights of women, it was still the Wild West in other aspects. For example, two years after statehood, powerful cattle ranchers invaded northern Johnson County trying to acquire grazing land from small ranches. Wyoming historian T. A. Larson called it "the most notorious event in the history of Wyoming." Even thirteen years after statehood, the incident at Lightning Creek between a sheriff's posse and the Oglala Sioux killed seven people.

In 1920, Jackson voted in an all-woman town council. The first female mayor of Jackson, Grace Miller, said, "The voters of Jackson believe that women are not only entitled to equal suffrage, but are also entitled to equality in management of governmental affairs." In 1925, Wyoming was the first state to vote for a female governor, Nellie Tayloe Ross; this confirmed Mayor Miller's statement.

Wyoming is still one of the largest states, nearly ninety-eight thousand square miles, though one of the smallest in population (in 2019, the population was still under 600,000).

Wyoming men needed to be resourceful and its women needed to be courageous. The copyright insignia of Wyoming, a bucking horse and rider, represents Wyoming residents' rugged, resourceful, and independent spirit. Wyoming's resourceful spirit certainly influenced my life choices

Maybe the myth of the ranch as an Indian meeting place was true. Before I started school, Dad held my five-year-old hand as we walked the newly plowed field to check the irrigation ditches. He dragged canvas dams to new locations along the ditch. With a shovel, Dad would set the dams to flood another area. As the water overflowed, the dogs chased the gophers displaced by the irrigation flood. It was a great game for them, even though they never caught a gopher. One day Dad saw a strange shape in the mud. He dug it out with his strong, calloused hands to show me. It did not look like much, just a longish, rough, rusted object. When we went back to the house, Dad cleaned it, then it was recognizable as a hunting knife with silver inlay in the handle. Dad smiled and said it probably had been traded north from Mexico; maybe an Indian had lost his knife at a summer hunting meet at White Grass. This seemed to confirm the myth of White Grass as a meeting place.

Dad seemed glad when I went with him to irrigate, repair plumbing in the cabins, doctor horses, start the diesel generator, milk cows, or feed the stock. To me, it was a good time of companionship.

During the winters, we stayed in one of the largest dude cabins, but in the summers, we stayed in whichever cabin was not occupied by dude reservations. I was six years old when I went on an all-day ride with a wrangler and several dudes. Afterward, I ran up to the cabin where we were staying, one with only two bedrooms and a bathroom, to tell Mom all about my wonderful day. I busted through the door and faced strangers. I was startled and embarrassed. Where were Mom and Dad? I ran along the central ranch road, screaming for Mom. I was out of breath, hiccupping sobs of fright. I found her in the Main Cabin's kitchen, sitting at the central work table with the cook, Ellen. She put an arm around my shoulders; her perfume and cigarette smoke drifted around her.

She said, "New dudes needed that cabin, so I moved us to cabin number eleven." Cabin number eleven was also a small cabin. As the sweet smell of spices and Ellen's cooking surrounded me, I calmed down.

As soon as Mom saw Dad, she said, "Frank, we must have our own house. Cindy was hysterical. This child does not know where her home is."

Shortly after, Dad went into the woods and marked the large lodgepole pines he would need for the house. Chainsaws sang in the forest, and trees crashed in the precise direction the cuts dictated. Horses puffed, shod hooves dug into the ground for purchase, and logging chains creaked tightly on logs which were skidded to a pile east of the barn near the ranch driveway. The foundation for the new house was laid with round river rock and cement. Two men lifted logs onto sawhorses. Drawknives skidded across them to remove the bark, which had to be done before they were used. In my shorts, I sat astride a log. I would pull a drawknife under the bark toward me. It was a sticky job; the sap made big blisters on my hands. I would be stuck to the logs by the sap on my pants and legs but I was proud to be helping to build our house.

The first few courses were placed by two men lifting the logs. Axes rang as the round notches were cut for the corners. As the walls grew taller, skid logs were leaned against the lower courses. Harnessed with a double-tree block and tackle, amid much shouting, the horses pulled the next log into place. The men, with axes in hand, tightrope-walked along the log wall, chopping a notch to fit the log underneath. When the notch was correct, the log was rolled into place. Skid logs and harnessed horses moved around to the next wall, and the process began again.

By the winter of 1949, we moved into the new Galey house. We had a kitchen, a living room, two bedrooms, and an office—a real home. I had a corner room with an outside door. I had Mom's special childhood bed from Germany, rather than one of the common pole beds that were in the cabins. I could have possessions, keep them in one place, and enjoy them. I knew where my room was, and it would stay there for me.

Mom and Dad kept an open house for dudes and help, which meant everyone was welcome to always wander through the house, but the bedrooms were supposed to be a private area. Dude children also were welcome, but they sometimes came into my room. I had collected butterflies and other bugs and carefully mounted them in shadow boxes, but a dude child crunched them into powder and damaged my one doll. I did not understand; when I visited other homes, I would not dream of touching their things. I stopped collecting anything, because I did not want the hurt that followed the damage. I liked having my room, but the barn continued to be my rock; it had been solid, unmoving, and unchanging since Dad first introduced me to Molly and Queenie.

Winter, A Time of Solitude

In winter, we had no electricity or running water. We kept our food in an icebox which was cooled by ice that was collected from a nearby ranch's pond in early winter. Our meat, usually elk, was hung in quarters on the back porch, where it would stay frozen. Dad would use an ax or saw to cut a piece for dinner. Much cut-to-length and split firewood was stored on the porch also. Each day, Dad would chop wood. It was my job to carry armloads to the porch or into the house. Before I was school-age, Dad taught me to chop kindling with his big pole axe to start the fire. We used a bucket full of water to flush the toilet once a day. When I helped, I felt like a big girl.

Since we had no electricity, candles, kerosene, or white- gas lanterns provided our light. They also were a fire hazard, as Mom and Dad constantly reminded me. But during the first winter in our own house, I almost burned the cabin to the ground. Mom sent me with a candle into the linen closet to bring her a towel. I thought I was careful to keep the flame away from the shelves. Upon returning to the kitchen, I gave the towel to Mom. Dad smelled smoke. He sent me to fetch the hired hand. Frightened, I ran slipper-footed through the crusted snow, calling for help from the one ranch hand who wintered on the ranch. Dad extinguished the fire. Thankfully, only a few linens were damaged. The incident taught me to respect fire.

In the evenings, Dad would often read stories to me of mountain men, such as John Colter, Jim Bridger, and Hugh Glass rather than stories of Cinderella. Western history showed me that one can withstand unbelievable hardships. And maybe I could be strong enough too.

When Mom put me to bed, she would fill a red rubber bag with a tight stopper, called an enema bottle, full of hot water. She would put it in my bed for warmth. By morning, I would have kicked the frozen-solid bag beyond my feet. I often awoke in the night feeling as if a moose were sitting on my chest because of the many heavy blankets. When I lay awake, I could hear avalanches roaring down the mountain right above us scaring me. None ever came to the ranch, but they sounded close. I would hear coyotes howl, inviting our dogs to play. Sometimes I heard a wolf howl. During the coldest temperatures, the logs contracted, causing a pop like a rifle shot. Even though I learned what the sounds were, I awoke with a start, causing me to burrow deeper under the blankets and cover my head for safety.

Dad was usually up first in the early morning dark, lighting the wood stoves as fast as he could. He then would jump back into bed until the room was warmed. When I heard Mom and Dad in the kitchen, I would crawl out of my warm cocoon, grab my clothes, and run barefoot on freezing floors to the warmth of the kitchen fire, where I would dress. As Mom started breakfast, it was chore time for Dad.

"Come on, pumpkin," Dad would call, and I'd go with him to the barn for morning chores. By the time we were living in our house, I was helping Dad regularly with the chores. Dudy and Little Man, our dogs, would scamper up the snow-packed canyon of a trail. Dad followed with a galvanized pail of hot water and a lantern. I trailed along behind, hampered by bulky snow pants, oversized boots, and a jacket. Mom attached my mittens together with a string threaded through each sleeve so I could not lose them. I watched Dad walk with the swinging lantern. It threw long shadows that raced across the snow one way, stopped, and raced back again, making Dad a giant and then a miniature of himself. The swinging shadow reminded me of a Robert Louis Stevenson poem that Mom read to me:

I Have a Little Shadow

I have a little shadow that runs in and out with me. What can be the use of him is more than I can see. He is very, very like me from the heels up to the head;

And I see him jump before me, when I jump into my bed.

The funniest thing about him is the way he likes to grow, Not at all like proper children, which is always very slow; For he sometimes shoots up taller like an India- rubber ball,

And sometimes gets so little that there's none of him at all.

He hasn't got a notion of how children ought to play, And can only make a fool of me in every sort of way. He stays so close to beside me, he's a coward you can see; I'd think it's a shame to stick to nursing as that shadow sticks to me!

One morning, very early, before the sun was up,

I rose and found the shining dew on every buttercup; But my lazy little shadow, like an arrant sleepy-head, Had stayed at home behind me and was fast asleep in bed.

Dad's first task at the barn was to toss hay from the outside stack onto the untracked snow, which caused the stock to reach and pack a larger area. Next, we would go into the barn to feed the teams and milk the cows.

The barn in winter was warm from the animals that spent the night inside. I liked the musty horse and cow smells and the acrid smell from the accumulation of manure. My job was to climb the ladder into the loft and throw hay into the mangers below. After using some hot water to clean her teats, Dad would milk Toby, a temperamental black cow who hated me. In summer, she would run all the way across the field and shake her wicked black horns at me. I was too frightened to stay around to see if she would really gore me; I would run and jump through the fence for protection. I milked Peewee; she was mild-mannered, and I liked her. The cats gathered expectantly for Dad to squirt milk from the cow's teat into their open mouths. They would have splashes of milk all over their faces; after, they wiped the milk away and licked their paws with a look of contentment. Dad would help me get Peewee milked dry. I did not have the patience to strip her enough to suit Dad. We rubbed Bag Balm on their teats and turned them out for the day to feed with the other stock.

In the chicken coop, Dad used the rest of the hot water to clean out the frozen mess in the chicken water container and filled it with fresh hot water. I would collect the eggs and scatter wheat. Often, I would take a mouthful of wheat. It was fun to chew it into a tasteless gum.

The chickens were important, not only for our food but also because we sold eggs. It was difficult to take the delicate eggs to town by team and sleigh. To prevent breakage, Mom cleaned the eggs and set them carefully in special boxes. She would put wood shavings on the bottom, put down a layer of eggs, and then repeat, adding more shavings and layers of eggs until the box was filled. Then eggs were safe to take in the sleigh to sell them.

As Dad and I returned to the house, the dogs would scamper ahead. We followed with the basket of eggs and steaming milk. Breakfast would be served: bacon from our summer pigs, eggs from our chickens and Mom's buttered fresh baked bread. The butter we churned in a big glass jar with a wooden paddle. I often had the job of churning it. Once, we had a clear plastic bag of mushy white stuff with a yellow- colored pill in it, called Oleo. I squished the bag until the color was even throughout the substance. I do not know why we were trying Oleo, when we had our own butter. Maybe Mom wanted to know what the new stuff was like. I hated it. Often, Mom set some milk in a warm place to make cottage cheese.

While we sat around the kitchen table, enjoying breakfast with the hissing Coleman lantern, Dad would turn on the battery-operated radio. Even though we were isolated, Dad kept up with world news. After breakfast, we would be back in the barn with more hot water.

I would help shovel manure from the milk cows' stanchions and the horse stalls. Dad would choose one of the teams from their night stalls for the day's work. The other team was put outside with the milk cows. Dad would dip the bridle bits in hot water. He told me he did so to prevent the horses' tongues from freezing on the bits. I doubted him, so I tried it: I put my tongue on the buck rake's metal handle. Sure enough, my tongue froze onto it. When I jerked it loose, tongue flesh stayed behind, leaving a fuzzy white coating on the machine. My tongue hurt for weeks, but I would not let Dad have a chance to say, "I told you so." I did not want him to know how stupid I had been.

Other winter chores included chopping wood for heat. Dad also had to shovel snow. The weight of the snow could collapse the cabin roofs. Dad also shoveled snow away from our windows so light could come inside. Snow covered the cabins, making them a row of hillocks along the edge of the field.

I liked to ski off the cabin roofs as if they were real ski slopes. Sometimes I would ski across the field. The six- foot buck fences were snow-covered; there were no obstructions in the expanse of white. When there was a crust on the snow, I could walk on top, but Mom and Dad would break through. I thought it was great fun that I could go easily where they could not.

Playing outside with the dogs, I dug snow tunnels and made a room at the back, where the dogs came to join me. I pretended we were an Eskimo family. I would bring treats for the dogs and myself into the tunnel, and we would eat together. I would take short naps in the igloo with the dogs lying against me for warmth. The temperature inside was about freezing but felt warm compared to the below-zero temperature outside.

In summer, the water supply was gravity-fed from the spring about half a mile into the foothills. But the spring froze between Thanksgiving and Christmas. The pipes remained frozen until late May, which meant we were without running water for half the year. After freeze-up, we collected our water from the lively ditch by the barn. Each morning, Dad used an axe to chop through the ice to free water for us and the stock. Dad hooked the team to the sleigh which had a fifty-gallon barrel on it, using a bucket he filled the barrel from the ditch. When the barrel was full, he drove the team to the house. The water would slosh and freeze on the sleigh floor, making the footing treacherous. Dad transferred the water to another fifty-gallon container in the kitchen. When Mom needed it, she would dip a metal bucket into the barrel and heat the bucket of water on the stove.

At evening chore time, Dad would walk ahead of me with the lantern swinging with his gait, again throwing long shadows and short shadows. We would herd the milk cows and team into the barn, throw hay to the outside stock, and throw hay down from the loft into the stanchions and mangers. Then we would milk again. The cats waited in anticipation. The flickering lantern light made the night milking

1945 Inge & Cynthia going to get the mail at Moose.
Snip and Bess pulling the sleigh.

feel intimate. The deep shadows contrasted with the soft highlights on the animals' bodies and the smooth logs walls. I loved to listen to the soft snuffling sounds the horses made as they pushed their hay around the manger and the sloppy crunching of the cows as they ate. I even liked the familiar smell of the stock mixed with the fresh milk splattering into the bucket. I liked the warm feel of the cow as I laid my head against her flank. When milking was done, we would go to the chicken coop. We brought the chickens fresh warm water, threw some wheat, and collected the eggs. With the chores done for the night, I would carry the lantern as we headed home, while Dad carried the milk and eggs.

A typical winter evening found us gathered at the kitchen table in the circle of flickering light from the white- gas lantern. Mom would sit with her knitting. She kept us in knitted wool socks and mittens. She said Dad and I could wear out socks faster than she could knit them. Dad would read with his aromatic pipe loosely hanging from the corner of his mouth.

Dad loved to read, as he had a reverence for the written word. Sometimes he would read aloud to me. Dudy and Little Man would stretch on the floor near the fire, happily twitching in their dreams. Another day devoted to staying alive in winter on an isolated Wyoming ranch would draw to a close.

Inge and Cynthia in the covered sleigh, which slid off the snow packed track.

1947, Cynthia fishing at Jackson Lake with Mt Moran in the background.

Every few weeks we needed to go for the mail in Moose. Dad would harness the team, and we would bundle up in our warmest clothes and put our feet and legs into sleeping bags for the trip. When the depth of the snow closed the road, Dad would ski to Moose. Sometimes he pulled the toboggan to bring supplies home. Once, he made a covered sleigh like a miniature Conestoga wagon or sheepherder's wagon, with a bench and a wood stove inside to keep us warm. On one trip to Moose, the covered sleigh slipped off the packed track and tipped over with Mom and me inside. Dad had to unhook the team and pull the sleigh backward onto the track. He then hitched the team to the front again, and we continued. At other times, we would use a flatbed sleigh, which was more stable, and we would bundle up in blankets and down sleeping bags for warmth during the trip to Moose.

During snowstorms, Dad would hitch the team to the flatbed sleigh. He attached a heavy logging chain between the runners, and the chain would drag and pack the center of the road. Dad would drive our road to the Moose Wilson Road and back to the barn for hours and sometimes into the night to keep the road open. Between Thanksgiving and Christmas, Mother Nature would win, and we would be snowed in until late May.

During Christmas Time on the ranch, before I started school, I would ski into the woods with Dad carrying an ax on his shoulder, to cut down a tree. We would drag it home where Mom would decorate it with real candles, oranges, apples, homemade ornaments, and German marzipan candies. Marzipan candies were a tradition in our family, as Oma and Opa, Mom's parents, sent them to us from Germany. Each of us received one gift, which we opened late on Christmas Eve, the only time the candles were lit. In the morning, Santa Claus would have filled my Christmas stocking—one of Dad's heavy wool stockings—with nuts, fruit, and maybe a special gift. When I was six, my first watch came in a Christmas stocking. I think they gave it to me so I would be home from exploring by four o'clock, which was my time boundary. Sadly, the watch did not last long; I took it apart to see how it worked and could not put it together again. Mom and Dad were disappointed in me. Another Christmas I got a ring with my birthstone; I still have it and treasure it.

It was common for Dad to be away on errands or business, leaving Mom and me at home. One time, Dad had gone to a neighboring ranch with the sleigh to cut ice for the icehouse. Mom and I were alone on the ranch. Mom needed supplies we had stored in the Main Cabin. She settled me for a nap and snowshoed to the Main Cabin with Little Man and Dudy at her heels. After taking her snowshoes off, she pushed them upright in the snow where they would be within easy reach on her return. She sat and slid through the small opening between the eaves and the drifted snow onto the cabin porch. She opened the door and entered the frigid cabin. She weaved her way around stacked and covered furniture and through the eerie, dark cold to the storeroom. With the aid of a flashlight, she retrieved the needed supplies and put them in an old pillowcase for easy carrying. As she returned, she was glad to see the stream of sunlight that shone under the porch eave.

She tried to climb up the snowbank but kept sliding in the loose snow. If she did not get out soon, she realized, she would freeze to death. She was also worried, unable to return to her child left alone. She had to think of a way out. She called her faithful companions, Little Man and Dudy. They stuck their heads under the eave, where Mom grabbed the scruffs of their necks. In fear, they pulled back as hard as they could, hauling Mom up the snowbank with the supplies.

1950's The Galey house in winter

Spring

In May, dog bones, pieces of wood, and escaped trash appeared as the snow melted. Even lost tools came into view, though the ground was mostly covered with snow and ice. Lavender spring beauties and yellow dogtooth lilies poked their heads through the edge of the snow. Early green leaves peeked through wet-packed pine needles. One afternoon, Dad and I could not find Toby, the milk cow, which was unusual. We were still feeding hay from the dwindling stack near the barn and expected her to come to eat. Dad and I spread out, sloshing through meltwater, mud, and snow, looking for Toby. Dad found her and called me. She was downed by bloat on the low porch of Bachelor Quarters.

Cows have multiple stomachs and cannot burp when they get gas, as humans do. The gas stays in the stomach, which expands and puts pressure on the heart, killing them. We had to act fast. As an eight-year-old, I thought I could run fast. When Dad asked, I ran to the barn to get the bloat tool: a sharp instrument with a hollow tube about half an inch in diameter and a sharp point. When I returned, Dad felt for the right spot to stab Toby. With a determined, quick thrust, he punctured through the hide into the correct stomach, and foul-smelling air swooshed out through the hollow tube. It was scary to watch him stab Toby, but I kept my mouth closed. Dad knew what he was doing. After no more air escaped, Dad removed the tool. He said the small wound would heal itself quickly. With our encouragement, Toby rose. She headed to the barn for food. How quickly animals recover from near death.

It was time to open the ranch road to the Moose-Wilson Road. Dad used the yellow Caterpillar, with its noisy tracks and big blade, to push snow off our road. It would be the first time that year to take the truck to Moose. However, he had difficulty in starting the truck. He opened the hood and fiddled, but the old green pickup would not start. Finally, he built a campfire under the engine to warm the block. He came into the house for a cup of coffee and a cigarette while the block warmed. The truck finally started. Even though he had pushed the snow off the road, there were humps and clumps of uneven snow. We were jostled and finally bumped over the plowed berm of Moose Wilson Road. It was a springtime milestone to drive instead of ski the six miles to Moose.

In May, the woods were still boggy from the snowmelt. There was snow on the north side of the barn, where we discovered Bess, the workhorse, had birthed her foal in an ice puddle. The little one was floundering, trying to stand. I haltered and led the anxious Bess, who had the placenta and sack still hanging from her hind end, into the barn. Dad lifted the foal out of the ice puddle and carried him into the barn. While Dad settled Bess in a box stall with her foal, I ran to the house for towels to dry the newborn. I had the job of rubbing him until he stopped shivering.

We named him Best. The colt could easily have died of exposure if Dad had not found him. Instead, he grew to be a fine horse. He was a black gelding with one white foot and lots of personality. As an adult he could jump any fence or cattle guard and go wherever he pleased. He often was near the Main Cabin, happily eating the sweet, tender lawn or sampling the flowers from the garden. When I opened the gate and yelled at him, he would trot back to the barn with his head held high. Many times, we would see his tracks in the soft, wet lawn and piles of manure, and he would eye us from the pasture with a laughing expression on his face. Obviously, he had jumped in for a snack and jumped back out to join his friends in the field.

Summers

The employees arrived by the end of May and into the beginning of June to prepare the cabins and barn for the summer season. Dad turned the water system on and repaired the inevitable leaks where the pipes had frozen and broken. Mom and the girls, and I hosed down the inside of the cabins. We wiped the logs dry, oiled them, cleaned the beds and dressers, and wiped them with furniture oil. Finally, we hung the crisp pressed curtains, made the beds, and placed the dresser scarves. In the barn, the guys had saddles and bridles to repair and oil, the barn to clean, and corral fences to repair.

Another early summer task was branding. I would watch the wranglers bring the cows and calves into the big corral and light a small hot fire. One would rope a calf, and drag the bawling animal close to the fire. My eyes stung amid air filled with smoke and dust. With hollers, curses, and bellowing cattle, one wrangler kneed the calf's head down while another held the back legs still for George, our Forman, to use his sharp knife to slit the calf's sack and squeeze the testicles out before slicing them off. Meanwhile, another wrangler would take the branding iron from the fire and burn H-B the calf's left rear. With the calf released, it would run kicking up dust with its hooves to its mother. Young horses that needed castration and branding got the same treatment. The wounds leaked for a day and healed without further treatment. I thought it cruel, but Dad said it was necessary and I should not concern myself with cowboy ways. So, when I saw other cruel behavior against the animals, I did not tell Dad. I felt he would only reprimand me for interfering with ranch work.

The ranch employees were mostly college-age, from eastern families, and former dudes who came to accept the rough raw ranch activities. They enjoyed time off playing pranks on one another, going to town on weekend dates, and occasionally taking a moonlight ride to Phelps Lake. They often went to the Saturday night rodeo in Wilson. Even though I had many of the same jobs, I was not included. I was not considered an employee. Even though I had had schooling like theirs, having attended girls' boarding schools from sixth grade, the dude youths did not accept me. I was awkward with no experience

The Hammond cabin in summer. Frank Galey is standing next to the horse, Inge sitting on the step with her cowboy hat.

Marian Hammond's sitting room inside the Hammond cabin.

with forming relationships or dating. Sometimes I thought I had made friends with dude youths but they left after a few weeks stay and when they came back another year, they were different, or maybe I was. At best, they were short-term friends. I knew I was thin with small breasts. Once I studied myself in a mirror trying to see some characteristics that turned people off. I saw that I had sandy blond ear-lobe length hair, and blue eyes too big for my face, but nothing grotesque. Oh well, my real friends continued to be the four leggeds who did not change personalities with the seasons. They had no hidden agenda, did not lie, and acted true to their character.

Dude season started at the end of June, but only a few dudes arrived that early. Usually, reservations were made starting in July. The Fourth of July was our first barbecue for the dudes, and Dad invited other friends to join us. It was always a great occasion. By July fourth, the ranch cabins were nearly all occupied. For fireworks, Dad would put a stick of dynamite in a garbage can and explode it for celebration. Frequently, we would get a smattering of snow, which excited the dudes.

Dudes who arrived by train were met by one of our wranglers at the Union Pacific station in Rock Springs. By the time the dudes arrived at White Grass, it would be dark. They could not see the shining mountains. But no matter how late it was, Dad would go to their cabin to greet them. They awoke to the Tetons, the expansive views of the Gros Ventre Mountains, and the surrounding forest. Many arrived with pale, pasty faces tight with tension. They tended to be gruff with their children and the hired help but after several days, they began to relax. Tension and the pasty complexions left, replaced by tanned faces and better attitudes. Their experiences at the ranch often shaped life-long values, influenced career choices, and helped determine the location of their residences and whom they married. Since the dudes came from cities that caused their anxiety, I wondered what cities did to people, perhaps cities had evil spirits. I saw the peaceful time at White Grass erase their anxiety and let them be their true selves.

Having our own house should have meant we had the same place to sleep and keep my treasures; however, if dudes arrived before their reservation date and no cabin was available, we moved to a tent under the nearby cottonwood trees for a night or two. The dudes would use our house. It did not happen often, but we moved into the tent about once per dude season. I thought it was a fine adventure to sleep in the tent next to Mom and Dad.

1945, Frank and Inge Galey as new owners and operators of White Grass Ranch.

Near Death Canyon Trailhead, only a mile from the ranch, a family lived in a tepee tent during the summer. Our tent was not a tepee but a wall tent about eight feet by ten feet in size. The family by the trailhead wanted to live like Indians. When I rode Eva to the trailhead, they would invite me in. Their canvas tepee was draped on a pyramid of lodgepoles. Inside was a half wall of canvas, the bottom of which was secured tight against the earthen floor, while the upper side was tied to the inside of the lodgepoles, creating an opening between for ventilation. Their beds were on the ground, delineated by logs along the walls, with fur hides and wool blankets for bedding. Their supplies and clothing were neatly kept in parfleches (rawhide boxes) placed between the beds. In the middle of the tepee was the fire circle. The smoke rose through the opening at the top of the tepee. The fire kept them warm and was used for cooking. It was a cozy and efficient home. By contrast, our tent was meant for short-term living, with no fire pit or protection of an inside half wall. We had folding cots with wool blankets, not on-the-ground beds with furs.

Summers on the ranch were like a beehive; people were everywhere. Dudes were constantly going to the barn for a ride or coming back from one. Dad and Mom often rode with the dudes. The barn buzzed with laughter and cheerful voices. The wranglers are busy with horses or mending tack. The Main Cabin housed a fine literature collection some of which had been Bispham's. Dudes sat on the porch, reading, or talking. The kitchen was filled with warm, delicious odors. Cabin girls wandered from cabin to cabin, cleaning.

The barn was the cornerstone where the guests, employees, and owners connected. The barn had a life of its own; it breathed cool air through the alleyway with dusty animal and acrid manure odors. From its tack room, with its oily counter, came heavy odors of leather and horse liniment. The barn felt safe, guarded by the animals; Dad kept sixty to eighty horses. I liked to sit on the barn's log ramp, leaning against the huge, rough doors, enjoying the sun, and listening to the horse's thump on the adzed log floor or their shuffle in the pole corrals.

The center alleyway was wide enough that a team with a wagon, or a pickup truck could drive through to unload. The grain was put in the inoperable freezer to protect it from mice. Sometimes mice would still get into the freezer if the lid was accidentally left open. I once found a mouse nest there. I removed it to find baby mice with their eyes still closed. I found them interesting and took them to show Mom. To say the least, she was not thrilled.

Saddle racks were secured to the south wall; bridles neatly hung from the pummels and saddle pads were laid on top upside down so they dried. I loved the cats, whose job was to decimate the mouse population but scampered to safety when the cows or horses stomped into the barn.

I thought summers were ideal; all the horses were home, wrangling occurred at sunrise, and I went on horseback rides with dudes. Many dudes experienced horse therapy. I observed pale, nervous people on arrival become tanned, outgoing ones after a few days on horseback. By age seven, I was exploring Buck Mountain and Static Peak foothills, following game trails bareback on my horse. The deer and elk made the best trails across steep drainages to access the grass-covered open areas good for their feasting.

I explored the mountainsides, where sometimes I would let my horse graze as I sat against a tree trunk watching the elk or lay on my stomach to watch ants carry leaves bigger than themselves. They held the leaves over their bodies with some of their legs while their

A White Grass Ranch overnight pack trip near Mt Hunt in the Tetons.

1950's, Frank and Inge packing a mule.

other legs propelled them forward. They marched in single file and dove down into holes in rotten logs or into the ground. I found their activity fascinating.

Sometimes I would walk, leading my horse, so I could examine the variety of plants and flowers. There was an enormous variety of sizes, colors, and forms scattered throughout the mountain meadows. Shadows striped the trail, wind whispered in the trees like Earth was breathing, and all around smelled of fresh damp soil and sweet pine tree sap.

One spring day, an unfamiliar car drove to the barn. Three people got it. "We are looking for lady's slipper orchids," one said.

"What are lady's slipper orchids?" the wrangler asked them.

"They are small purple-and-white ground-growing orchids. They are rare but may be in this area."

"Haven't seen any," the wrangler said.

"I think I have. There are some not far up the trail," I tentatively interrupted as I approached.

I guided them to where I had been watching ants destroy a rotting log. I had seen the flowers they were describing nearby. They looked happy and took many pictures. I was proud I could show the visitors something I knew from my explorations that the wrangler did not, and I learned the name of the interesting-looking flowers.

In the mornings, when I was not wrangling, I went to the Main Cabin, where Ellen would be preparing breakfast for the help, and I would eat with them. Mom and Dad awakened later and ate with the dudes. I would do whatever task I had been assigned. At age five, I picked up cigarette butts that dudes tossed off the porch during their morning coffee. By eight, I washed cocktail glasses filled with butts soaked in the alcohol dregs and ashtrays left over from the previous evening; I gagged over the sink from the stale, foul odors. As a preteen, my assigned job was to clean the Main Cabin before the dudes arrived for breakfast. After completing my tasks, I was at the barn and on a horse, ready to ride.

Since the horses were let out of the corral to wander the mountainside during the night, they needed to be collected—wrangled—in the morning. I especially liked wrangling to find the horses first thing in the morning. In fear of being left behind by the wranglers, I would get up in the dark and go to the barn. I would make myself a nest out of saddle blankets and canvas manti tarps—special-sized tarps for packing—and wait for the wranglers to arrive. Usually, the foreman, George Clover, would stomp into the barn for his horse, which would awaken me.

George was an opposing figure who stood more than six feet tall, had well-muscled arms, a stern countenance, and talked gruffly. George was an Idaho farm boy, who had served in the navy, so he knew horses. Early mornings, he would saddle up, ride out to the pasture, and bring in the other five to ten horses who were kept close for wrangling. I would put the saddle pads and manti away. Soon the other cowboys would arrive to choose their horses from the ones George had brought in and saddle up. I would quickly catch mine and saddle for myself. There were no fences between the ranch and the farms on the west side of the Tetons in Idaho. Grand Teton National Park had no fences around us. Only the Rockefellers' JY Ranch on the south side of Phelps Lake had their acres fenced, but the horses could go past their property, which made it extra hard for us to find them.

Wrangling horses from the pasture. Main Cabin in the background.

George would assign the various areas where we were to go in search of the horses. Areas included the sides of Buck Mountain and Static Peak, the Big Meadow, Phelps Lake moraine, and Wister Draw, east along the lodgepole pine benches and north to the marshes near Trail End Ranch and the avalanche area. I would go alone to the area assigned to me. I was sure none of the wranglers wanted to babysit the boss's daughter. Regardless, by ten, I knew how to herd the horses in by myself. I hated going into the marshes. I was afraid the horse would sink belly-deep in mud and be unable to get out. I was fearful of Wister Draw. It had tall dense trees with thick branches creating an ominous darkness, I thought, maybe vampires lived there.

Hunting horses could take most of the day. Horses, like people, have friends who stick together, and there is a leader in each group. For instance, a big black horse, Koon, liked to go with his herd to Phelps Lake. Sunny Boy liked Wister Draw, and Arapaho liked the Big Meadow under Static Peak. Rarely did they go over the mountains to Idaho but necessitated driving around and bringing the group back by trailer. Occasionally, a group of perhaps fifteen horses would go north to the Grand Teton National Park's Beaver Creek residence area, about a three-hour ride from the ranch, where, in front of the two-story gabled log houses were juicy green lawns. Someone from the Park would call immediately for us to remove the horses. The grazing permit for White Grass Ranch did not include the Grand Teton National Park Superintendent's lawn!

Ellen was gracious about fixing late breakfasts after we came from herding horses to the corral. After breakfast, we would saddle horses for the dudes. Each of us working in the barn would catch one horse at a time, lead him into the barn, brush him, and choose a saddle and saddle pad to fit the specific rider. The saddle was swung on top of the pad, and the cinch was secured. We would place the bit into the horse's mouth, adjust the neck strap, and lead the horse outside to the hitching rail. There usually were forty or more horses to saddle.

The horses had to be available for dude rides by nine o'clock in the morning. If any dudes wanted to go for longer rides, they could sign up at dinner time and have a sack lunch prepared for them the next morning by nine. Wranglers were available as guides, but often, dudes, especially the many who returned year after year, would go out by themselves. One returning dude, Sukie, sometimes acted as a hostess and she loved to fish, another was Curt who played the guitar and sang cowboy songs around the fire at the Sunday barbecues. Employees and dudes alike often formed lifelong friends and relationships during their time on the ranch.

People who knew White Grass agreed it had a quality like gravity. It could not be seen, but it drew a person back again and again.

Using a team and wagon to bring in the hay to store in the barn for the winter.

Even during the historic reconstruction (2006-2016) of the cabins, this quality attracted the workers. One said he could not know what Hammond had thought as he built the cabins, but he could see why they had been built in their locations. Each cabin faced east to the rising sun and had a wonderful view. There was ample spacing between cabins allowing privacy.

The ride to Phelps Lake was everyone's favorite. On the way, we would pass the huge, speckled gray granite boulders that had been strewn ahead of an ancient glacier. Marmots lived in the caves formed by the tumbled rocks. I often saw marmots sitting on the rounded granite tops, their sunning patios. The marmots whistled a chorus of warning of intruders to their friends. The whistle seemed to squeeze from the rear and finish with a pursed mouth and a flick of the tail. Their fluffy gray-red coats made a beautiful contrast against the dark granite. When we reached the top of the moraine, we would stop at the overlook. Below, the lake shone cobalt blue, and snow-browed Prospector Peak rose from its western shore. Arriving at the lake, I held the horses as the dudes dismounted, tied them to trees, and loosened cinches. I watched as neophyte riders walked gingerly and rubbed their sore buts as they went toward the sandy shore for a picnic. It was fun to swim the horses in the snowmelt water. If I swam, I ran as fast as I could into the icy water. With that strategy, I could not back out at the last second.

By age eight, I often took my favorite Sunday ride to the Chapel of the Transfiguration in Moose. Sometimes we would have a long string of riders. Dudes from other nearby ranches such as the Bar BC, Elbow Ranch, and Bear Paw, to name a few also rode to church. White Grass riders tied their horses to the buck rail fence and walked into the chapel with spurs jingling against the rough wood floor and emanating odors of horses and leather. I looked out the big window behind the altar to see the luminous Tetons, my mountain cathedral. My heart soared at the sight—surely that was where God lived. On those mountain slopes, I had always found solace. I connected the joy, comfort, and peace I found on the mountainside in the wild to the feeling I found in church.

Injun's Death

The mare Injun introduced me to death, and her gelding friends showed me what friendship should be. Injun was not anything special, just a mousy roan with a white blaze running crookedly down her face. She had a foal. When the horses were let out each evening, she would run to the grassy slopes to graze with them. But one evening, she stayed behind. I climbed through the corral fence to watch such unusual behavior. Two geldings remained in the corral also; shoulder to shoulder, they pushed the foal out of the corral with them. The foal was a bit young to be weaned. He did not want to leave his mother. He whinnied, stamped his little white feet, and shook his dainty head in defiance, but the geldings prevailed. It was unusual for the geldings to leave their friend and unheard of that they would take a foal without the mare. Injun usually interfered with anyone bothering her foal, but that evening, she stood in the corral corner, watching, her head hung low. Horses and mules are smarter than people give them credit for; the geldings and the mare knew of the impending death, as humans we were unaware.

When the geldings and foal left, the mare laid in the corral's deeply shaded corner by the barn. If a horse lies down for too long, it can die. I was afraid for her. Later, I went back to check on her. She was still down. I climbed into the corral and lifted her head to encourage her to get up. When I let go, she let her head drop onto the ground. I ran for Dad. He came to tend to her, but nothing helped. It was not long before she died.

I sat with her head in my lap. My tears dripped onto her mousy gray head. I ran into the woods to hide my tears and nurse my pain; in the woods, I found peace. It was where Spirit Guide, my guardian angel, was close. Maybe she had died of a twisted gut or intestinal obstruction. In the following days, I saw the geldings continue to protect the foal. I wanted to be a loyal, caring friend like the geldings, to stand by my friends and family and contribute however I could.

First Grade

When it was time for me to go to school, Mom or Dad would drive me the six miles of dirt road to Moose, where I caught the school bus. I disliked the school bus. I tried to sit in front, where I felt safe from a boy who would spit pomegranate seeds at me or pull my hair. As winter snows set in, it became obvious that going to school from the ranch was not feasible. Dad bought a lot in Jackson with a two- room log cabin on it. He moved another cabin next to it and built a long room in between. During the construction, I saw two shiny wires sticking out of the wall. I picked up a piece of metal rod and touched them. Sparks flew everywhere. I was not hurt, but I learned that electricity could bite, and I gained respect for it. When the snow was too deep to keep the ranch road open, we moved into the house in town.

Since I acted differently, the first-grade teacher singled me out. She sat me at the back of the classroom to draw and color; it made me feel dumb. She did not try to teach me or find out why I was not responding as she thought I should. Mom was beside herself but could not budge the decision of the teacher. The other children teased me. Even though Jackson was a small town, I was a stranger who lived on a ranch. I could not distinguish among the children. I had a difficult time finding my way around the school building and grounds. I failed first grade.

Oma and Opa

In 1949, during the end of first grade, Mom's parents were finally able to leave war-torn Germany and come to live with us. Mom had been worried about them. I had little contact with other family members since Dad's family lived on the East Coast, so when Oma and Opa came, I was excited to have family nearby. Mom had already taught me to call them by the German words for Grandma and Grandpa, which were Oma and Opa. Opa spoke with a heavy accent, and Oma spoke little English. They greeted me with gentle, loving hands on my shoulder. They moved into the small cabin next to our house. Opa helped Mom with the ranch office work, putting precise numbers in columns in a large ledger; his cigar smoke filled the office. Opa loved to feed the chickens and collect eggs. He would use his penknife to peck a hole in an egg and then suck the raw egg out. Oma scraped the leftovers from our plates into a soup pot, saving every morsel. They were careful about saving food since they had nearly starved to death during the war.

Opa and Oma, Inge's parents, with the painting that is the cover of this book.

World War II was not the first war they had been in. During WWI they lived in Morocco, in 1914 when the French invaded, Opa was taken prisoner, and Oma with one child, my mom, was roughly deported to Switzerland. Oma sewed many coins in her clothing to save them from the French; everything else was lost. During WWII, Oma told me they had moved out of their home in Frankfurt to their farm in the country in hopes of survival. On one of Opa's birthdays, she had been determined to put meat on the table. They had not had meat for a long time so Oma asked their retainer to get sparrows. He had snared several which were cleaned, plucked, and roasted. Oma had been proud to serve meat to surprise Opa. I had always had plenty of food and could not imagine living without, as they had.

In the summer, I would see Oma standing out in the field, painting. She had been trained as an artist, but Opa forbade her to sell her paintings. It was not proper, in their time, for a wife to have an occupation. I still have many of her paintings hanging on my walls.

Oma was a good housekeeper and wife, and she took pride in those roles. Oma took care of their cabin and repaired our torn clothing. She wanted to teach me those skills. She tried to teach me to sew and embroider. It took me a full winter to finish four simple cross-stitched napkins and a tablecloth as a Christmas gift for Mom. After that ordeal, Oma gave up on me and sewing.

I always came to her call and was glad to do her bidding. Instead of learning homemaking skills, I built her a corner shelf in her living room. Dad had taught me to use the Skill saw at ten. I searched the shop and found lumber. I cut the pieces with the saw—there were no safety features in those days—and then nailed them together. Oma was pleased with the shelf.

As I became an aggressive rider, Dad thought I was too tough on the elderly Eva. She continued to teach young dude kids to ride. I was assigned Judy, a lean strawberry roan. She was not as bad as the strawberry roan in the Western song, but she was mean- spirited. She would bite and kick when I saddled her. I tried to break her by kneeing her in the ribs which did not deter her one bit. One day I lost patience with her abuse. I grabbed her ear, pulled it into my mouth, and gave it a hard bite. We were both surprised. I was surprised because her ear was dusty and gritty—yuck! She was surprised because she had never had her tricks turned against her. She quit biting me, but she kept kicking.

One day George guided a few dudes up to the avalanche area looking for lost horses and I went along. The avalanche area was a steep hillside slashed by gullies where trees had been flattened by tons of snow exploding down the mountain. Interspersed among bushes and deformed stunted trees was a riot of wildflowers and good grass which the horses seeked.

"My saddle is slipping," I called to George.

"You are all right," he said as he continued forward.

"I'm not alright," I insisted as Judy jumped another gully. Her saddle slid right up her narrow withers.

My balance kept it from tipping to one side, until she dropped her head. I landed on the ground. George laughed. Judy lowered her head to graze. I scrambled to my feet. Soon, George reset the saddle and we continued our search. We saw elk in the high meadows but we did not find the lost horses. The dudes were thrilled with the adventure. I learned new territory that I could come back to and explore on my own.

At age ten, I took my first pack trip with Dad into the Tetons. It was one of the several summers when my cousin Fran, who became one of the most constant people in my life, visited the ranch. Several dudes and Fran were on the trip. We rode past Phelps Lake and up Death Canyon. I rode bareback, as usual. The first night, we camped near the vacant Death Canyon Ranger Station. In the morning, dudes' duffels went back into canvas panniers that hung on each side of a packhorse. After taking the tents down, we folded them to the correct size to fit across the packhorse's back, covering both panniers, and secured them with a diamond hitch. Another horse would carry the wooden panniers with the kitchen canvas fly folded over the top. When everyone was mounted and the pack horses were loaded, we rode over Static Peak. Misty, my horse, quietly walked along and rocked me into sleep. We descended into Alaska Basin, a boulder-strewn alpine meadow. Snowfields were melting into many rivulets bordered with stunted, wind-bent trees; spring wildflowers; and moss-covered rocks. The landscape seemed otherworldly with the unfamiliar vegetation. We set up our second night's camp near a copse of gnarled wind-bent trees. Dad and I hobbled the horses and turned them loose to graze. They could not go far with their front feet tied together.

Dad erected several small tepee-type tents in which the dudes slept. The kitchen area had a canvas fly attached to a couple of trees, with a pole holding the front up. I helped Dad cook over the open fire, clean up after dinner, and wash dishes. Dad and I slept under the kitchen fly between cans of food and panniers. The wooden panniers, being stronger, were used to save most of the food from marauding scavengers. The bacon received special treatment; Dad's custom was to sleep with it under his head to protect it from bears.

The next morning, we followed the rocky trail over Hurricane Pass named for its strong winds; the horses' tails flew at a right angle from their bodies. We rode with one hand holding on to our hats, the other holding the reins. When the trail dropped out of the wind into Cascade Canyon, it was a relief. We passed Schoolroom Glacier, which fed the creek with opaque light turquoise meltwater. On the third night out, we camped at Lake Solitude. Fran and I had a great time exploring, climbing, and sliding down the snowfields. The last day was a long ride back to the ranch along the Valley Trail. I loved the days of camping out, riding, and ranging over the mountains. It was my first pack trip, and I thought I was in heaven. After that first pack trip, Dad frequently used me as an extra hand on pack trips.

Before I was school age, the ranch caretakers Marmie had hired, Ollie and Twila VanWinkle, lived in the farthest-north cabin, near the fox pens. It was smaller than the Hammond cabin and very warm.

Unlike the dude cabins, which were for summer use, this cabin was insulated with a drop-down ceiling. I remember it being nice and warm when I visited. During the winter, salt was put on the eaves to melt the ice, and the salty water dripped onto the protruding corner logs, which attracted salt-hungry porcupines during the summer.

In the 1950s, Larry Messler and his family had reservations for that cabin in July during many successive summers. We started calling it the Messler cabin (we named the cabins by the dudes who stayed in them most). One summer, Larry complained to Dad.

"The porcupines keep us awake all night," Larry said.

"What do you mean?"

"They gnaw on the corner logs."

"They must be after the salt on the logs," Dad said. "Might as well kill them, because there is no other way to stop them." And that is what happened.

George came to help. Skinning a porcupine is done carefully, starting at the belly, where there are no quills. Larry and his daughter Ann helped. A few years later, Ann returned as the first female wrangler.

"I read that porcupine was good to eat," Mom said. "Why don't we cook them and feed the dudes? It will be a great Western treat." And that was what Mom and Ellen did.

"Did you enjoy the meat tonight?" Mom asked after dinner. Much of the response was positive.

"That was a porcupine," she announced. A few dudes, whose faces paled, left the table.

Each September, we closed all the cabins for winter. Winterizing included covering the chimneys with coffee cans to keep the snow out. If snow drifted down the chimney, the stove used for heating would rust and shortly be unusable. Years after the porcupine dinner, some skiers entered the Messler cabin and built a fire to get warm but were smoked out since they did not know the chimney was blocked by the coffee can. They left a fire that eventually engulfed the entire cabin. It was a major loss.

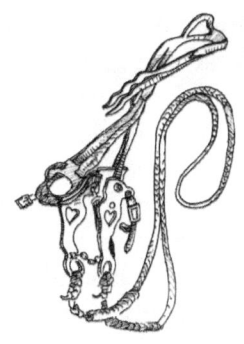

CHAPTER 2

Childhood Challenges

OFTEN IN MY LIFE, I HAVE FELT AS IF I AM ON A RAFT FLOATING ON a river, at the mercy of the strong currents.

There have been peaceful times of good weather and quiet waters; at other times, vicious waves have bashed me against inhospitable shores where I have no control. I thought my vigorous rowing against the menacing currents might direct me away from danger. If I study the way the water boils past boulders and rushes around sharp turns, I might learn the reason for those currents and be able to face the challenge of navigating the river of life with a modicum of safety. I must be aware of my surroundings and conscious of my Spirit Guide's directions to stay safe.

When I was in first grade for the second time, we stayed on the ranch. Mother ordered the Calvert Home Study Course. She insisted I keep the book twelve inches from my nose when I read.

"You must keep this distance from the book, or you will ruin your eyes," she said as she placed a ruler between my forehead and the book.

But I could not determine the letters or numbers unless they were four inches from my nose. It was a constant struggle to read. Mom seemed so severe. I also spent much time practicing cursive writing, forming each letter between the lines. The math involved pages of difficult problems to solve.

In response to my final tests, the Calvert people said I had learned two years' worth of studies in one year. I had caught up with my class in Jackson. I think I did well because if Mom was not watching, I could hold everything close and I had no distractions from other children. The following fall, Mom enrolled me in third grade back in the Jackson public school. Mrs. Ferris's punishment was an exercise of writing, "I will not …," fifty times on the blackboard. I had learned enough from Mom to follow along adequately. I tried hard, but at each parent conference, the teachers said I was not applying myself. However, I was learning my way around school. I loved playing on the monkey bars, and I had finally found a friend.

One day in third grade, I was called to the classroom door. Standing in the hall was a tall boy I did not recognize and the unknown person frightened me. Previously, Mom had taught me to recognize her unique handwriting and told me never to go with anyone without a handwritten note from her, and he did not have one.

"Your mom and dad are at my parents' house. You are to come home with me on my bus. I'll meet you outside after school. OK?" he asked as he shifted from foot to foot. But he didn't have a note written by Mom.

Feeling danger, I looked at him with big, startled eyes and nodded. I felt like a deer blinded by headlights, paralyzed by fear. I wanted to run, but I stood and listened. I was not going with strangers into the unknown; if I did, I would never see my way home. I was determined to find my usual bus. After school, I hid in the big, curving silver tube of the fire escape until the buses began to pull out. I made a furtive dash to my regular bus.

I arrived in Moose. No one was there to meet me. I stood watching the road, expecting to see Mom or Dad at any time. It was getting dark; I was getting cold. I was frightened. I could not walk the six miles to the ranch in the dark.

The postmistress saw me, invited me into her home, and fed me dinner. Her home was the only one for miles around. Her son was three years older than I was. I was surprised that he lowered himself to play cards with a little girl like me. Mom called to see if I was at Moose. She said she would pick me up on her way home. I was still glad I had not gone with the strange boy.

When Mom and Dad picked me up, it seemed they were disappointed to leave the party sooner than they would have liked. They thanked the Postmistress, and Mom put a hand gently on my head.

Dad put an arm around my shoulders. We climbed into the car to go home like usual.

About that time, I started having nightmares. Since I seldom had dreams, it was particularly puzzling. It was about a mother moose chasing me from the high meadow near the Phelps Lake overlook into a thick aspen grove. I ran as fast as I could, with my lungs nearly bursting, but the moose kept gaining ground. I would climb one of the slick-trunked aspen trees out of her reach. But she would dig with her sharp hooves until the tree fell. I would awaken in a sweat and breathing hard in fright.

I continued to have the dream for months. It was always the same. Once, while on horseback, I was chased by a real moose, but as we entered the woods, she stopped. If Spirit Guide was sending me a message, I did not understand it. But I became wary of moose.

White Grass Ranch had a three-month dude season, and Dad's hunting camp extended our earnings for another six weeks, but four and a half months failed to provide enough earnings to last all winter and to open the ranch in spring, so Dad often found other employment. He once had a job in Southern California welding storage tanks several stories tall. He hated the heights but continued for several months before we returned to the ranch.

As winter snows closed the ranch road, we drove to Florida where Dad had secured a winter job at the Rosemere racehorse farm near Ocala. On the way, Dad gave me the highway map. I looked at the map as he asked me which road to take. That was my map-reading lesson. Along the way, I was surprised at the waitresses calling me "Dearie". I also had my first taste of frog legs, which I liked.

I was enrolled in the public school near the farm to continue third grade. I was taught "Silent Night" in German and was the only child in the class to know the spelling of Florida which I had learned from the map. School was close enough to the farm that I often walked to school—a big change from the commute to school from the ranch.

We lived in a rusty gray travel trailer. Every time Mom opened a drawer, cockroaches skittered out of sight; how Mom hated the cockroaches. I found a turtle under the trailer for a pet, and Mom helped me fix a box for its home. I was allowed to ride the farm's ancient, rotund workhorse along the sandy farm roads. Only the hired hands were allowed to go into the racehorse pastures or barns, but Mom and I could stand by the fence to watch the mares and foals frolic in the brilliant green pastures. Mom would go with Dad into the barns at night feeding time. She especially loved the foals' soft, velvety noses, which they presented to her in their curiosity. One morning the manager reprimanded Mom for going into the barns; her bright red lipstick on a foal's white nose gave her away.

That winter in Florida, Dad took a few days off, and we drove to the Clearwater beach. Dad, Mom, and I went out on the gulf in a rowboat to fish. I felt a tug on my line, pulled it up, and swung my catch into the boat. Mom screamed as the crab dropped onto her lap. She almost capsized the boat. I thought fishing in the ocean was lots of fun.

After ocean fishing, we went back to the kitchenette for Mom's special spaghetti dinner. We sat around the green Formica-topped, chrome-legged table. Dad invited me to sit on his lap; lap-sitting meant serious business. I was uneasy; what had I done? I struggled to make sense of the world around me.

Dad lifted me onto his lap, the unusual behavior made me uncomfortable. I suspected Mom and Dad, whom I respected, believed, trusted, and loved, had something important to say. I felt I was facing another strong, unpredictable river current. I felt insecure without my familiar mountains nearby, where I could go to think or for solace. My parents looked pleased with themselves but a bit nervous. What was coming?

"Your mother couldn't have a baby. After looking at many places, we found and adopted you," Dad said as he bent closer.

I was speechless. Adopted! Who was I? My whole world turned inside out; the river current dropped off a cliff flying me through the air and landing me in turbulence. My world changed in a second.

"I love you very much," Mom said, reaching to touch me. "We wanted two children, so you could have a playmate."

"Oma and Opa tried to find a war orphan from Germany, but none were allowed to leave Germany."

"Our only regret is that we couldn't find a baby to give you a little brother."

They continued to speak in soft, reassuring tones, but my mind was in turmoil; my heart was beating double time. I could not breathe. I did not hear all their words. All I could think was, "They lied to me all my life. They aren't my real parents. I put my trust, love, and respect into imposters." I felt deserted. I bit my cheek to hold back tears. I was not going to let them know how confused and hurt I was. I needed to be alone to think this over.

"I am tired. I want to go to bed," I said, still fighting tears. When the lights were out, I lay, staring at the ceiling trying to get my thoughts together. I needed to be outside, where the wind, stars, and moon, with their reliable, consistent rhythm, could comfort me. They never deceived me.

When all was quiet, I crawled out the window. In my pajamas and barefoot, I headed over broken pavement to the beach two blocks away. I ambled along the edge of the waves, my tears mingled with the salty seawater splashing at my feet. I watched the thin, high-flying clouds as they passed in front of the big moon. I cried to the moon, "Why?" My heart screamed at the unfairness of life. The moon shone a silver path along the beach. I followed it. "I'm not going back to those imposters," I said to myself.

The soothing rhythm of the waves gently lapped at my feet. I began to hear the waves talk to my soul, calming my spirit: "Ker-splash. Ker-splash. Go back. Go back." I felt the grip of anger and confusion weaken as the moon's silver path began to disappear. The solid, gritty sand helped me to gain a sense of security; Earth was there for me.

My resolve softened. My parents have been good to me but I wondered if I would be treated differently? Would I still have a right to be part of the ranch? I especially loved the mountains, where the essentials of life never changed and where dogs and horses were my best friends, companions, and playmates. Besides, where would I go? I was in a strange land where there were no quiet mountain swales or surrounding forests to enfold me, comfort me, or warm my soul, where I had no horse to nuzzle me, no matter how confused or angry my mood. I resolved to learn whatever I must to be able to take care of myself. Obviously, I was the only person I could trust and depend on. "I'm not doing them or myself any good by running away," I said aloud as I resolved to return to the motel.

With new determination, I straightened my back, pushed out my chin, stomped back up the beach, and walked the two blocks over the hard, cold pavement. "Ker- splash. Ker-splash. Go back. Go back," the waves called to me. I felt it was Spirit Guide talking to me. I climbed back through the window into the bunk bed. I shivered. My feet were sore and raw from the hours of walking on the wet sand. I vowed I would never let Mom and Dad know my anguish. I did not want them to feel hurt like I did. Finally, I fell asleep. I believe they never knew I had been gone; they never spoke of it.

I knew I must act the same as I always had. The sun would rise from the east; I would get dressed, eat breakfast, go to school, and come home; and the sun would set in the west. I would act as if nothing had changed. But my soul was walking on shifting sand; my footing was precarious.

Years later, Mom told me that once while she was in the hospital with another miscarriage, the doctor brought her a baby because its mother had died in childbirth. The doctor thought the live mother and live baby should be together. That baby was me. However, in time I would learn that the story was not quite like that.

I have come to believe people do the best they can with their knowledge and abilities. They may not mean to be hurtful; they may not even know they have been hurtful. I forgave. Sometimes forgiving is not easy.

As an adult, I decided to view the advantages of being adopted. I am what I make of myself. I cannot make excuses and say I am a certain way because I am like or unlike my mother or father. Looking back, I see they were good parents, giving me the freedom to discover life for myself yet giving me boundaries. I make a special effort to take responsibility for my actions. Whatever I like about myself I try to keep. As for the characteristics I do not like, I can choose to change them. I do not want to make excuses. One friend thinks I am German; another thinks I am Irish. Others say I am unique or different. Great Spirit, preserve me from the normal, I say to myself, whatever normal is, maybe borning. I will not fashion myself by labels.

Amiable St. John's

After most of the winter in Florida and two months left to finish third grade, we were back in Wyoming, staying in the Jackson house Dad had built until the ranch road could be plowed and opened. A neighbor invited me to go to Latter-Day Saints, Mormon, primary Sunday school. Mormons are strongly against smoking and drinking; both my parents smoked and imbibed. The church's strategy seemed to use children to influence adult habits. After attending a few times, I reprimanded Mom for smoking, and she put a stop to my going to primary. I knew that my paternal grandmother, Marmie, gave her gambling winnings (gambling was open in Wyoming until the 1950's) to St. John's Episcopal Church, and when she lost, she would match her losses for a donation to the church. Being curious and looking for friends, I decided to see what St. John's church was.

I walked across town by myself past the Jackson Drug Store to Sunday school. St. John's was a log church standing under tall pine trees and looked inviting. I found there were chocolate brownies made by Mrs. Vincent, the priest's wife. I was converted! Not only were there brownies, but it was a place with many friendly people. I had fun playing, drawing, and learning about Jesus with other children. We sang a song with the lyrics "All creatures great and small, the Lord God loves them all." We were all loved, the song made me believe it; I did not feel so alone. I felt a connection to the child Jesus, who was also different from other children. I had been ridiculed in first grade. I lived on a ranch; the other ranch children I knew, instead of going to school in Jackson, moved to their city homes in the winter.

On Easter morning, I started for church, and Mom said, "Don't you dare bring any more candy home. We have too much as it is."

"OK, bye," I said as I skipped out the door.

In my exuberance, I ran several blocks to Sunday school. Of course, I was given candy in a brightly decorated Easter basket. It had yellow cloth daffodils, red cloth tulips, jelly beans, chocolate eggs, and a big chocolate bunny. It was so pretty, but I could not take it home, and I could not refuse it either. Mrs. Vincent was so thoughtful and had spent time and money to make an Easter basket for each Sunday school child. As I walked home, I remembered a family who were living in a garage near my home. They had five or six children. Previously, I had watched as they took turns playing outside in the snow. It seemed there were not enough winter clothes to go around. When no one was watching, I placed the basket on their doorstep, knocked, and ran to hide behind a snowdrift. I didn't want them to refuse it, as they may have if they thought it was charity. I heard the door open and the happy squeals and the children took the basket inside. It made me happy to give them some cheer on Easter Sunday. I walked home proud that I solved the conundrum.

My first male teacher was Mr. Ellingston in fourth grade. I was again seated near the back of the classroom. I was puzzled by the waving of the teacher's arms in front of the class. Mr. Ellingston helped me with the work and I liked him. One day he moved me to the front row of the class. There I discovered his arm waving was really writing on the blackboard. But I still could not see the lettering clearly until I got closer after class.

Later that spring, as Mom and Dad were driving me home from the school bus stop in Moose, Mom said, "See those elk?" She pointed toward the mountain.

"No," I answered honestly.

"Up by the aspen trees."

"What aspen trees?"

She swung around and glared at me. I cowered in the corner of the backseat. She thought I was sassing her.

"You really don't see the aspen trees?" she asked when she saw my reaction.

"No," I said hesitantly. I was afraid of Mom; she was always so direct, and her reprimands seemed more like a hammer blow than a nudge.

"My God, Frank," she said to Dad while staring at me. "This child can't see." She asked me, "Why didn't you tell us you couldn't see?"

How could I have known I could not see? I had never seen. I could not tell what other people saw. I thought the world was what I experienced. How could a person who could not hear describe sound? How could I describe what I had never seen? I was confused. What had I done wrong?

I discovered that I must have been born severely myopic, near-sighted. Obviously, my parents did not know I could not see. I now realize my poor vision affected my perception of the world and thus my responses. I felt insecure and shy, especially in new places or around new people. My horse served as my eyes and my guide around the forest. I only knew a world filled with great, soft fuzzy blobs of diffused color, light, and dark, as if one was looking at the moon through a layer of clouds. I could see no details and no facial features or expressions. Trees were tall green ovoid shapes. Stones were dark shadows that tripped me; stumbling made me seem clumsy. I heard creeks before I saw the dark line of water at my feet. I'd learned to find my way around the ranch and its environs by a system of memorizing the large splotches of dark and light patterns. With my horse, I could find my way along any game trails and explore the mountainsides behind the ranch. If I was lost, my horse would always take me home with her. She always accepted me, no matter my mood. She always behaved in a predictable manner that I could trust.

I could recognize familiar people by their tone of voice, the rhythm of their footsteps, or their mannerisms, but new people were a mystery. In my insecurity, I would not call anyone by name, in case I made a mistake. My intuition gathered the information for me. I could only see detail when an object was four inches from my nose.

Soon after my parents discovered my poor eyesight, we drove to Salt Lake City to get my thick, heavy glasses. The sight of all the sharp edges was a shock. I was overwhelmed by detail. I was lost in a new world of chaotic, harsh lines and abrupt edges of contrast and color instead of my old world of soft forms and diffused color. I was lost on the familiar trails and woods around the ranch. I often took my glasses off and used my old system of landmarks to navigate. I had to relearn all the horse trails and game trails with the new set of visual signs.

Sight did not change my feeling of well-being in the forest, but the forest sure looked different. Sight was a miracle; I explored its possibilities endlessly. I would stare at people, even those I knew to study their features I had not seen before. I could see freckles, frowns, smiles, and moles. People's facial expressions, which I had never seen, fascinated me. I would match the familiar sound of the wind to the sight of leaves quivering in the trees. I watched the light reflect on the ever-moving and shifting clouds. And flowers—what a variety of intricate shapes, colors, and sizes. I will never tire of seeing the Creator's works; I will never take the blessing of sight for granted.

Looking back, knowing I could not see details; I marvel at how I learned the individual horses in the herd of sixty to eighty. They were all sizes, including untrained young horses, geldings, mares, and foals. The paints, with their large black, white, or brown patterns, and the horses with large white stockings or white blazes were easy to distinguish. But there were many horses that had no large distinguishing marks. I must have learned their mannerisms, because before I had glasses, my job was to catch the horse whose name the wrangler called out to me, which I did successfully. It was important to me to know the horses, maybe like others recognizing their friends.

Unlike other children I knew, play, for me, meant working or going with Dad, not playing games with other children. I remember October when I was eleven and went to Dad's hunting camp on Pilgrim Creek to help. Dad's hunters wanted to bag an elk or bear. Dad would drive to his base camp, where there was a big tent for storage and corrals. From base camp, he would pack horses with supplies going to the main camp several miles up Pilgrim Creek. The main camp had a large cook tent, several smaller teepee-type tents for the hunters and guides, corrals, and poles tied high between trees for hanging meat out of predators' reach. The cook tent had a wood range with an oven, a long table with benches, and boxes stacked on their sides for shelves. One corner had a folding cot for the cook. It took many days to pack everything into camp on packhorses. I loved to visit the hunting camp.

Bear hunters were scheduled for a week. It was common practice to leave a carcass to attract a bear. In preparation, Dad bought an old, sickly mare for bear bait. With her came a roly-poly foal whom the cook named Bearbait, since that was going to be his fate also. Dad took the mare out to shoot her. The first hunters bagged their bear. By the time the next group arrived, everyone had fallen in love with the cute, friendly Bearbait. He became the mascot of the camp, as well as a nuisance. He feared nothing. He would wander into the cook tent as readily as the corral to eat. He learned to get handouts by watching Koon get cookies or pie from the cook. Bearbait had a long, useful life at White Grass. He became a favorite reliable riding horse and an excellent packhorse.

One morning, Dad took me to find and pack out an elk. The hunter, having succeeded in bagging his elk, stayed in camp. Dad and I rode most of the day, trying to find the kill on Wildcat Peak. The sun was getting low in the west. My ears were frozen, my nose dripped, and my toes were numb. Dad found the kill gutted and quartered on the side of a steep slope. We tied our horses to trees near the bottom. Dad led the packhorse to the lower side of the kill. I held the horse while Dad lifted a quarter elk onto one side. The slope was so steep I had trouble standing. I led the packhorse to a more level place to turn him around. He stumbled because he was off balance from one quarter, but I managed to position him for Dad to load the other quarter. I took the first packhorse to the bottom of the hill and tied him next to the other horses. I led the second packhorse for Dad to load the remaining quarters. He put the antlers on top of the second pack, with the points hanging down on each side of the loaded quarters.

With the horses' packs covered with tarps and tied securely, they lined out behind Dad me taking the end. With my collar turned up, a bandanna tied around my neck, and Stetson pulled to my ears, Dad rode toward the last rays of the sun along a precipitous drainage and I followed.

"This should be a shortcut to camp," he said. I trusted Dad because it seemed he had an internal compass.

The sun went behind pink clouds. A sliver of moon was visible near the horizon. I listened to Dad's tuneless whistle ahead of me. I could see the white tarps on the packhorses undulating ahead. Suddenly, the white tarps disappeared. I heard a splash. My horse and I were suddenly in the air and then splashed wet. We all jumped down a small dry waterfall into the catchment puddle below. It seemed I would be riding forever in the dark void; the only hints of life were the clomping of horse hooves, Dad's reassuring whistle, and an occasional owl call. We followed the drainage, and then Dad turned right over a ridge. I could smell the campfire before I saw the camp. Exhausted, I was grateful the ride was nearly over.

"Hey, good to see you. It was getting late." The cook greeted us with a smile and the lantern.

"Glad you are still up. I could use help in hanging the elk," said Dad. I helped to unsaddle and feed the stock. The elk quarters were hung high between the two trees.

"I'll heat leftovers for you. Do you want coffee?" asked the cook as we all trouped into the tent.

I hated coffee, but with lots of sugar and canned cream, it was great to have a hot drink. I slept on the ground with Dad in the cook tent. The cook slept on his cot.

Each morning, the cook started the fire in the wood range. A hot cooked breakfast would be ready for the hunters before sunup. The range warmed the tent. The coffee smelled inviting. Everyone was in good spirits. The hunt had been a success. The hunters were prepared to pack up and ride the thirteen miles to base camp, where their cars were parked.

One year, Dad had yet to bag his elk, the meat on which we depended. He was disappointed and concerned about our winter food supply. While hauling the horses from the hunting camp, on entering the ranch, he saw a herd of elk eating his hay, which was stacked to feed our stock. He desperately wanted to shoot one, but Marmie was entertaining the Grand Teton National Park superintendent on the porch overlooking the haystack. Since there was no hunting or shooting in the park, Dad could not kill an elk for our meat, nor could he shoot to scare the elk off our essential winter feed for the stock.

Attack Walking Home

Unfortunately, having glasses did not prevent me from getting shot in the butt one afternoon while running home from school. Several older boys chased me. There was no place to hide as I had already passed the drugstore where I knew I could have entered and been safe. I quickly made a run for home. I was quite a distance from the boys, when they shot at me. The shot stung like crazy, even though my heavy coat. I could hear them laughing as I turned the last corner toward home. I felt like the ugly duckling, and like him, I did not know why I was treated differently. My coat must have protected me, as I only had a big bruise. I thought I must have done something wrong to cause the attack.

Being shot was nothing compared to another attack that occurred when I was in fifth grade. I usually walked to and from school across town and past the Jackson Drug store. Mom had planned so I could stop at the store or the nearby B&W market to get a treat on my way home—fruit, not candy. One day, after school, I was on my way for a treat. I walked by the tall fence made of colorful old skis set vertically. I liked the cheerful multicolored spot. As I passed the ski fence, two older boys jumped out of the alley, grabbed me, dragged me, and threw me to the ground. I did not recognize them.

My heart jumped from fear. What was happening to me? Who were these boys? I fought and twisted but with little success. They were big. When they began ripping my clothes off, I became a wild thing—biting, kicking, hitting, screaming, twisting—and managed to break away. Holding my tattered clothes on, I ran like a terrified horse to save my life.

If I could make it to the drugstore, I knew I would be safe. I crashed through its back door; plopped on the floor behind the nearby magazine rack to hide. No one came to me, so I guessed no one noticed. I was content to have the quiet time to calm down as I tried to catch my breath and calm my fear. I put my clothes in order as best as I could. I was scared and embarrassed. I was afraid to show myself. I was afraid to walk home. But I was determined to take care of myself. It did not occur to me to use a phone. The phone on the ranch was a hand crank—we cranked the long or short rings to reach the desired person—and was only used for business. Several minutes later, after my breath slowed and my heart settled to a near-normal beat, I knew I had to go home on my own. Looking out the windows, I could see no one lurking. I cautiously went outside, made a mad dash across the town square, and ran the several blocks home, where I arrived out of breath. I never told anyone about the attack, because I thought it must have been my fault, and I wanted to avoid trouble. But I suspect Mom knew I had, at least, been in a fight because of my damaged clothes.

I felt like the nearly frozen, chirping chick Dad had found in the hayloft. He took it to my grandmother Oma, who named it Petelle. She held him in her gentle, gnarled hands under a Coleman lantern to warm him and fed him brandy from an eyedropper. She talked baby-talk to him in German. He learned to come when his name was called and ate with the dogs. Like the dogs, he slept in front of the fireplace. Unlike the dogs, however, he never became house-trained. Mom needed to follow him with paper towels.

"Petelle is a chicken; it is time for him to join the others in the coop," Dad said as he picked up Petelel. It was spring, and the snow was mostly gone; it was no longer freezing in the coop.

Dad put him in with the chickens; however, the other chickens did not recognize him as one of their own. He acted differently. They picked on him and eventually pecked him to death.

Unlike Petelle, I was determined to survive. I had to find a way to walk home safely. I hoped there would be safety in numbers, so I closely followed a group of kids from the school to the drugstore. I was not attacked again. I thought, if I told Mom and Dad, what could they do? Mom was strict. Would she blame me? The attack had happened; it was over. I learned to be wary of others. I made a habit of taking care of my problems with Spirit Guide, who had come to me from the Creator.

Looking back, I realize my family did not talk about feelings; doing so was an unspoken taboo. Conversation was about the conditions of the animals, dude reservations, the inventory of supplies to last until the next resupply, or the funds available until we had income from guests. I could not learn how to talk about feelings.

By 1953, Mom needed help with managing the growing dude business. She advertised for a hotel manager. One of the responses sounded like an experienced middle-aged woman. Rachel arrived in the spring; however, she was not middle-aged but a twenty-year-old trained and experienced manager. She was from England and was cheerful but firm in the way things should be accomplished for the dudes' comfort. She became Mom's best friend, and I had a new boss, one I could not get around.

"Cindy, when you clean the Main Cabin, it must be completed before the dudes come to breakfast," Rachel told eleven-year-old me. "Cindy, you must clean behind the books in the library too. You missed the furthermost corner under the couch." When setting the dining room, "The silverware must be placed just so." She demonstrated. "Tighten the hospital corners—no wrinkles"; she directed me on how to make a bed properly in a dude cabin.

1956, Frank, Inge, and Rachel in the Main Cabin
dining room planning meals for a pack trip.

The Main Cabin, the lodge, was built as a gathering place. The ranch kitchen, dining room, library, and game room were in the Main Cabin and a big porch facing east. One row of dude cabins overlooked the field. Another row was nestled at the edge of the lodgepole forest. The centrally located log bathhouse was constructed in 1939. The huge wood-fired water heater filled the center and warmed both the men's bathroom facilities on the south side and similar facilities for the women on the north sides; linens and supplies for the cabins were in the back. When fences needed repair, the old grayed rails and posts were randomly stacked near the bathhouse to fire the water heater. Hot water was available in the afternoon and evening only as Dad lit the water heater early afternoon and let it burn out after dark.

The cabin girls and waitresses gave Rachel the nickname Wretched in a teasing way. But everything looked good and worked well. She was always the consummate hostess, and the dudes loved her. By the time I was twelve, at the end of the dude season, Mom, Rachel, and I would get together to allot the tips. Each dude would recommend one or more employees who had spent extra effort on their behalf. Mom and Dad would recommend exemplary employees too. After figuring the allotment, we awarded the season's tips. End- of-the-year tip dispersal encouraged the employees to stay for the whole season. Also, Mom taught me billing and payroll methods. I was not an employee and was not a guest. I was not being paid; I was expected to contribute to the business; be part of the Galey team, with the goal of everything on the ranch working well. For instance, if a dude asked me for toilet paper, I delivered it; I did not go to the cabin girls to have them deliver the toilet paper.

Daddy's Little Girl

The dude season was over, but there was still much work to do. The cabins had to be closed, and all linens, blankets, and towels had to be washed and put in mouse-proof cupboards in the bathhouse storage. Beds were hung from the rafters with baling wire so mice could not chew the mattresses. Instead, we placed old mattress fluff on the floor to satisfy the mice. Chimneys were topped with coffee cans to keep rain or snow from rusting the stove stoves and rendering them useless. The ranch water system was shut off and Dad drained each cabin's pipes. The Main Cabin kitchen was cleaned and closed; all open food and perishables came to our house. Other unopened containers and canned goods were placed in the Main Cabin pantry storage. The icehouse was cleaned out, and new sawdust was placed, ready for new ice when the pond froze. In the barn, all the saddles, saddle pads, and bridles were hung from the ceiling to prevent mouse damage. Only the harnesses and items in the tack room were easily available.

One fall evening, when all the dudes were gone for the season, Dad, Mom, the dogs, and I were sitting as a family on the east-facing porch of the Galey house overlooking the ranch pond toward Blacktail Butte and Sheep Mountain on the horizon. We heard elk bugling.

"Let's saddle up. We'll see if we can find the elk and watch them bugle," Dad said.

"I'll go," I said as I headed out toward the barn.

"I'll keep the dogs here and start dinner," said Mom.

A bull elk bugles to attract cow elk and also warns other bulls away, protecting his harem from competing bulls. Sometimes two elk will fight, causing the clash of their antlers to ring through the forest. A hunting guide once told of seeing two elk carcasses with the antlers locked together. However, that was uncommon.

Dad and I rode quietly through the thick lodgepole forest. The low-hanging sun filtering through the trees caused bright streaks on the huckleberry bushes and flashed in our eyes as we passed. The air was fresh from a dusting of snow. We dipped into Swamp Creek; the colder, moist air penetrated my clothes, causing me to shiver. Our horses clambered up the other side. We traversed a small ridge paralleling the creek to the marsh. We sat silently, letting our horses drop their heads to graze. The air was heavy with the sour odor of rutting elk. A six-point bull elk came into the opening; he sniffed the air and grunted as he searched for the scent of cows in heat. He tipped his head back with his antlers straddling his back. He let out an ear-piercing bugle. Three grunts punctuated his bugle, causing his stomach to contract with each sharp exhalation. He was challenging any bulls in the area. The sound gave me goosebumps; it was a beautifully wild sound. He wandered through the park and stopped again to bugle. Occasionally, he would attack a sapling, as if scraping the little remaining velvet from his antlers.

The marsh was a large, low area where thick clumps of willow thrived and surrounded by higher ground covered with lodgepole pines. Between the willow clumps were open grassy parks, areas frequented by the elk and our ranch horses. The seeps created narrow, deep channels that had grass growing over the edges, which made them difficult to see. Years of heavy snowfall had made the marsh so boggy that a horse could become mired. During dry years, there was a well-defined dry game trail traversing it.

On the way home, Dad and I followed the game trail in the hope of seeing more animals. We came around a clump of willows and saw a small herd of grazing cow elk with a large bull standing guard. As soon as he detected our presence, he circled his harem, chasing them from the willows into the protective pine timber. The bull stood blatantly looking at us as a rear guard.

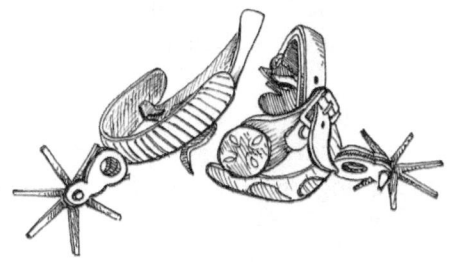

CHAPTER 3

Leaving Home, 1952–1957

"WOULD YOU LIKE TO GO TO BOARDING SCHOOL?" MOM ASKED me as we sat one evening in our house. "It would solve the problem we have in getting you to school in winter. When we lived in town, Dad still had to take care of the ranch animals and shovel snow from the roofs, which made for impossibly for long days. When the snow is deep, he must ski into the ranch. You could get a better education and make friends."

Fear of the unknown grabbed me. Leave my mountains? Leave the ranch? Leave Jackson Hole? I was twelve, going into sixth grade. Would the classwork be similar or harder? There was so much unknown.

After pondering their proposal, I realized it sounded somewhat reasonable as I understood their reasoning but disliked it. I could still be in my mountains and ride into the woods with my horse in summer. I felt better about being in Jackson Public School, but I hated being teased, accosted, and shot. That was hard and left me hurt somewhere deep inside. My strategy, which I had learned by observing the horses and elk, was avoidance. I saw that it helped to keep peace in a herd, and I discovered it worked somewhat with fellow students.

I recalled the winter when Mom and Dad had taken me to Florida, where Dad had worked at Rosemere Farm, where they had told me I was adopted. Though that had been two years ago, the feelings of desertion and insecurity lingered. But despite those feelings, I decided I was willing to explore new possibilities, and learn more, by going to boarding school. Besides, it would have been useless to fight the inevitable; if they had decided I was going, I was going. It was not really my decision. I thought they just asked because they wanted to avoid seeming heavy-handed.

Boarding school meant there would be no more winter family time around the kitchen table with the hissing lantern. I would no longer be Daddy's little girl, going to milk the cows, care for the stock and chickens, or go to hunting camp, all of which was a joy. Boarding school would change my life much more than only schooling. I felt sad about those losses.

"Where would I go?" I asked, expecting I did not have a choice.

"We have found a nice Episcopal school in Salt Lake City. It is close enough that you can come home on vacation. The Crenshaws live in Salt Lake City and have been friends since Dad's army days. You could visit them sometimes."

Mom bought my uniforms: two straight gray wool skirts, six white blouses, a grosgrain ribbon colored to designate my grade level, and a long camel's hair winter coat. The school had strict rules, confinement to the campus, and long hours of study hall, and it was in a city. It was noisy and smelled bad. I was used to running free. My boundaries had been time-related, not hard land boundaries.

The dorm mother, Aunt Henry, put me in a room with another child who had no siblings. She thought we would have lots in common. What did we have in common? We had no social skills to help us share. Barbara split the room in half. That was fine by me. I had the window, and I did not want her in my things. Everything was fine by me until I had to go to the bathroom. I tried to cross her section to the door. She stood with her hands on her hips and said, "You are not allowed," as she firmly blocked my way. I attacked and quickly had her on the floor with my hands around her throat. Her screaming brought Aunt Henry who decided Barbara and I would do better in rooms of our own. But I was still living with a gaggle of girls.

I wrote home once a week. I did not tell Mom about my difficulties but told of my activities. When she wrote back, there was little affection or comment about what I had told her, but she wrote much about my mistakes in spelling or punctuation. I knew she was trying to correct me, but I felt I was being attacked and belittled. I wrote to her less and less to avoid being hurt.

A difference in opinion regarding porcupines caused the next fight. Porcupines lived around the ranch. One had gotten into the horse corral. I had to protect the horses. I tried to chase it out, but it would not leave. One horse already had quills in its nose. I found a discarded fence rail and hit the porcupine on the head repeatedly while screaming at it. The rail bounced off the quills. Porcupines do not die easily. They do not throw their quills, but if you touch a porcupine, the quills stick into you easily, as they did on the rail and the curious horse's nose. A classmate insisted porcupines throw their quills. After we slugged each other a few times, we went to the encyclopedia. It said, "Porcupines can throw their quills." I was mad and frustrated. I knew I was right for a change, but I could not prove it; I learned that a trustworthy source could be mistaken.

The girls knew how to navigate the city, knew the Yankees, Dodgers and the World Series, I had not even heard of them. On the other hand, I knew how to navigate the backcountry and knew animal characteristics. None of which was a benefit at school. It made me different and vulnerable to bullying.

The school had chapel services each school morning before classes and twice on Fridays; we walked to the St Mark's Episcopal Cathedral on Sundays. The quiet time in the church helped me accept the changes:living with others, playing, eating, studying. There was no alone time. There was much to learn. On the ranch, I had not learned how to have a friend. The dudes were there for only a few weeks and then were gone again. The hired hands were there for only four to five months. Parents are parents; mine did not really teach me how to interact with others. I was lonely. On the ranch, I had my four-leggeds, my friends; it was easier.

During my four years at Rowland Hall, I missed the ranch terribly, especially the horses. I missed the big log barn, the acrid smell of manure, oiled leather, and horse liniment. I missed the horses snuffling hay in the mangers. I missed the scraping sound of the barn door's slide closures opening and closing. (They were made with a smaller pipe sliding into a larger one.) I missed the cool summer breeze drifting through the barn's alleyway. I especially missed my quiet, contemplating time alone in my cathedral mountains. The mountains are steadfast; they are solid. I found peace; a sense of well-being in them.

At school, reading helped waylay my loneliness. I could escape into the book's story. My desk in the study hall was against a bookshelved wall. When homework became tedious, I furtively, as I was supposed to be doing schoolwork, searched the shelves by my desk. I discovered *And Quiet Flows the Don* by Mikhail Sholokhov and *Anna Karenina* by Leo Tolstoy within easy reach. Reading them was my way to avoid study hall assignments; I could get lost in winter stories of horses and sleighs that reminded me of winter on the ranch.

When I needed to write a research paper, I would thumb through National Geographic to find something that interested me and then look in the encyclopedia and other books for more references. It was easier to find available information and write about it than to dream of a subject and not find resources.

During short holidays, such as Thanksgiving, I often visited the Crenshaws, Mom and Dad's army friends. They had three children younger than me. I observed how a large family interacted. Learning from them helped me to mesh with the kids at school. The Crenshaws became my second family.

I especially remember one Christmas vacation, I flew to Idaho Falls, where Dad picked me up, and drove to Jackson Hole. Along the high open plains, which were wheat fields in summer, snow was blowing, drifting, and there was poor visibility. A moose appeared in front of us. She was confined to the highway by the high snow banks on each side of the road. She kept trotting in front of us on the black ice. I feared that she would slip, do a splits, and we would hit her. I kept asking Dad to slow down, but he ignored my plea, saying, "Be quiet. I need to concentrate on driving." The moose finally found a lower snowbank and jumped off the road. I saw her land in snow up to her belly, but she was safe. I let out a sigh of relief.

One Easter break, flying to Idaho Falls again, I hurt all over and felt nauseous. I was so weak I could hardly walk off the plane. Dad and I had a several-hour drive to the ranch. I slept most of the way. When Mom saw me, she insisted we turn around to go to St. John's Hospital. Dr. McLeod, who had skied to the ranch when I was an infant, sharpened a large needle on a stone before he used it to take a blood sample from my arm. The needle felt as if it had a hooked point. The diagnosis was mononucleosis. I spent my spring break in the hospital; no fun.

At school, I had no common ground to develop friendships. I had helped birth calves, doctored seriously injured horses, and pulled foals out of frozen puddles to save lives. The girls were interested in which color of lipstick or plaid skirt was prettier. Once, the girls pulled me down the hall, dragging me by my hair. I wanted them to quit, so I made no defensive response. Practicing avoidance, I placed my arms across my chest and made no facial expressions. It was no fun for them, so they quit; my strategy worked.

Sale of the Ranch

In the summer of 1956, Dad came into my room and sat on the bed next to me, which meant there was something important to say. I wondered what was up. Previously, such revelations did not bode well.

"The Grand Teton National Park wants to annex all private property on the west side of the Snake River," Dad said. "The Half Moon Ranch sold. The Elbow Ranch made a deal to move near Kelly. Your mom and I have sold the ranch, but we bought back a life estate so we can live here as long as one of us is alive. With the sale, we will have money for improvements. You will probably marry and move away."

I was astonished; how little he knew me.

The earth quaked beneath me; the river turned into a tsunami. My nest was the ranch. My comfort corner was the barn. Now it is gone. There was nothing solid to hang on to. Why had Dad taught me ranch plumbing, electricity, and horse management? Why had Mom taught me bookkeeping, reservations, and tip dispersal? What was going to happen to me? What about the horses? I was confused, hurt. I tried not to show my feelings, but felt disregarded; abandoned.

Dad seemed pleased. I did not want to hurt him. As soon as Dad returned to his project, I caught my horse and rode into the mountains to my secret grotto. I was not going home again. Did I even have a home? I lived at school for nine months of the year and at White Grass for only three months. Maybe school was my real home but my time at school was finite; in a few years I would graduate, then what?

But with quiet time by the murmuring stream, Spirit Guide talked to me. I calmed down. It grew dark and I realized my time on the ranch would soon end. I decided that feeling sorry for myself served no purpose; that it was useless to fight the inevitable. What was done was a done-deal. Fran, who knew of my grotto sanctuary, came to take me back. What else was there to do? I had nowhere else to go. I had to pretend everything was the same. I knew I could only trust myself. Maybe, if I expected less, I would be disappointed less. I told myself I must put one foot in front of the other, balance, and keep forging on to what Spirit Guide would reveal to me sometime in the future.

With the sale of the ranch, Mom and Dad would no longer spend the winter on the ranch. They wanted to travel and look for a place for a winter business.

Planning for school break the following Christmas, Mom and Dad wrote to me. They were in Mexico, so I was going to meet them at Mazatlán to celebrate the holiday. I was excited and looking forward to visiting Mexico. Maybe it would be by the ocean. Instead, plans changed, I met them at one of Dad's cousins in Santa Barbara, California. It was a great disappointment. Her house overlooked the city, with the ocean in the far background. I found a package under the tree wrapped in tissue paper with sharp points poking through. It turned out to be a pair of silver-plated Mexican spurs. They were beautiful; I still treasure them. However, I knew I would never use them on a horse because they were too severe.

I returned to school, where life was normal. On a spring weekend, three of us walked to the ZCMI department store downtown. The other girls were looking for pleated plaid skirts, the present fashion rage. In comparison, though it was an old-fashioned hand-me-down, my favorite dress was a roughly woven mahogany-colored jumper with a white blouse brought from Germany. Each girl purchased a plaid skirt, but Mom and Dad had given me no pocket money. When on the ranch, I picked up the coins off the floor that fell from Dad's packets. If he did not want them, I figured I could have them. But I had no money at school. I went into the dressing room and put a red, blue, and white plaid skirt under the plain skirt I was wearing. The others paid for their purchases, and we walked out of the store. I was terrified I would be arrested and jailed, but I was not stopped.

Living with the knowledge that I had stolen was a huge burden. I would not do that again. Also, I learned that wearing the right pleated plaid skirt failed to make me popular. Clothes do not define a person. Instead, I learned to follow directions and was exposed to a lifestyle and culture normal for people not living on a ranch. I learned to exist in peace with the other girls. Four years at the Utah boarding school molded this wild ranch creature into a relatively socialized student.

In Jackson Hole, every July, there was the Dude Ranchers' Rodeo, a friendly competition among the dude ranches usually held at one of the ranches. As it became larger, it was held at the Rodeo Grounds in Jackson. Some of the competitions were novelty races, slow horse races, and horse packing. The novelty race was walk, trot and run race and in the slow horse race, each ranch traded horses with another ranch according to a draw. It was the ranch's horse that won being the slowest, not the rider.

During my summers at home from Rowland Hall, I participated in the rodeo. Once I was out in the lead with a field of eight horses coming up behind, when my horse fell. As I rolled to the edge of the track, the heel of a horse's metal shoe caught my nostril, tearing it. When Mom saw me, I had blood running down my face and spotting my shirt.

"I'm going to take you to Dr. McLeod for stitches right after the rodeo," said Mom.

Stitches! I was afraid of stitches. I caught Shane, a coal- black horse who would not be used this late in the rodeo, and rode the many miles back home. I avoided stitches, and my nose healed.

That was not the first time I was injured by a horse, and it would not be the last. During the next Dude Ranchers' Rodeo, Mom and Dad had left to guide a river fishing trip with dudes. Tony, my cousin, another wrangler, Willy, and I had several horses in the hay field to practice for the races. We needed to match each child with an appropriate horse and an appropriate event. We felt everyone should have a chance to ride in a race.

I was holding a horse when he threw his head and smashed my glasses. I put my hand over my eye. There was blood. I handed the horse to Willy and ran for the house. I locked the door behind me. I would take care of myself. I wanted to look at my injury without anyone else around.

I saw my eyelid was cut. Blood was running down my face. I was afraid there was glass in it. On further inspection, I saw that my eyeball was not injured. I would be all right. Tony came and pounded on the door. I would not let him in.

Soon, I heard the rough voice of the foreman, George, at the door. "Let me in. I want to see what happened." Tony obviously had gone for backup.

George's voice brooked no defiance. I opened the door. He put his manure-covered hands from shoeing, on my forehead, tipping my head back, to get a better look. The curious cowboys and children crowded around, staring at me.

"You gotta go to Doc McLeod. If there's any glass in your eye, it has to be removed." I was the boss's daughter, in my parents' absence, he had the authority.

"I don't want to go."

"Willy, you drive Cindy to town," George said, completely ignoring my plea.

"Can Tony drive me?" I asked, giving in to the inevitable.

Doc McLeod washed out my eye and confirmed my eyeball was not damaged. He covered the eye. Before my parents arrived home, I had the bandage off. Since it was not bleeding, I reasoned, I did not need it. I hoped my folks would not notice my black eye without the telltale dressing. Looking back, I suppose they would have noticed that my glasses were gone. I still have a small calcified piece of glass in my eyelid, but it is no bother.

The glasses were a constant nuisance, falling off, breaking, and giving me sores behind my ears. My prescription changed twice a year, and each time, Mom or Dad would take me the five-to-six-hour drive to Salt Lake City. The ophthalmologist was hesitant about fitting a fourteen-year-old with the new hard contact lenses. He said the contact lenses should mitigate my constantly changing sight. He showed me how to put them in, take them out, and take care of them. When my eyelids touched the contacts, I felt as if sandpaper were grinding my eyes! I was instructed to put them in for five minutes, take them out for a while, and then put them back in, eventually extending the wearing time. Mom and Dad's plan was for me to stay with the Crenshaws for the week I had to accomplish wearing them.

The Crenshaws had a balance board intended to help skiers, but I used it to take my mind off the sandpaper in my eyes. I would wear the contacts, balance them on the board until they were excruciating, and then remove them. I spent lots of time putting them in, balancing, and taking them out. Each time I put them in, I extended my wearing time. I was determined to make them work. I was tired of my glasses sliding off my nose, falling off when riding, and fogging up. My parents were tired of replacing glasses two to three times a year. By the end of the week, the doctor was surprised I could wear them for eight hours at a time, and I was released to go home. Dad drove to Salt Lake City to get me.

As with any resort lodge, people came and went in quick succession. There were families who stayed for a week or two; others stayed for a month or more. People drifted in and out of my life, but the same ranch animals were always there. They were my constant companions and friends.

George taught me how to braid leather to make belts and reins. He taught me to back-braid to make lead ropes and trusted me to hold recalcitrant horses while he was shoeing. When shoeing, he wore a wide homemade saddle-leather brace buckled around his middle; leather wrist cuffs; and short, scarred chaps. He hot-shod, using a forge, for the horses who had foot problems. With his six-foot-plus frame, he had difficulty bending to shoe the small horses, so he taught me how to hold the hoof so he could tack the shoe on.

Dogs hung around the barn, chewing horse hoof trimmings, looking for attention, or chasing a cat. I spent hours watching the wild barn cats. I wanted a pet that would sit with me when the horses were out grazing, so one day, I lay by a hole in the split log floor in ambush. When an unsuspecting kitten popped up, I caught it. It was a skinny, frightened, fuzzy gray one. I held it quietly to calm it. I did not want it to go under the floor again because I might not have another chance to catch it. I knew better than to put anything around its neck, so I carefully tied a string around its middle to use as a leash. The kitten managed to scratch me; I let go, and it ran back into the hole. I tried to pull it by the string but failed. I was in a quandary. If I forced it up the hole, I could hurt it, but if I let go of the string, it might get hung up. Hoping it might chew the string off, I finally decided to let it go.

Later, I heard the dogs yipping and barking. They were jumping at the buck fence between the barn and the kitchen. Something was bouncing from the ground back onto the fence. I ran nearer with fear clutching my chest. It was the kitten, with its string caught in the crossbuck. The dogs nipped it with each bounce. I scared the dogs away and grabbed the kitten. I freed the string from the fence and tried to get it off, but it was too tight. I ran to George in the barn, because I knew he had a pocket knife. Before I reached George, the kitten died in my arms, a quivering bloody mass gasping for breath,. I had killed the kitten by my selfishness. It had been perfectly happy,

Cynthia with the visiting flicker on shoulder.

healthy, and useful as a wild barn cat. I cried until I was sick to my stomach. I became determined to respect others' lives and freedom forever after.

In contrast to my effort to control the kitten, one morning, as I sat on the barn ramp, lazing in the morning sun with my eyes half closed, a red-shafted flicker landed on my shoulder and settled happily, closing his eyes. He had a little black bib, rows of black speckles on his fat chest, and cheeks of bright orange. He matched my plaid shirt. I wondered if the shirt color made him think I was a safe place. I rose slowly to walk to the house to show Mom what a wonderful wild creature had come to visit me. I felt no need to control or catch him.

He was perfect just the way he was. After several minutes, he flew away. I was not going to try to keep him or cage him. I felt blessed by one of the Creator's beautiful wild critters befriending me.

The barn was my playground and my sanctuary. I could climb into the hayloft from either the log horse mangers or the cow stanchions. It was more fun for me than climbing the jungle gym at school. A pair of giant logs were strung across the middle of the hayloft, with a cable paralleling them and attached to both sides of the barn. When the barn was full of hay, the logs formed a cave with hay bales as walls. It was a good place to be alone with the peaceful sounds of shuffling animals below, the occasional snort of a horse blowing its nose, or the muffled sounds of conversation. No one found me in the hay cave. It was one of my special places.

One day Dad found cigarette butts in the hayloft. He confronted me. "Why were you smoking in the hayloft? You know the fire danger," Dad said, accusing me.

"Dad, I don't smoke. It wasn't me," I said.

Cynthia age 15 with Littleman and Dudie

"Now you won't get a car. Our agreement was if you didn't smoke before age eighteen, you would get a car." Dad ended any discussion. He was skeptical and I knew I could not change his mind.

But previously, one spring day, I had been working with the cabin crew, cleaning cabin number eight. I was elected to climb into the miniature attic. I was the smallest and fit into the tight place the best to remove a massive mouse nest. When the nest was removed, I scooted to the opening and was helped down. I coughed from the dust. One of the cabin girls suggested I have a smoke and lit one up for me. I took a few puffs but hated it. A few years later, I tried smoking again, but I did not want to waste my money, and I was too proud to beg any. I doubted that one experience would have been enough for me to lose our agreement about a car. At least it was an action I did, not one I was accused of unfairly. Every action has a consequence.

I avoided going to my parents when I needed to ponder something that disturbed me; I would ride to one of my sanctuaries up the mountain side. One of which I had built on a bluff about a half mile from the ranch. I made the structure by using an overhanging tree on the edge of the hill. I dragged another log to place against the forked one, forming a tripod with one long leg. Against the long leg, I leaned many small logs, sticks, and bush branches. It made a wonderful hidden shelter in which I could sit looking out over the countryside and ponder. Sometimes I would take a nap inside my shelter enjoying the shade and solitude. The only downfall was that it leaked when it rained. After I left White Grass, the wranglers rode to the lean-to and developed a legend about a renegade Indian who had built it as a hideout.

Instead of riding horses for fun in an arena as most girls with horses did, I not only ranged through the mountains but I also doctored injured horses. With a herd of eighty horses, there tended to be much squabbling, kicking, and biting. Morning wrangling brought the horses running down the mountain jumping fallen timber and thick brush, causing leg injuries, punctures, and cuts. If the wounds were not doctored, infection was imminent, and the wranglers avoided doctoring. I would tie an injured horse to the corral fence and would talk quietly and pet the injured horse until it calmed before I could squat under the horse with a rag dipped in a bucket of hot Epsom Salt water. I would remove the dirt and pick and pull the dried pus from the wound. It had to hurt, though I tried to be gentle. The animal would stand calmly. The horses willingly accepted my help. After the injury was clean, I would use gentian violet on minor cuts and Sulfanilamide on deeper wounds to inhibit further infection. Each injured horse needed treatment for several successive days; it kept me busy.

Mom and Dad bought Golden Rock, an abandoned sugar plantation on the ninety-three- square-mile Caribbean Island of Nevis (known as Alexander Hamilton's birthplace) to develop as a winter guest business using the $165,000 from the sale of White Grass. They moved me to a school closer to the Caribbean than Utah. Larry and Alice Messler, dudes from White Grass, recommended Foxhollow School in Lenox, Massachusetts. The Messlers lived near Foxhollow, in northern Connecticut, so I would have someone I knew close by. One of their daughters had attended Foxhollow and enjoyed the school, which was in the Berkshire Mountains, with trees and lawns, a riding program, and a large campus with wonderful mansions. The property was included originally in the Edith Wharton estate and an adjoining Roosevelt estate.

Mom and Dad decided Foxhollow was a good school for me. However, skill testing in math and reading established that I was not prepared for the stringent preparatory school curriculum of Foxhollow. Miss Farrell, the headmistress, suggested I go to summer school in Maine. At age fifteen, I faced my first summer away from the ranch, the horses, and my mountains. The remedial camp was located by a lake, with bunk cabins lining a path to the centrally located lodge. Tall trees overhung the cabins. Instruction included reading Dr. Seuss' books out loud. His writing forced me to look at the words carefully. I spent much time studying math. We also had time to swim in the lake, which was as cold as Phelps Lake back home. I was asked to lead a few of the craft classes, which I loved to do. My favorite was making platters out of sheet aluminum by pounding the middle until it was the right curved shape. But I missed White Grass, the horses, and the solitude I found in the mountains.

Foxhollow School, Autumn 1958–Spring 1961

Flying to school in Massachusetts was much different from my flying experience between Idaho Falls and Salt Lake City. Foxhollow was way across the United States, and I discovered there was an immense, diverse world beyond the Rocky Mountains. By myself, with trepidation, I traveled through various cities and airports and transferred from planes to trains. A few times, I missed the plane because I could not find the proper gate, which frightened me but went to the desk for directions.

The Eastern United States was different. Family background and connections with "important" people defined who you were. In the West, you were what you made of yourself, regardless of your connections, breeding, and associations. Even though Dad was from cultured Main Line Philadelphia stock and Mother was from aristocratic German stock, in Wyoming, it did not make a difference, since those connections were unknown in Massachusetts. At school, my parents' lineage should have helped, but my Wyoming upbringing erased that. I was the strange western- ranch freak of a cowgirl thrown in with a flock of cultured Eastern city debutantes.

Mom had bought me a western-style leather-like jacket which made me feel out-of-place. After study hall, we walked nearly a mile to the Mount, our dormitory. One evening, I slipped and fell on the slick hill and slid to the bottom, saving much walking. Soon the other girls wanted to wear my jacket so they could purposely lie on the snow to slide to the bottom of the hill. It was a lot of fun, and they befriended me so they could use my jacket.

With the cold weather and there was less snow than in Wyoming, the lagoons that traversed the school property froze. Some days, we skated for our activity instead of playing ball games. Field hockey was my favorite. We played in shorts and sweatshirts, even when the temperature was freezing. While playing lacrosse, I threw out my hip, so that was the last I was allowed to play lacrosse.

The British headmistress, Miss Farrell, saw how much I loved books. She appointed me to the library club. I helped to keep the books organized in the sunny pale-blue library next to the study hall. I learned how to repair them, build new spines, or secure loose pages. I felt Miss Farrell respected me. Many of the students came from diverse backgrounds. There was a French girl who lived in Chile; her parents were diplomats. There was a beautiful girl from Cuba and one from Hungary, but most were from well-to-do eastern families. Miss Farrell viewed all the children equally, accepted their differences, and treated them with respect.

In October, Mom and Dad came east to gain clientele for White Grass on their way to Nevis. Mom called and said, "We are driving to Foxhollow to see you and take you out to dinner next Friday." On Friday, while all the other girls ate dinner, I was dressed and waiting downstairs in the foyer for Mom and Dad to pick me up. Miss Farrell came to me and said my parents had called and could not make it. It would be months before I heard from them again.

One evening, after dinner, I was in study hall, as my demerits demanded. The other girls were getting ready to go to a concert. Miss Farrell came in.

"What are you doing here?" she asked.

"I have demerits to work off," I said as I looked up from my book.

"It is best for you to go to the concert," she told me. "You have five minutes to get changed and on the bus."

Even though I was different, with Miss Farrell's example, the girls treated me and one another well. There was no bullying. Each senior was assigned a new girl to show her the ways of the school. No one was left to fend for herself in the new surroundings.

The school's curriculum was much like that of a junior college. We used college textbooks for biology and chemistry. We studied English language writings from the Old English *Tristan and Iseult* to the authors Chaucer, Shakespeare, Blake, and Swift. The French teacher was from France and taught Latin too. The math teacher made us memorize the geometry theorems verbatim. Memorizing was the greatest difficulty for me. History of art and music was taught with the same timeline as world history, so we had a concept of what was happening in history, art, and music in each time period. Classes consisted of eight to ten students, so we received individual attention. I was made to toe the line.

Miss Farrell took our class to see the musical *Camelot* in New York City, to coincide with our study of early British history. We stayed in a hotel and walked to the theater. New York had more people than I had thought possible; they seemed to live on top of each other in the tall buildings. There was no quiet place.

The school was in the mountains. They were not like the Rockies but green and rolling, with lots of snow in winter. I learned to ride English style. I loved to ride Chico, the only western horse in the school stable. The instructor said we fell into bad Western ways, so I was usually assigned an Eastern-trained horse. When one acted up, I dropped the short stirrups, wrapped my legs around its barrel, and made it mind. This action made the instructor crazy. It was not a proper riding style, the instructor said. I liked riding best when we rode trails through the Berkshire woods, when the horse was allowed to go with loose reins and allowed a natural gait.

During my senior year at Foxhollow, Miss Farrell, recognizing my creative ability, suggested I visit Garland College in Boston. I took the train and then a cab to the college. I was interviewed. They let me attend a class. I was enthralled with the artistic direction of their curriculum.

On another senior trip, I went to Boston to interview for Colorado State University. I got lost in the city and, despondent, walked in the slush in high heels, trying to find the way, and missed my interview appointment. I finally found the hotel, rescheduled, and was interviewed. But I was so overwrought I was sure I did a poor job. My Foxhollow diploma reads, "Honors in Geometry, General Science, Appreciation of Music, and Biology and credits in English Literature and History, French, Algebra, Chemistry, and History of Art. *** Cynthia has learned to add effort to her naturally artistic perceptions." I was surprised and pleased with Miss Farrell's comments. Utah boarding had socialized me, and Foxhollow School had formed me into a somewhat cultured young adult. But I wondered where my life was going.

Looking back, I now realize that when I went to boarding school, my family's connection ended. I had no time with my parents. I was gone for nine months. In the three months of summer, they ate in the dining room with dudes, while I ate in the back with the help. They were busy managing the ranch. I was mostly guiding kids or dudes in the forest. We seldom saw each other and had no time together; family life died.

Tilly, My Companion

Before I started school at Rowland Hall, Dad bought a pair of piebalds, black-and-white horses. Their names were Tilly and Timmy. Dad said he bought them from a family whose children had outgrown the small horses. I rode Tilly during my summers home from Rowland Hall.

Tilly was part Shetland and part quarter horse and had a white chest, which made her look as if she wore pantaloons. Whereas Eva was patient and tolerant of me, I saw mischief in Tilly's honest eyes. Tilly needed a determined rider; Timmy was a better- behaved horse. George chose me to ride Tilly and Fran for Timmy. My first ride on Tilly was wrangling with George through the high mountain meadows. In the early morning, the horses were frisky, but Tilly behaved. Tilly and I were a good match; we were both strong-minded. She became my substitute for my family. However, she was never an easy ride; if I was not paying attention, she would leave the trail or brush me against a tree trunk. I was continually challenged to keep her in line. She had a wonderful fast walk and loved to run. We often went full speed along the dirt road below the ranch. She would stretch out with her belly close to the ground. I could feel the power of her rippling muscles with my legs. Sometimes, like a jockey, I tucked my head against her neck, which was easy without the hindrance of a saddle, and went full speed. Other times, I would sit up straight with the reins loose on her neck, my arms straight out from my shoulders, and my hair flying wildly in the wind; it gave me an exquisite sense of freedom.

During many of my preteen and teenage summers, my cousin Fran came to stay on the ranch, and we chose to ride together often. One hot day, Fran and I rode to the Phelps overlook—as usual, bareback. He was on Timmy, and I was on Tilly. He dared me to shortcut to the lake for a swim. Because I wanted to be tough like the guys, I accepted the challenge. We rode Snowy River–style off the moraine. Tilly's haunches slid on rocks, and I gripped with my knees and hung on to her mane for dear life. That ride scared me, I did not want to hurt Tilly and I did not want to be hurt. I think it scared Fran too, as we never took that shortcut again. I often took my frustrations out on Tilly, kicking her to a full run over rough ground. I made her climb steep mountain slopes where it probably was not safe. It was fortunate that she was tough. Spirit Guide must have been always near, as we came to no harm due to my mistreatment.

Tilly had a peculiar trait: she loved airplanes, or so we thought since she would disappear from the herd only to be found later watching the planes at the airport many miles away and across the Snake River. George thought he could break her of the habit, so he rode her hard and swam the river back to White Grass. It was quite a sight, with George's six-foot-plus frame draped over the little mare and his feet nearly dragging on the ground. She was not even out of breath on arrival. Soon she was back at the airport.

Tilly had a foal who seemed to fly with the wind across the hay field in front of the Main Cabin. I named him Windy. When I returned from boarding school, I saw that his tail had been broken by the kink in it. His shoulder was dislocated. He limped. The cowboys had been much too rough in trying to train him to lead. I was angry. I hoped they had not broken his spirit. I only brushed him and did not train him during the summer, because I wanted him to heal for a year.

The following summer, I started to train him again. He showed his spirit by bucking every morning before settling to work. Loping home once, I pulled right to go around a tree; he wanted to go left. Showing his strong-mindedness, we went through the tree, which caused a road-rash type injury on my neck. With patience and gentleness, he became a much-prized ranch horse. One day, Dad told me his mother, Tilly, died during another birth. I was heartbroken. She had been my best friend during my preteen and beginning teen years, when I had been in such turmoil. She had been my rock. I would miss her sorely. I wanted to see her to prove to myself that she was gone, but Mom would not let me. I knew Mom and Dad were trying to protect me, but I needed closure.

I recalled one winter in the house Dad built on Kelly Street in Jackson when Sniffer disappeared. I disliked that dog because he would knock me down and hump. One day I came home from school and Dad said that his cousin came and wanted Sniffer to live with him. But I suspected that Dad had put him down like he did severely injured or sick horses; I suspected he put Tilly down or sold her. I didn't really want to know the truth so I avoided searching for her body. I decided I would not allow myself to wallow in disappointment; I needed to continue doing what was expected of me.

On a rare trip to town with Mom, I saw a hackamore bit at Mercill's Mercantile store. I thought it would look good on Windy. It had a heart-shaped cutout and etched design on the shank. It had a sheepskin noseband, which would be comfortable for him. I was not going to ask my parents, for I was sure the answer would be, "No. There are lots of bridles and hackamores in the barn. Use one of them." But I wanted my own. Maybe I could make money to buy it.

"Mom, may I borrow your leather- engraving tools?" I asked.

"What do you want to do with them?" she asked. She was probably remembering the silver fork, spoon, and knife she had given me etched with Cynthia. I regretted that through my neglect, I had lost all but the soup spoon which I still use.

"I want to make hat bands," I answered. "I'll be careful and not lose them," I added.

"OK, I'll get them for you. Keep them in their box when not in use. Do not leave them outside."

With the leather draw knife, I cut narrow strips off the large hide in the barn's tack room. I took the leather strips and tools to the bench under the big Douglas fir tree next to the Main Cabin. There I would be out of everyone's way but centrally located. I could watch the ranch activities. I spent many days building inventory. When the dudes walked by for meal times at the Main Cabin, they saw me making hat bands. They liked them and bought them. When I placed them on their hats, they were emulating the cowboys, which they especially liked. By the end of August, I had enough money to buy the hackamore.

I hitched a ride to town with Mom. As she conducted her business at the Mercill's Mercantile, I bought my hackamore. I still needed a headstall and reins, so I collected long black hair from horses' tails and braided a headstall using the method George had taught me. It was not a good job; hairs stuck out every which way but I used it. For the reins, I cut a medium-sized strip from the barn hide and made two cuts along its length, leaving a few inches of solid leather at each end. By weaving and pulling the end piece through, I had a three-strand-looking braid. The solid ends made it easy to attach to the hackamore bit.

I was angry when the wranglers used my hackamore. I had worked hard to buy it and to braid the headstall and reins. It was mine, and I was proud of it. But what could I have expected? The wranglers continued to use the saddle delegated to me. I had bought a quick buckle for tightening the cinch, and my silver nameplate, a gift from Mom and Dad, was screwed onto the back. They stole the quick buckle, removed the nameplate, and then used my saddle. I was constantly looking for it. I decided to take my hackamore to my room each night. It was not going to go away. I still have the hackamore and silver nameplate but not the saddle. Each time my saddle was gone, I mumbled complaints to anyone within hearing in the barn. It did no good, and I was not going to tattle to my folks. I learned early in my life that everyone else was considered before I was.

Marmie's sidesaddle hung in the tack room. For fun, occasionally, I would put it on my horse and ride through the field. I especially enjoyed loping and jumping the irrigation ditches while riding with it though I never rode it on the trails.

"Pumpkin, I am going to Turpin Meadows to pick up the pack trip horses. Do you want to go?" Dad said as he casually came up behind me and, using his strong hands, pulled my shoulders back—his way of showing affection. "Stand up straight," he would say. I knew that the day before, a pack trip had come back to the ranch. I presumed we were going to pick the horses up to bring them home.

"Yes," I said. Anytime Dad asked me to go with him, I was all in. It was usually an adventure, as I never knew what would happen, and I enjoyed the unexpected.

Dad threw several halters behind the seat of the International snub-nosed green horse-hauling truck, and we were gone for the day. At Turpin Meadows corals, where they had been left after the pack trip, the horses whinnied in welcome. They were easy to catch. We led them up the wood ramp to load into the truck. They were well behaved—they probably knew they were going home.

On the way home, Dad pulled into Dornan's Chuckwagon in Moose and parked in front. It was rare for Dad to pass Dornan's without stopping. We walked into the bar. I slid onto one of the tall stools next to Dad.

"Hi, Frank. Is Cindy of age to be in the bar?" Jack Dornan, the owner, asked.

"Do you think I would bring my daughter in here if she wasn't of age?" Dad responded. I was fourteen. Dad ordered a martini for himself and a Coke for me.

Nevis, West Indies

My first visit to Nevis in the Caribbean was for Christmas 1957. Golden Rock would be Mom and Dad's winter home and business from October throu5.5gh April, while White Grass was still their summer home and business from May through September. I took a train from Lenox to Idlewild Airport in New York City. I flew to San Juan, where I changed planes to land at St. Kitts, British West

Indies. Dad met me with his boat, and we bounced over the waves to Charlestown, the port town on Nevis. Since Golden Rock did not have a place for Mom and Dad to live yet, they rented a cabin on the beach. I ate mangoes with the surf slapping my shins as sweet juice dripped from my elbows. No worries, I relaxed.

They drove me around the small inland. We went to see the abandoned 1800s sugar estate, Golden Rock. There was a round hand-hewn stone mill that once had squeezed juice from the sugarcane, and under the mill were dungeons reminiscent of slave times. There was a longhouse that Mom said would be the lodge. There were a few small buildings, all made of huge hand-hewn rock nearly two feet thick. Besides repairing and modernizing the mill and longhouse, Mom and Dad were building two duplex guesthouses. They were excited about opening for guests the following winter.

In the rented beach house, we had a thorn tree as a Christmas tree, with candles as lights and a few homemade decorations hanging from thorny and leafy
branches. We boated to St. Kitts for the Steel Band Contest, for which each village had its own steel band. Each band played and danced their way into Basseterre, the main town, followed by innumerable dancing fans. It was a great, colorful festival.

By their second winter on Nevis, Mom and Dad had moved to Golden Rock, their new resort. At Golden Rock, Mom coordinated with the local Gingerland School and invited the children to a Christmas celebration, where she gave each child clothing and candy as gifts.

The following summer, I was back on the ranch with Mom and Dad, as usual. Mom and Dad, at the suggestion of several dudes, decided to have someone hired to entertain the children, whom they called the kid wrangler. That summer, Judith, a former dude now with a summer job at White Grass, and I were kid wranglers. She would lead the rides, and I would take the rear of the line, riding Windy. When the slow horses fell behind, they tended to trot to catch up with the giggling children bouncing on top. I held Windy at a walk to catch up. Since he wanted to be with the other horses, he went as fast as he could walk. When the children loped along the trail, I would keep him at a fast trot, forcing him to extend his gait. The following year when I first asked him to run, he was awkward, but he learned quickly. I was teaching him for the novelty races at the Dude Ranchers' Rodeo held each midsummer. In the following years, Windy won often; he would take the lead early in the walk and keep the lead in the trot. If the run had been a longer stretch, his short legs might not have held the lead against horses with longer legs.

Eventually, I wanted a big horse. Eva, Judy, Tilly, and Windy were all small horses. I chose Bud from the seventy or more horses on the ranch. He was a tall, rawboned horse. Standing on my tiptoes, I could verily see over his back. Whereas I could leap onto Tilly or Windy, it was impossible to leap onto Bud. It would have been uncomfortable riding him bareback, because he had a bony back. He was a bay with three white feet and a snip of white on his nose. I liked his dark brown honest eyes. When riding him, if I held the rein tension just right and used my knee pressure just so, he would pace. A pace is a gait in which the left legs move in unison, and then the right ones move in unison. It creates a fast-moving, swaying gait, and it was a comfortable ride. By the time I rode Bud, I used a saddle most of the time as I had become interested in boys and did not want my jeans covered with horse sweat and hair.

The job demanded Judith and I get up each morning at four thirty. We helped to bring the horses in from the mountainside. We ate breakfast and helped to saddle the dude horses. By nine o'clock, the dudes would come to ride. Judith and I oversaw children from as young as four to age eighteen or older if they wanted to come with us. Unexpectedly, halfway through the summer, Judith had to go home because of a family illness.

At fifteen, with Judy gone, Mom and Dad put me in charge. I taught children to ride and took them on day rides and picnics. The trick to make everyone happy was to pick the right horse to best suit the child, as Dad had done for me. I had to know each horse's personality to be successful, which I did. After the rides, I supervised the children during their evening meal. Then I cleared and cleaned the table in preparation for the adult dinner. I entertained the kids outside until their parents finished eating. Typically, I had them until seven or eight pm. It was more responsibility than I realized at the time. It was my first paying job, except for picking up rocks for Marmie. I could finally buy things I wanted, such as a new headstall. I refused to beg Mom when I needed something. I did not have to pick up Dad's discarded coins. The income gave me a sense of freedom and control.

One day I had several children on a ride, when the weather turned; angry dark clouds sailed over the Tetons, and it started to rain. It quickly cooled and threatened to hail. I turned the ride back toward the ranch, trotting as fast as I dared, hoping to beat the pelting hail that could sting the horses into bucking. I envisioned children scattered on the ground, screaming, as horses ran away—chaos. The hail caught us before we reached home. I had the children follow me into the thickest patch of trees I could find for shelter. We were crowded, ducking into the low branches; the horses were restless. Bud was a rock, obeying and staying calm. I talked to the children in quiet, confident tones, as I would have talked to an injured and frightened horse. Soon the summer storm passed, and we rode home wet. The children thought we had had a great adventure, but I knew we had narrowly escaped disaster; Spirit Guide protected us. Also, my choice of horse to fit each child's ability helped to prevent disaster. For example, I often chose Koon for the youngest children to ride, as he was a great child sitter. I saw him, time after time, step under a young child who was losing his or her balance. It was the same way he kept packs balanced when used as a packhorse.

When Koon was turned out to graze, he liked to graze near the shores of Phelps Lake. When I wrangled, I would see him hide in thick trees, holding his bell against his neck to silence it. He would stay still. He was smart and wanted to stay out to graze all day instead of going to work! At hunting camp, he loved to eat pies and cookies and sometimes entered the cook tent. Chocolate cream pie was his favorite. On picnics, the children loved to share their cookies with him, which made the children giggle.

These four-legged siblings taught me that I could be strong but still gentle. I learned their behavior could tell me when something was amiss or threatening. Communication does not need to be verbal. I learned horses and people respond better to patience better than anger.

The summer I was seventeen, I met Pete on the trail. He worked at the neighboring Circle H Ranch. He must have been nineteen or twenty, and we became friends.

I had become cocky about my riding ability. I could ride every horse at White Grass and had trained a few of them. I was barrel racing at the Wilson rodeo and had tried several ranch horses, but my competition rode expensive quarter horses professionally trained.

"You did pretty good at the barrels last weekend," Pete said as he limply leaned against the corral rail.

"You should ride our horse, Reno," a wrangler friend of Pete's from the R Lazy S Ranch said.

"He can turn on a dime and give you change. But he might rear over backward when you stop him," Pete warned. Reno was a rangy dark-red roan. I rode him around the pasture a few times. He was alert and did turn well—so well that he almost turned out from under me. I decided to try him at the arena. He ran the barrels fast, clean, and with a good time; I thought I might win money with him. But when I pulled on the reins to stop, he reared. I had to bail off. Once, at the barrel racing competition in Wilson, as I jumped off, he went all the way over and landed on his back. I was not scared easily, but I could imagine a thousand-pound horse on top of me, with the saddle horn impaled in my gut. I decided Reno was not for me. That ended my barrel-racing days.

Pete and I planned a ride to Marian Lake after the dudes had gone. Harold Hammond had found the lake and named it after his wife, my grandmother. Dad frequently took one-night pack trips to the beautiful little lake, but I had not been there. I wanted to see it. We chose the fastest walking horses from our respective ranches and started at dawn. I used Bud. We were excited to be out with no dudes and no worries, going our own speed and aiming for new territory.

We made good time past Phelps Lake, into Open Canyon, and over a divide into Granite Canyon. We stopped to give the horses a quick breather and used the time to eat our lunch of squashed sandwiches and oranges from our saddlebags. Granite Canyon was much longer than I had thought. We finally saw talus slopes, indicating our elevation; threatening clouds boiled over the next ridge. It started to snow. We had to turn back. I was disappointed to miss Marian Lake. Our jubilant mood turned quiet and thoughtful. Our horses were worn out, stumbling occasionally. The sun set; no moon rose. Now I understood why Dad took a full day to get to Marian Lake and another to ride home.

Like most ranch employees, Pete moved on, and I never saw him after that summer. Years later, I backpacked up Granite Canyon to Marian Lake and was thrilled to see the lake named after my grandmother for the first time. It is nestled below gleaming granite cliffs, with sky-blue water reflecting cumulus clouds and jade-green grass hugging its edges.

On weekends at White Grass, we often played games on horseback. Capturing the flag was a favorite; the curving ranch driveway was the middle line between the two teams, fences on the north and east were side boundaries, the pond was the west boundary, and a line of trees was the south boundary. We split into two teams. To start play, the flag was thrown into the air at the centerline. Everyone scrambled to catch it and run for the opponent's goal. It was fair to grab the flag from another's hands.

Once, I was galloping to the goal, when my horse stumbled in a gopher hole. My knee was crushed under the horse. I would not whine. The horse jumped up. I climbed on. I excused myself from the rest of the game and put my horse in the corral. My stubborn young body healed well.

In the excitement of another capture-the-flag game, we were chasing Ben, one of the wranglers, who rode out of bounds to keep the flag from the opposition. The electrical- pole guy wire caught under his chin. It flipped him off his horse. He landed flat on his back on a pile of rocks. We dismounted and went to see if he was alive. Since Ben was a veterinary student, he recognized that he had probably broken his neck. We called an ambulance from town. Ben gave them directions on how to lift a person with a broken neck. He was taken to the hospital, where he was put in traction with pins in his head and weights on his legs. Remarkably, he healed with no signs of permanent damage.

Ben was kind. Once, I was curled up in the manger, crying. A horse was pushing hay around me, chomping, and dribbling saliva on me as tears dripped down my cheeks. The horse's presence was comforting. I was trying to make sense of my loneliness. I wondered what my mother looked like. I wondered if we shared similar characteristics. Did I have another family somewhere? Why did I always feel different? I looked up, and Ben was bent over the manger, looking at me. He must have heard my sniffling, and he asked what was wrong. I talked to him. It was the first time I had confided in anyone. He was kind and made me feel better. He was my hero.

Another favorite game was musical chairs on horseback. We would place old chairs in a big circle in the field. Curt Winsor, a longtime dude, played the guitar as we rode around the circle. When he stopped playing, we jumped off our horses and scrambled to sit in a chair. We had to hold the reins of our horses and sit, not stand, on the chair.

Whoever lost a seat or lost hold of his or her horse was out of the game. A chair would be removed from the circle, and the remaining riders would circle again. When only two riders were left with one chair, things were rough. We played with lots of laughs and good spirits.

Dad preferred to play polo. He would gather the wranglers and play in the rough field. It was fun to watch grown men carry sticks and gallop around chasing a ball.

Even though I liked playing games on horseback, I still chose to ride alone, observing wildlife, finding new elk trails, and seeking solitude. I never knew what I would find, but it was exhilarating to explore. One time, I went to Phelps Lake to swim, but hikers were picnicking on my favorite beach, so I rode around to the inlet, which was seldom used. I tied Shane to a nearby tree. I took off my boots, jeans, and shirt and swam parallel to the shore, when I saw a Western

Frank Galey and the wranglers playing cowboy polo.

Garter Snake swimming toward me. I moved out of its line of travel. It changed directions to follow me. I knew it was not poisonous, but it felt creepy to be stalked by a snake, especially in water. I tried to go faster, but it caught up with me. As my feet touched bottom, I grabbed the snake by the tail and swung it far into the lake—but it came right back at me! I continued to hurry toward shore, but it caught up with me again. I threw it farther. By then, I was really scared of that snake. It was still stalking me as I reached shore. I grabbed my jeans, shirt, and boots; swung up onto Shane's bareback with my clothes in hand; and loped away. I never went back to the inlet to swim.

Only a few years earlier, my friend Bethy, whose family had been coming to the ranch for many years, and I had caught snakes, put them in our hats, and rode bareback to the ranch to show off. We would feel them squirming around on top of our heads, which did not bother us. When I showed Mom my catch, she was not impressed. That Western Garter Snake taught me to be wary of snakes. I had become too trusting; the danger is always present in the backcountry.

I also liked to ride to Moose, where a sign read, "Population: 2 in summer, 1 in winter." Dornan's Chuckwagon and Bar was across the Snake River, accessed by an old steel truss bridge. Menor's Ferry was once the only way across the river. It was attached to a cable secured on each side of the river. By angling the ferry's bow, the current would push the ferry across. In the 1960s, Menor's Ferry was managed as a historical tourist attraction, taking visitors across. When I rode to Moose, the narrow steel bridge crossed the river to Dornan's. I was afraid to take my horse across the bridge because of the busy car traffic, so I did not go to Dornan's.

While in Moose, I usually stopped at the Trading Post for a soda or ice cream, using coins I picked up from Mom and Dad's bedroom floor. The Trading Post had all kinds of Western wear and Indian crafts. Next door, Carmichael's Tackle Shop had colorful fishing flies, rods , reals, and fishing-type clothes. In the back of the tackle shop was our post office.

The Chapel of the Transfiguration was near Menor's Ferry. I could look through the chapel's big plate-glass window at the Tetons, my cathedral. Looking out the window reminded me that the Creator had made the mountains beautiful and awesome. I felt the Creator's spirit in the trees, meadows, and glades. His actions were reflected in the elk, grizzlies, marmots, and ants—in all the animals great and small. His Spirit invaded my soul. The church represented formal worship, but the mountains were my place of private faith. The chapel brought them together. I was confirmed and married in the Chapel of the Transfiguration, and both my children were baptized there. In 1985, Dad's memorial service was held there.

Whereas most kids had someone to drive them to activities, I had my horse for transportation. But my curfew was four o'clock, and if I missed it, I would be in big trouble—no excuses! I was desperately trying to find friends. I once rode to the Bar BC, where a fellow student from Foxhollow School was spending the summer. With young people my age, I swam in the earthen pool. I enjoyed their company so much that I lost track of the time. When it began to get dark, my parents phoned the ranch. They came for me in the car, and I had to leave Windy for the night. The next day, Mom drove me back to Bar BC to get Windy to ride him home. I was not allowed to talk to anyone; I had to saddle up and ride. My punishment was being grounded: no horse riding for a week. That was the worst punishment they could have thought of.

When I was married and moved away from White Grass, I asked Dad if I could take Windy. He said Windy was too good a horse for the ranch to lose. It reminded me that nothing of my parents or anything of the ranch would come to me. I never was given a horse, only assigned one to use. I had learned to accept hurts from my parents, but it was still painful. I refused to ask anything from them. I reasoned that if I did not ask, they could not hurt me.

I graduated from Foxhollow preparatory school and flew back to Jackson, dragging skis and two big suitcases. I settled into the required spring ranch work, as usual. That spring, a new employee, Jim, came to work at White Grass with a good recommendation from the manager of Jenny Lake Lodge, where he had previously worked. He was not a former dude, nor was he from the East Coast; he was from the Midwest. He was going to Utah State University with the GI Bill grant. Jim invited me to see a movie in Jackson with others from the ranch. Another time, we all went square dancing at Jackson Lake Lodge. Jim took me with him when he went fishing. He fished; with a book in my back pocket, I read, watched, or enjoyed wandering the shore, looking at flowers and gnarled sticks and listening to the sounds of birds. The Creator made Earth marvelous and diverse; I thought it amazing. It was also amazing to me that someone invited me to go to the movies, square dancing, or fishing. It was my first. No one had included me before.

Independence in Philadelphia, Winter 1961–1962

I had graduated from Foxhollow, and another winter was approaching. Jim had left for university, and Mom and Dad had closed the cabins. Saddles hung in the barn, and the water was ready to be shut off. Before they left for their winter business in Nevis, my parents had to place me. They decided I was not going to be accepted into Garland College or University of Colorado. Though I eventually received acceptance to Garland College, it came too late, according to Mom and Dad. They had sent an application and admission fee to Philadelphia School of Office Training in downtown Philadelphia. It was a done deal; I had to go. Soon Mom and Dad would be going for winter to Nevis in the Caribbean. I felt the home was on the ranch, but in winter, the water system was closed. Dad no longer kept pigs, chickens, or cattle; the horses went to Lander for the winter pasture. White Grass would be closed and locked by the many feet of snow. White Grass was not a home during the long winter anymore.

To encourage me, Mom said, "With office training, you can get a job anywhere. I tried to go to college to be a veterinarian. I was the only female. I was basically run off by the male students. Office training is better." She insisted. I thought her experience did not define what would happen to me. I would do what I must and wait for the Spirit Guide's direction. With patience, I accepted the inevitable, but I was not happy. The river had taken control of my raft. I was floating on a slow current with no paddle, no direction, and doldrums, waiting. I had finished the state- required schooling.

When Mom and Dad were in Nevis, there was no place for me. In a town or city, if homes were closed and locked, one could still break in and turn on the electricity for heat and light, whereas the Galey house was snowed in, with snow covering half of each window, no electricity, no heat, and no water. To heat the house, I would have had to find firewood, which was buried under five or six feet of snow— an impossibility. However, each summer, I was on the ranch, biding my time and taking advantage of the ranch for what time I could. Since I was not paid for my work on the ranch, I had no money. I was at the mercy of my parents. I had to ride the slow river current. I would wait. In the future, I would get control of my life, and I could use the current to go toward a goal. I was hopeful the Spirit Guide would direct me. I look back now and realize how right my folks were about Garland College. If I had gone to Garland, it would have prepared me for a job in a city, and I would have hated working and living in a city.

About that time, I realized Dad's family's culture did not pass possessions on to the next generation. Dad had to buy White Grass from his mom. He had sold it away from me. The only thing he had of his father's was an elephant tusk, and from his mother, he had a grandfather clock that was supposed to be mine but was in safekeeping with Dad. Mom had written in the family album that it was to come to me on my twenty-first birthday. But when I was twenty-one and asked Dad for the album, he said no. During a visit when I was thirty-three, I concealed the album under my coat and took it. He must not have missed it, because he never said anything.

As fall approached, I went east to Philadelphia to stay with Dad's sister Mopsie and attend business school, which would last until May. At Christmas, Jim used his break from Utah State University to come to see me. Even though we had been writing to each other since fall, his visit was a surprise; I had doubted he cared that much. He stayed at a nearby motel but ate dinner with us. We drove to visit some historical sights and had a fun time together.

To get to school each day, I trudged a mile through slushy snow to the Penllyn train station teetering beside the road, wearing heels and business clothing that had little warmth. I arrived in downtown Philadelphia's dreary underground passages, where the homeless and drunks lurked along seeping walls, seeking protection from the foul weather. The passages were permeated by sour, foul odors. I was appalled by the living conditions of those people. Philadelphia felt like a caustic, alien place.

In lieu of walking to the train and encountering the dangerous, frightening underground, I wrote to Dad, emphasizing my safety and need for a vehicle. He sent me a hundred dollars to buy a car. Cousin Fran took me to a dealership owned by a distant relative in nearby Conshohocken. The only car that fit my budget was a sage- green compact 1942 Plymouth sedan with bare tires. It amused me that the car was the same age I was. I named her Sage, and she was a character. She worked well if I filled her with Sinclair gas; other brands made her engine knock. I kept a box of ashes from Aunt Mopsie's fireplace behind the driver's seat, so when I drove the slippery, snowy roads, I could open my door and throw the ashes under the back tires. Sage refused to start on cold, wet mornings until I wiped her spark plugs dry. A fellow at a business school gave me a discarded radio from a Buick. It fits upside down between the dash and seat. I enjoyed the company of music. You would not think such an old car would be safe, but I felt safe in her. The best part of having a car was that I could drive to the Main Line train station, arrive closer to school, and avoid the underground passages. Also, to soothe my loneliness, I could drive to visit my cousin Fran, Lori, and baby Francis, the only people my age I knew in Philadelphia.

Aunt Anna Ingersoll held a formal tea each Sunday afternoon. Previously, I had attended tea with Aunt Mopsie, and I liked the elderly Aunt Anna. One Sunday, there was more than a foot of new snow. No vehicles moved. I bundled up and walked a few miles to Aunt Anna's. Her butler was surprised to see someone at the door. With his help, I shed my outer clothing and wet brogues in the hall. Aunt Anna was sitting in her usual place on her worn leather couch. She was surprised but welcoming. I pulled a chair near the fragile tea cart and sat. She poured tea with her pale, delicate hands, into translucent China cups asking if I wanted sugar or milk. She asked what my interests were and how I liked business school and the city. I answered honestly. Aunt Anna was the first adult to ask me what I thought. We had a delightful conversation.

With the help of the butler, I bundled up. I trudged back through the knee-high snow to Aunt Mopsie's. As I walked back, I thought about how thankful I was to have Sage so I would not have to walk to the train station in heels through so much snow.

When spring came, my cousins invited me to a pool party. Aunt Mopsie took me to a department store to buy a swimsuit. I had no idea what kind to get, and neither did Aunt Mopsie. In Wyoming, I swam in my clothes at Bar BC or underwear by myself in Phelps Lake. I chose a blue cotton boy-shorts type of suit. When I arrived at the party, I felt as if I had on a 1920s swimming costume compared to the others' skimpy, tight-fitting ones. I was out of place again. They let me know it by laughing or ignoring me. On the ranch, those same youths would have been out of place. But I never would have thought of treating them the way they were treating me.

During many weekends, Aunt Mopsie took me on outings that outweighed some of my suffering through business school. She took me to Merion, Pennsylvania, to a private fine art museum; to Valley Forge; and to the Philadelphia Museum of Art. I was amazed at the quality of color and shape of the artwork in person compared to seeing photos of them at school. When we went to historical sites, I felt the history; it was much more meaningful than only reading about it. My time in Philadelphia was the loneliest of my life, especially because there were many people physically near, but I was invisible to them. I was glad when I graduated from business school. I knew the East was not for me. I knew I had to go back west to Wyoming, back to my cathedral, the sacred mountains, and the forests, where I thrived. Back to my friends, the four-leggeds, who seemed to like and understand me and had patience.

I wanted to drive Sage west. She was running smoothly, with no indication of problems. I figured if I got tired, I could stop, lie down in the backseat, lock the doors, and sleep. But Dad and Mom insisted I not drive Sage. I could not even drive following my cousins Fran and Lori west. So, I sold Sage to my uncle, who shortly drove through a stop sign and totaled her. I knew it was not true, but as with passing a pet on to a neglectful person, I felt responsible and sad. Looking back, I feel I should have stood my ground and driven myself west.

Instead, I rode with Fran and Lori in their blue Ford Fairlane. It had a broken thermostat, which caused many stops. Baby Francis was sick and crying; Fran was stressed. After several days of driving, we came to a junction in mid- Wyoming. Fran asked me to look on the map for directions. Before I could unfold the map, he turned north. With the wrong turn, we arrived in Cody instead of Jackson, adding another day of driving.

"If I am not back by morning, take Lori and Francis to Jackson," Fran huffed as he turned and stalked off to a bar. I was prepared to drive us to Jackson, but he made it back before morning and took over driving again.

By the time we reached Moose, he refused to make the six-mile detour to take me to the ranch. He dropped me off in Moose. I was glad to be out of the Fairlane full of tension. I used the post office phone to call Mom and Dad for a ride home. As I waited, I breathed the rare mountain air I had sorely missed. After nine months away, it felt like a precious elixir lifting my soul. Jim picked me up as he had known I would be coming home and had come from Logan to stay at the ranch for my arrival.

Mom and Dad greeted me at their house and helped carry my two suitcases into my corner room. Jim carried my skis to the shop for safekeeping. Mom had prepared a nice dinner, and soon we moved to the kitchen and all sat around the table together. Mom and Dad related all the work still to be done and the prospects for the coming dude season.

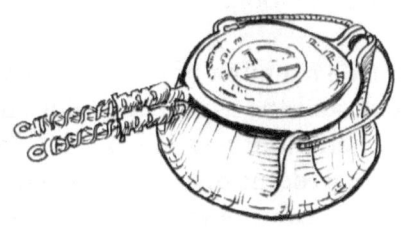

CHAPTER 4

Practicing Marriage, 1962–1967

AFTER DINNER, JIM AND I TALKED AS WE WALKED NORTH PAST THE row of cabins. Jim's arm draped across my shoulder, made me feel soft and pliable. We turned around at Sky Ranch, surprised at how far we had gone.

Dad met us as we came by the Main Cabin. "What have you been doing? It's dark. Follow me."

At the Galey house, we stood like recalcitrant children in front of Mom and Dad, though we had done nothing wrong.

Mom confronted us. "We are not going to have starstruck-lovers working here. You won't get your jobs done. Does Jim want to find a job elsewhere, or do you two want to get married?"

Thoughts flew through my head. I could cause him to lose a summer job that paid his university expenses. He was a good worker, so he had prospects. He was the only male to have interest in me. I was desperate to have a friend. I knew I had not done well enough at Philadelphia School of Business to get a job using office skills. I was lost. Living at my parents' ranch was only a three-month option, as they were gone in winter, and the place was snowed shut. I knew there was no place for me in Nevis. The time I had tried to get a job at the veterinarian's office in Jackson, Dad had put his foot down, saying, "If you are going to work, I need you on the ranch." So, I had no connections in town to even look for a job or find a place to live. After school, what came next? I guessed marriage. If we married, I could leave my parents' house and have a full-time friend. I did not know what Jim thought, but he looked at me smiling and said he wanted to marry me.

The spring hillsides were a sunburst of yellow balsamroot interspersed with blue larkspur, and the aspen trees glowed with early spring chartreuse leaves when Mom sent me to Salt Lake City with Mimi Crenshaw to pick out a wedding dress. Later, Mom and I picked bouquets of wildflowers to grace the pews and altar. My bouquet was wildflowers and calla lilies. Mom insisted on calla lilies. I do not know why. To me, they represented a formal life, not what I envisioned for myself. The ceremony was in the Chapel of Transfiguration, with the Crenshaws and many of my parents' friends present. A few of Jim's friends and Jim's parents attended. As Jim and I stood together, the sunlit Tetons shone through the picture window above the altar—the mountains, my cathedral. Even though I had reservations about marrying Jim, I was a happy girl. June 1962, I was nineteen, and we were married before the dudes arrived.

The reception was held at White Grass. Mom and Rachel, the ranch manager, decorated the Main Cabin with wildflowers. They put on a great hors d'oeuvre spread, easily enough for a meal, including plump, juicy shrimp in a huge glass bowl with a tangy sauce. There was a small band. Jim and I danced, as did many other people. Oma, Opa, Fran, and Lori were there, which greatly pleased me. We opened a mountain of gifts, utilitarian ones, and aesthetic ones. Sixty years later, I still use the ironing board and treasure the Steuben glass bowl we received as wedding gifts.

I overheard a neighbor say, "I'll give this marriage a couple of years. Jim thinks the Galeys have money because they have a ranch." My mulish spirit emerged. I was determined to make this marriage work, no matter what. I wanted to prove the respected neighbor wrong. We were given a week to honeymoon and then were expected back to work on the ranch. We drove to Las Vegas and visited Zion and Bryce National Parks. I enjoyed the colorful and unusual rock formations. We stayed in a small Las Vegas motel. We saw a young Waylon Jennings at one of the old-town casinos and had dinner at a show on the Strip. It was crowded, and the food was mediocre, but I enjoyed the show. I only had ever seen the shows that came to Jackson, such as Sons of the Pioneers, which I sneaked into as a seventeen-year-old. At that time, one needed to be twenty-one to enter the bars in Wyoming.

When back on the ranch, we stayed in a cabin for a few weeks. One morning, Jim and I were arguing. He demanded something I was not going to do. He started screaming at me. I screamed back. Frightened, I ran out the door. He sprinted after me and tackled me like a football player. I landed facedown. The wind was knocked out of me. I thought marriage was a partnership, not a boss-and-slave or master-and-doormat relationship. Mom and Dad, though having difficulties occasionally, were a good partnership. The incident frightened both of us. I learned not to confront him directly. But I was not necessarily going to obey. He bossed me less. As E. E. Cummings said, "It takes courage to grow up to who you ought to be." I wondered does one ever stop growing up?

With my marriage, it seemed the other employees accepted me as one of them by practical jokes. One morning, I was going to town. I sat in the VW Bug, turned it on, put it in first gear, and went nowhere. I looked behind me, where three grinning cowboys held the wheels off the ground. It was a milestone; I did not feel so alone.

The dudes arrived. The cabins were needed. Female employees had their bunk cabin near the Main Cabin, and the males had bachelor quarters south of the barn. There was no cabin for Jim and me. We moved to a leaky eight-by- twelve-foot wall tent. I was a kid wrangler,

1962, Cynthia Galey and James Kinker wed at the
Chapel of Transfiguration, Moose, Wyoming

1962, Cynthia Galey and James Kinker at the reception on White Grass Ranch.

officially this time, with a salary. I started work at four o'clock in the morning to wrangle horses, help with saddling dude horses, and make sandwiches for the all-day rides. After breakfast, with four hours of work accomplished, it was time to take the children riding. Sometimes we went on all-day rides with a picnic; other days, we went for morning and afternoon rides. The rides had to be back in time for the horses to be unsaddled and let out to graze at four o'clock. After unsaddling, I had an hour or so to rest and bathe. Then I was back to work; I ate dinner with the children, helped clear the table, and reset it for the adult seating that followed. I occupied the children with outside games until their parents were through with their evening meal. I often worked a fourteen-hour day. Looking back, I do not know how I had the energy.

The summer of 1962 was wet. At the end of the workday, I climbed a rickety ladder and painted the aged gray canvas tent roof with Behr canvas sealer to waterproof it. It took several evenings. First, I covered the area above the bed and dresser, so we could sleep dry. Jim usually played cards with other employees or dude children after he finished working. I felt put upon, with no help in making our tent dry. About the time I had it waterproofed, the wall tent was needed for dude children. Jim and I set up a small canvas camp tent farther into the woods. We slept on the ground and had our clothes in duffel bags. It was so damp and miserable that Charlie, our yellow Labrador, deserted us. He went to sleep in the dry house with Mom and Dad.

I became sick. I thought it was the stomach flu, maybe caused by the damp living conditions.

"You are going to the doctor," Mom said.

"You are pregnant," the doctor told me.

Dad had recently asked me to go on a several-day pack trip into the Thorofare country south of Yellowstone National Park. He wanted help with packing, horse care, setting up camp, and cooking. I was looking forward to the trip. I remembered a previous trip to Thorofare when I had fun helping Dad. But Mom was anxious. Her own difficulty with carrying a child caused her excessive worry about me.

"No more saddling horses. You can take rides out and take care of the children, but you are not going on the pack trip," Mom said. "You will make sandwiches and help Ellen," she added, as if it were an afterthought. I thought riding on a pack trip was easier than taking care of the children on horseback.

At the end of the dude season, tips were calculated and dispersed to the help as the dudes requested and with consideration of the bosses. Mom came to me and said, "You received more tips than Jim, so I am adjusting them so his feelings won't be hurt." Was I being punished for getting married? I lived in leaky tents, when everyone else had better housing, and I was being docked tip money. No one had ever said life was fair, definitely not the Bible. But I resolved to move on. I had to do to others as I wished they would do for me. It seemed others must come first. But my time would come.

Dude season had ended, and university was about to start. We packed Jim's white Buick sedan with our few belongings and moved to Logan, Utah where Jim attended Utah State University, studying wildlife biology and education to become a science teacher. Our apartment was one-half of the second floor of an ancient white clapboard farmhouse. At the time we were there, it was surrounded by newer 1950s houses. I had cooked outside for years, and transferring that experience to inside was a challenge. Mostly, I undercooked our food. As a Midwesterner, Jim preferred food cooked well done, but I preferred my meat pink and vegetables crunchy. Jim did not want me to work, so to fill my day, I often walked up the hill to meet Jim after classes or to the mom-and-pop market several blocks away.

We drove back to the ranch in October to say goodbye to Mom and Dad before they left for Nevis. When we were ready to leave my parents' house and I was sitting in the car, Jim went back inside. Shortly, he came out with their television. Later, I learned that Jim had talked them out of the TV even though Mom and Dad would be on the ranch for several weeks. He disregarded that it was their TV, that they would be without. We could have picked it up after they left. I was beginning to recognize his selfishness, and I disliked it.

Back in Logan, life was difficult. The mom-and-pop grocery store gave free kidneys to customers for cat food. I thought I could save money if I served one meal a week with free meat, so I brought kidneys home. I cleaned and cut them and made a sauce like Mom had. Jim came home. He threw a fit. I grabbed the iron and threw it at him. He ducked out the door, closing it and saving himself. I was struggling to live on the little we had made in the summer. I sewed my maternity clothes, and anything we needed I purchased at Deseret Industries thrift store. I scrimped on everything.

During my teen years, I had saved several 1800s silver dollars. One day I looked in my special jewelry box to admire them. Most of them were gone. I asked Jim about them. He had taken some to buy onion rings and root beer at the A&W fast-food. So little was mine that I treasured what I did have. I lost trust in Jim, and I was livid.

On a warm April day, with the snow gone from the flatlands but still painting the mountain peaks, Jim took me with him to fish for carp. The stream meandered through a horse pasture. Yellowed leftover timothy grasses hung over the edge of the sluggish stream, making it look like a furrow. Jim had a spear with which to stab the carp. He killed them and left them to rot on the bank. I thought it was wasteful. More interested in horses, I walked toward them. I felt tired, and my back was hurting. I turned back, and soon Jim took me to the hospital.

I had watched many foals and calves being born. Childbirth is a natural occurrence. The medical staff tried to tie me and gas me. I fought. I knocked the gas mask away. I lay on my hands to prevent them from tying them, trying to appease the medical staff. I was fighting the hospital system while giving birth. Despite the medical help, David was born in the evening. Nursing is also natural. I am a mammal. But the nurses kept giving David water in the nursery. Then, on their four-hour schedule, a nurse brought him to me. The nurse pinched his face and pinched my sore engorged breast to get it into his screaming mouth.

Once we were at home, everything went well. David ate on a three-hour schedule, not the hospital's four-hour one. When he was hungry, I fed him like the horses and cows on the ranch; life was good. Mom came to visit. She would have come earlier, but she thought she had the flu. As it turned out, she had been having anxiety attacks about my delivery. She had had such difficult times with her pregnancies that she was overwrought, expecting the worst for me.

On laundry day, I filled the wringer washing machine in the communal hall with a hose attached to the kitchen sink and draped it through the door. After wringing the clothing and diapers, I hauled them outside to hang on the line. An elderly neighbor came over to show me the right way to hang the clothes. The socks were to be paired and hung together. Shirts hung by the collar, and diapers hung next to each other. It made sense and saved time. When the items were dry, I could fold them as I took them off the line and pile them together in the basket. When I dropped them into appropriate drawers, I averted the need to sort them again. I still hang clothes with this strategy.

The farmhouse where we lived was in a Mormon neighborhood. I would sit with David on the lawn, enjoying the sunshine. The neighbor children playing outside would stare but were not allowed to visit baby David, nor would the adults talk to me. Only the friendly laundry-hanging expert talked to me. She was also a quilter and showed me how to piece a star quilt together. Decades later, I started quilting. It was lonely being ostracized by the neighbors.

I ironed the sheets, Jim's shirts, and his underwear, as his mom had and as he wanted me to do. He wanted me to make weekly menus too, as his mom had. I preferred to plan meals when I saw the sales at the market. One day I was ironing as David peacefully napped in the playpen near to me. The sun was slanting through the window across the multicolored linoleum floor. Ironed clothes hung from the closet door. Mom and Dad's TV was on. I saw a cavalcade of cars and a body slumped over—Kennedy's assassination came over the air. I stood with my mouth open, unbelievingly staring at the news. Things like that did not happen in the United States. My feeling of security in living in the United States was shaken. After that day, I quit ironing sheets and underwear forever; it seemed insignificant compared to the assassination.

Home in an Army Wall Tent

At the end of May, university classes ended, and we moved back to the ranch. Jim was expecting to work, but I had my hands full of a newborn. Following Dad's example, Jim guided fishing and scenic trips on the Snake River for White Grass Ranch. We erected a large green army wall tent that belonged to the ranch. It was maybe fourteen by eighteen feet, with no leaks. Jim built a plank floor in it. We had a bed, a crib, and one dresser inside. I fastened a rope for a closet rod between the end supports. We moved in with one-month-old David with no heat or electricity; we used Coleman lanterns for lights. We were living by the irrigation ditch in the woods, out of sight of the ranch buildings. My dad had taught me how to camp in a tent, but now I was living in one for three months with an infant. I was nursing, so feeding was easy. I rinsed cotton diapers (there were no disposable ones in those days) in the ditch and took them to the ranch laundry machines to wash. I hung them to dry on a rope I tied between trees near the tent. I kept our food cool in the ranch icehouse. I cooked over a campfire, mostly in my Dutch oven.

Jim used an inflatable raft with one paddle, following Dad's example, to guide fishing trips, unlike most river guides who used two oars. With infant David, I shuttled the trip upriver and brought the vehicle downriver to the takeout. I would nurse or change diapers alongside the roadside. Since Jim was too busy, between driving Jim's trips, I installed a small wood stove in our tent for heat and warm water for bathing David and making coffee.

Sometimes Jim would invite his fishing clients to dinner without warning me, which meant I had to make a quick twelve-mile round trip to Dornan's to purchase a steak, potatoes, and salad makings; come back; and cook. It was easy to grill steak over the fire, wrap potatoes in foil, and place them near the coals to bake. Once, I was baking potatoes by the fire, and they were not getting soft. I opened one to test. It was a solid black misshapen ball. I had placed it too close to the fire—another learning experience. How embarrassing it was with Jim's clients there for dinner, sitting on the log seat, watching me, but the steak and salad were good. At other times, Jim took moonlight trips, creating another shuttle for me. I would make potato salad and send a large sirloin steak and fresh fruit. He cooked over a fire along the riverbank with company and a good dinner while I was alone eating something quick and boring.

"Jim, would you teach me how to fish?" I asked one day. We had no activities we did together. I wanted to join in the fun of fishing with him. I felt that without shared activities, we would grow apart, and I wanted the marriage to work.

"You need a rod first," he said as he turned and walked away.

We were too poor to buy a rod, but as Dad had demonstrated throughout my childhood, I could repair or repurpose it as needed. I found an old discarded fiberglass rod at Dad and Mom's house that had lost the ferrules. With silk thread, by reading about restoring fishing rods, I wrapped the ferrules in place according to the directions. I used a special varnish to finish it. I was ready to go fishing.

"Look. I made myself a fishing rod. When can I go with you?" I was sure we could spend some time on the riverbank together.

"You need to make your flies," Jim said.

I was disappointed. Jim was pushing me away. I had taught myself to cast by watching dudes practice on the Main Cabin's lawn. Years later, I learned to tie flies, but Jim never took me fishing with him.

In the winter of 1963, Dad and Mom wanted Jim and me to stay on the ranch as caretakers until the snow closed the road. In September, we moved from the tent into the Homestead cabin. It had plumbing, a coal-and- wood-burning cook range in the kitchen, and an oil- heating stove in the bedroom.

We settled into the Homestead cabin, anticipating moving out at the first blizzard, which we expected before Christmas. David's crib was in a wide hallway between the kitchen and the bedroom, where he would be warm. To prepare for a few months, we had wood stacked and had the oil tank filled. Surely it would snow, and we would move to town before we ran out.

Jim was gone for several days to bird hunt with some buddies in northeastern Wyoming. Mom and Dad were preparing to leave for Nevis. Daily, I went up to their house with David to help Mom with preparations. One day I fell ill with a stomach bug. I managed to give David a bottle in his crib but could hardly get myself from bed to the toilet. When I reached the toilet, I did not know which end to put over it. I crawled back to bed. At dark, Dad walked by to see if I was OK. He saw me through the window; I was prone and incapacitated. He went for Mom. Poor David had been in his crib all day with no diaper change and only two bottles I had managed to get to him. Mom took over. She cleaned David and fed him. She wiped me with a cool washcloth.

Two days later, Jim came home with a pheasant and a chukar. Mom cooked the birds for their dinner at the Homestead cabin. They had a delicious-smelling dinner. I was feeling better but weak. I wanted to have a wee taste, but Mom said no. I have yet to taste either bird.

The last of October brought the end of hurricane season in the Caribbean, and Mom and Dad left for Nevis.

Jim was working at Teton Village Ski resort, so he took our only vehicle, a sage-green VW Bug, leaving in the dark and returning at dusk since winter days were short, and his work hours were long. I stayed on the ranch with David. I spent much of my days carrying David as I wandered the deserted ranch, with no animal or human around. The horses were in Lander, on the Wind River Reservation, for winter pasture, and the dogs had gone to friends. I searched the barn. Everything was familiar, except for the saddles hanging from rafters and the quiet. I missed the happy repartee and laughter that usually filled it. Instead, I heard cold silence or logs popping from the cold. It was not the happy, warm place I was seeking. It was eerie. The Main Cabin, usually busy with dudes planning the day's activities or relaxing to read, was still. The kitchen, usually filled with good cooking odors, was boarded up and smelled stale, almost moldy. The only activity was the crisp mountain breeze flowing down from Buck Mountain. I hugged David closer to assure myself I was not totally alone in the world.

On a particularly blustery day, I stayed inside. I explored hidden corners of the Homestead cabin. I found a trapdoor to a hand-dug cellar. The passage had earthen walls, which emanated a musky smell—maybe death. I crept down the rotting wooden stairs, brushing my shoulders on the solid earthen walls. It was a small cellar. I saw a hard edge of iron—a heavy, muddy shape. I dug it up and brought it into the light of the kitchen. David watched from his high chair, gurgling, and kicking his feet in joy. I scraped and burned off the mud and rust. A cast-iron waffle iron emerged from the mass. I saw the lettering Griswold and the date 1908. It must have been Marnie's as she had lived in this cabin when I was a child picking up rocks for her. After I cured the cast iron, I made waffles. It still makes the best crispy waffles.

With more wandering, I went into a shed next to the abandoned diesel generator room. I found an assortment of hand-painted plates spilling from boxes deteriorated by moisture and covered with dust and mouse droppings. The dishes must have been Marmie's, I thought. I collected several that I liked and cleaned them thoroughly, and I have used them for decades.

The pattern of Jim's and my marriage was of itinerant seasonal moves that continued a schedule like the one I had had when going to boarding school. Except for the availability to live on the ranch property, we were homeless. We were working together to make our lives better. I was frugal. He worked. We saved a little. We were a team as I drove his trips and prepared meals for clients. He guided me but, I knew, we needed to move on.

Finally, February brought the first major blizzard, much later than anyone would expect. I was thankful we were going to leave the deserted ranch. Overnight, two feet of snow fell. Drifts piled deeper with the bitter north wind. If we were snowed in, Jim would be unable to work. There was not enough fuel to last much longer. We had little food. We had no skis or snowshoes like I had as a child. It was imperative that we leave, or our lives would be in jeopardy.

I found a discarded pickup truck hood by the shop. After overturning it, we packed our essential items on, using it like a sleigh, Jim chained it to the back of the VW. With Jim behind the wheel, I held tightly to David. He gunned us through the drifts. David and I were thrown from side to side as Jim yanked the steering wheel left and then right, trying to stay on the nearly invisible road. The engine howled. Snow flew over the windshield, blinding us. Three miles later, we bumped over the hard snow berm onto the plowed Moose Wilson Road. I sighed a grateful prayer that we were safe. We moved into a cinder-block rental house in Jackson.

From the cinder-block house, I often walked, pushing David in the buggy, the many blocks into Jackson to shop. There was a little extra room in the buggy to put groceries. I had taken over the bill paying. I opened a joint checking account at the same local bank Mom and Dad used. For the first time, we had checks to pay bills. Maybe our itinerant days were coming to an end. Sometimes Jim rode to work with a friend and left me the VW. I sometimes visited George, our former ranch foreman, and his wife, Elise, and their three children. At that time, George had a hunting guide's license and his own business, took summer pack trips, and had a fall hunting camp. He also cut and sold firewood. With four months by myself, I had difficulty making conversation, even with my longtime friends George and Elise. I took advantage of the Bug for grocery shopping or to haul laundry to the Laundromat. On one laundry trip, the VW stalled. I pushed it several blocks into town for repairs.

Before Christmas, I called my obstetrician and said, "Jack, I am bleeding badly. Jim has the car at work."

Jack Crenshaw, MD, a dear family friend, had by then, moved from Salt Lake City to Jackson. "Be right there," he said.

He carried me to his car over the mountain of plowed snow. He drove me to the hospital. I was put to bed, and he gave me a shot. I miscarried at four months. The pain was like David's birth. But there was no thrill of a new life in my arms. A nurse balled her hands into fists and pushed with her considerable weight on my stomach to remove the afterbirth. It was like squeezing toothpaste from a giant tube.

Jim came from work at the ski area. "We'll have another one right away," he said.

I avoided thinking of another pregnancy but kept my mouth closed. I hoped my expression spoke volumes.

Home at the Fish Hatchery

Spring arrived, and we moved back to White Grass and erected the tent. Jim was back to guiding float trips. Our life pattern continued. But by fall, with the help of a family friend, having earned a bachelor's degree in wildlife and a teacher's certificate from Utah State University, Jim was able to secure work at the fish hatchery outside Jackson.

Finally, in the fall of 1965, after three years of virtually being homeless and moving twice or more each year, Jim was using his knowledge and had a full-time job with benefits. At the end of dude season, we moved from White Grass to a camp trailer next to the Jackson Hole Hatchery. I was pregnant again. The air was ripe with the smell of animal entrails; ground and fed to the fish. To help Jim with his job, I siphoned dead fish eggs from egg- hatching trays Jim brought me.

After the winter in the cold, cramped trailer, Jim was promoted to full-time permanent employment. With the promotion, we were able to rent one of the hatchery employees' houses. It had three bedrooms and a bathroom with a tub, and it was warm. It seemed big after tents and trailers. I ordered curtains from Sears and bought furniture from the thrift store.

In spring 1966, the hatchery scheduled fish stocking in southern Wyoming. It would be an overnight trip. Jim wanted to go, but he also wanted to see the birth of our next child, so we had labor induced. Tami was born in Jackson on May 11. It was a much better experience than David's birth. Jim left right afterward for his overnight trip in the big hatchery truck to deliver fish in southern Wyoming. When Jim got back, it was time for Tami and me to go home. Mom and Dad came from the ranch to see Tami. After they left, I sat on the bed with pillows supporting my back and with my feet extended on the bed and nursed her.

Shortly, there was a quiet voice at the door. "Mom, can I come in?" asked David.

I had been told it was damaging to let older children watch a sibling nurse. *Should I let him in*? I hated secrets. David surely thought he was shut out. Something secret was going on behind the door. The unsolicited advice seemed wrong.

"Come in. Here—sit by me," I said. "See your little sister eat. When you were a little baby, you ate like this. Now you are a big boy and eating at the table." I tried to explain. "When she gets bigger, she will play with you, and you will have fun together."

David watched. I could see his little brain working. With his curiosity satisfied, David scooted off the bed and ran outside to play with the neighbors. I put Tami into the baby basket. I put a roast in the oven.

I heard a scream from outside. Running to the door, I saw David with blood running down his face. A piece of bone stuck out from the side of his nose. The neighbor kids had golf clubs in their hands and fear on their faces. I called Jim at work and grabbed a receiving blanket to catch the bleeding. The hatchery building was nearby. Jim was home in a few minutes; we took David to the hospital. As we waited to see the doctor, I suddenly remembered that Tami, the newborn, was sleeping in the house alone, and the oven was on. I called the neighbor, who rescued Tami and turned the oven off. David spent overnight in the hospital with a packed nose. He had two black eyes and a slightly crooked nose. I felt sorry for him.

David was intrigued by Tami. He would watch her sleep. At her first wiggle, he would call me.

"Mom, Tami is awake. Mom, Tami is hungry. Mom, Tami smells. Mom, Tami turned over." David wanted to hold her. I let him if he was sitting on the couch with Jim or me beside him. They still have a close connection; when I am gone, they will still have each other.

About two weeks later, Jim received a call from a long-standing fishing client who wanted several guided fishing trips on several different Wyoming rivers. Jim asked his boss if he could take July off.

" Do you want to work or fish," asked his supervisor.

"Guess I'll fish," Jim replied.

He did not consult me on the matter of family concern. We had lived in the hatchery house for about a year. By June, we were back in the green wall tent in the woods on the ranch. Tami woke with frozen diapers. I rinsed them in the stream, and we washed clothes and ourselves at the main bathhouse. I cooked on a campfire. I drove float trip shuttles twice a day and prepared dinners in the tent to feed clients on the evening scenic trips. I dragged two children with me; changed diapers and nursed Tami along the roadside. At least I was familiar with the routine, but with two children, everything was more difficult.

I learned my parenting skills by watching the animals. There were no neighbors or friends nearby who had children I could observe. I learned by watching, the animals did not shove their young around or scream at them. A mare would whine to her foal and then walk off. The foal, wanting protection and food, would follow. Sometimes the foals were left for brief periods with a gelding or another mare as babysitter. So, the babysitters were all right. The cows acted much the same. When I wanted my children to follow me, I told them I was leaving. I would walk away, and they followed. The method worked especially well in the food market. When we first entered the market, I bought them an apple or banana as a snack, and happily eating their snack, they would follow as I continued to shop. When I drove float trips, I kept snacks of fruit, cheese, or jerky. They lived much of their days in the VW Bus. David was toilet- trained to pee in the bushes. Later, Tami was taught the same way.

That winter, we replaced the VW Bug with a bigger vehicle for Jim's fishing trips. The vehicle needed to carry the raft, two or three customers, the children, and myself. One January day, Jim decided to make the change. He thought Denver was the place to buy a new vehicle. The VW Bug had no heat, so we bundled the children in sleeping bags in the backseat. We slipped our feet and legs into sleeping bags also, which made driving difficult. It reminded me of traveling with the team and sleigh as a child. Denver was a long day's drive from Jackson over snow-and-ice-covered roads.

In Denver, we found an attractive blue-and-white VW bus. We purchased a twin mattress for David, as planned. Even though we were short of funds, Jim decided to buy a TV too. I was firmly against the purchase and said so, but to no avail. On our way home, we stopped in Dubois, about one hundred miles from home, for gas. We dug to the bottom of our pockets and found thirteen cents to buy gas. We did make it home but apparently on fumes, because the bus would not start in the morning. Jim had put us in danger; if we had been marooned in January, we could easily have frozen to death. I knew it had happened to others.

When summer came, we were back in the army tent. Jim guided, and I drove and prepared meals, as usual.

The following winter, we purchased an ancient twelve- by-thirty-foot house trailer in a run-down trailer park in Jackson. Jim was working at Teton Village ski hill again. His fishing buddy, George, was living with us and slept on the pull-out couch. He took care of pulling it out, putting it back, and folding his bedding, which surprised me. Jim would have left it to me. He and Jim drove together to work, so I had the VW bus.

In mid-February, on a sunny day, I stripped the windows and beds for a spring cleanup. I loaded it all into the van to take to the Laundromat. On my way home, I went to Fred's Market for food and the post office for mail.

When I arrived home, Jim's folks were there for a surprise visit and had checked into a nearby motel. I liked Jim's folks but was embarrassed the trailer was torn apart, looking a mess. But Mom Kinker helped put curtains up and make beds. They enjoyed entertaining

Tami and David. We had a good visit with much laughter and a dinner out, which was a great treat for me.

To Nevis with Infants

"Can you come help me?" Mom pleaded on the phone call from Nevis.

Tami was nine months old, and David was four. It was the end of February 1967, and Wyoming was in deep winter. Jackson's streets were enclosed by snow piled on each side by the plows; snow-packed and icy. Mom was at Golden Rock on the island of Nevis, and she had broken her wrist and needed help typing and driving for the resort.

"Sure," I said as I thought of the complications involved. Jim could take care of himself and encouraged me to go. I would need to take diapers, bottles, food, and clothing for us all. I wanted to take the camera too. Could I fit in two toys and a book to read? I would have to carry the nine- month-old Tami and everything else since I could resupply little in Nevis. Mom said she would rent a native open-air house and a nanny for the children.

Jim drove us to the railroad station in Rock Springs as an arctic wind blew across the central Wyoming plains, and snow drifted against fences. Antelope huddled together against the wire highway fence; many would die because their habit was to crawl underneath, not jump over fences, and they could not crawl under those. So sad. The sky was a cobalt blue, and the sun shone blindingly on the bright expanse of blowing snow.

We boarded the train. Jim helped with the luggage. The three of us had two reclining seats. I held Tami on my lap. I read to them from the book I had wedged into the diaper bag. I occupied them with simple games. We went to the diner for dinner. As the sun went down, I put Tami in her sleeping bag and laid her on pillows on the floor under my legs. David curled up, like a puppy, on the seat next to me. The train clacked and rumbled along. I soon fell asleep. When I awoke, David was still curled up on his seat, but no Tami. I jumped up in a panic, looking for her. A grandmotherly lady several rows down the aisle held Tami up.

"She was lying in the aisle. The conductor started to pick her up as he thought she was a doll. She laughed and really scared him. I was happy to enjoy her until you woke up. I miss my grandchildren," she said.

"Oh! Thanks so much. She scared me when she disappeared," I said walking to retrieve her.

Our surrogate grandma helped me with the children for the rest of the day. They were doing well, with no crying or fussing. I had snacks for them but cotton diapers were a bit of a problem. I changed Tami in the bathroom and cleaned the diapers as best as I could. I kept the dirty ones in a thick plastic bag while the three-year-old David stayed and guarded our belongings at the seat.

We arrived in Chicago. I had to change trains for a commuter to Philadelphia, where Fran would meet me. The commuter had bench seats that did not recline, but I could flip the back of one so it faced the other, making a miniature compartment for us. We had another night on a train. Tami slept by me, and David had a whole bench seat to himself.

When we arrived in Philadelphia. I gave David the camera bag to carry. I carried the enormous suitcase, a diaper bag, and Tami. Fran was nowhere in sight. Once we were inside the cold, drafty station with our luggage, I had to go to the bathroom, badly. It was upstairs. I stacked the luggage, sat David on top, and put Tami on his lap.

"Do not let go of her, no matter how much she screams or wiggles," I said as I grabbed my purse and ran for the toilet.

When I came downstairs, David had a determined look on his face. Tami was screaming, arms flailing and legs kicking, but firmly held by David. Surrounding them were several elderly ladies watching and guarding. I picked Tami up and explained to the audience. They were surprised I was traveling cross-country with babies all by myself. I called my cousin on the nearby pay phone. He had overslept and said he would get there as soon as he could. As I waited, I thought how wonderful taking a shower and sleeping horizontally would feel after three days and nights sitting up.

After we spent a night, Fran drove us to the Philadelphia International Airport. He helped me check-in. I settled into my seat with Tami on my lap and David beside me. I was happy that half the trip was behind me. After a flight to San Juan and another quick plane change to St. Kitts, Dad would meet me for the boat ride to Nevis. The plane leveled off, and I relaxed.

Suddenly, the speakers crackled. "We are having mechanical problems. Nothing serious. We will fly around to use up fuel before landing at New York's Idlewild. Sorry for the inconvenience," the pilot announced.

The airline took care of everything, changing us to another plane. Our arrival in San Juan was too late to make our connection. I went to the airline desk and discovered the next flight to Basseterre, St. Kitts, was the following morning. The gal at the desk could not help me with lodging. But following her directions, I traipsed into the manager's office with David and Tami. The two tired children were quiet, and I explained our circumstances.

"I have no place to stay and must get to St. Kitts. Can you help us?" I asked.

He looked at the restless Tami on my lap and a pouting David hanging on to my pant leg. "Let me make some phone calls. Wait here a moment," he said as he left the office.

When he came back, he had found a room in the Airport Hotel and adjusted my plane tickets to St. Kitts for the morning.

"Here is your room key. The stairs are by the airline desk where you came in," he said, but he neglected to offer help in carrying everything upstairs to the hotel rooms.

"Thank you," I said. I was grateful indeed.

I left the large bag on the turnstile while I took David and Tami into the room. I left my purse, camera bag, and diaper bag there. With one child in my arms and one holding my hand, I went back downstairs to retrieve the large bag. I cannot remember what we did for food that evening, but I do remember collapsing in bed next to the children. We had a good sleep and, in the morning, room service helped carry the luggage to the flight check-in.

On arrival at St. Kitts, I looked for Dad. The airport was on a hill overlooking Basseterre which was by the ocean. We were shuffled into British customs where they opened my big bag and rummaged through everything. Afterward, I half carried and half dragged the bag with the lid ajar and articles dragging and held Tami awkwardly with the other arm. I put her and the bag on the ground outside the building. I folded and replaced items allowing the bag to close. I was embarrassed, stooping on the ground with two children, trying to save our clothing.

"I am Stu Green. You must be Cynthia, Frank and Inge's daughter," a voice behind me said.

"Yes. Hello, I was expecting Dad to meet me."

"I didn't see his boat when I docked. Must be running late," Stu said. "Why don't you come to town with me? I am sure he will be in soon."

I knew no other options. I remembered Stu Green from my teenage visits to Nevis and accepted his kind offer gratefully.

"I see Frank's boat," Stu said as we were close to town. I looked at the strait between St. Kitts and Nevis. I saw a white spot, presumably a boat wake. How could he determine it was Dad's boat? When we reached the pier, Dad had docked near Stu's boat.

"Sorry I'm late." Dad turned to Stu. "Thanks for helping Cindy."

"My pleasure," Stu answered, shaking hands and then turned back toward town.

"Hi, Dad," I said, giving him a big hug.

"I have a list to fill for the resort," Dad said. "Do you want to go around town with me?"

"No, I'll stay on the boat and rest."

Dad, with a huge smile, took David by the hand and headed to town to show off his grandson. I carried Tami into the cabin, and we lay on the bench. The boat rocked, splashed, and bumped against the dock, and soon both of us were asleep.

When Dad came back, he looked worried. "Are you alright?"

Golden Rock Hotel, (left to right) the stone water cooler, the sugar mill and the lodge.

"Yes, just really sleepy," I answered as I sat up.

"Most people would be seasick lying in the cabin with the boat rocking at the dock," Dad said.

For the first few days on Nevis, I only slept and ate. Mom thought I had reverse-altitude sickness. Mildred, the nanny, took care of Tami and David. She fed them the native rice dishes, a mix with vegetables with a little meat, which they both loved. After the rest, I was busy helping Mom. It was much like running a dude ranch in the tropics. Each day, we offered car rides to either the windward or leeward beaches, and hiking was available as was the tennis court.

Once I took a family up the gut canyon to Golden Rock's water source. Overhanging vegetation dripped with tropical moisture,

1967, Tami and David when we visited Nevis

monkeys howled from treetops, and some threw fruit at us. The trail was a mudhole, and the youngest child decided she was afraid of the mud. Her parents could not stop her fear, so I took her hand in mine and stomped in the mud, making a game of it. I began to sing, "I'm not afraid of the big, bad mud [wolf]." She lost her fear and arrived at the hotel muddy but happy and the parents were thankful.

Guests could also go sea fishing. Dad's friend Bob was at Golden Rock, and both were avid fly fishermen. They decided to dry fly-fish in the ocean. They bought a live chicken and went out in a rowboat. They tied the chicken to a line and threw it. Shortly a shark longer than the boat came for the chicken, and they cut the line to save themselves. Later, they tried the same method in a larger boat and had fun.

Jim came to Nevis for a week after his ski-hill job ended. It had been nearly two months since I had arrived in Nevis, and we were all glad to see him. I was especially glad I would have help in traveling back to Jackson.

Mom and Dad shopped in Canada for Nevis, as it was a British island with no tariff on goods from Canada, whereas there was tariff on goods from the United States. One of Dad's trips to Canada with a list for Golden Rock, he came back with Nona, whom he had befriended in Canada during shopping, and Dad wanted Mom to be hostess to his paramour. Mom told him to remove Nona from Golden Rock. He did, but he went also. Dad came back to White Grass with Nona, who supposedly was the new manager, taking the place of Mom and Rachel. Rachel said she would not go to White Grass under the circumstances.

Mom spent the summer in Vermont with Rachel. In Mom and Dad's divorce, Mom got the Nevis business with four of Dad's friends as partners, and Dad kept White Grass. Mom was 49 percent owner and the manager of Golden Rock, so she would spend her winters there. The next summer, Mom built a summer home at Skyline Ranches, a subdivision west of Jackson.

With an invitation from Dad, Jim and I moved the house trailer to White Grass. It was the first time Nona would be there instead of Mom and Rachel. The road was muddy from snowmelt, and we could not pull the trailer into the forest west of the Main Cabin, where Dad wanted us to park. What a mess it was living in it without electricity or water for eight days. We finally backed the trailer into the woods with the big ranch truck and connected to water and electricity. The trailer sat near where we had previously had the army tent. I loved being back in the woods, listening to the nearby rippling irrigation ditch and the wind rustling the lodgepole pines. Jim built a porch across the front, which made the old trailer more of a home.

Even though I was ashamed at Dad's behavior, as a welcoming gesture, I invited Dad and Nona to dinner. I knew Dad could be easily swayed; his best friend was always the last person he met. In preparation, I went to Moose and asked Dorman's, the store and bar, what Dad's favorite wine was and bought a bottle, along with a special steak. I wanted to show Dad support, even though I disagreed with what he was doing. Dad seemed pleased. He sat the children on his lap, was his natural charming self, and talked fishing and hunting with Jim. But Nona's face showed bored disinterest or, at intervals, was tight with disapproval, which made me uneasy. Perhaps she saw us as competition. Dinner was a great failure, and we were never invited to his house. Dad hated confrontation and avoided conflict. Instead, his charm attracted many friends.

One sunny morning at the trailer, I was washing dishes while Tami played in the dirt outside, babbling to herself. Suddenly, it became very quiet—a bad sign. I looked out the window. I saw her with her diapered butt pointed in one direction and a finger stretched in the other, within a foot of a black bear cub's nose; two curious youngsters. I ran off the porch, grabbed her, and headed for the Main Cabin. A cub might not have been a major danger, but a mother bear definitely was. The most dangerous of any species is a mother with a threatened baby.

Bears were a constant problem on the ranch, as they would break into the ranch kitchen, looking for food. Dad had installed metal bunk bed springs over the kitchen windows to prevent their entry. They were often seen near the cabins, scaring the dudes. We often had to have bears trapped by Wyoming Game and Fish to be relocated.

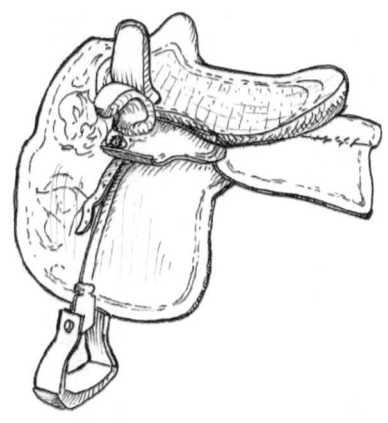

CHAPTER 5

Laramie, 1968

J IM ENROLLED AT UNIVERSITY OF WYOMING IN LARAMIE IN THE FALL of 1968 with the intention of earning a master's degree in wildlife biology. It was five years into our marriage, and we were still homeless, tenting in summer and living in inadequate housing in winter. With two children, we had accumulated more essential belongings to complicate moving. In Laramie, we lived in the long one- story student apartment complex. That winter brought the worst snowstorm in recorded history. The wind piled snow high, covering student housing except clearing only the end unit. As soon as that occupant freed himself, he dug others out. When we climbed out of our apartment, I could see only a few vehicle radio antennas sticking above the snow. Student housing was a snowdrift, a Lilliputian hump in the expanse of blinding white. The university was closed for a week. Interstate 80, across southern Wyoming, was closed, where people were marooned in their vehicles. Snow machines were sent out for the rescue, but it took nearly a week to open the interstate across southern Wyoming.

Jim decided I did need to work; our funds were so low. I found one waitressing in the down-town hotel. As expected, it only brought in a little. Once a business man asked me to work in his office but I declined saying I was leaving Laramie in the spring. I have wondered how the office job might have changed my life.

Nearby, Rosemary, a friend from the Circle H Ranch near White Grass, was also living in student housing with her husband, who was going to university. She knew of a weekend job in Cheyenne, which was fifty miles away across a mountain pass and necessitated spending a night. Jim, with no classes on a weekend, stayed with Tami and David. The job she offered would be less time, but more wage. I drove over the pass every Saturday afternoon to work at the Hitching Post Inn. I set up the banquet, served cocktails, served dinner, served more drinks, and cleaned up afterward. I would sleep for a few hours with Rosemary at her mother's home and work Sunday brunch. By afternoon, I would drive home, exhausted, and find a mess of toys strewn all over, food left out, and dishes unwashed. I thought the least Jim could have done was put things away, out of respect for my working to put him through university. Instead, I cleaned up his mess. On one trip home, I was fighting the wind, struggling to stay on my side of the lonely highway. A semi truck came from the other way, when the wind swung its empty flatbed trailer into my lane and narrowly missed me. I could have been beheaded, but Spirit Guide saved me. My heart raced, and my hands shook, but I continued along the narrow highway.

In late November, I received a letter from Dad "inviting" us off the ranch. Dad had encouraged us to put the trailer on the ranch, we had not presumed. I did not understand, except for Nona's mean-spirited attitude. All Wyoming roads were icy and snow-packed from a series of blizzards. The letter said we had to move our belongings out of the trailer immediately, and Dad would buy the trailer. We were settled into student housing and were 380 miles away—a seven- hour winter drive—from Jackson Hole. It was a dangerous and tedious drive, especially with restless children. On the ranch, late in the day, we threw what we could into the back of the VW bus. We stayed with George and Elise in Jackson for the night. Jim was angry because he had such a long drive. I felt thrown away, as if I were worthless; a piece of garbage. We arrived back in Laramie after another long, tedious drive.

By spring, Jim completed his classwork for a master's degree and had trapped a collection of specimens, rodent phalluses, for his final research project. But he never completed writing his theses for his master's degree. I felt it was a great waste. However, I managed to take one class at the university, a pottery class, the only one that fit Jim's schedule. I hoped that eventually, I could take more college classes, as I really wanted to have a degree. With a degree I would feel valued; have a marketed skill.

Summer came, and we returned to Jackson Hole. Since we were banned from White Grass, we rented the Moulton cabin on Antelope Flats, near Moose. The cabin's amenities were electricity and a wood cooking range but no plumbing. The wood range was wonderful for heating the cabin on cold mornings. I would put the enamel dishpan on the edge of the range while I drove the float trips with Tami and David, on my return, the water was hot, and the dishes were easily cleaned. But by the end of a summer day, the cabin was too hot to light a fire, so I cooked one-dish meals in the electric skillet.

Across the footbridge over the nearby irrigation ditch was a small bathhouse with a toilet and crude shower stall; outside were wringer washing machine and wash tubs. I bathed the children in the wash tubs under the expansive western sky; the shining Tetons in front of me. For all water needs, including drinking, dishes, and minor washing, I hauled water from the bathhouse in a bucket. It aggravated me to haul the dirty water back out. Hauling water was so reminiscent of tent living.

One day, while I was doing laundry by the bathhouse, Tami fell off the footbridge. David, at six years old, grabbed her by the shoulders and pulled her out of the lively flowing ditch. I was only a few feet away, but David was quicker. My heart missed several beats in fear; if she had fallen in, she would have drowned. I was proud of David.

My days were filled with caring for the kids and driving the float trips; Jim was working for Vern Bressler at the Moose Tackle Shop. At the end of September, we had our first winter storm. Snow blew through the cracks between the logs, and we awoke to snowdrifts across the floor by our bed. With winter closing in, the Moutons turned off the water and drained the bathhouse pipes, much as the ranch did, so we had to move. With an invitation, we moved to the cabin of my friends the Huebners south of Moose, as they had gone east for the winter. It was a nice log house with plumbing and electricity—such a pleasure—but since it was a mile or more to the highway and miles from town, Jim was anxious about being snowed in, as we nearly had been at White Grass. In early November, when

Mom left for Nevis, we moved into her house at Skyline Ranches and were closer to Jim's work and town.

Our Own House, 1969

With Jim's additional education, he secured a science teaching position at Jackson Middle School. Six years of moving two to three times a year with small children had become untenable; we had to find permanent housing. Except for the gift of living in Mom's Skyline cabin one winter, I knew there would be no help from my parents, so I asked two of the most conservative men I knew to cosign a loan so we could buy property in the Skyline Ranches subdivision. If they declined, I would know our buying was a poor idea because I trusted their knowledge. But they agreed to cosign, and with their signatures, the bank gave us a loan. The conservative duo also gave us a lecture about responsibility and repaying the loan. I smiled to myself because they were telling me exactly what I intended to do. I thought it was a great compliment that they trusted me. Since Jim was a veteran, he applied for a Farm Home Loan under the GI Bill to build a house.

We built a split-level milled log home on the hillside below Mom's. We stayed in Mom's house at Skyline until she came back from Nevis in April. Vacating Mom's house, we moved into our unfinished one. I looked forward to the end of our itinerant days; surely life would be easier.

Existing in our house without a functional kitchen or spigots was difficult. Jim expected a latch-key house and expected me to do homemaking tasks that could only be accomplished in a finished house. It seemed to me that tent living was easier than living in a nonfunctional house. I did the best I could but seemed to always fall short, which made me irritable and short-tempered.

One day I lost my temper with David; I slapped him. I was appalled at my actions. I sat on the floor and held the frightened boy in my arms, apologizing profusely, tears running down my cheeks. I thought I had damaged him for life. I learned I must never strike out in anger, and I had to better our circumstances to lessen my frustration and anxiety. Since Jim was not motivating the contractors to complete their work, I started calling. Finally, in January, I begged them to finish the last task for my birthday near the end of the month, and they did; it was a relief. Years later, I again apologized for striking David, but he did not remember the incident, which relieved my guilt.

By the time Mom built a home in Skyline Ranches outside Jackson, Mom and Dad's divorce was final, and Mom had lost her fighting spirit. She had faced too many changes. But thinking ahead to another winter of managing Golden Rock in Nevis, she asked me to make long dresses for her. It was the custom at Golden Rock to dress for dinner. Women dressed in simple, long dresses, and men wore Bermuda shorts with knee-high socks and ties. Mom chose the material. I cut and sewed, and Mom ironed. The dresses were a great success. Our time making the dresses stood out because we seldom did anything together.

Mom's residence at Nevis from late October into May meant she was my neighbor for only six months. It was almost the reverse of my school years; she was gone to Nevis instead of my being gone to school. However, the habit of being near her on a part-time basis did prevent making for a closer relationship. She still strongly expressed her ideas. She said she had raised me, and it was my job to raise my children; she was no babysitter. However, she did watch them a couple of times. Tami and David loved to climb the hill to her house and visit for short periods of time, but Mom wanted me to be home as backup in case something happened. I wondered if she was afraid of being responsible for them.

By autumn 1969, we were in our finished house at Skyline. David started school. Tami was bereft without his company. One morning, I was sorting clothes to wash, and suddenly, it seemed too quiet. I went to look for Tami, who had been playing in her bedroom. I looked everywhere— no Tami. Where could a three-year-old have gone? Then, I heard a car drive into our driveway. Looking out the door; Tami exited the car. A friend had picked her up at the junction of our street and the busy highway. With hands on her hips and a pouty face, Tami said she was going to school to join David. The school was several miles away. Twice, I caught her leaving to meet David at school. To keep her safe, I tied a rope around her waist, with the other end tied to the tree in their play area. She usually loved playing there but she was mad. She sat with her lower lip protruding, arms crossed, and back turned toward me for fifteen minutes, which was a long time for a three-year-old.

Jim and I depended on game for meat, fortunately, Jim loved to hunt. On one of our autumn hunts, I drew the special elk permit to hunt on the east side of the Snake River in the Grand Teton National Park. Most people hunted the sage-covered flats, but Jim decided to hunt the river bottom north of Moose. Before the sun rose, we slogged through knee-high snow, descended to the riparian area, and weaved through trees and underbrush. When the sun rose, the mountaintops glowed, but long shadows still engulfed the river bottom. I was cold and wanted the hunt to end. I was following Jim, but I saw the bedded elk first.

"Shoot it! Shoot it!" I whispered against his ear as I yanked on his sleeve.

The elk slowly stood up and took a step. She fell with a single shot. With her on the ground, the work really began; we cut her open, pulled out guts, and skinned and quartered her. We covered her with snow and hiked back up to the highway to our Land Cruiser. The elk was much closer to the river than the road, so Jim thought it would be easier to retrieve the elk using his raft and the river. We drove home on the raft. I drove Jim to launch it upriver at Deadman's Bar and then drove to Moose, where I left the Toyota and drove the Bug home.

Time passed; Jim was late. I began to worry. When he came home, he told me that park rangers had met him at the takeout which was on the west side of the river, where there was no hunting. They wanted to know where he had shot the elk; they presumed it was an illegal kill. Jim explained, but he had to take them to the kill site to prove his kill was legal. They warned him to never take an elk out on the west side of the river again. If they had decided he was in the wrong, he would have lost the coveted Grand Teton National Park permit to float the upper Snake River, and we would have lost a big part of our livelihood.

It was time to butcher the elk. We moved the big oak dining room table onto the kitchen's linoleum floor so dribbling blood could be cleaned easily. We butchered a quarter at a time, cutting the meat off the bone as best as we could since we had no knowledge how to butcher properly. Having meat in the freezer for the winter made me feel secure. It was excellent to eat, and we had good laughs in telling friends about the hunt.

Since I loved creating with my hands, I joined the Art Guild where I could use their equipment. I took silversmithing classes where I made earrings out of the elk ivory and a twisted silver bracelet. In the pottery class I made a few small bowls to bring home. I met new people and had a great time.

After the fiasco of my asking to fish with Jim and making my fishing rod, I knew Jim avoided my joining any of his fishing trips. In spring, Jim and his buddy George went camping and fishing for a week at the Henry's Fork River, over the Tetons in Idaho. Even though we would not be fishing, George's wife and I thought it would be fun to go join them. George and his wife had two children about the same age as Tami and David. Even though she and I cooked for them, the men were unhappy with our arrival. While the men fished, we enjoyed two days of exploring with the children. The children especially liked the paddleboat at Big Springs. We went home on the third day, leaving the men happily to their own devices.

Another year, I went over to the Henry's Fork River with the children to meet Jim and George in their camp. As expected, the guys went off early to fish. I decided I could fish too. I drove the VW Bug near the river and carried each child over the fence to the bank. Next, I carried my fishing gear over. With one eye on the children, who were sitting and playing with insects, and the other eye on the river, I saw a big fish rise to floating bugs at a riffle by a huge rock. I cast my fly. I let it float by the fish's feeding spot. I cast it again and again. I watched the fly float past seemingly in slow motion, and the trout rose and grabbed it. I brought the fish to shore. It was about thirteen inches long. As I looked downriver, I saw Jim and George look toward me from across the river, which made me anxious. I knew they would be angry if I trespassed on their river, so I hustled the children, the fish, and the equipment across the fence back to the car. That evening, they came back to camp scowling. They had caught nothing, but I thought my trout tasted mighty good at dinner. I was never again brave enough to go to the Henry's Fork when they were there.

However, there were a few times when I fished by myself. Once, Jim took the kids on a rare float trip from Schwabacher's Landing to Moose. Usually, rafting was for paying customers only. I had some free time while waiting to pick them up at the takeout. I parked by the Moose Bridge. I walked with my rod to an aspen grove by the shore. I cast, expecting to catch nothing, only passing the time, enjoying the rustling leaves and the sun dancing on the water. To

1969, Gina, Cynthia, Tami, Jim, and David Kinker

my surprise, I caught a ten-inch trout. I had packed a picnic for Jim and the kids but no food for myself. I built a small fire, cleaned the fish, and impaled a small aspen branch into it. I held it over the fire. Soon it was ready to eat. At first, I was surprised by the slightly bitter taste caused by the aspen, but I soon decided I liked it. I treasured my short peaceful time alone as I listened to the rippling river and enjoyed the musty smell of the damp ground.

During the winter of 1970, Jim taught middle school and coached the school's cross-country ski team. He invited me to come ski with his fellow teachers on weekends. I had missed downhill skiing; I could no longer afford it. But cross-country was even better; I could go anywhere I wanted, exploring, whereas skiing downhill, I had to stay on the trails. I often took the kids cross-country skiing, beginning when they were five and eight years old. They took to it like fish to water, and we had a great time.

That same winter, I wanted to take an overnight ski trip to Goodwin Lake, under Jackson Peak. Jim invited a ski patrolman from Teton Village and Laurie, an airline stewardess who was renting a room from us. I wanted to go to the well-known ski cabin. Mom agreed to look after the children. But we started skiing late, and after a few hours, we approached a steep side hill, the patrolman recognized it as a potential avalanche area. To avoid the danger, he directed us to ski across slowly and one at a time. When we were near the cabin area, the sun was hanging low in the west, and angry clouds were coming our direction from over the Tetons. We searched for the cabin but it remained elusive. Laurie and I wanted to camp inside an enormous Douglas fir tree. I explained how branches hung low to the ground and were covered with snow, making a great shelter. We could break the dry dead branches off the trunk to make a good fire, we said, and there was enough room for all of us. But the guys wanted to head home. In the dark, with the moon hidden by the storm clouds, we retraced our path. Near the bottom, the snow was patchy, so we carried our skis and poles. Several times I fell facedown, skis and poles cutting into my chest. Instead of being in jeopardy of turning an ankle or breaking a bone, I thought of how safe and snug we could have been inside the Douglas fir tree.

The following winter, Jim was no longer coaching the ski team. I still wanted to go cross-country, so I would invite him to go. After he declined, Tami, David, and I would go. We had great fun exploring the summer horse trails behind the ranch and skiing to Taggart Lake or sometimes toward Jackson Peak, behind the Elk Refuge, but not up the mountain to Goodwin Lake.

As a teenager, I had become close to the Huebners, a family who had been dudes at White Grass for many successive years and had eventually built the cabin south of Moose where Jim and I had stayed one autumn. They treated me like a daughter they never had, and I loved them in return; it was a rare and precious relationship. Having spent many summers at the ranch, they knew all the trails around White Grass and preferred to ride by themselves; however, I helped them clear their favorite game-trail routes. They loved to mountain climb and treated me to a class at Teton Climbing School, where we climbed Disappointment Peak, learning to self-arrest with an ice ax. It was a lot of fun.

Betty Huebner also taught me how to identify many wild plants, which eventually and surprisingly, led to my getting a job. Once, we rode together into the cirque between Static Peak and Buck Mountain, where I saw pink snow for the first time, which they explained was caused by minute organisms that lived in the snow. To return their kindness, I wanted to show them territory of which they were unfamiliar. Walking with a day pack, I took them with Tami and David to Goodwin Lake, under Jackson Peak. I was still looking for the ski cabin that Jim, our friends, and I could not find on our aborted overnight ski trip. At lunchtime, I surprised Mr. Huebner with an angel food birthday cake I had carried in my backpack. Tami and David wandered the lakeshore, found bugs and pretty stones, and waded in the cold lake, which turned their toes blue. I found the cabin too. On the way back to the trailhead, four-year-old Tami was exhausted, so I carried her. David, who was seven, carried my small backpack. Betty took one of my favorite pictures of the children by a stream.

I was constantly looking for a way to earn money. Jack, a fishing friend of Jim's, who had a guide service and store in Jackson, taught me to tie fishing flies. Working from my house was best, as I could tie and still watch Tami and David. He came to our house each weekday to tie flies at my oak dining table, which left feathers, animal hair, and hooks covering and caught in my carpeted floor. In the evenings, when Jim came home from teaching, he usually invited Jack to stay for dinner. Sometimes Jim would tie some flies for himself while I quickly decided how I should prepare the elk or antelope that I had defrosted. That winter, I tied five hundred dozen flies to fill Jack's order from Orvis and Company. My payment was three dollars per dozen; however, flies sold for $1.00 to $2.50 each at the sporting goods store. However, it afforded much needed income. As a thank-you for my helping him, Jack gave me The Galloping Gourmet Cookbook. Another of my enterprises was knitting and selling children's sweaters, which sold well at the Christmas bazaar. I did not believe in spending family money or Jim's money to buy Jim gifts. The sweaters were one of my best money-making ideas, earning money made me feel I had some control over my life. With the knitting money, I bought Jim nice high-powered binoculars for Christmas.

Jim worked with Jack in guiding fishing trips. Muddy waters make for poor fishing, so while the northern rivers were still muddy from snow melt, Jim's spring fishing trips were in southern Wyoming. The

Tami and David at a creek along the trail to Goodwin Lake, Jackson Hole, Wyoming

Green River, south of Jackson and near Big Piney, ran clear before the Snake River did. At the end of each day, Jim usually came back to Jackson by five o'clock. I wanted to know when he was back. I needed to know if he was having dinner with us or with clients. Jim seldom called. I had asked him again and again to let me know. The children asked, "Where is Dad?" I wondered if he had drowned in the river. Had he wrecked on the mountain roads? I could only tell the children I wondered too.

One evening, as night fell and Jim again did not call as to his whereabouts, I fed the children. As their bedtime passed, I called Mom so she would not worry if she found us missing. I packed the children, cereal, and milk, and sleeping bags into the Bug. I drove up Teton Pass and found a relatively flat spot, and we curled together on the ground to sleep. In the morning, after cold cereal, knowing Jim was at work, we packed up to go home. I was not only worried but also mad that he did not care enough to let us know he was alright. I wanted Jim to feel the uncertainty of not knowing where or how his family was. Mom said Jim had not called her either to find us. Did he even care about us?

For the following two days, he called home, but then it was back to normal: no call. I was struggling to make our marriage work. I wanted to prove the White Grass neighbor I had overheard at our wedding wrong about the marriage only lasting a few years. I felt I was carrying too much of the burden of the relationship and was coming to the end of my patience with Jim's behavior.

Tension grew between us. When we spoke, it seemed neither of us heard or understood the other. We went to counseling, and his only complaint was that I wore a nightgown to bed. I figured if that was his level of concern, the marriage was hopeless. I felt I was losing it; I was going mad. The next stop for me was the state mental hospital in Rawlins. Jim's actions made me feel worthless. I doubted my value. Why was I there? Was it worth my effort to continue? Did Jim care? I prayed to Spirit Guide the words of a song I remembered from church:

Open mine eyes that I may see glimpses of truth thou has for me.
Open my ears that I may hear voices of truth thou sends so clear
Illumine me, Spirit Divine.

Eventually, I found purpose, but meanwhile, I had other challenges to overcome.

Failing Marriage

About that time, I was driving into town on the snowy and black-ice-covered road to pick up Tami and David from school. I shifted down when approaching the junction of WY 22 and US 89, knowing I had no brakes. But I automatically applied the brakes. Of course, nothing happened. I slid and skidded through the busy intersection. Luckily, no one crashed into me. I was grateful for Spirit Guide's protection, but I wondered if I was worthy. It would have been easier to stop fighting, let go, and avoid confrontation.

A few weeks later, as I was turning a corner in town, a flatbed semi truck was right in front of me. I applied the brakes and stopped, even though there was no brake mechanism to make them work. If it had continued, the flatbed would have crashed through the window and decapitated me. I was convinced Spirit Guide saved me again. I wondered if I had to have replacement Spirit Guides because I wore them out trying to protect me. But those near-death events made me realize that for some reason, which I did not know, the Creator wanted me there. Shortly after those incidents, I was able to save enough money to repair the brakes, and eventually, my relationship with Jim was resolved.

That spring, Jim came home from a Green River fishing trip and bragged to me about how great sex was with the bartender in Big Piney. After eleven years, that was the end; I was so angry that I wanted to leave the house, but I thought better of it because of the children. The house was a convenient shelter. I knew I could have sheltered in tents, in trailers, or even under a Douglas fir tree, if necessary, but the children needed a house. I finally confided in a friend.

Mesa Verde Escape

"Take a trip. Cool off. I'll take care of Tami and David for a while," my friend said. "You can spend quiet time with no interruptions; you can determine what to do."

"Where will I go?" I asked. I had never thought of taking a trip or camping out for myself; too much of my home life had been camping out.

"Don't you have a place you would like to see?" she asked, looking expectantly at me.

I responded with silence. I did not, but I started thinking. "Why don't you head south? The weather should be perfect."

How could I go anywhere? I did not have the funds.

A few days later, I dropped the children at a matinee. While I waited, I went into the Wort Hotel coffee shop for a cup. I saw Cookie, Dad's army friend, sitting in a booth and having coffee. He invited me to sit with him.

"How are you doing?" he asked.

I was near tears. I was beyond the ability to hide my emotions any longer, I exploded with my concerns and frustrations. The waitress, whom I knew, came by with more coffee. She sat beside me in sympathy. She and Cookie looked at each other meaningfully.

"Here." She pulled fifty dollars tip money from her apron and handed it to me.

I knew she could not afford to give fifty dollars away. Cookie opened his wallet and handed me two hundred dollars. I knew he could not afford it either. But I accepted the offerings with sniffles and much gratitude. Even in my anguish, I recognized Spirit Guide was helping me.

I looked at road maps and considered Mesa Verde, which looked interesting. Making the decision, I packed a cooler, a sleeping bag, a change of clothes, and food for myself and Gina, my dog. Tami and David stayed at my friend's house and Gina and I headed south over Togwotee Pass. The high-altitude sun shone on the snowpack, causing it to look like a field covered with sparkling crystals.

As I descended into Dubois, the sun was close to the western horizon, and the striped shadows from the pine trees flickered in my eyes. I needed to find a place to sleep. After passing Dubois, I turned up the Wiggins Fork dirt road. I found a corral with a three-sided salt shelter and stopped. For dinner, I nibbled on jerky and fed Gina. Emotionally exhausted and physically tired, I dropped the sleeping bag onto the dried manure ground; Gina curled companion against me; and we fell asleep.

The next morning, my route took me to Rock Springs. I turned south on a dirt road entering Utah and went by the Gates of Ladore, where there were abundant mosquitoes but no facilities. However, there was a beautiful canyon of the Green River, which the road followed. Indian petroglyphs speckled the cliff faces. The road then climbed onto a plateau, where I camped. I fired up my miniature camp stove and boiled water for a dried soup mix and added jerky crumbles for dinner. I shared some jerky with Gina. Scanning the barren plateau to the horizon, I imagined I could see the curve of the earth. How small and vulnerable we really are. Could my life have any meaning in such vastness? I especially found Gina's company comforting in such emptiness.

Morning brought difficulties. The VW's engine sputtered into Grand Junction, Colorado, where I pulled into a garage. The mechanic said it needed work but with luck got back to Jackson. I needed to arrive home before the car died; I had to change it. It would be disastrous if I were stranded in the middle of a vacant plateau. I reasoned that at least at home, I would have shelter while the Bug was being repaired. But I decided someday I still wanted to see Mesa Verde. What I read about it piqued my curiosity.

As I headed back north across the high plateau, a butte's spire looked like a fist with the middle finger pointing up. I drove farther, and another butte with a fist and finger came into view. Was the earth, which had always been my comfort and place of renewal, saying, "Eff you"? Despite the trials of the trip, I loved sleeping under the awesome stars. Gina's undeterred loyalty helped my spirit; at least she cared about me. I arrived home with new determination to take care of Tami, David, Gina, and myself. I was no longer going to be a victim of circumstances. I put Jim's belongings on the porch and called him to come retrieve them. Jim moved to the Aspens subdivision with a gal who had two children and a trust fund. How was I going to provide for us? But I had Spirit Guide to help me.

It was 1973. After eleven years, I was a failure at marriage. I had kicked Jim out of the house. I had tried hard and struggled to make a home. I took good care of our two children. As an example of the pioneer women, I was a working partner, assisting with his boating business and helping with his work at the hatchery. I was ashamed because I had failed. I wondered how any marriage succeeded. Jim was from Ohio, I from Wyoming with different values and backgrounds. It was not as if we used a well refined wheel, but created a new one. We were young and ignorant. We began divorce proceedings.

I had been my true self before I met Jim. I had been self-reliant and strong-minded, had developed ingenuity, and had moved forward during difficult times. Mrs. James Kinker was a label, a thing I did. I had let myself be molded to meet Jim's expectations and had become submissive. That role abandoned my individuality, my nature, and was a poor fit for my soul. I needed to be my true self again. I knew I could do that and still have the precious part of my family, my joy: Tami, David, and Gina. I might have been losing Jim, but I still had my uniqueness and Spirit Guide. It was another rough river rapid to navigate, but I trusted all would be OK in the end.

To pay the mortgage and feed us, I worked at a deli, cooking, and driving the deli truck, taking the kids along. I cleaned houses and catered private parties. I bought adult clothing at the Orville's and St. John's thrift shops, took the clothing apart at the seams, and sewed the material into clothes for the children. I also used the good wool uniform material saved from my boarding school days to repurpose into their clothing. I thought of Jacob's coat of many colors, but sadly, these clothes had little color. Soon I was able to pay Cookie and the waitress back.

I was the only one I could depend upon to take care of the children, so when school was out, I rented my house. I took the children and Gina to Dubois, where I cooked at the Bitterroot Dude Ranch, where cousin Fran was managing. I was again living in a small one-room cabin with no plumbing. It had one lightbulb hanging from the ceiling, three beds, and one dresser. I started work at four in the morning, baked breakfast cinnamon rolls, and cooked breakfast first for the employees and later for the guests. I cleaned up afterward. Then it was time for lunch and preparation for dinner. At three o'clock, I had a break and spent time with the kids. I bathed them and myself. Then they were back outside, amusing themselves with the ranch dogs or insects; with no expensive toys, they amused themselves well. I was in the kitchen to cook and serve dinner, struggling for our survival. Work often ended at eight o'clock. I was grateful for Ellen in the White Grass Ranch kitchen who taught and prepared me for a marketable skill, though a low-paying one.

When I had a day off, Tami, David, Gina, and I would drive into Dubois. I thought the children should learn to drive. On about eighteen miles of dirt road, David, age ten, would steer and shift while sitting on my lap. On the way back, Tami, age seven, would steer the same way. They became good enough drivers that if I had been hurt, one could have driven for help. The lessons were part of teaching them to be self-sufficient, able to take care of themselves. Bumps and bruises were good learning experiences. It was important that they learn to take responsibility, gracefully accept praise when appropriate, and admit to wrongdoing. I knew life was seldom fair, but I wanted my children to learn to move forward, putting one foot in front of the other. I wanted them to choose happiness, not dwell in anger or bitterness. They had lost a full-time dad, which I knew was hard because I had lost mine in other ways.

Autumn arrived, school started, and I still owed money on the VW. I parked it under the bank president's window. When I talked to him about adjusting the loan, I pointed out the window at the faded Bug. He canceled the small amount still owed. Shortly after, I was hired by Western Development Company, which was building the Ramada Snow King Inn. One boss needed blueprints copied, another needed innumerable letters typed to advertise for conventions, and a third wanted tasks done to open the ski hill. They kept me busy; each really wanted me full-time. I was relieved I had a real job with a salary on which I could depend. I bought one Christmas gift for David and one for Tami.

However, the position ended. At Christmastime, I left work four minutes early to walk across the street to attend a service at St. John's Church. I never shortened their time, as one evening, I had worked more than an hour and a half late to sell ski tickets for Snow King. Tami, seven, and David, ten, had been at home alone; I had been anxious. Dinnertime was near when I finally closed the door. I was fired, and the day I left, a new secretary was already on duty. I felt the convention boss only wanted to hire his friend. However, I did not think she would stay late to sell tickets or walk a few blocks away to copy blueprints.

I was glad I had bought the gifts, but my second thought was that maybe I should have saved the money for food. When I had only ten dollars and had a house payment due, I went to Teton County for help, and was given food stamps. The county employee asked me to help some elderly folks with cleaning and cooking, which I did, and I became friends with the couple. Another friend gave me the front quarter of a moose with its hide on. I was grateful that Spirit Guide was on duty, bringing me help in the guise of friends and county. I cut the moose up, packaged it, and put it in the freezer. We ate lots of oatmeal and moose that winter. I found the food stamps generous, as I made the stamps last a month longer than the time they were allotted. We would survive another winter.

I tried to teach Tami and David that loyalty, honesty, and love were the important things to be, that money only helped you buy food and shelter; cleanliness was important, but their looks were unimportant. What was important was generosity, good nature, and a sense of fairness.

On Saturday, January 27, 1974, about a year after Jim's and my divorce, Dad and Nona were having a winter party at the ranch, and Dad invited the children and me. The invitation surprised me because we had been unwelcomed on White Grass since Dad kicked us out in 1968.

When we arrived, they had Madam, a big bay mare, harnessed to the sleigh and were giving rides. Since I was anxious about Nona's reception of us, I chose to drive Madam for several rides. When I got cold, I went inside with Tami and David for some food and warm-up. Nona ignored us, which was fine by me. Glenn Exum, the famous mountaineer, suggested a cross-country ski trip behind the ranch. I asked if the children could go since I was concerned they might be slow and hamper the trip, but they took the lead along a summertime riding trail, and we all cheerfully followed. When we prepared to leave for home, Cookie gave each of us a hug. I told Cookie my secret that I was pretending this was my surprise birthday party, but Dad did not know. Cookie told Dad, and before we left, Dad came to wish me a happy birthday. He said he could not remember which day was Mom's birthday, February 2nd, and mine since they were a week apart.

As spring approached, I was again looking for income. I contemplated renting out the downstairs, but the stairs led into the area I would rent, which would warrant the renters no privacy. I looked at the back hall. If I disconnected the stairs and turned them around, the stairs would enter the laundry room, a communal area. I could build a platform above the stairwell and place a mattress on top for my bed. A dresser would also fit in the back hall, across from the bed. So that was what I did. I moved onto the platform, giving each child his or her own room. I rented out the downstairs to two young people who had been recommended by friends.

With summer coming, work opportunities opened. I worked at a deli, cooking, and driving the sandwich truck, always with the children. We went to construction sites at Teton Village and drove the Moose Wilson Road to meet the plane's arrival at the airport. Tami and David were good about coming quickly when I called to leave.

As autumn approached, the deli released me as business slowed. I catered a business party, where the host kindly took David by the hand and walked to the creek to see the fish. By winter, I was hostess at the Pink Garter dinner club, and cleaned business offices during the day. When I could not take the children, they stayed at Miss Woodward's Day Care. I hated to leave them there as it smelled of urine, and they hated it, but I saw no other option. I again had a difficult time in paying the mortgage and utilities and buying food; only trying to survive.

To save money, Jim convinced me to share a lawyer in the divorce settlement. Eventually, I was awarded thirty-seven dollars a month per child and no alimony. I could live in the house and pay the mortgage, but upon sale, we would split the proceeds. I had worked to help him through university; had supported his rafting business by driving and fixing meals; and was raising his children. I was appalled with the settlement; I felt I was being punished for dissolving the marriage, Jim was untrustworthy for support or bill paying. Previously, he had neglected to pay the electric bill because he was saving for a Canadian fishing trip with his buddies, causing the electricity to be turned off, jeopardizing his family, when nightly temperatures were below zero. He did not have the cojones to go into the electric office to pay the bill himself, as it would have been embarrassing, so I went and paid it.

After Jim moved, he would call, wanting to talk to Tami and David, but first, he would berate me, saying I was spending the children's money on myself, I was a poor mother, he would take the house from me, and he would take my children from me. I told him I would hang up if he was uncivil. I hung up a few times before he learned.

Tami was mad at me for making her dad go away. One day I put her down for a nap and went downstairs to do laundry. I was surprised when an angry Jim arrived at the door with a squalling Tami. She had run away, dragging her sleeping bag with her important toys inside. She had walked cross-country until she came to the Snake River and then had followed the dike to cross the river at the highway bridge. A friend of Jim's had recognized her, picked her up, and taken her to Jim and his sweetie. Tami was unwelcome and brought her right back home. Since I was not always told the truth as a child, I was determined to be open with Tami and David. They asked if Dad was coming home. "No," I said, but I reassured them we would be fine. The three of us would remain together, no matter what.

Jim eventually moved to the Pacific Northwest with another gal. When he became sick with cancer, Tami and David went to spend his last days with him. I am proud of them for their loyalty to their dad.

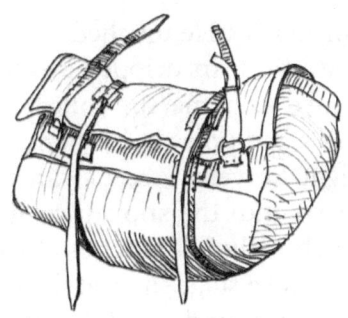

CHAPTER 6

William King Peck, MD, 1974

ON A FEBRUARY SUNDAY 1973, THE CHILDREN WANTED TO GO SKIING. I drove Tami and David to the Teton Village ski area to meet Jim's acquired children before going to church. I arrived at church late and followed the choir to a vacant seat by the aisle. The gentleman next to me was not using a hymnal, so I offered to share; he did not sing. I accidentally brushed against him. His jacket was as soft as chamois. After church service, he introduced himself as Bill Peck. I went to the Lenten class. He sat behind me. To my embarrassment, he heard my stomach growl.

"Could I take you to dinner?" he asked as the class ended and we were all trooping down the stairs.

"I have children to pick up at the Village," I said. "Don't they need to eat too?" he asked.

We drove in his fire-engine-red 1970 Ford 150 to the Village. Bill opened the door for me and placed his hand gently at the small of my back, it was so mannerly. In contrast, at the ranch, when I opened a door, I stood back as the rush of cowboys or dudes went through.

We found the children in the downstairs game room at the Mangy Moose Lodge, as planned. He helped Tami and David order pizza and took me upstairs to the nicely appointed dining room. During dinner, he shared that he was widowed, was the radiologist at St. John's Hospital in Jackson, and traveled to Alpine through the Snake River canyon to read x-rays. I told him of my divorce and struggles.

I felt I was carrying the world and managing poorly with no support emotionally or financially. He touched my cheek in sympathy. His touch broke my reserve; tears dripped down my cheeks.

When he returned us home, the children scampered inside. Bill was left holding skis and poles in his hand, he leaned forward and kissed me good night, I felt effervescent with butterflies in my stomach and he fell sideways into the snowdrift. It was the beginning of our romance, which included lunches at Ridenour's Open Range restaurant, movies, and a stage show at the Pink Garter dinner club. As the days grew longer, we drove Teton Pass, parked, walked over crusty snow drifts, and picked pussy willow buds to decorate my table. They represented a hint of spring, an awakening in more ways than one. I was a mother, but I was a woman too.

I needed to get away from the emotional chaos with Jim. Judith, my kid wrangler cohort from the ranch, invited me to visit her in Denver. It was the school's spring break for Tami and David. I packed us into the Bug, headed south; stopped for gas in Laramie. The Bug quit going down the pass to Ft. Collins. I managed to pull it to the edge of the highway. Snow covered the hillsides, and tall snow banks bracketed the road. Spirit Guide brought us an elderly rancher driving a dilapidated truck overfilled with wood poles, who stopped and offered help. He chained us to his bumper and pulled us. The many protruding logs pointing at my face made me glad my brakes worked. He left us at a garage in Ft. Collins, where it would take a day to fix the Bug. I had no funds to cover the repairs. I pictured us living on the streets and begging for food, with no shelter, trying to find work in a strange place, like a picture out of Dickens's David Copperfield. But I found a cheap motel that accepted Gina.

In desperation, I decided to call Bill, vacationing in Tucson, which I found embarrassing. He offered to wire funds, and I was overwhelmed with gratitude. The next day with the bug repaired, we arrived at Judith's by late afternoon. I sat in the kitchen, visiting, as she fixed dinner. Tami and David played with her children. After dinner, I settled Tami, David, Gina, and myself into the guest bedroom; it was a relief to feel safe and tucked into a comfortable bed.

Judith woke me for dinner the following day and told me she had taken the children to the zoo. As she was the zoo photographer, she even took them behind the enclosures, where the public was not allowed. I slept for another twelve hours before I could join the activities. I had forgotten what it felt like to be rested.

Bill called to say he had changed his plans so he could come through Denver on his way home. When he arrived, we walked the hill behind Judith's house. He surprised me with a turquoise bracelet. Later, we all went to a nice restaurant for dinner. Leaving Denver, Bill followed me across Wyoming in his red Ford, named Bessie. The wind was blowing so hard that I had to steer quartered into the wind to stay on the road. We turned north toward Lander and picked up a tailwind, which made the driving much easier.

"Bill, do you ski cross-country?" I asked one beautiful spring day with snow still on the hillsides, inviting outside activity.

"Sure, where do you want to go?"

"A friend gave me the keys to the Diamond L Ranch. We could ski in and spend the night. We will need to backpack our food and sleeping bags; everything else is in their cabin." My friends were creating an off-the-grid ranch. After felling trees on their property, they had sawed the lumber to build a cabin. Their cabin was insulated with the sawdust waste from the sawmill. They heated with wood and cooked with propane but had no electricity.

"We could drive to Spring Creek to park. We can follow the drainage to the ranch." I had not made the trip before, but from the map, it looked straightforward.

The highway was narrowed by the snow berm, so we were unable to park at the place I wanted. The trip would be longer than I had planned. But it was a sunny weekend morning. We donned our packs. The drainage I was following was turning the wrong direction, so I corrected it by turning easterly. I reasoned that if I paralleled the foothills, I would intersect the correct drainage. When I looked up, I saw threatening clouds coming over the Tetons; the wind was picking up. The day was half gone. I calculated that we still had a long way to go. I crossed a small creek with snow- corniced edges. I stepped wide over it.

"Bill, step wide; the banks are fragile."

As I called back, I heard cursing. Bill was on his back, weighted down by the pack. He looked like an overturned turtle. I laughed. But this was serious. The circumstances were dangerous. He was wet to his thighs; it was cooling off quickly and would be below freezing when the sun set. I helped him remove the pack and skis. I realized I needed to adjust our destination immediately. I vaguely remembered a small log cowboy cabin somewhere nearby. It had been decades since I had seen it. With his skis and pack on, I moved faster, to find the cabin but also to keep Bill warm. Visibility was diminishing, and the pelting snow bit my cheeks.

"There is a cowboy cabin near here." I tried to encourage him.

"I'm freezing," he answered. The snow was falling heavier; Bill was in jeopardy of frostbite.

With relief, I saw the shadow of the cabin under the cottonwood skeletons. As we neared, I also saw a chain through a hole in the wall and through another hole in the door, with a big padlock threaded through the links.

"I'll go around back to find another way in," I called to Bill as I kicked my skis off. I went around the corner of the cabin, saw a window with no latch. After pushing it up, I crawled over the low sill. I opened the ghost-locked door. In desperation, Bill was pointing his pistol at the lock. It was also pointing at me!

"I was going to shoot the lock to get in," he said sheepishly. I wondered if he was affected by the cold, or had he not listened when I said I would find another way in? There was no time to be afraid or rebuke him. I needed to warm him. I had to focus on the essentials: shelter, warmth, and food. It was time to practice ingenuity.

It was as cold inside as outside, but we were out of the wind. I quickly started a fire in the cook range with the dry wood that was stored by the stove. I took inventory of what else was available in the cabin: a bed with no mattress, an empty honey can, and an ice cube tray on the rustic shelf. There were large pieces of cardboard in the corner. While Bill changed into his dry long johns, I went outside to see what else I could find. I found a nicely cupped Ford hubcap. OK, I thought, *we will do just fine.* I washed my finds, thoroughly scrubbing them with sand and freezing creek water. Then I was ready to utilize the supplies in my backpack.

Bill was close to the fire roaring, his feet against the stove, and his wet clothing hanging on nails from the rafters. Soon I had coffee boiling in the honey can to warm our insides. From my supplies, I baked biscuits in the ice cube tray and heated beef stroganoff in the hubcap for our dinner. We put the cardboard on the bed springs for insulation, with our sleeping bags on top.

The morning was sunny, with a new layer of sparkling snow. Bill lit the fire. I fried bacon and eggs in the hubcap and made more coffee in the honey can. According to the code of the West, you may use a cabin but must leave it in good condition and must replace what you use as best as you can; it is a matter of respect. Bill and I gathered dead wood to replace what we had used. I washed the can, tray, and hubcap and put them on the shelf for the next person.

With renewed spirits and happy companionship, we skied toward the highway. The area was rife with moose tracks and reeked of moose urine, an odor of danger. My feet were moving slowly and quietly, but my heart was beating double time. Bill followed. With trepidation, I continuously looked left and right, watchful of an attack. If a mean-tempered moose attacked, my plan was to ski into the thickest willows. Moose do not see well, but their hearing is extraordinary. If we hid in the willows and stood absolutely still, they might not gore us. Luckily, we saw no moose. When we reached his truck, Bill found a note under the windshield wiper; he was needed at the hospital. His X-RAY license plate had given him away. We had arrived back to the populated world that demanded our attention.

Bill had three teenage girls whose mother had passed shortly after they moved to Jackson. They wanted him available, even though one was spending significant time in Rock Springs, one was in college, and one was finishing high school. They resented the time Bill spent with me and may not have understood why he was dating a woman twenty years younger. I felt no difference in our ages; we both had farm or ranch backgrounds and had similar morals and ethics. After several months of lunch dates and day-long car trips, he asked me, my children, and Gina, to accompany him on a summer trip. He was taking a leave of absence from radiology. I accepted.

When school was out, I rented my house to the Teton Symphony again. There was nothing holding me in Jackson. Bill drove his Ford pickup, Bessie, with its camper shell, pulling his small camp trailer. We had no destination, only an idea of going through Idaho and heading west. On our first night of camping, the children complained of having nothing to do; they were addicted to TV as was their dad. After a few days, they were entertaining themselves, with TV forgotten; the great outdoors beckoned exploration. At another camp by a lake, they swam and tried to catch a fish with their hands. The Olympic Peninsula was their first experience with the ocean. Fascinated by the unusual creatures, they squatted for hours watching and touching the variety of life in the tide pools. We turned toward home at Cannon Beach, Oregon; school would start soon.

I doubted my judgment of men after Jim. I felt that Bill was wanting a commitment when he offered to take care of us all. But I was afraid to commit. It was difficult for me to trust anyone. I felt I must be able to take care of my children financially; however, I could not see a way to accomplish that. I called for guidance from the Creator and received a response that I should follow Bill.

Bill accepted a job as dude wrangler at Tanque Verde dude ranch east of Tucson, Arizona, for the winter of 1974–1975. He wanted me to come along, but I would not go without a job. To my surprise, the ranch hired me as a kid wrangler, reminiscent of the job I had had as a teenager, riding and entertaining dude children.

We made a quick trip south to Tucson in Bessie to find housing. The Tanque Verde ranch had housing for single employees but not for families. We looked at several houses. I joked about how this one or that one would fit our needs, not really expecting him to purchase. At dinner, Bill asked me which one I liked best. I mentioned one with Mexican stonework on its front, on Avenida Aguila, the one closest to the ranch. He said he would buy it. I was shocked. He would buy a house so I could come with him for a winter job? Filled with emotion, I started to cry. Embarrassed by my tears, I walked outside. I wandered the open desert near the hotel, finding solace in the outdoors. When I had my emotions in control, I joined Bill at the table. Bill had been distraught by my disappearance. He said he had looked in our room and told the waiter to hold madam's dinner. After I explained my reaction, all was good.

Moving to Tucson, we caravanned with a U-Haul truck that Bill drove and I drove Bessie, pulling the Bug filled with my houseplants. Gina and Gretel, Bill's dog, rode in the truck shell. We took turns having Tami or David ride with us. We stopped in Utah at the home of his daughter, who was embarrassed by the hillbilly way we were moving. As we arrived at Avenida Aguila and opened the gate to our new house, I told Bill, "This will be a happy home."

Both Bill and my hours working at Tanque Verde were long. Tami and David became more self-sufficient; they made their lunches before school, and they caught the school bus. They occupied themselves after school until I arrived home.

When work ended at the ranch in spring, Bill went to trade school for welding. He was contemplating a change of careers. But he discovered welding jobs required long, arduous hours and involved lifting heavy machinery pieces, which was too grueling at his age of fifty-six, when he was unused to manual labor. However, he enjoyed welding small items for us during the following years.

The jobs brought Bill and me to Arizona and to our life commitment to each other. In the summer of 1975, we had a small marriage service at St. John's Church in Jackson. The reception was at Mom's home at Skyline Ranches. Even though the reception was small, Mom outdid herself with a lovely table and delicious finger foods.

She looked the part of the regal hostess, a position she was accustomed to at White Grass Ranch and at Golden Rock. Only one of Bill's daughters came, and brought her boyfriend. I felt I could trust Bill; he would pay the bills, and he would not put us in jeopardy. I felt safe. Eventually, his girls came to accept me.

After Bill and I were married, I sold my Skyline house. Mom had been forced out of Golden Rock. She sold her house at Skyline. She came to stay with us in Tucson. Within a few months, she bought her own place a few miles from us. Her house was a quaint old adobe. She drove her Mazda through the washes and over the in-between hills with gusto, giving the kids a thrill. She worked the front desk at Tanque Verde Ranch, doing many of the same tasks she had at White Grass.

Back to Rural Living

We worked two winter dude seasons at Tanque Verde Ranch. Their dudes did not know that the wrangler Bill was a radiologist, until eventually, another physician recognized him. The National Enquirer magazine picked up the story of the highly respected radiologist who had left a lucrative practice in Ft. Lauderdale, Florida, to go to the wilds of Wyoming and become a wrangler. The *Arizona Republic* came to interview Bill and took pictures of him riding horses.

The *Arizona Republic* Sunday section caught Eddie Bashas attention. Basha was a major grocery owner in Arizona and was on the Chandler Hospital board and invited Bill to develop a twenty-four-hour service for the emergency room. We were looking for a life outdoors, maybe managing a dude ranch. Moving and working

In 1975, Cynthia & Bill Peck wed; Tami, Gina, & David joined the ceremony.

into the fast-growing Chandler and Mesa area was not in our plan. But Bill felt he needed to work and he loved a challenge. We sold the Tucson house and bought one in Mesa designed by a Frank Loyd Wright student, because the price was right.

After setting up the emergency room in Chandler, Bill was hired by the Lutherans to "form a presence" in Apache Junction. He established a clinic inside an old convenience store building at the corner of Idaho Road and US 60 and was the physician at a clinic. The clinic was operated under the Lutheran umbrella. When the Lutherans applied to build a hospital in the east valley of Mesa and Apache Junction, they stated that they had demonstrated their commitment to the area because they already had a clinic there. They eventually built a hospital on Power Road, accomplishing their goal.

When we moved to Mesa, our neighbors came to greet us. They asked, "What are your interests?"

"We like to follow dirt roads through the mountains and camp," said Bill.

"You must go to Young, which is about thirty miles of dirt road from the highway," one told us. We decided we wanted to investigate the mountains and the village of Young but we had commitments first.

When Mom sold her house in Tucson, she moved in with us in Mesa. One of Bill's daughters, Helen, broke her ankle and came to live with us. Mom wanted me to shop, explore the city with her, and have lunch out. Helen needed to be driven to and from Arizona State University in Tempe. My children needed transportation to after-school activities. Bill was working from four o'clock to midnight at Chandler Hospital. He needed meals at unusual hours. I tried to accommodate everyone's needs, but it was impossible. By spring things eased up, Mom decided Bill and I were unsettled. We moved from Jackson, to Tucson, and to Mesa so she left us to go live with her sister, Renate, in Connersville, Indiana. Helen's ankle healed, and she went to Oregon to be near one of her sisters, and enrolled in a master's program. Bill's work changed to days.

Life became easier with only Bill, myself, Tami, and David in the house, so I enrolled in classes at Mesa Junior College, taking sociology, psychology, and pottery. I again had an opportunity to pursue a college education. I still hoped someday to earn a degree to gain self-security.

The following February, Bill and I finally headed to Globe and north to Young. Leaving the highway, the road was muddy; Bessie's four-wheel drive was faulty. After much slipping and sliding, we arrived at a quaint roadside gas station in Young. A friendly gentleman greeted us and filled the tank.

"I'm Merle. What brought you to Young?" he asked. "We enjoy exploring the mountains. We were told about Young," Bill answered. "By the way, is there any land for sale?"

"The man in that white truck has land for sale." Merle pointed to a white truck leaving the parking area.

Merle gave us Onis Jones's contact information. We tried to follow the white truck but lost sight of it. Bill tried to phone, but there was no answer. Finally, Bill wrote Onis a letter, but we received no response.

Two months later, we got a call from Onis. He said, "Are you still interested in the land?"

We met him, next to the property for sale, as he was plowing his bean field. We squatted in a furrow. Onis made a map of the acreage by drawing in the fresh-turned earth and stated a price. Bill counter offered his price.

"Do you want the land or not?" Onis asked; he raised his head to look at Bill.

We made a handshake deal for full price on twelve acres. The land had a decrepit barn and a few falling-down corrals. There was a small log house with no plumbing, one electric light bulb, with an outlet and a black cord draped to the refrigerator. No one had lived there for nine years except vermin; scat was everywhere. There was an orchard with a dozen standard-sized apple trees. I thought that with much work, the place could be an awesome home. The valley in which it was located was like a miniature Jackson Hole, with surrounding mountains. Even though the mountains were lower, unlike the spectacular Teton peaks. They made me feel as if I had come home. The property included a forested hillside; at its base was the house, with a field stretching to the riparian vegetation by the creek. Both Bill and I were looking forward to leaving city life behind. We planned to meet Onis in Globe the following week to register the sale and go to the bank to plan for payments. How simple the real estate sale was.

As we squatted in the bean field, Onis told us about his family. "We was coming from picking jobs in California. Charlie, Red, Bertha, my brothers and sister, and I wanted to stay in Young. We forced our parents to buy land. We camped by the creek. Mom always planted iris at our camps. You can still find patches. Later, Dad purchased logs at the Red Lake Sawmill. He traded the logs for a pocket watch and a gun. Later, the watch was returned. We asked for help, but the carpenters wanted a paying job, so they wouldn't help. We had a dull saw and a hammer to build the house. After Dad died, Mom lived by herself in the house for years. She walked several miles to the store. She would not accept a ride. Everyone in town called her Granny Jones."

The cabin that Onis's family had built nestled under huge alligator juniper trees. It was a square cabin measuring about thirty-by-thirty feet, built of three-quarter-cut logs, with an exterior of asbestos stucco. After Granny's death, the rodents had moved in; surfaces were covered with scat. The inside log walls were chinked with dish towels, underwear, and pieces of worn-out oilcloth. In places, it was wallpapered with newspapers using flour paste. It had an enameled cast-iron farm sink with dish drains on each side sitting on a white metal cabinet, but there was no plumbing. Granny had carried water in from the hand-dug well and carried the dirty water back outside. A wood cook range sat on the floor with no legs, which had caused its base to melt into the linoleum. I enjoyed cooking on a wood range. I thought the cabin had possibilities. I climbed a ladder and investigated the dark, dusty attic. The rafters and supports were placed where their inherent lengths allowed, not conforming to any construction standards.

The house was divided into four corner rooms: two were intended as bedrooms, another was a kitchen, and the last was a living room. There were a few sad-looking pieces of furniture covered with rodent droppings. The curtains hung in threads from drooping rods. Outside was a 1935 Great Depression WPA (Works Progress Administration) outhouse. The outhouse had a wood vent behind the rustic seat, which I had never seen before and the whole outhouse tilted to the southeast, door ajar, half buried in the ground. It looked as if it would topple over at any time. It too was overshadowed by enormous alligator juniper trees. Our plan was to remodel and live in Young during the summers. Bill and I would move to Young after Tami and David finished high school.

We learned that Young was first called Pleasant Valley, but when the mail was brought in, it was delivered to the Young sisters' home, which became the Young Post Office. Arizona maps mark the location as Young, but inhabitants say they live in Pleasant Valley. It is seated in a valley at 5,200 feet elevation under the fault of the Mogollon Rim which is at 7,400 feet elevation. The first white men rode into Pleasant Valley in the early 1800s. Cowboys brought cattle into the belly- deep grass and abundant water. They lived in tents or built one-room log cabins. An occasional rock house was built.

Young was the central point of the Pleasant Valley War, which was the bloodiest of any feud in the United States. Even before the feud, the place was hounded by Apache raids, cattle rustlers, and horse thieves. In 1885–1886, the war erupted as a combination of family feud and cattle and horse rustling with a running iron to change

1979, Granny Jones house as we found it. We purchased the house with 12 acres.

brands. Shootings were wide-ranging from Holbrook throughout the Rim country to Tempe.

In the 1980s, the University of Arizona conducted a cultural anthropological study and declared Young was the smallest complete community in Arizona. Bill and I liked to eat at the Antlers Café and frequented Hogland's old-fashioned general store, received mail in a box at the post office. Electricity came to Pleasant Valley in 1964, followed by phone service. In 1980, eight acres of land were donated to the community. The local people combined efforts to build the Pleasant Valley Community Center as a place for community events. A volunteer fire department was established in the 1990s. Internet and cell service arrived later. When we bought property in Young, the population was about eight hundred, including the outlying ranches.

Young is a village like many small, isolated villages, which tend to cling to the past more than reaching toward the future. We are influenced by the seasons: spring planting, summer forest fires, wood-gathering for heat, fall harvest, winter repair of equipment, mending clothing, and such.

In September, Young hosted the oldest Gila County fair, Pleasant Valley Gila County Fair. I entered my needle crafts and canning at the community center, where there was judging of canned goods, needlework, wood crafts, fine art, and photography, to mention a few. There were many entries from the schoolchildren. As it was an old-fashioned county fair, there were no Ferris wheels or other rides; instead there were horse events and small animal judging. The fair committee served a free hot lunch to everyone attending; a time enjoyed visiting with friends and neighbors.

I became one of the Pleasant Valley Homemakers, who were instrumental in raising funds to start the Young Library and the Pleasant Valley Medical Center. We made quilts, all by hand, and raffled them; they were good money makers.

When we bought the property in Young, the north road was twenty-eight miles of dirt road climbing the Mogollon Rim to State Route 260. The nearest town was Heber, nearly fifty miles away. But Payson, about seventy miles away, had a Safeway and more shopping opportunities. The road south toward Globe was even farther away. As of 2020, both roads have some pavement but most miles are still gravel. One does not come to Pleasant Valley by mistake. It is an adventure.

Spring 1979 arrived. I was excited to start making Granny Jones's house livable. The children visited Wyoming for much of the summer. Tami helped the Crenshaws at their ranch in Bondurant, and David stayed with Jim. Bill was working at the clinic in Apache Junction but came to Young on weekends. I had the cab-over camper from Bessie parked by one of the enormous alligator juniper trees. Living on a property abandoned for years was interesting. One night, I was awakened by what I thought was a frantic child's scream. I jumped from bed and flew out the camper door. The saliva-wet kitten Pierre leaped onto me and climbed my leg into my arms. I must have surprised the coyote attacking Pierre, which saved his life. I also had seen cougar tracks by the barn. Wildlife had moved in when Granny left.

I knew we would have to install plumbing, so when I spotted a cast-iron claw-foot tub in a field in Mesa, I bought it. I slid it into the back of the Datsun station wagon. Arriving in Young, I placed the tub under the juniper tree nearest the cabin. To bathe, I would heat water on the wood cook stove, empty the boiling water into the tub, and add cold water from the hose to achieve the right temperature. I would wear a robe and hang it on a branch to take my bath. Only one time, I was caught in the tub. Our neighbor from Mesa came for an unexpected visit. I jumped out, put my robe on over my wet body, and pretended there was nothing to be embarrassed about.

My first task in cleaning the house was to strip the walls of glued-on coverings. I found flat-faced logs, which I sanded. The inside walls were inch thick rough-cut planks with buckets of vermin manure in the crevasses and had been nailed to the floor joists and ceiling beams before the floor and ceiling had been installed. I sawed at floor level with an antique carpenter's hand saw to remove the wall between the kitchen and living room, making an open floor plan. My bloody knuckles and bloodstained floor attested to the difficulty of that task.

I was determined to sleep in the cabin by August when Bill took his vacation and the children would return from Wyoming. On weekdays, I worked on the cabin til mid afternoon, at which time I would sweep sawdust away and organize construction materials for the next day before I relaxed and ate.

We hired a country contractor to build onto Granny's four-room cabin, adding a bathroom, a dining room, and a master bedroom. We had planned to wait for the children to finish school before we moved, but life in the city became intolerable for us; noise, pollution, and traffic increased. Bill sold the Mesa house, and we moved full-time to Young as soon as the addition was finished. The children went to the country school, of about one hundred students, kindergarten through high school. Coming from the large Mesa school, it was a big change for them.

Winter brought lots of snow, and as the snow melted, Cherry Creek flooded which was between the village and our home. Sometimes Tami and David walked a log across it; at other times, the creek was so high they had to stay with acquaintances near school. At one time, the creek was up so long we could not cross for three weeks. It was a productive time for me, as I organized all the tools, nuts, screws, and nails. It would be a long time before we resupplied, because I could now find what I wanted.

Bill was commuting to the Apache Junction clinic. Many times, during the floods, he was unable to cross the creek. Sometimes he stayed with friends, or he stayed in Apache Junction. He hated the creek flooding. He became irritated by the gravel road to Young. One time he crossed the flooded creek when it was flooding. Bessie was washed downstream as the water splashed over the hood and Bill had to drive along the bank to gain the road. I watched and was so frightened my knees collapsed.

I became domestic, baking all our bread, English muffins, and making noodles. I was quilting. It reminded me of being snowed in at White Grass, as I was alone for much of the flooding time. I fed our horses, Joe and Freckles. I had cats and dogs to feed. I had wood to chop and carry into the house.

Eventually, after purchasing another twelve acres from Onis's brother Red, we owned a twenty-four-acre property. Many of our friends called it a ranch, and maybe it was. In Arizona, one needs only ten acres of private land to hold a grazing permit on public land and be a cattle rancher. My ranch upbringing held me in good stead for rural life. When the electricity went out, I knew how to cope. I cooked on gas, heated with wood, and had Coleman lanterns for light. Only the refrigerator and freezer were dependent on electricity. To remedy saving frozen food, in 1985, Bill purchased a generator to keep food cold during electrical outages.

Also in 1985, I remodeled and opened the Apple Orchard Restaurant in the building we had recently bought that was adjoining ours to the south. I planned to open Friday through Sunday for lunch and dinner. Bill and I opened the restaurant with a keg and free steaks. The opening was a great success. Inside, I had a cozy dining room furnished with antiques, old photos, and shaded lamps, all from our own possessions. We averaged serving fifteen dinners each weekend, which was good for Young's small population. Our second summer opening, the insurance company doubled the premium, which made the restaurant financially impossible, so I closed at the end of the summer. Since the restaurant was not a possible income source for me, Bill began worrying about what would become of me when he was gone. I could only answer that I was a survivor.

Pleasant Valley Medical Clinic

In the early 1980s, the Pleasant Valley Homemakers built a metal building for a medical clinic. Bill, as an MD, had worked for the Lutheran Hospital organization. Nelson Turner, a Young resident, had been an officer at Lutheran, so Bill and Nelson went to talk with the Lutherans to sponsor the clinic, which culminated in their giving Bill a salary and supplying medical items in return for referring Young patients to their hospitals. The Homemakers supported the janitorial service and building upkeep with the Thrift Shop earnings.

Again, following the example of pioneer women helping their men, I studied to become a licensed Emergency Medical Technician to help Bill. The classes were held in Young, through an extension of Eastern Arizona College from Safford, Arizona. He was the only doctor in a more than fifty-mile radius of the village and over mostly dirt roads. Bill and I manned the clinic one day a week, but we were on twenty-four-hour on-call for six years. I acted as his medical assistant, office administrator, and janitor as a volunteer for three years before I had a salary.

One day, when we were coming home from the clinic, the creek was flooded. Bill had rigged a cable across the creek, from which a three-by-three-foot platform on which to sit hung. Using ropes, we could pull ourselves across. This time, Bill sent me across first with his leather medical bag. As I stepped off the platform, Bill's bag tumbled into the creek and quickly floated downstream, bobbing on the whitecaps. In my tall irrigation boots, I galloped along the rock-strewn and brushy edge of the stream and finally saw the bag caught in an eddy where I could wade in to retrieve it. I was greatly relieved, because Bill's medical tools were inside.

When the creek was not in flood, many medical calls came to our home. More than once, I placed a board across the bathtub on which a bleeding patient could sit while Bill sewed his hand or leg laceration. Another time, we rolled a screaming, squirming child tightly in a large towel so Bill could doctor her. One evening, a husband drove in at dusk with his dead wife necessitating a call to the sheriff and a long wait. Another time, a lady arrived in a hatchback with her granddaughter presenting a half-born baby. Amazingly, the mom and baby were fine but Bill called the medical helicopter to assure their health. Often, we would grab the medical equipment and treat injuries in the field. Bill would radio a helicopter to the accident location while I held a strip of toilet paper high as a windsock. I was his partner in picking up broken bodies along the road, sewing and bandaging what we could, delivering precipitate babies, and holding clinic hours where we fought illness.

During the same time, I was elected to the board of Young Public Library, a small borrowing library started by the Pleasant Valley Homemakers. I served on the local board for eighteen years and the country library board for a term. I enjoyed serving the community.

The Young Public School was not meeting David's needs, so he chose to live with his father in Denver to receive a better education. He went to high school in the morning, studied drafting at trade school in the afternoon, and worked at a pizza café in the evenings. His dad went to pursue his own interests, leaving David to fare on his own. Tami and I drove to Denver for his graduation. I was proud of how he had managed the difficult situation.

David worked one summer for my dad on White Grass, but Nona and the head wrangler gave him so much grief that it became unbearable. Feeling guilty, he left three weeks early. As with my experience, Dad did not support him against the bullying, which was heartbreaking for me. Another summer, he worked on geological survey as a "juggy", placing sensors in the plains of Wyoming. He arrived home so thin he looked like a Dachau survivor of World War II but he completed his commitment and I was proud of him.

Next, he drove to Texas, where he thought he had a job. On that journey, his engine mount broke. Friendly ranchers helped, but it turned out there was no job in Texas. Finally, answering an ad with on-the-job training, room and board, he found himself enlisted in the US Navy. After the Navy, he used the GI grant to earn his bachelor's degree in art and design. He became a budding commercial artist in Oregon and then a partner in a fine art gallery, where he shows and sells his landscapes and teaches art at the college. He is also a commercial river rafter and has guided many trips on the Colorado River in the Grand Canyon of Arizona. He was invited and went to Peru and Ecuador on exploratory trips with the goal of saving the free-flowing rivers from proposed dams.

One late March afternoon when Tami was a high school senior, I was cooking a special dinner—baked potatoes, Bill's favorite french-fried parsnips, and steak—and was putting the steak on our plates, when the phone rang.

"There was an accident across from Bingel's. Tami is hurt," a breathless voice said.

Bill grabbed his medical bag, as usual, and we headed a few miles to the roadside accident. We found Tami unconscious and hanging like a rag doll over a barbed-wire fence. She had been catapulted out of the bed of the rolled- over pickup truck, had slammed against a giant juniper tree, and slid onto the fence. Her head inflated like a party balloon, someone helped Bill lift her off the fence, and support her neck in fear that it was broken. Others were shoveling dirt over the truck's spilled gas to prevent fire. Bill controlled himself from thrashing the drunken pickup truck driver as he treated Tami. The deputy arrived and called the helicopter. It landed on the road, and Tami was on her way to Phoenix.

While Bill stayed home to take care of our animals and be on medical call, I grabbed an overnight bag and headed to Phoenix, a three-hour drive. I was terrified I would arrive in Phoenix to find my child dead. I listened to Sally Jessy Raphael's talk radio show to keep my mind from exploding with gruesome thoughts. At the hospital, Tami was still unconscious; surgery was scheduled for the morning to put her smashed jaw together. Large, ugly stitches secured a gash in her arm. At three o'clock in the morning, exhausted, I was not calling to wake my friends in Tempe. What was I going to do?

Meanwhile, Tami's friends had called a young man from Pleasant Valley who was living in Mesa, and he arrived at the hospital. The hospital staff pushed us out of the intensive care unit; no visitors were allowed at that hour, and in the daytime, only family were allowed, visiting for ten minutes at a time. The young man invited me to stay at his place. It was a smoke-filled, filthy bachelor pad, but I was thankful for a place to put my head. The next morning, I called friends in nearby Tempe and told them what had happened. They invited me to stay with them. For the next five days, the nurses let me stay quietly in Tami's room while knitting, even though it was against protocol. I was grateful I could stay. On the sixth day, Tami woke up, sat up abruptly, and began walking, with innumerable lines attached, to the bathroom. I called for help as I stopped her. Nurses came and disconnected the medical equipment.

2000, Cynthia and Bill Peck in Young, Arizona.

Later that day, Tami was rolled into an MRI machine. My heart pounded double time. I was so distraught I started having a panic attack, but I convinced myself it was only a test; she was not entering a wood chipper and coming out in little pieces.

Eventually, at home, with her jaw wired shut and a paralyzed left arm, she needed to learn to live with a new reality. She managed to catch up on her schoolwork, and she walked with her class, with her arm in a sling, raccoon-like black eyes, and a wired jaw, at graduation. Nothing kept her down for long. A month later, she received an invitation to go boating on Roosevelt Lake. She jumped off the boat to see if she could swim one-handed, and she did.

She had won a full-ride four-year scholarship to Northern Arizona University. She took advantage of the scholarship for only a year. She married a young man who was a Forest Service firefighter. After almost two ye ars of rough marriage, he used a rifle up his nostril to commit suicide. We were horrified by his actions.

It took Tami six years to achieve an associate's degree after she left Northern Arizona University. She then worked for the US Department of Agriculture's cotton division, first in Phoenix, then in Corpus Christi, and then in Washington, DC. She moved up to a position in

Phoenix with Western Power Administration. I respect her courage and the choices she has made for her life journey.

After a change in support and the physician's assistants manning the Pleasant Valley Medical Clinic, Bill worked radiology elsewhere as locum tenens, (filling a position) when another physician was on vacation, at a meeting, or during busy times. Often, I followed him, living in a Residence Inn, a rented apartment, or a townhouse in Tucson, Tempe, or Phoenix. I took a trunk filled with essentials and could set up housekeeping quickly anywhere. I stayed home at other times to manage the property and take care of the apple orchard and the animals.

The End of an Era

Most summers, Bill and I took Bessie with the camper to Jackson Hole for vacation. We enjoyed walking familiar trails and visiting friends. In July 1985, Dad invited us to a Fourth of July dinner party on the ranch. I was surprised and excited. I went to an upscale shop in Jackson to buy a skirt and a fancy blouse for the occasion. The evening included pleasant conversation and a good meal. Bill was good in social gatherings, whereas I felt awkward, especially in Nona's presence. Hugs and smiles ended the evening. Bill and I planned to leave for Arizona the next day.

In mid-Utah, where we had stopped for the night, we received a phone call that Dad had passed. He seemed an immortal fixture; I had a hard time believing he was gone. After years of alcohol consumption and smoking, he had been in poor health. But he had balanced his alcohol intake and smoking with naps and light activity and still had been a gracious host to dudes. He still had encouraged rides and pack trips, though he no longer took the pack trips himself. A wrangler became the pack trip guide.

Dad's death also meant the end of White Grass Dude Ranch, the end of the lively Western dude ranch era. The few remaining dude ranches tended to be resorts with swimming pools, tennis courts or golf and the rides, scheduled one slow, one fast, Wednesday lunch ride were all guided by wranglers. The freedom that White Grass afforded its dudes was forever gone, the age of insurance companies controlling the dude business had begun. The city-run insurance companies thought it was dangerous to ride without a guide. It was so sad.

I felt Dad's passing heavily. We had been buddies during pack trips. We had been a team working on the ranch. Bill and I offered to go back to Jackson but received a strong NO from Nona. I waited to hear of a burial or memorial service, but none came. Dad's goddaughter; Bethy; my cousin Fran, and I were in constant phone contact, discussing whether Nona was going to have any closure. July wore on, and August arrived, with September near. I felt too much time was passing between his death and a closure.

I was told the circumstances of his death. The night before Dad's passing, the cowboys in bachelor quarters were fighting; knives and maybe a gun were involved. Dad called the sheriff. They were up all night solving the altercation. In the morning, Dad went to the Main Cabin for breakfast. After breakfast, he went to his house, sat at the desk with paperwork before him, laid his head on the desk and died. No one told me who found him. Later, a friend of Nona's put Dad's body in a van and took him to Salt Lake City to be cremated. The ashes were brought back to Nona, who was emotionally paralyzed. Finally, a pastor convinced Nona to bury the ashes. The pastor, Nona, and a wrangler with a shovel over his shoulder went to the White Grass Ranch cemetery and buried him. Dad was laid close to Opa, my grandfather, under the sturdy Douglas firs and white-trunked quaking aspen trees. A carpet of wildflowers surrounded him.

The employees, in loyalty to Dad, decided to fulfill Frank's contracts and reservations with the dudes for the rest of the summer. They continued the rides and all services, with no direction from management; they did an excellent job.

Nona chose not to have a service or reception for Dad. Bethy and I needed closure. Dad was a respected rancher in Jackson Hole and had many friends, ranchers as well as several business owners in Jackson. Bethy and I decided to have a memorial service at the Chapel of Transfiguration in Moose. Dornans graciously offered to host a reception afterward. In respect of Nona's feelings, Bethy and I did not want to have the memorial advertised in the local paper. Instead, we talked to a friend who was good at spreading the word. Nona found out about the service and reception, which was no surprise. She told the employees they were not to attend. They came anyway, as did a multitude of people who had known Dad.

After the reception, the cowboys asked Bethy, Fran, Lori, and me to Bachelor Quarters on White Grass. We sat around a campfire companionably, sharing stories about Dad; the guys passed a bottle of booze around.

"In remembrance of Frank, let's catch the horses, saddle up, and take a moonlight ride," said Fran and the cowboys cheered, thinking it was a great idea.

As they stumbled to the barn for halters, Fran called to me, "Come on, Cindy! It'll be great fun."

"No, you all have fun," I replied. I thought the ride was going to be a wreck—too much alcohol had been consumed. While the guys took their ride, Bethy and I wandered through the sleeping ranch, the moon making eerie shadows. "Let's find one of Tucker Bispham's books or one of Owen Wister's," Bethy said.

The scavenger hunt was on. We went into one of the large cabins presently occupied by sleeping guests, whom we knew. We fumbled through the bookshelves in the living room. We found one of Tucker Bispham's books, with his ownership sticker on the front cover and Owen Wister's *When West Was West*. Wister's book is still on my shelf.

When we arrived back at Bachelor Quarters, the wranglers who stayed behind had Dad's worn-out jacket from the machine shop and Marmie's sidesaddle from the barn to give to me. I was pleased and grateful. Those are the only items I have from Dad.

According to the life estate agreement Mom and Dad had signed at the sale in 1956, they had the right to stay and operate the ranch as long as one of them was alive. In the divorce settlment, Mom signed her rights away but the Park did not award them to Nona. After Dad's death, Grand Teton National Park gave Nona a year to remove portable possessions from the ranch; the cabins had to stay.

On September 18, Nona held an auction, selling horses, furnishings, and even bathroom fixtures that were ripped out. Cousin Fran purchased a few things. He said the eighty horses especially brought high prices, as did many other items. A few years earlier, I had gone to an auction at one of the oldest ranches in Jackson Hole, the Bar BC Ranch. Seeing a lively part of Western history sold off to the highest bidder had brought me to tears. Those once-treasured historic items were sold and became scattered all over the United States, perhaps the world. It would have been too hurtful for me to attend the White Grass auction, so I didn't.

Cabin #8 at White Grass 1989 while the ranch was abandoned.

On November 5, four months after Dad's death, the Galey house burned to the ground. It was thought to be caused by an electrical fire, but Dad had electrified all the cabins, there had never been an electrical fire. Those who knew Nona speculated that she had set the fire for the insurance payout. A friend who was later in Nona's home in Jackson said she had seen many of the ranch treasures from Dad's house there.

For the next twenty years, the ranch buildings deteriorated; a tree fell across Sukie's cabin breaking the ridge pole, many of the roofs leaked, and some cabins leaned as the lower logs sank into the ground. It was heartbreaking.

My backpacking group wanted to hike the Tetons so I planned a hike up Death Canyon to Alaska Basin and down Cascade Canyon, but first, I wanted them to see the ranch. I acted cavalier, pointing out cabins and telling stories, but soon my emotions took over. I wanted my fellow backpackers to view me as strong, not see my emotions and tears; I picked up speed and ran-walked toward the north pasture. I slowly got control of my external emotions, but my heart and soul still cried.

I was devastated at the damage. No one cared about the buildings or the history even though White Grass Ranch had been the oldest continuously operating dude ranch in Jackson Hole and the second in Wyoming.

The hike with my backpacking friends brought back memories of Dad and me riding into the Alaska basin with dudes. As I descended into the Basin, I saw a new sign stating no horses were allowed beyond this point. Dad's presence was so strong that I turned to tell him about it, but of course, he had been gone for years. The only constant is change.

The barn was sold for one dollar and removed log by log. After several years, it was restored on a property near Wilson, Wyoming. Twice, White Grass Ranch reunions were held at the reconstructed barn and others at the ranch. It was wonderful to see the logs back together, but instead of being on the rise with its iconic inviting log ramp, the barn was on flat land, and the inside was gutted, with no stalls, and no slit-log floor. It was a huge box with a large open space perfect for parties.

In 2005, The Western Center for Historic Preservation was created to adapt reuse of the ranch as a training center for preservation techniques. The Park thought the Main Cabin was the first structure, perhaps a small one-room part of the Main Cabin was. The barn had been built the first year of homesteading and continued to be the primary focus of the ranch. In the north country one took care of their animals first.

About this time, visiting the ranch, I met Roger Butterbaugh who was the volunteer caretaker. He was instrumental in developing an oral history and timeline history of the ranch. We became friends and then he became my writing mentor.

As the saying goes, nothing remains the same. I was glad the barn had been rebuilt and the ranch had been preserved, but it did not feel like the ranch where I had been raised. It had a new function as a training center, which was much better than rotting into the ground.

CHAPTER 7

Pleasant Valley Ranger District, 1991–1992

I HAD ALWAYS LOVED THE OUTDOORS, BEING IMMERSED IN THE BACK-
country; poor weather or other difficulties did not deter me. With
Tami and David on their own, I finally had time to pursue my own
interests in wildlands and animals, and saw their need for protection.
I had studied archeology at Pima College in Tucson while Bill was
working there. Later, I took Wilderness Management classes, off
campus, at the University of Montana, Missoula. I had backpacked
or ridden into many wild areas. Those activities eventually brought
me to a job with the U.S Forest Service.

The sweet-smelling spring air, filled with odors of pine and fresh-
turned earth, wafted through the window; the sun peeked over the
mountain, painting the tops of the cottonwood trees gold. What a
glorious morning to be alive, I thought. I slipped my feet from the
warmth of my bed to the cool rough wood floor. Wrapped in my
cozy plaid flannel robe, I ambled to the kitchen. I filled the coffee
pot with tap water from our well and tossed in a handful of grounds.
I leaned against my homemade cutting-board table and crossed my
arms tightly to hold in the sleepy warmth while I watched the blue
flame of the stove bring the coffee to a boil. After it boiled for a few
seconds, I added a cup of cold water to settle the grounds and poured

myself a cup. With the cup of steaming coffee cradled in my hands, I was startled by the sound of insistent pounding on the front door.

Through the window, I saw a stern-looking cowboy; a fringe of white hair peeked from below his battered black hat; a ribbon of brown stain emphasized the line between the brim and crown. A plaid shirt, jeans worn to a gray tint, and pointed-toe packer boots completed the image. His blue eyes, one slightly squinted, looked at me as cold as glacial ice. I was not afraid but curious. What was this cowboy doing at my door?

In a small town, you know about everybody, even if you have not been introduced. I recognized Tommy Jones, the Wilderness Ranger for the Pleasant Valley Ranger District, a retired stockman for the White Mountain Apache tribe. He had spent most of his life riding the rough, mountain ranges, taking care of the Apache herd of two thousand registered Hereford cattle, as his father had done before him. But, I wondered, what was he doing there?

I opened the door. I tried to act nonchalant, as if I always entertained men while I was barefoot in my robe at seven o'clock in the morning.

"Good morning. Want some coffee? I was about to have a cup." Western manners dictate always offering food or drink, which I was glad to offer.

"Yep," he said.

Tommy sat across from me at the table, slowly sipping his mug of coffee. He said in a contentious tone, "Ranger Jordy says ya want to measure trails."

"I'd be interested," I answered. I hiked regularly with the Payson Packers, a small hiking group, and often backpacked with several of them.

During dinner one evening at Merle's, Ranger Jordy had told me he was looking for someone to measure trails. I was in my fifties, my daily mothering was not needed, Bill was often out of town, working. I needed to be serious about finding work to achieve a sense of security. I had been told volunteering for the Forest Service could lead to a paying job. Measuring trails would be hard work, few people I knew wanted to walk as much as the job required—but I was used to hard work. Ranger Jordy had said Tommy's bad knee would prevent him from walking great distances, nor could he push the measuring wheel from a horse.

"Would ya consider volunteering?" he begrudgingly asked me. "We start work at six in the morning. Everyone takes care of his own things. If ya want breakfast, ya fix it. Ya saddle yer own horse. No one'll wait for ya," he growled.

I realized, *Tommy doesn't want no woman in his camp, messing things up.* But I was used to roughing it in Dad's camps, where everyone, man, or woman equally, was expected to arise early, take care of him or herself, and participate in the day's progress. I knew there was no time to pamper folks in the backcountry. By the age of ten, I had been working regularly with stock and camping out. I cooked in camp. I helped set up tents. Tommy's orders were nothing new to me. I met Tommy's stony, cold glare without

Blinking.

"We'll start this ten-day tour of duty Wednesday," he grumbled. "They're two trails to measure where we're working'. Can ya make it?"

"I can't stay the whole ten days," I told him. "But I could bring my truck up on Thursday, walk those trails for a few days, and then drive myself home."

"We're camped up Billy Lawrence. Road's pretty bad." "Where's Billy Lawrence?" I asked.

"South of town. Ya turn up Reynolds Creek Road. Turn past Cienega Springs to the end. Our camp's on the saddle."

"See you Thursday evening then."

I had lots to do before Thursday; plan meals, a canteen to take on the horse, changes of clothes, walking shoes, camp shoes, a sleeping bag, a tent, a toilet kit, and a warm jacket for the evenings. I would take my own saddle, saddlebags, saddle pads, and bridle. There would be a horse in camp for my use.

I thought, since I had walked the Grand Canyon rim to rim with a forty-pound backpack, walking a few miles of trail should be easy. Bill was used to my going on hikes or on backpacking adventures, and he encouraged me to pursue those interests.

I left at noon on Thursday and headed south on the Young Highway, a graded, washboard gravel road. I followed Tommy's directions past Cienega Springs into the Sierra Ancha Mountains. The road, if you could call it that, climbed sharply above the springs. It became a big rut full of boulders, but Bessie, our four-wheel-drive Ford, took the terrain like a trooper. Even going so slowly that the speedometer did not register, I was thrown around like a rag doll, bruising my shoulder and bumping my head on the roof. The saddle was a comparatively level spot before the land dropped abruptly several hundred feet into the Billy Lawrence drainage. It was surrounded by towering ponderosa and Douglas fir trees that shaded the camp. I felt a cooling breeze, which made it a pleasant place. I saw the trailer, a large rock fire circle, and a wire corral with a portable canvas water tank. A canvas bag hung in a fir tree over a large, flat rock; that I presumed was the shower.

The trail crew came into sight on wet, tired horses. They were three grimy figures with sweat-stained Stetsons pulled to their ears; bandanna sweatbands tied over their brows; and worn, dusty clothing hanging from their lean, muscular frames. They wore sturdy lace-up boots with pointed toes and high heels made for heavy work and riding. I was used to working men, so their rugged garb and grim countenances were not frightening.

There was no greeting. Each went about the business of unsaddling his own horse and putting it in the corral. Each slung his saddle on a log rail set between two ponderosa trees. They tossed flakes of hay into the corral and spread them so each horse had a pile. They checked the giant water tub to make sure there was enough water for the night.

"I'm cookin' steak and taters tonight. There's enough for ya too." It was Tommy's first effort to be hospitable. He put a big Dutch oven over the fire and wiggled it around to set it securely. He added a large dollop of bacon grease. He rolled the steaks in flour and dropped them into the sizzling grease. I pitched in, peeling and cutting the potatoes, which were dropped into another Dutch oven with bacon grease. Meanwhile, Scott, one of the crew, sliced onions, which went into the potato pot. I needed something to eat that was not greasy, so I prepared a salad from my supplies. Bryan put a two-gallon coffee pot full of water on the fire for washing dishes later. We sat on logs cut and upended for seats around the campfire, eating noisily from paper plates.

There were no introductions. Names and associations became known as listened. They went about the business of preparing for the night. They joked among themselves but ignored me, except for a few shy looks. Bryan was a strong twenty something man with brown hair, brown eyes, and an easy smile. I learned that his wife was a biologist at the Canyon Creek fish hatchery, north of Young.

Scott, a large, quiet man, was an engineering student from Phoenix. Tommy was the crew foreman.

As I crawled into my tent, the faint smell of wood smoke wafted from the dying cook fire. I heard the shuffle of horses, and an owl called. All was calm and peaceful as I fell asleep. In the morning, I heard pots rattling. Peeking out of my tent, I saw a weak light from the trailer window. I hurried to dress, crawled out of my tent, and splashed my face with icy water from my five-gallon container. As I entered the trailer, Tommy was putting the coffee pot on the gas stove to make the ubiquitous boiled coffee. I placed my small pan of water on another burner.

"What's that for?" Tommy growled.

"I'm boiling water for instant oatmeal," I said. Tommy emitted a disparaging grump.

The crew came in and ate their breakfast of cookies and coffee and began to make their lunch sandwiches, white bread with slabs of bologna. I was glad I had brought supplies for myself, as camp food planning seemed sparse at best.

Remembering I was there on sufferance, I was careful not to be a nuisance. After I ate my cereal, I washed my bowl, spoon, and cup and put them away.

"Ya can use that sorrel horse with the big blaze," Tommy said as we approached the corral. "Name's Easy."

I caught Easy without difficulty; he was appropriately named. I bridled him and tried to saddle him. I was suffering from a frozen shoulder and could hardly lift my arm, much less the saddle.

Embarrassed, I called to Tommy, "If you can throw the saddle for me, I can do the rest. My shoulder won't let me do it."

To my surprise, he was not grumpy and threw the saddle onto Easy for me. I managed the cinch and put my sandwich and water into the saddlebags. I was prepared to go, with the measuring wheel in hand, before the crew was ready to leave. The measuring wheel was like the ones used by police when measuring roadway accidents. Every time the wheel rotated, it measured the distance and recorded it on a counter. I led my horse with one hand and pushed the wheel with the other. I was measuring the Lucky Strike Trail, which was a steep trail contouring around ridges downward toward Cherry Creek Road. I walked as fast as I could so the crew would not think poorly of me; I wanted to be part of the useful wilderness team. Easy was coming along, except for each time he sneaked a bite of grass.

When the crew caught up with me, they followed for a while. When we came to a wide spot, I stepped aside to let them pass. I relaxed a little and caught my breath but still made good time, despite the wheel alternately catching on rocks or in holes. Easy either kept going when the wheel stopped or stopped to grab a bite to eat as the wheel kept going. I felt like a bungee cord caught between two objects at odds with each other.

I met the crew cutting through oak brush and tangled manzanita and digging roots out of the trail with pick mattocks and Pulaskis. They raked the trail with a Mcleod, a clumsy hand tool with a rake on one side and a broad hoe on the other. A Pulaski was a hand tool with an ax on one side and a narrow hoe on the other.

Tommy pointed. "Ya go across a small drainage and over a rise. You can see Cherry Creek Road from there. Ya go on downhill and through a gate. The trail ends at the road." Until then, I had had tracks and a newly maintained trail to follow, but now I saw a faint trail in front of me. *I had better figure it out. No time to waste. Let's go*, I said to myself with trepidation. The trail ahead of me had been unmaintained for several years. The manzanita and oak brush clamped over it. Though meager, Tommy's directions were a help.

After opening the gate near the finish, I reached the road and stopped to catch my breath. I drank a little of the sun- warmed water from the canteen and folded the measuring wheel. I walked back and closed the gate, I found a large rock to help me mount. I balanced on it to swing my leg over Easy without wrenching my shoulder. The wheel's size and shape made it difficult to tie onto the saddle, so I carried it in one hand and the reins in the other. Easy climbed the trail back to the crew.

"Did ya see the barricade to keep the trucks out?" asked Tommy as he walked toward me.

I wondered what he meant and tried to visualize the trail near the road. "Do you mean the two big posts on either side of the trail?" I said, stopping Easy.

"Yeah," he said as he turned back to the trail work.

I added to his back that the trail was five miles long, and from the topo map, I estimated an elevation change of 2,800 feet. Typical of cowboy culture of few words, there was no further response, so I rode back to camp.

As I relaxed to the rocking motion of Easy's gait, I pondered Tommy's question and realized I had been tested. His real, unspoken questions had been "Did she really get all the way to the end of the trail? Can I trust her?"

The next morning, I smiled to myself when Scott came into the trailer and asked, "What's that pot of water on the stove?"

"None of your business," answered Tommy, as he had put the water on for me but was not going to admit to his thoughtfulness; he was softening my presence in camp.

The next trail to measure was the Grapevine Trail, which branched north from the Lucky Strike. We rode to the junction together; I chose to ride behind everyone. I watched the men and their mounts. Waltz, the mule Scott was riding, stopped suddenly and ducked his head, throwing Scott forward so he nearly fell. But Scott picked up the reins and kicked him. Waltz was a smart mule and would take advantage of a rider who was not paying attention. Scott had better stop daydreaming while riding Waltz. In front of Scott was Bryan, who surveyed the scenery from his plodding paint horse. Tommy was in the lead on his alert, big black horse, Duke. Tommy's shoulders were hunched as he watched the trail, inspecting the quality of work. At the junction, I dismounted and unfolded the measuring wheel handle.

Tommy said as he pointed with his chin, "The Grapevine Trail has not been cleared for seven years."

I looked in the direction he indicated. The path was obscured by a thick tangle of manzanita brush, catclaw, and scrub oak. I shouldered brush aside as I went with one hand on the wheel and one hand leading Easy. There was a slight overgrown indentation in the ground that indicated the trail; nothing else was of any help. The brush became so impenetrable that I had to scout. I tied Easy to a small oak tree and leaned the wheel against it. Cattle trails wandered this way and that under the tangled branches. I saw cloven hoof tracks too big and wide to be elk or even most cattle. As I continued to search for the trail, I ducked under a thick manzanita bush. Two beady black eyes surprised me. A monstrous red bull with curled horns bellowed and shook his head, splattering me with snot from his dripping-wet nose! I made a speedy retreat as I wiped my face on my sleeve. I felt I had narrowly avoided being chased or gored by his wickedly hooked horns.

Relieved, I finally found the route and returned to retrieve Easy and the measuring wheel. As I pushed my way through the brush, the wheel continually tangled in the stiff brushy branches, and I freed it with sharp jerks. When the trail descended to cross a drainage, where there were tall, shade-making oak trees, I took advantage of a short rest stop. I saw cougar tracks in the mud of the intermittent streambed, which made me uneasy, but I did not think the cougar would attack me in broad daylight, as they tended to be night hunters. I knew danger always lurked in the backcountry, so I stayed alert.

I decided it was a nice, shady spot for lunch, so I tied Easy to a tree as I thought, What have I gotten myself into? Walking a trail was familiar since I had hiked and backpacked many overnight or five-day backpacking trips. This so-called trail was more like beating my way through African bush. But the job needed doing, and I had said I would do it. I was determined to keep my word. Tommy nor the conditions were going to make me quit.

Looking around the small glade, I spotted a mine monument. The can buried inside revealed a discolored paper bearing the familiar Gila County name Haught. I sat against the oak tree to enjoy my saddlebag-mashed peanut butter and jelly sandwich. As I ate, I thought about the history of mining in the area.

During World War II, the Atomic Energy Commission built innu-merable roads in the Sierra Ancha Mountains prospecting for uranium and asbestos. Luckily, the quality and quantity of uranium discovered was not worth the extraction of it, leaving the area appropriate for the Wilderness designation under the 1964 Wilderness Act. The state mine records said the ore from the Lucky Strike mine (from which the trail was named) was packed down the steep mountainside by mule, surely an arduous task. Many of the prospecting roads were incorporated into the non motorized trail system. For instance, most of the Lucky Strike Trail was an abandoned mining road.

I took a large swig of sun-warmed water from the canteen, which was not very refreshing, as I prepared to move on. It was a relief when I arrived at the small grassy knoll and saw Cherry Creek Road, the end of the trail. I found a stump to climb onto Easy, and happily, he stood patiently. As I started back, nothing seemed familiar. I couldn't have come through that thick brush, I thought. A feeling of panic rose in my chest. I was lost. Then I saw Easy and my tracks and the thin line made by the wheel. Whew! I was on the right track.

When I reached the junction, I checked in with the crew. "Did ya see the sign by the road?" Tommy asked.

"You mean the one with the hiker and staff?" I asked. He was testing me again, but I was better prepared. I knew he needed to know if he could trust me to complete assigned tasks.

"That's the one." With a slight smile, he indicated I had passed. I must have gained some respect in those few days; he talked more and even smiled.

Being out in the wild is always an adventure. One never knows what will be around the next corner or what will happen. But the challenges faced and decisions made are the building blocks of self-confidence. I was determined to bring Tommy around to have confidence in me and respect for my work ethic. Reliability made for a better work environment and might even give me a recommendation for a paying job. After all, I was still trying to find a way to support myself.

After two days in camp, I drove Bessie back along the boulder-strewn road past Cienega Springs to go home.

McFadden Horse Trail

"Do ya want to measure another trail?" Tommy asked as he came seeking me.

"Sure, when do you want to do it?" I said, I was dressed and working at the barn.

"Next week," said Tommy as he stood, weight on one leg, John Wayne style.

"Where do I meet you? What trail do you want to measure?" I bombarded him with questions.

"Camp is on Aztec, up Workman Creek. The McFadden Horse Trail is the next one," he responded.

"I could come to camp on Thursday," I said, knowing that Wednesday was used to move and set up camp.

I found camp under tall ponderosa pine and Douglas fir trees below Aztec Peak where there was a Forest Service fire lookout tower. There was a new trail crew member, Jeff, a tall fellow who kept up a monologue even if no one was listening. The camp area was larger than the Billy Lawrence one and flat enough to accommodate a better wire corral, with the portable canvas water trough as well as the old camp trailer. A big wooden cable spool served as a table. The shower was hung from a rope slung over a stout branch of the immense Douglas fir tree. It was surrounded by hanging canvas on two sides and a curtain of tree branches on the others.

Tommy broke into Jeff's monologue, asking me, "Do ya want to ride to McFadden Horse Mountain with me tomorrow? There isn't enough gas to drive and pull the horses closer. Someone used the trail truck and didn't fill the gas tank." I knew the only gas station in Young did not open until nine in the morning. The trail crew came to work at six and were supposed to leave the station by seven-thirty so Tommy could not fill the gas tank in the morning.

"If you can do it, I can too," I said with some angst. No vague directions—we were going together. I thought I must have moved up in his estimation!

Tommy put the oatmeal water on for me again but had no harassment from the other crew members. As usual, Tommy ate his breakfast of cookies and coffee, and I ate mine of oatmeal.

Afterward, Tommy automatically put my saddle on Easy as my shoulder was still sore. We were on our way by six o'clock. Tommy kept his horse, Duke, at a fast walk. To keep up, Easy had to trot occasionally. The pace was rough. Soon my stomach and knees hurt. I gritted my teeth and kept quiet. Five hours later, we were at the end of McFadden Horse Mountain, having crossed two major drainages and worked our way around Aztec Peak, over Center Mountain, and onto Cienega Springs Trail, an old mining road grade.

"McFadden lived on Reynolds Creek and used this area, in summer, to graze his horses, on top is a grassy mesa," Tommy said. "That's why it's called McFadden Horse Mountain."

When we reached the end, we tied our horses to trees. Tommy ambled to the cliff edge.

"Come closer, and I'll show ya an old trail used by rustlers," said Tommy. He was standing on the cliff edge with a mischievous twinkle in his eye.

By that time, I knew Tommy enjoyed practical jokes. I did not trust him. I hate heights with drop-offs. I sat on the big, flat rock and scooted to the edge. If he tried to scare me, I felt safer sitting; that made him laugh—a great, booming sound of pure mirth.

He pointed to a talus slope between two peaks. "About the turn of the century, renegades drove stolen horses through that pass with the vigilantes hot on their tail. The vigilantes didn't find the pass

Cynthia and Duke backpacking Paria Canyon, Utah to Arizona.

and never caught the thieves. It was said they took the horses across Cherry Creek to the Indian reservation."

I looked at the area he was talking about. It consisted of steep talus slopes interspersed with cliffs and a deep drainage. I could not imagine any horse getting through there without breaking a leg. He stepped back. I scooted from the precipice, stood, and went to the shade of a scrub oak tree for lunch. To my surprise, Tommy chivalrously spread his chaps on the ground. He motioned for me to sit and he sat beside me to eat our saddlebag-mashed sandwiches and drink sun-warmed water.

Tommy pointed to a small nearby peak next to McFadden Horse Mountain. There was a precipice between us and the peak. "See the walls round the peak?" he asked. "That is an ancient Indian ruin.

I climbed over there once. There is a whole prehistoric pot on the south side that I found and hid from pot hunters." Pot hunters were people who searched ancient burials for the pots, which they sold for high prices. It was an illegal activity.

After lunch, Tommy, riding Duke, led Easy. I pushed the wheel. Even with the wheel sticking at rocks and holes, it was easier without leading a horse. Sweat ran into my eyes, stinging and blurring my vision. Duke slowly followed me until his impatience caused him to butt me with his head to hurry me, nearly knocking me over. Before long, he learned to follow close behind without pushing. Tommy unexpectedly poured water from his canteen over me. It was a shock but it cooled me. Three miles later, we came to the junction of the Cienega Springs Trail. Another trail measuring was completed but it was a long way to camp.

I mounted and tied the wheel to the back of the saddle and we headed back. Following Duke's fast walk, Easy again trotted to keep up. At six-thirty, twelve hours later, we rode into camp.

1991, Cynthia sidesaddle on a misbehaving Easy ready for
the Pleasant Valley Days Parade, Young, Arizona

"Did you have any trouble? I was starting to worry," said Bryan as he stood and came toward us with his hand held out to take Easy.

"No, just a long way," I said as I dismounted and handed the reins to him. I was exhausted.

Bryan put Easy away. I took hot water from the two- gallon coffee pot, poured it into the shower bucket, and began to take a shower. I thought I heard footsteps to the side where the canvas had an opening. Looking over my shoulder, I saw Jeff pretending to feed the horses. The horses were not ordinarily fed in that part of the corral. Was he spying on me? It made me angry, but I stayed quiet. I would keep a lookout for his tricks.

With my shower finished, I dressed and sat on a stump. Tommy brought a plate of dinner to me. We ate. I was exhausted beyond anything I had done previously but felt good that I had completed the task and kept up with Tommy, even though initially, I had doubts I could. I crawled into my sleeping bag, not even setting up my tent, but on the extra bunk in the trailer. I was so tired that I had no energy left to warm myself in my sleeping bag. Even though I was cold, exhaustion made me fall asleep.

Searching for My Birth Certificate

Lewis Pyle Memorial Hospital in Payson hired Bill to fill the radiology position. We rented a house in Payson for the work week but went home to Young on weekends. I spent Tuesday each week hiking with the Payson Packers. I also took oil painting classes with Bill Ahrendt of Arizona Highways magazine fame. He was planning a group trip to Europe to visit museums. I had taken history of art at Foxhollow, and I wanted to see the masters' paintings in person. Bill and I made an agreement: if I made half the cost of the trip, as a supportive husband, he would contribute the other half. I also had to have a passport, but I did not know where my birth certificate was.

I went to Mom, but she did not have my birth certificate and did not know where to look. I was born in Oregon, so I called Salem, the capital. They did not have it. But I learned that census information, a letter from someone who knew me at an early age, and school records would suffice. I doubted I would be in the census, because Dad had been such a free spirit, but fortunately, I found myself on it. Next, Ellen Dornan wrote a letter stating she had known me when I was a very young child who came to Wyoming with Inge and Frank Galey. I looked for school records, but the school had burned—no records.

I got back on the phone. Maybe New Mexico had records of my adoption, but no, they did not. However, the gentleman on the phone spent time explaining the record system. My records had to be in Salem. I called Salem again, and this time, a lady with a mature voice answered. She looked at the computer—no information. She asked for my birth date again and then told me the 1942 records had not been entered into the computer system. She went upstairs and looked in the boxed files, and yes, I did exist. I was relieved. With a fee of five dollars, she made a certified copy and sent it to me. In an adoption, only the names of the adoptive parents were listed, along with the date of birth; no other information was even hinted at. I mailed the birth certificate with an application and obtained the passport successfully.

To pay for the Europe trip, I harvested and sold apples from the several standard-sized apple trees on our property. I parked Bessie under a tree and used her to climb into our large, worm-free Macintosh apple trees. Once, I climbed onto her roof and dented it. Bill was unhappy about my abuse of her. To fix the dent, I lay on the bench seat and kicked the dent out. I thought all was good.

When I had the truck bed filled with apples, I drove to Forest Lakes, parked in a busy area, dropped the tailgate, set the scale on it, and sold apples. I had bags and a knife so I could cut apples into quarters for tasting. People were glad to pay twenty-five cents a pound. I filled the truck many times and sold them by the roadside, and I made half of the trip cost, with a little extra.

Going to Europe and seeing the paintings and sculptures in person was much different from looking at pictures, especially turning a corner and seeing one of Monet's water lilies in front of me. The use of color was magnificent, genius, and so beautiful!

More Adventures Measuring Trails

"Moody Point starts near the Aztec camp and goes to Cherry Creek, near Flying F Ranch," Tommy said.

I knew the camp was still on the shoulder of Aztec Peak at 7,200 feet of elevation. Reading the topographical map, I saw the ranch on Cherry Creek was about 2,700 feet in elevation. It looked like a long, arduous task.

"Could I invite Allen and Gary from the Payson Packers hiking group to go with me?" I asked Tommy.

"Sure. Good for ya to have others on this trail," Tommy answered.

Allen, Gary and I slept one night at camp so we could start early. Instead of cookies and coffee, Tommy kindly fixed us a delicious breakfast of bacon and fresh eggs from his wife's chickens. By six thirty, we were on the trail. Since I knew it was going to be a long, strenuous day, I was anxious about successfully walking the grueling terrain.

We were well prepared; in our day packs, we each carried a gallon of water, our lunch, rain gear, and a small first-aid kit. Soon my legs complained because of the steep, continuous downhill. With each step, my legs acted as they pile- drive to brake, preventing my falling. The trail leveled for a bit along a ridge and gave us some relief. The measuring wheel's behavior was normal, sticking on rocks, running ahead on steep slopes, and catching me off balance; my body ached in response. Sweat soaked my hat brim and dripped into my eyes, stinging and blinding. I wiped my eyes with my sleeve and continued onward. Behind me, Gary and Allen suffered the same effects without complaining.

As the day wore on, reaching lower elevations, we were in a hot country. There were no taller, shade-making trees. Once, seeking shade, we sat shoulder to shoulder under a scrubby juniper on the steep hillside, ate lunch and drank warm water from our packs. Moving on, I stumbled with cramping legs, sweat running down my torso and forehead, burning my eyes. When we reached the creek, we looked at one another with the same idea: girls downstream and guys upstream. No matter how hard it was, I wanted to succeed. Dad used to say, "Hardship makes you stronger."

When we reached the road after six hours, nine and a half miles, and a 4,200-foot drop in elevation, we saw Tommy leaning against the dusty green truck. I was proud I had completed another difficult task.

He greeted us with "I saw ya stumbling those last miles but lost ya by the creek. Didn't have any trouble, did ya, on the ridge?" It sounded like he was concerned about us instead of testing.

Since I'd signed up to measure all the trails in the district, there was more to come. The following year in early summer, Tommy came to our house again. "Do ya want to go on a pack trip?" he asked.

I wondered if he hated using phones as much as I did, since he always arrived at my house instead of calling. "What do you mean?" I asked.

"Need to go to Boyer cabin and Hell's Hole. We'll drive hay one day and then ride from Reynolds Creek Trailhead another. I figure we'd have one night at Boyer and one at Hell's Hole."

"Sure, can you tie a diamond hitch?" I teased as I was more relaxed in his presence.

"Been a long time. Usually used a squaw hitch." These hitches were used to tie loads onto a pack mule. I had finally gained enough respect that we joked.

Driving with the hay, we followed a harrowing track with washed-out gullies toward Boyer cabin.

At one, "You'd better drive," Tommy said as he hopped out of the four-wheel-drive truck. "I'll put a rock in the gully and direct you to put the wheel on the rock."

I could see that if the truck slipped off the rock, we would be high-centered and thoroughly marooned.

"Slowly turn to the left—no, right. A little more."

The truck bumped over the rock. I could breathe again. Tommy returned behind the steering wheel and we crossed the spectacular sunflower-covered Thompson Mesa to the Boyer cabin. It was a well-locked cattleman's line camp with a two- room board-and-batten cabin. Looking through the grimy windows, I could see a dusty wood range, rough pine-board shelves lining one wall, a table with chipped pale green paint, and two equally disreputable chairs. The second room had two steel bunks with mouse-chewed and soiled mattresses. Cobwebs and vermin scat covered everything. I preferred the clean ground outside. In the three-sided large barn there was a stack of the rancher's hay. We added our bale and a bag of grain. It seemed cleaner than the cabin, or maybe the sweet hay smell made me think so.

The following day, we trailered the horses and mule to the Reynolds Creek group site. Tommy saddled Duke and Jimmy, the mule, and I was able to saddle Easy since my shoulder was better. We combined our efforts to load gear and food onto Jimmy, a small, mean- tempered black mule. Tommy snubbed him tightly to the tree to keep him from bucking while we packed. It took a couple of tries with our rusty packing skills and Jimmy's reluctance to secure the pack. Thankfully, Easy and Duke were well-behaved.

The previous year, while measuring that trail, I'd slipped and found myself looking up Duke's nostrils, with his legs straddling me. Tommy had laughed when he saw my frightened look.

"Duke's never stepped on ya," he'd said, but I hadn't been so sure.

I had been seeing double; the world was spinning— signs of heat exhaustion. I wandered around like a crazed cow, looking for shade, but the only shade was under the horses. I was in trouble. Tommy offered me water from the canteen hanging from his saddle horn. It tasted of metal. He poured some over my head, which spilled onto my shirt; evaporative cooling at work.

"Let's get out of here," I told him. As we had passed a stagnant pool, I declined dipping in it; we would be back in timber and shade soon, and then I could take time to cool.

I was thankful this trip was in cooler weather. We laughed and poked fun at each other as we rode, checking the trail condition, and to spend a night at Boyer cabin. The next day we replaced a trail sign on the way to Hell's Hole. It was dusk when we wound our way into Hell's Hole Canyon. We strung a tarp between trees and placed our sleeping bags underneath the crude shelter. We fed the horses hay and grain pellets and turned them loose. We closed the dilapidated wire fence across the gap that led toward home. The other exits to the canyon were blocked by logs and brush jammed between boulders and cliffsides. The only way the horses could leave was up an extremely steep, overgrown hillside with scattered boulders. Tommy did not think they would go there after such a long day.

We had a meager dinner of heated canned chili. After dinner, the horses were not finding their way to water so I caught Easy with my belt and led him to the boulder- strewn stream. Easy pulled back, causing the hook on my belt buckle to rip through my index finger.

"To hell with you! You can find your own darned water!" I shouted, released him, and walked back to the shelter holding my hand up, blood streaming down my arm.

"What happened to ya?" Tommy asked. "Let's see that. Looks like it should have stitches. Should we load up and go in?"

"No, I don't think so. By the time I could get to a doctor, it would be too late for stitches. Just help me wrap a Band- Aid tight enough to stop the bleeding," I answered. Bill had told me that stitches must be done within eight hours of the injury. I knew the trip to town would take too long: a half hour or more to load the animals, another four hours of riding to the trailhead, an hour to unpack and load the animals in the dark, an hour to drive to Young, and another two hours to drive to Payson. Gritting my teeth against the pain, I settled myself against a tree trunk, holding my hand above my head. I knew in the backcountry, one had to accept the possibility of injury and the consequences thereof. I expected, if injured, to solve whatever came next. Certainly, endangering other lives was not worth going for stitches. I heard thunder.

"Hooves on the hillside. Run up the trail to cut'em back," Tommy called over his shoulder as he hobbled up the hillside to waylay Jimmy.

When I heard the bushes rattling near camp and Tommy's swearing at Jimmy, I figured I could return to camp. We tied Jimmy for the rest of the night, but Easy and Duke looked content to graze the sparse grass near the creek. We ducked into the shelter just as the rainstorm hit. Lightning flashed nearby, thunder echoed off the narrow canyon walls, and my finger throbbed. I threw the sleeping bag over my clothed body. I braced my elbow against my side to hold my hand up. I tried to sleep, but it was a restless, long night.

In the morning, we still had all the stock. My finger still hurt, throbbing like a bad toothache. I took the old blood-soaked bandage off. Tommy helped me apply a new one, the bleeding had stopped. We gathered garbage left by other campers along the creek and in the campsite to pack out, which was the purpose of this trip. Tommy said that once, he had found a twin bed mattress here. People tended to pack junk in, but obviously, they were not going to pack it out. I have often wondered if the people who leave trash at a camp leave trash around their home yards too.

Tommy helped saddle Easy, and I helped pack Jimmy one-handed. We climbed out of the canyon with the fresh smell from the night's rain. We looked for smoke in case lightning had started a fire; thankfully, we saw none. If we had, we would have reported it on the handheld radio we always carried, though it worked sporadically in our mountainous area. My finger healed with no infection, though I do have a scar and diminished feeling at its tip.

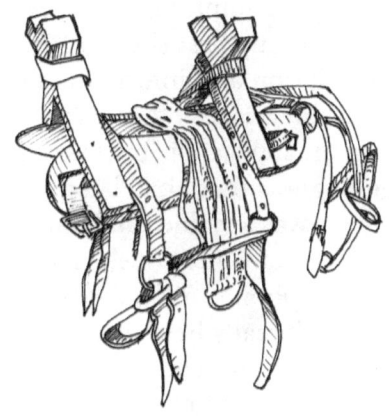

CHAPTER 8

Montana Wilderness, Summer 1992

"WHY DON'T YOU GET A JOB WITH THE FOREST SERVICE?" TOMMY asked me, as he knew I was looking for permanent work and had contributed 1,500 hours volunteering. "You know the trails and how to handle the stock." I knew Tommy was approaching retirement.

I went to Ranger Jordy. "What openings will there be next summer, so I can apply?"

"Why don't you wait two years and join the senior citizen volunteer program?"

I knew the senior program accepted people fifty-five years or older. I wanted paid work now; I wanted to use my knowledge. Age fifty-five was a few years away, and the senior citizen program meant cleaning outhouses, picking up garbage, and emptying garbage cans with no pay. I was riled. I was being disrespected. I felt that my work ethic and skills with stock and outdoor survival were significant and valuable. It had taken me nearly forty years to find a possible market for them. I told Ranger Jordy I would find a Wilderness job elsewhere, and I started looking.

One winter day, Ranger Jordy told me he had seen a job announcement for a seasonal Wilderness guard position in Montana. I guess he realized I was seriously job hunting, or maybe he was testing my commitment. It looked like my best shot so I called the district in Montana for a job description and information on how to apply. I applied to their Helena supervisor's office, as per instructions. They could not ask my age on the application, but looking at my experience, they could make a good guess that I had been around for a while. I wanted them to see that I was a viable candidate.

"I may be coming to Montana next week," I told Charley, who had introduced himself on the phone. "Would it be possible to come by and visit with you?" I didn't really have plans to go to Montana, but I thought the trip might help me acquire the position.

"That's fine." I heard confusion in his voice. Interviewing was not part of their system for lower-level jobs. Usually, an applicant sent the information to the employment

office, and then the district would request the applications when they had a job to fill.

"What day would be best for you?" I asked.

"We'll be at the station all day Wednesday."

"I'll check with the station when I arrive in Lincoln to see what time is best for you," I told Charley.

Eventually, I mailed seven applications throughout the western states. One application to Powell, Idaho, involved backpacking while carrying clothes, food, tools, a stove, water, and a radio—everything needed to live in the Wilderness for ten days at a time—and working by myself. As I dropped the envelope at the post office, I prayed I would not obtain that job. Why did I even apply for it? Even though I had backpacked lots, I knew I could not carry an excess of sixty-five pounds for ten-day tours of duty.

I drove three days to Montana. The village was nestled in a valley with snow-capped mountains on either side. It was a quaint western town with a few businesses spread along both sides of the highway. Tall ponderosa pines and Douglas firs stood sentinel over rustic wood buildings. Snowdrifts remained everywhere. I almost passed the motel, as its small wooden sign was hidden among the trees. I was directed to one of the log cabins where I found a homey, well-kept room.

Lincoln had a single flashing yellow signal light swinging leisurely above the intersection. A sign pointed toward the dirt road indicating Fletcher's Pass. On one corner was a gas station, another a deserted building and one had a sign announcing a bar and restaurant. It was surrounded by pickup trucks. This was the center of town! I felt at home. I lived in a community of only seven hundred people, and from what I could see, this village was larger.

At the Forest Service office, an attractive brown-eyed gal met me. "Can I help you?" she asked.

"I'm interested in getting a map of the Scapegoat," I responded.

"What are you particularly interested in?"

"I'm Cynthia Peck. I'm applying for the Wilderness job. I'd like to see what the Scapegoat area looks like. I have an appointment to visit with Charley Hester or Jerry Burns tomorrow. I need to make an appointment time that would suit them."

A lanky cowboy walked along the hall towards the front desk. "Jerry Burns. Glad to meet you." He stuck out a callused hand as he introduced himself and offering a firm handshake. "I don't have any time now; I'm on my way to a meeting." Jerry was tall, thin and wore tight jeans, a wide belt with a big buckle, and black cowboy boots with bright red tops. He had a handlebar mustache above a wide smile.

"I was wondering what time tomorrow would be best for you," I said.

Jerry turned to call down the hall to someone else.

"What time will you be here tomorrow?"

"Nine o'clock would work well," answered a disembodied voice.

"Sounds fine. See you then," I said standing tall to look confident.

"I think the map can be an administrative expenditure under the circumstances. Here is the Bob Marshall Wilderness Complex Management Plan, if you want to look at it. The Scapegoat is managed under this plan." He handed me the thick document.

"Thanks. I'd like to read it."

Boy, do I have homework for tonight to read and learn what's in the management plan. But first, on the way back to the motel, I stopped at Garland's department store. Its rustic front porch and outdoor clothing window display caught my eye. The cheerful sales gal was visiting with a friend but welcomed me. "Hello! May I help you?" she asked. She was much friendlier than salespeople I'd encountered in cities.

"Just looking. Thanks."

The store was one large room. To the left was women's clothing, including jeans, sweaters, and long-sleeved shirts. In front was a wall of boots—snow boots, galoshes, riding, and hiking boots. There was an aisle of long underwear, wool hats, warm gloves, camping gear, heavy wool jackets, and rainwear. I saw a few mid calf-length oiled canvas raincoats made for horseback riding, cut with a long pleat in back, labeled "The Australian Outback Collection " and tagged

$185. I had wanted an Australian duster for a long time but could not justify the expense. They were rugged and waterproof and would last the rest of my life. I had little use for it in Arizona, but if I secured the job in Montana, it would be essential.

"My sister has one. She uses it all the time," the sales gal said when she saw me inspecting the duster.

"I am applying for the Wilderness job and might need it," I told her. I knew if I bought the duster, I was taking a nearly two-hundred-dollar chance that I would land the job and need it.

"You won't be sorry," she told me.

"OK, it's a sale." I took a dull brownish-green one off the rack but I had a feeling I would need it; I would be in the village for the summer.

Back at the motel, I stayed up till midnight, reading and comparing the plan to areas on the map. On the Canadian border is Glacier National Park, with one road crossing it from east to west. Below Glacier is the Great Bear National Wilderness. Contiguous to Great Bear is the Bob Marshall National Wilderness. Continuing south of Bob Marshall is the Scapegoat Wilderness. Several miles south of Scapegoat is the next road through the northern Rocky Mountains. On this road is the village of Lincoln, Montana. The three adjoining Wildernesses are all managed under the same plan, the Bob Marshall Wilderness Complex. The management plan begins:

> The Bob Marshall Country stands as a monument to the wisdom of people, from both past and present, who so cherished its wilderness that they spent much of their lives achieving protection of the land in its natural state. This plan provides a uniform system for protecting or restoring the resources and social conditions needed to comply with the Wilderness Act of 1964. The central management thrust in the Bob Marshall Complex will be to permit natural processes to operate uninhibited by human influence. Man, however, will be viewed as a natural part of the ecosystem, so long as his stay is temporary and he lives by primitive means.

In a nutshell, that described the job I hoped to receive: to see that natural processes operated without man's influence and to erase any influence man had left in the Wilderness.

The management plan continued by saying, "Consequently, this management program is to be applied by rangers capable of communicating the land's mystery, geography, history, and culture to others, and its purpose is to perpetuate the opportunity for each visitor to enrich his or her experience to the fullest without unduly limiting the freedom to interact alone with nature." The plan continued to outline my job.

The next day, at the station, Jerry greeted me with another handshake and said, "Do you want some coffee? Come on into the office."

"Yes, thank you. Black." Western perspective of coffee doctored with sugar or cream was sissy. I'd learned to like it black in my mid-teens when I emulated the ranch cowboys. I really preferred honey in it.

"This is Charley Hester. Charley, this is Cynthia Peck." Jerry introduced me.

"Have a seat. You came all the way from Arizona?" Charley greeted me with warm brown eyes and a serious countenance. He stood up to shake my hand. He was a stocky man as tall as I was, about five foot seven. I handed him the management plan.

"Yes," I said as Jerry handed me a cup. I sat up straight and looked into his eyes, acting assured. "I'm extremely interested in the Wilderness job and want to convince you I am the right person for you." Wow. I could not believe I was so forthcoming to say that. Where had that come from? I was usually more reserved but hoped it sounded convincing.

"It means working by yourself, riding, and packing supplies on a mule. You need to be able to lift fifty-pound bags of grain cake." He sounded doubtful.

"I don't think that's a problem. I was raised on a ranch in Wyoming. I have ridden since I was very small and helped Dad pack since I was ten years old. I manage bags of grain and bales of hay at home. We have two horses."

"You will need to wear a uniform."

"I would expect to. If I wear my own hat, chaps, and rain gear, is that considered out of uniform?"

"No. That's fine. Do you understand the LAC—Limits of Acceptable Change—monitoring system?" he asked.

"I went to a San Juan National Forest Wilderness Management workshop, where David Cole, the expert on Limits of Acceptable Change, explained it. I haven't worked with it but am willing to learn," I told him.

The LAC is a management tool used to monitor the effects of man's imprint in Wilderness. The first step is to inventory existing trails, campgrounds, and any other use sites. In other words, it's intended to inventory man's impact on the area and then decide what an acceptable amount of change is. The inventory and continued monitoring give management the information they need to determine when an unacceptable amount of change is occurring and take steps to control that impact.

"Do you want to look around the station?" Jerry asked. If they were not considering me, I doubted they would have offered a tour; maybe I had a chance.

There was a board-and-bat-sided barn with pole corrals behind it. It had a wide door on the side and a gable door for moving hay into the loft. Huge ponderosa pine trees sandwiched the two bunkhouses, where seasonal personnel could stay for a minimal fee. I sensed the people in the station worked together and stayed in communication with one another. They seemed proud of their workplace and the work they did; it was a nice environment. I left with a good feeling.

I headed home via Helena since Jerry suggested I change my application at the job service, as I had understated my qualifications on my original application. But I left a copy with Jerry, as he requested.

Calling home, I told my husband, "There were no promises. There are other applicants, and my qualifications only give me a chance for a GS 4, minimum wage. They had advertised a GS 5, but they were very informative, open, and friendly."

Three weeks later, a message was left on my answering machine: "Charley Hester of the Helena Forest in Montana with a message for Cynthia Peck."

When Bill and I had talked about my working, we had known it would mean my being away from home a few days a week, but we had thought I would be working in Arizona; we had not thought I would be moving to Montana for four months. However, if I wanted to work, I had to go where the work was. It was 1992, and I was fifty years old, facing my first job with the Forest—perhaps a job that could turn into a career that would support me.

I called Bill, who was working as a radiologist in Tempe. I said, "It's time to put up or shut up. There's a message on the answering machine from the Forest." Since Bill had raised two families and was twenty years older, I knew I was going to have to support myself soon.

"Go for it, gal." He sounded pleased with me. I called Charley back.

"We have the GS 4 Wilderness job open. Do you still want it?" asked Charley.

"I sure do."

"It's only a four-month job. It will start May 31 and go through October 1."

I had a week to prepare my house for my absence and put the camper on Bessie, the same Ford truck we had taken on our first summer trip. She had helped us move to Arizona and again to Young. Her fire-engine-red color had faded to an orange, and she was a bit battered from her years of faithful service, but she was a reliable old friend. To save on gas and time, I had taken my '89 Toyota 4Runner on the first trip to Montana, but this time, I needed the camper and space to haul my gear; I wanted to be self-sufficient. I packed everything as if I were living in the camper all summer, plus everything needed on an extended horse pack trip and a few good clothes. I had some business to finish as the chairperson of both the town and the county library organizations. Then I needed three days to drive to Montana. I must hurry as I did not have much time.

Lincoln Ranger District

By the end of the week, after the Ford was serviced in preparation for my drive to Montana, I drove to Payson to spend the night with Mom and Aunt Nati. They were unhappy about my leaving for the summer, as it meant no weekly visits, no one to complain to, and no one to run errands. I was not really abandoning them; I made sure Bill and Tami were committed to visiting regularly. I was excited; I was going on an adventure, a road trip, to new territory with new people and perhaps new tasks from which I could learn. I was especially looking forward to earning the benefit of rehiring rights with the Forest near home.

As I left Payson the following bright, sunny morning, I noticed the mirror and the gas gauge were not registering; they were supposed to be fixed. It seemed that dealerships preferred selling new trucks to fixing old ones. But Bessie had been faithful and dependable for years. I did not expect her to let me down now.

I spent Thursday night at a KOA (Kampgrounds of America) site in the middle of Utah. It cost fifteen dollars with no hookups. I thought that was too expensive; I would avoid that in the future. On Friday afternoon, I stopped for gas fifty miles north of Idaho Falls. The engine made a sizzling sound. It was bleeding antifreeze and water onto the cracked and pitted asphalt of the rural gas station. The local diagnosis was a bad water pump.

"Fill 'er up with water, and backtrack to Idaho Falls as fast as you can. There's an Exxon station that stays open till six. They do repairs," said a rough-looking fellow hanging around the station.

As I turned onto the interstate, black clouds were rolling in. The wind tossed and rolled a semi-opaque object ahead of me, which bounced into a ditch. I briefly wondered where it had come from. But my mind was on the truck, I hoped it did not quit.

As I pulled into the Exxon station, a truck stopped behind me. A rancher in scuffed cowboy boots and a stained cowboy hat stepped out. He handed the camper skylight cover to me. "Here, I think it can be repaired."

What a thoughtful person he was. Now I knew what had blown by me and knew I had a hole in my camper roof right over my bed.

I took advantage of the time it took to repair the truck by eating dinner at a nearby café. Home-style cooking was advertised on the flashing window sign. After I'd downed a large meal of crisp fried chicken, real mashed potatoes with homemade gravy, and a fresh salad, Bessie was repaired. It started to rain. I wanted a dry bed. I parked on a side street and inspected the camper skylight cover. The mechanism that held the skylight on was broken. I could not fix it. I needed to figure out a more substantial way to install a lid. After taking a mental inventory of material available in the truck and camper for repairs, I wrapped a garbage bag over the hole and duct-taped it as a temporary fix.

I parked beside a secondary road for the night, the wind rocked the camper, but only a few drops of rain fell. My fix-it job held. In the predawn light, I was back on the road. I knew my temporary fix would not survive a stronger storm, and one was threatening on the northern horizon. Towns are few and far between in Montana. I stopped at the next one, Dillon, and bought two pieces of plywood cut a little bigger than the skylight and four bolts with nuts. I borrowed a drill, took my materials onto the roof, and bolted the pieces of plywood together, with one on top and one inside, and clamped them together so they could hold. People stopped and gawked at me perched on top of my camper parked on the street in front of the lumber yard. I did not care as long as my patch held. From my camper's roof, I looked again at the great black front drifting in from the north. I was a little anxious because I was driving into it.

I exited the interstate west of Butte on a Montana state route. I drove through a series of lush green valleys. Rivers ran between cottonwood groves; hayfields had buck rakes and beaver slides standing idle. Mountains dominated the view. Buck rakes and beaver slides are relics of the days when horses were crucial to hay harvest and when haying was accomplished with horse-and-man teamwork.

My mind wandered back to childhood. I remembered Dad at White Grass, walking the hayfields of contoured ditches with a shovel over his shoulder. The hay grew tall under his care. When its golden seed heads bobbed in the sun, it was time to use the sickle bar mower. As the horses pulled the mower through the field, the hay lay in tidy rows. The sweet smell of fresh-cut hay filled the air.

The sun would dry the hay in a few days. When it was dry, horses pulled the buck rake that scooped the hay into piles. Tines pinged on rocks, dust blew, and excitement was in the air. An old truck with a large pole fork mounted in front picked up the loose piles of hay and carried them to the beaver slide. The beaver slide was a one-story contraption with a steep log ramp on one side and a mesh of support logs. The hay was placed on the forks at the bottom of the ramp. By means of many ropes, pulleys, and horses, the hay was pulled up the ramp and dropped over the top onto the stack. The horses had the most boring job, walking forward till the hay went up and backing until the empty forks came down, all day long. Two people were on top of the stack with pitchforks, leveling the hay in a special way to shed rain. The properly built stacks had much less water damage than bailed haystacks. It looked as if this valley used the old labor-intensive horse-and-man teamwork.

As a youngster, during hay season, I made lemonade in gallon jugs and delivered it by riding bareback to the hay crew. I also brought tools as needed for repairs. As a teenager, I drove a team. When Dad bought an old baling machine (he seldom bought anything new), the John Deere cat pulled the baler. We hand raked the hay up the ramp, which was supposed to pick up the hay and drop it into the hopper. With an excess of squeaking, clanging, and banging, the ram in the hopper would compress the hay into a long square that would emerge from the back of the machine. Fran and I sat precariously on the bouncing seat, grabbed the wire that was pushed through the bale, threaded it through a loop, and twisted it several times as the bale continued to move along the belt. We worked from the time the dew was off the hay until dark. I have wondered which work was more intensive: using the ancient baler or stacking the hay with horse-drawn equipment and beaver slides.

I was brought back to the present by chilly air blowing through the truck window. I was self-sufficient; all I needed was in the truck and camper. As I closed the window, I saw the Blackfoot River running parallel to the highway. It was made famous by Norman Maclean's book A River Runs Through It, which was later made into a movie starring Brad Pitt.

On my first day of work, another bank of clouds rolled in. My first task was to order my uniforms: two shirts, two pairs of pants, a name tag, and a pair of socks. Then Jerry sent me with the trail crew—Keith, Carol, Race, and Tim— to Indian Meadows to work. Carol was a lively gal in her early twenties. She had a giggle always ready to explode. Her long blonde hair was controlled by a big Stetson. Keith, a few years older, treated her like a sister. He knew how since he had six siblings several of which were sisters. Keith was a tall, muscular young man with a black handlebar mustache who wore a big black hat and a silk neck scarf Gene Autry style as easily as he wore his smile. When working in Wyoming one summer, he had adopted Carol as a sister. He had invited her to Montana. Ever since, she had had a room available in his home. She lives there now. They invited me to drive with them to Indian Meadows, a Forest administration site, which was about ten miles east of the village by highway and dirt road. Keith and Carol acted as my tour guides.

"This highway goes to Helena or Great Falls," Keith said as we turned right onto the highway. "In winter, it's a treacherous, steep winding pass to the east slope of the Rockies."

"That's the 7-Up Ranch. It has the best food," said Carol as she pointed to the sign beside the driveway.

Keith turned right at a Y in the road. "If you go straight up the canyon, there are two forest campgrounds." Our road was a narrow, rough dirt road cut into the side of the mountain. The road's potholes were filled with water. "To the left is the Mainline Trailhead, with hitching posts, corrals, and camping facilities for horse use," he said.

Ahead, I saw the large fenced meadow, a tack shed, corrals, hitching rails, and a cabin set at the edge of the pines. The truck that Race and Tim drove was backed to the porch of the tack shed. The cabin was a reconstruction of the previous historic log cabin. Our task at Indian Meadows was to move the furniture from the tack room into the new cabin and install the wood cook range and wood heating stove for the upcoming orientation meeting. However, the chimneys were not finished, so we used a propane camp stove as a substitute. Race made boiled coffee, which we all appreciated.

Race had many construction skills. He took control of the project and directed us as he also pitched in. Race and Carol smiled at each other and kept making eye contact with a smile. Carol lit the Coleman lamps to warm the cabin. We used the truck as a shuttle to move everything. Between loads, we warmed our numb fingers near the Coleman lamps.

The bunk beds went into the loft by way of a steep, narrow ladder. With Keith pulling on ropes tied to the bunk and Race on the ladder to steady it, they lifted each bunk into place. Tim helped Carol and me heat water to wash all the dishes and clean the tables, chairs, bookshelf, and cupboard. We put the enamel dishes in the cupboard, hung the cast-iron skillets from the ceiling beam, and left the blue enameled coffee pot on the stove. Carol and I especially wanted the cabin clean and inviting.

Tim looked to be in his late fifties, had a pale, drawn face and dull brownish-gray hair. He did not have the energy the rest of the crew so easily displayed. Tim, like the other members, had worked previous summers there. The crew easily pitched in to help one another, intuitively seeing where help was needed. Banter, jokes, and laughter abounded. I thought about how next week, we would be cooking, eating, and sleeping there for the orientation meeting.

However, the first day of orientation was held at the station. Jerry arranged a barbecue in the evening for all new employees, and most of the full-time employees joined to greet us. The employees seemed to enjoy one another, sharing stories, laughing, and eating with gusto.

The orientation at the Indian Meadows cabin was specifically for those of us who were going to work in the Wilderness. It included staff from the Forest supervisor's office, who wanted to introduce themselves. They stayed for two days and were friendly and eager to answer any questions. We were shown how to use the portable radios, when to use them, and which tones and frequencies to use. If we encountered suspicious (illegal) activities, we were not to interfere. "S and W" was the word—smile and wave and hurry out of there. When at a safe distance, we were to report the incident by radio to the station. Jerry gave us canisters of pepper spray and taught us how to use them.

"These are to be used for bears only. Even though there has been illegal activity with aggressive, armed people in the Scapegoat Wilderness, this is not for use on humans."

"How will the spray affect a grizzly bear?" I asked as I turned and examined the small spray can in my hands.

"It may blind him for a few moments; then he will be a very angry bear. The idea is to give you a moment of advantage before the bear wants revenge. Whatever you do, your safety must be considered first." To me, it did not seem a good idea to use the spray.

North of the Scapegoat Wilderness are Great Bear National Park and Glacier National Park, which are within grizzly reach of the Scapegoat, as a grizzly's territory may include a hundred-mile radius. Grizzlies can open cans with ease and tear into a tent as if it is butter. Since it was spring, the bears were coming out of hibernation hungry. They were opportunists, always looking for food. They would take advantage of anything they thought was food. We had to stay aware of our surroundings to stay safe.

Jerry and Charley showed us how to fill out many forms, including the one for my paycheck. Jerry would be my immediate supervisor, and Charley was his. If a matter was urgent and Jerry was not available, I could go to Charley.

We learned that only Congress can designate Wilderness Areas. The first Wilderness Act was passed in 1964. The act proclaims its intent to "establish a National Preservation System for the permanent good of the whole people and for other purposes." In the Act, the definition of Wilderness is:

A Wilderness, in contrast with those areas where man and his works dominate the landscape, is hereby recognized as an area where earth and its community of life are untrammeled by man, where man himself is a visitor who does not remain. An area of Wilderness is further defined to mean in this Act an area of undeveloped Federal land retaining its primeval character and influence, without permanent improvements or human habitation, which is protected and managed so as to preserve its natural condition.

The Scapegoat was the first Wilderness to be designated by the federal government under pressure from the locals. A new highway was slated to go through the backcountry which was an excellent hunting area. There was also talk of mining. The locals wanted neither in their backyard.

With the meeting finished, Max from the supervisor's office, Carol, Race, and I chipped in to cook steak, hash browns, and salad for dinner. Charley, Jerry, the crew, and I slept in the cabin. The others went back to town for the night. With eight people sleeping in the loft, all the bunks were used. Race and Keith slept on pads on the floor. I kicked off my boots, slipped off my jacket, slid into the sleeping bag and slept in my clothes.

On the weekend, Carol invited me to go with Keith and Race to purchase supplies in Missoula. I was as old as their parents, but they included me. They showed me where to find bargains on western wear, horse supplies, and food. I bought myself a wool shirt because I had been cold since I arrived. We picked up Keith's girlfriend, Trish, and went to dinner. Keith sat next to Trish, Carol snuggled against Race, and I perched at the edge of the booth. We filled ourselves with hot stew, biscuits, and fabulous homemade apple pie.

On my second day off, I stopped at the post office to rent a box and pick up my mail. I had received a funny card and a letter from Bill. All was well at home. The dogs had moved to Bill's side of the room to sleep, and Straycat curled on his lap every time he sat. He would be leaving for Mississippi next week, to a military hospital where he would replace the radiologist who was going on vacation. It was good to hear from home. Since we lived in a rural village with no opportunities for work with remuneration, it was common for folks to work at great distances. If you wanted to work, you went where the work was, as Bill had been doing, going to Tucson, the Grand Canyon, and now Mississippi to work, while I had gone to Montana.

When I was back in my truck, it would not start— another truck issue. I walked to a nearby station for help. The voltage regulator had gone bad. It cost fifty-one dollars. I did appreciate Bessie's timing; each time she had a problem, we were close to help, Spirit Guide at work. But I was short on cash, and I was determined to stay within the budget I had set for myself and save a good amount of my salary. This was a summer job, but if I did well, I would have rehire- rights back home with the Forest. That would give me an advantage over new applicants and a greater possibility of a job closer to home.

In preparation for my first trip into the Scapegoat Wilderness, I packed two changes of clothes, extra socks, chaps, a duster, a toilet kit, a wool sweater, and an old wool jacket of Dad's. I laid out my spurs, a hat, gloves, and a large silk scarf. The scarf added warmth when wrapped around my neck twice and tied in front and offered many other uses as needed.

I was anxious about grizzly bears and wolves who lived in the Scapegoat Wilderness. Elk and deer were there too. There were more than a hundred miles of trails and landmarks to learn. I had horses to meet. Like people, horses have their own idiosyncrasies. I love a challenge, and I was eager to start my paying job.

Wilderness Work Begins

The first morning I was expected to go into the Scapegoat, Jerry gave me a pile of three-ring notebooks: Wilderness orders, special closure orders, and rehabilitation site closures. The orders needed to be copied and covered with waterproof clear plastic. Once we were in the Wilderness, Jerry would point out where the orders were to be posted.

Meanwhile, he dumped several books into my arms: *Wilderness Guide Guide, National Handbook for Wilderness Personnel, Montana State Hunting and Fish Regulations, and Campsite Inventory for the Scapegoat Wilderness.* I had to be informed to answer questions. He also included a safety handbook, a guide explaining hazards and safety measures. I had to read and study the 1992 Wilderness Monitoring Report, a compilation of last year's work in the Scapegoat Wilderness. On top of that, he gave me trail encounters and occupied campsite forms to copy and make into booklets for myself and the trail crew.

I was staggering under the load of books, manuals, and papers sliding every which way, with no place to set them. Then Maggie, the cheerful and energetic gal from the front desk, came to save me. She helped find a place to put them. I tried to organize the mess and copy the appropriate pages. I nearly had the copies made, with the pages cut to size and stapled—obviously, Wilderness patrol was much more than riding around and enjoying the great outdoors—when I saw Jerry bolt along the hall.

Jerry marched toward me. "We're leaving at noon," he said. "I'm going to show you many of the trails and the cabin where you will stay."

I was already overwhelmed, when he handed me a list of items to purchase. Angst gripped me, I did not know where or how to obtain funds or the district system for purchases. I knew Pleasant Valley's District system, but I was not there. The list looked insufficient; I wanted to buy more items in order to have a balanced diet.

"Get the money from Karen," he added as he abruptly turned and walked into his office.

Karen was a large, forceful-looking woman who brought to mind a drill sergeant, and she was the treasurer. Her stern countenance made me uneasy. Was I doing something wrong?

After signing her voucher, I went to the local market; it reminded me of the market in Young, which had narrow rows of shelves with a limited variety of products. I gathered the supplies, marking everything as Karen had directed. When Karen checked my receipt, list, and change, I passed muster.

At noon, Jerry had the four-horse gooseneck trailer hooked to the truck and parked by the office. We drove to the pasture a few miles west of town. I saw it was large, with a stream flowing through. The horses, about twenty head, were on the far side of the marsh.

As Jerry turned off the highway onto a dirt road beside the pasture, he honked the horn and called to the horses, "Come on, boys! Come 'n' get it!" He honked some more.

"When I feed them in winter, I honk to train them to come in," he told me, as if I couldn't figure out what he was doing. The horses and mules perked up their ears and looked toward us but continued to graze the tender spring grass.

Jerry parked beside the grayed wood corrals and two sheds with weather-warped silver boards attached. I recalled abandoned ranches

I had seen throughout the west that had the same weathered silver
board walls.

Without a word, Jerry handed me two halters and grabbed the grain
bucket and two halters for himself. He opened the gate and went to
the pasture. He looked at me expectantly. Uneasy, I presumed I was
to follow. He was already way ahead. I ran to catch up over rough
ground, which was wet in places and frozen in others and filled with
holes made by horse hooves when the ground was soft.

Jerry had not told me what he wanted me to do. I was suddenly
assaulted with doubt. Was I supposed to follow, or was I to wait? I
slowed to a walk.

"Come on, boys! Come 'n' get it!" Jerry hollered as he shook the
bucket, rattling the grain cakes. One horse began to come at a trot.
The others wanted some so they started to run. Jerry turned toward
the corral with twenty horses and mules running at him and toward
me. Feeling silly that I had not understood the game, I reversed and
ran out of the way to prevent being trampled before I had a chance
to even start work.

Jerry walked and flapped his arms like a goose taking flight to
keep the horses from running him over. They wanted the pellets,
and he was trying to keep the pellets from spilling. He ran into the
corral with the horses on his heels, spreading the pellets along the
fence as he walked the perimeter. Each horse tried to grab a bite,
kicked, and turned to protect his bit from the others. They were like
children scrambling for the treats from a broken piñata. Horses can
step on you, turn and mash you against the fence, knock you down,
or trample you. I was trapped in the middle of the milling herd.

Jerry caught a tall sorrel horse with a long mane and tail. I stood
ready to help. "Here's Rambo. You can use him," he said as he handed
me the lead rope. Rambo had a small lightning-shaped white blaze
on his forehead, a velvety dark nose, honest eyes, and a white right
hind foot. The horses were still milling around, biting each other,
with their ears back. I dodged to keep from being stepped on.

Next, Jerry handed me the lead rope of a rangy roan who was
jumpy and nervous and had eyes showing distrust and fear. "This is
Ribbon," Jerry told me.

He gave me the lead rope of a white mule who looked warily at
me. I put out my hand to calm her, but she stepped back. Obviously,
she disliked being touched. Now I was holding three animals and

trying to keep the leads from tangling. Jerry had caught a sorrel mule, who was calm in all the turmoil. The mule plodded behind Jerry as they came toward me.

"The white mule is Skunk. This one's Charlie," Jerry said, introducing them.

We loaded them into the trailer, all tied to one side. They stood at a slant, the easiest way for them to ride. Jerry closed the trailer door and flipped the bar across to lock it. We hopped into the truck cab. The remaining stock would go back to graze after they finished the grain cakes.

Jerry drove along the highway out of town toward Indian Meadows. We ate our sandwiches as we traveled in silence. When we turned onto the narrow road cut into the hillside, I wondered what would have happened if someone had been coming down at the same time. A Volkswagen Bug could not pass on that hill. Luckily, no one came.

At Indian Meadows, the familiar log cabin came into view. Jerry backed the trailer near the shed and hitching post. Jerry's movements were quick and efficient, and he was always watchful. With his work ethic, he accomplished much. We spread two eight-by-eight-foot tarps, called mantis, on the tack shed's porch. We put our personal duffel and sleeping bags in two piles of equal weight on the mantis. Each was wrapped with a series of half hitches and slipknots, so all was secure and dry. We packed Skunk first. The big white mule looked at us askance but stood still as a good mule should. We put panniers on the decker packsaddle with the two fifty-pound grain sacks, food, a shovel, and small tools on Charlie. We bent the crosscut saw over the top of the pack and secured it with a small rope under Charlie's belly.

The decker pack saddles had two bent metal bars screwed into the wood saddletree frame: one in front and one in back. The underside of the tree was covered with sheepskin to better protect the mule's back. The breeching went around the mule's butt, and a breast collar circled his chest. They kept the saddle from slipping when going up or down steep hills. A double cinch under the mule's belly served to hold the saddle on. After we placed the full manti against the saddle, he looped a rope over the manti, tightened it, and then brought it under and tied it where it crossed the manti. One manti hung from each side of the mule. Tying the manti thus allowed it to swing if it hit any trees. It was the first time I had seen this method of packing.

I remembered that Dad had bought a few new deckers, which he had thought were expensive. White Grass used mostly the old wood sawbuck pack saddles. Dad had stacked sleeping bags and other soft items on top of the panniers, covered them all with a tarp, and secured them with a forty-foot lash rope and diamond hitches. A diamond hitch is a time-proven way to tie a load onto a pack animal. It is the hitch about which Aldo Leopold, who accomplished the Gila Wilderness designation, said, "When no one knows what a diamond hitch is, it's the death of wilderness." He meant that when pack animals would no longer be used, there would be no wild country to explore.

Jerry, leading the two pack mules, and I left Indian Meadows at two o'clock. Work was supposed to end at four o'clock, but we had a four-hour ride to the Webb Lake guard station; it was going to be a long day. We wound through giant Douglas firs and stately lodgepole pines. My breath caught and my heart swelled at the sight of the Scapegoat Wilderness sign. I was really in the Scapegoat as a Wilderness Guard. Could I succeed? This was not like guiding dudes in the Tetons of Wyoming or the Superstition Mountains in Arizona; each of those areas could have been put inside the Scapegoat Wilderness with lots of room to spare.

"There is some wire that needs to be picked up." Jerry pointed as we rode on.

I guessed I was supposed to pick it up at another time. He talked in a kind of shorthand.

Further on, he said, "There're fire circles that need to be removed," as he pointed along a small stream. Then he said, "There're old batteries left from the telephone to the fire lookout tower. They should be picked up." He used passive verbs and military abruptness; he was a veteran, which I admired.

The melting snow left the grass matted. Along shallow pools and rivulets were a kaleidoscope of colorful spring flowers: violet shooting stars, yellow dogtooth violets, creamy globe flowers, shiny buttercups, and marsh marigolds. Despite the overcast sky, the colors cheered me.

When we rounded a hill, I saw the varied sky of blue with angry black-bottomed clouds gathering and reflecting on Webb Lake. It was obvious a storm was coming our way, and we needed to take care of everything before it poured. The cabin sat at the far end of the lake, under the ubiquitous pines. Its covered porch beckoned and promised a time to relax. I dismounted. I was struck with pain that brought tears. My legs could not bear weight. The saddle had a very flat seat. Where it dropped to each side, it cut the circulation to my legs. It had been uncomfortable, and now my legs were numb. I hid my pain from Jerry. "If you hurt, bear it," as the western song says. I hung from the saddle as the blood flowed into my legs, causing severe burning and tingling like when your hand goes to sleep. Slowly, I stood. I untied my duster from the saddle, took my few personal items from the saddlebags, and unsaddled my horse. I helped unpack the mules, putting the tack and feed into the small shed. I found the tack shed a treasure-house of tools, extra rope, veterinary salves, Coleman fuel, dry stove wood, and a mouse-proof bin.

"The pack saddles go on these back racks. Riding saddles go on the front ones," Jerry said. "Pour the pellets into this mouse-proof box."

As the sun disappeared behind the western hill, I felt the chill seeping into my jacket. Together we tied plastic netting to the manger poles in preparation to feed the stock. The netting kept the stock from trampling the hay, causing waste, or getting sand colic by ingesting earth.

Work had technically ended, but we still had to unlock the heavy wooden door and unlock the split-log shutters of two windows, light a warming fire, and unpack groceries. Five mattresses were stored on the central table for mouse protection. I put three mattresses on the lower bunks, and Jerry put the others on the top bunks. Opening a cabin in grizzly country required extra effort. While I put covers and sheets on the mattresses, Jerry went to clean out the spring so we and the stock had water. Returning, he put water on the stove to heat for washing the table and counter.

"One year, there was a dead beaver in the spring. Spoiled the water. I removed the carcass, dug the spring deeper, and let new water flow for a week before it was safe," Jerry said. Beavers can carry giardia, a potentially deadly organism that gets into the water.

A cold drizzle pushed by the wind had buffeted us on the trail. Needing a substantial meal, I offered to cook steak and fry potatoes so I could stay near the stove. I boiled coffee. I began to feel better. After dinner, Jerry did the dishes. Soon we were snuggled in our respective sleeping bags. Many of the field jobs require living circumstances with the opposite gender. However, the Forest Service had strict regulations against sexual harassment. Orientation taught that any physical or verbal advance that might be construed by someone as objectionable was considered sexual harassment. Knowing what the living arrangements were, Bill must have trusted me. Despite the strange bed, there was no problem in getting to sleep after such a long day.

I woke up before Jerry and went outside. I looked around. The Webb Lake guard station would be my primary duty station in the Wilderness. The cabin faced down- canyon southeast, overlooking Webb Lake, which caught the morning sun as the clouds had passed. The one-room log cabin had a steeply pitched wood-shingle roof. Three steps led up to the covered porch and its centered front door. The door was really three doors: a heavy split log door to discourage grizzlies, a regular wood door, and a screen door.

The inside logs had been whitewashed and caulked with black tar, which gave the room a curious look of black-and-white-striped walls. The room was the size of a generous bedroom, with hardwood floors and four small windows. To the right of the door was a shelf on which the two stainless-steel water buckets sat. Next to the buckets was a small window. A barrel wood heating stove stood in the corner. The white enamel wood cook range was by the window shedding light on the cooking area, making it a good work area. Iron skillets hung on the wall. The cupboard held all the dishes and canned food. Next to it was a small propane refrigerator.

Two sets of bunk beds were built against the back wall. My bed was the lower one in the corner, behind the edge of a cupboard, which gave me a little privacy. That cupboard held the dish towels and sheets. There also were books, an AM radio, batteries for our handheld radios, and a first-aid kit. Behind the front door were a mop, broom, wash bucket, and wood box. We ate at the big, centrally located table with six chairs. There was a loft, which I imagined was home to spiders and vermin. I hoped none would filter through the ceiling.

Charley had told me a story that had happened several years ago. Jerry was sleeping at Webb's cabin, when scratching and grunting outside awakened him. Jerry grabbed a flashlight as a big grizzly looked in at him. Jerry shouted, cursed, and beat pots and pans together to scare the bear away, but the grizzly did not scare. When the bear broke the window, Jerry climbed into the attic and closed the trapdoor. He spent the night listening to the bear destroy the inside of the cabin. When he climbed down, the bear had broken into the cupboards and bitten into the tin cans, and the cabin was dusted with flour and sugar. The grizzly had broken and scattered the furniture. The story reminded me how strong and dangerous grizzly bears were. After that incident, heavy split-log shutters for the windows and door had been built. With the repairs, the cabin was secure.

"You must secure the shutters each time you leave overnight and may open them when you are here. Sweep and mop, replenish water and wood supplies, do all the dishes, and fill the Coleman lanterns each time you leave. Take all the garbage back to the district dumpster for disposal." Jerry explained the strict rules. "Keeping the cabin clean will help discourage bears. If a grizzly smells food or anything he thinks might be food, he will try to break in. Each time he is successful, his behavior is rewarded, creating a dangerous bear and eventually a dead one."

I knew that from living in grizzly country in Wyoming, but I kept quiet.

The privy (outhouse) was set in the woods. I could sit and look through the open door and see the stock munching hay or deer nibbling grass under the trees. The horses and deer shared the area without dispute.

While Jerry went to feed the horses, I emptied the ashes from the stove, lit the fire, and started coffee. We used the wood range to conserve propane, which was packed in on a mule. Eggs and bacon were breakfast, and I made toast in a skillet. Cooking seemed to be my duty; dishes were his. There was no discussion, but we intuitively knew who did what, as in most camps.

We were on the Mainline Trail by seven thirty in the morning. Two hundred yards past Webb Cabin, all the stately lodgepole pine trees were carbon black. No trees were alive; no trees were green. We were in the 1988 Canyon Creek fire area. Lodgepole pines need fire for germination; the heat from fire opens the pine cones, and the seeds pop out onto the soil made fertile by the ash. I saw the ground covered with new trees from one to three feet tall. Elk thistle, fireweed, lupine, and other seeds blown in on the wind had also started to sprout.

Jerry stopped and tied his horse, leaving Skunk and Charlie tied to his saddle. "Every time you come across a tree fallen on the trail, you need to remove it," he told me. I dismounted, tied Rambo, and helped to unpack the crosscut saw.

A crosscut saw is a six-foot-long two-man saw. One man pulls the saw straight to full extension, and then the other man pulls toward himself, sawdust dropped to the ground on both sides. Sawyers must stand with feet far apart. Of course, one tends to pull in the natural arc of the body, which will cause the saw to bind.

Jerry stepped over the log and positioned the saw where he wanted the cut. I stood on the other side and stepped into position. Jerry had a longer reach than I, so I had a hard time keeping up with his rhythm. Eventually, we cut the log with log sawdust dropping to the ground on both our sides. With a second cut, we had a piece to remove from the trail. The slang saying "It's the pits" comes from the time when sawyers used to saw lumber with a crosscut. One person would stand on the log, and the other would be in a pit below the log. During cutting, the sawdust would fall, and air circulation was poor, making it a miserable job.

Sweaty and out of breath, I helped bend and retie the saw onto Charlie's pack. As we rode, silence reigned, except for the hooves splashing and the wind singing through the blackened tree trunks. I was thirsty; I had forgotten to bring water. Dumb and compounding my misery! I said to myself. I should have taken the time to go behind a tree to relieve myself, even though there was little cover in the burn.

"The year after the fire, mushrooms were abundant, especially morels. We had a mushroom war," Jerry said.

"What do you mean a mushroom war?"

"Illegal commercial pickers invaded the Wilderness. They fought each other over good picking areas, even shooting at each other. They needed a permit to pick and sell mushrooms which they seldom had. It was really challenging." Jerry sounded as if he'd enjoyed chasing the pickers.

His conversation reminded me of my first trips with Tommy. The only talk was to give orders or relate items of interest—typical of many cowboys I had known on ranches.

As we rode by a heavily used area, Jerry said, "The hitching rail needs to be moved farther from the trail soon."

Remembering Jerry's directives from the day before, I had put a notepad in my saddlebag, and I added to it.

We forded Meadow Creek. "That trail leads to Hoeffner's outfitter campsite," Jerry said as we took the left fork. "Last fall, hunting guides at Hoeffner's camp heard gunshots coming from the Meadow Lake area. In the morning, they went to investigate and discovered a large area that had been recently dug up, but no one was around. They notified the Wilderness Guard, who notified me by radio. By the time I arrived, a grizzly had already dug up a horse and was eating it. Apparently, the horse was sick and dying, so the campers put it out of its misery. The people had been in such a hurry they left the halter on it. Hoeffner's guide removed it and used it.``

I realized this trip was twofold: to inventory trails and hunting camps and second, to show me the territory.

Jerry said, "Authorities decided the dead horse was a bear attractant. An elk or other indigenous animal carcass would have been considered natural and left for the grizzlies or other carnivores, wolves, black bears, and birds. However, people brought the horse into the Wilderness, so it was considered unnatural. Such influence by man does not comply with Wilderness Management directives. To discourage the bear, the trail crew buried the horse and covered it with lime." I was thinking that must have been a very smelly and distasteful job.

As we approached the horse burial, Jerry called his dog to heel. As it is dangerous to surprise a grizzly, he also whistled. If a grizzly was in the area, the noise from Jerry's whistling would let him know we were near, and he would *probably* leave. Jerry and I knew a surprised grizzly might be aggressive and attack—not good for one's health! If you run from a grizzly, you are prey. However, if you offer him a way to avoid people, he prefers to do so.

No grizzly was in sight, thank goodness, but I could smell the rank grizzly odor and the rotting horsemeat. I read the story the tracks told; I saw a big hole with a large, hairy butt print on one end and twelve-inch-long bear tracks at the other end. The bear had sat in the four-foot-deep hole, balancing himself with his hind feet against the sides while digging and eating with his front feet. The rear end of the horse had been excavated. A piece of leg and part of the vertebrae were scattered. The bear had thrown the lime; globs of it were around the hole. Damn big bear! Spooky! Obviously, lime did not deter a grizzly. I later learned that Wilderness management had approved the use of explosives to remove dead domestic animals from the Wildernesses where the remaining pieces would be no bigger than a spool of thread. The pieces would dry or rot so quickly that the smell was diminished enough to not attract bears.

A game warden had talked to us at orientation about what to do if you encounter a grizzly. To demonstrate, the warden told us about his hunter friend.

"Pete was surprised by a grizzly on the trail. It stood up on hind legs, grunted, sniffed the air, and showed his large, sharp yellow teeth. Pete, knowing the proper way to act, backed slowly to climb the nearest tree and climbed it out of reach before the grizzly could grab him. The grizzly shook the tree so violently that Pete fell out. Pete kept a clear head and tucked into an armadillo-like ball with hands locked behind his neck. The bear ambled over and rolled Pete around like a cat playing with a mouse. After a while, the grizzly left; it wasn't trying to kill, just warn the human away. Pete had fang punctures from being bitten and claw marks but nothing fatal and was able to walk out for help. Following the proper procedures in a grizzly encounter surely saved Pete's life."

I had a high respect for them; my first grizzly encounter occurred when I was a teenager. While wrangling, the horses were strung out ahead of me through a thick stand of Douglas timber. Sunnyboy, a dark reddish horse, had a habit of breaking away from the herd. I glimpsed Sunnyboy up to his old tricks and turned to chase him. I came around an enormous, spreading Douglas fir to confront a grizzly standing up on his hind legs and waving his long-clawed front paws at me, like a horror movie, but this was real. In a flash, my frightened horse did an about-face and ran. I hung on. When I arrived home, no one believed me. They may have thought I was only a delusional teenage girl, but a few days later, a wrangler saw the grizzly, and then they all believed me. It was unusual for grizzlies to be so far south of Yellowstone National Park.

Jerry and I stayed on our horses, looking at the horse burial hole. "He's been here recently," Jerry said, stating the obvious to me. "We need to get some warning signs posted to let people know the danger of this grizzly feeding area."

On the way back to Webb Lake, we took a shortcut through Hoeffner's deserted hunting camp, fording Meadow Creek, I had to lift my feet high to keep them out of the water. I felt Rambo lose his footing, which made me uneasy, but he quickly recovered as the stream became shallower.

Hoeffner's outfitter camp had been closed for the winter. All tents had been taken down, and the poles had been stacked against trees to prevent rotting. The corral was still standing. The logs around the tent sites were in place, and one fire circle was evident. The management plan directive for outfitter camps stated that everything brought in must be removed. This was a good example of a closed camp.

My legs were killing me. It was impossible to stand after nine hours in the saddle. My shoulders ached from my hunching to hold in warmth. Dad's old worn-out wool jacket was not keeping me warm. I was miserable, but I would not let Jerry know. I was not a wimp.

We worked side by side, unsaddling the horses and mules, putting everything in its place, and feeding them. That far north, summer daylight extended to nine o'clock at night. I sat on the porch edge, watching as Jerry stretched out on the grass with his dog, Wink, near a ground squirrel hole. Many small excavations surrounded the cabin. If all was quiet, up would pop a shy ground squirrel's furry little head squeaking and whistling. Wink would sit by a squirrel hole with ears perked until a head emerged and then pounce. The squirrel was always faster and ducked down his hole. Wink would stick his nose into the hole, making snorting noises, but Jerry would not let him dig. To please Wink, Jerry took him and a small piece of cord up the hill to make a snare, placed it over a ground squirrel hole, and crept away to lie in wait for a squirrel to pop up. While Jerry and Wink had a good time, I decided to take advantage of their absence to heat water and bathe.

Bathing was difficult compared to home, where I could turn on a faucet for hot water. I had to haul the water from outside in a bucket, pour part of it into the large enamel coffee pot, and heat it on the woodstove. Then I had one gallon of water to bathe in. I checked to make sure Jerry was still hunting. I took off my upper layers of clothes, washed using a small amount of soap, rinsed, dried, and redressed that half. Next, I removed the clothes from the lower half, washed, rinsed, dried, and redressed. If I used too much soap, the water would become so soapy that I could not rinse properly. Also, the soap was bad for the ground, though I had to scatter my bathwater on the ground. I cleaned the basin and hung it back on the wall.

In comparison, in the backcountry of Arizona, my preferred bathing method was to walk downstream from camp, dip water from a stream into my pot, soap and rinse a distance from the stream so my soap did not pollute the stream. There at Webb Lake, ice was still on the shadowed edge of the lake—way too cold for me.

As the sun slipped behind the western hill, I cooked dinner: more steak, potatoes, and canned corn. I needed to do better with meal planning. Jerry did the dishes. After dinner, we made the bear warning signs and covered them with clear plastic contact paper for weatherproofing.

The next day, dreading that saddle, we retraced our route during the cold, drizzly rain to post the warning signs at the grizzly feeding area. There was no sign of the grizzly.

I again followed Jerry. As directed, I posted the signs in appropriate areas as we passed. We went out the Middle Fork Trail, which had been rerouted after the 1988 Canyon Creek fire to contour along the side hill above the Middle Fork of the Blackfoot River. All the trees along the way were black skeletons. I found the route interminably boring since it had little interest. But it kept people from the riparian area, protecting the fragile habitat, and welcomed wildlife to the stream to drink.

Jerry fumbled in his saddlebag as he rode along and pulled out a sandwich. He unwrapped it and began to eat. "I won't stop to eat," he said. "It's just a waste of time."

I also discovered he did not stop to go to the bathroom; I was in misery. But followed suit, pulling my lunch out of the saddlebag. I was shivering, as Dad's jacket, which I was wearing for old times' sake, was not adequate for Montana temperatures.

Jerry dismounted. I followed, gritting my teeth, trying to hold back a cry of pain. I vowed that once back at the district barn, I would find a different saddle—I wondered if I would survive that long. But my priority was to head for the bushes.

"The sign at this junction needs to be replaced." He showed me an old gray post that leaned precariously and had holes where a sign must have been bolted. I added the new tasks to my notebook.

He mounted. I hobbled after him and mounted Rambo. We turned toward Webb Lake cabin. My knees were hurting; my legs had no circulation. I wondered if it would be better to walk in my high-heeled packer boots. But that would have let Jerry know how much I hurt. I would not be a weak, complaining female; I would cowboy up. We stopped once to cut a log from across the trail. We spent fifteen minutes without letup, pulling, reaching, and pulling as fast as I could. When we finished, we each grabbed an end of the cut piece and lifted it out of the trail, packed the saw, untied the mules, mounted, and left without a pause. I bore my misery.

When we reached the cabin, I was nearly crying in pain. I slid off Rambo and hung from the saddle until blood flowed to my legs and I could walk.

I knew I was being tested—a type of hazing. I sort of understood; it is better for an employer to know if an employee can handle the job early on, when a replacement can still be found, rather than later, when that option may not be available. Jerry needed to know if I could handle being thrown from a horse and kicked by a mule, find my way in new territory, and confront wild animals safely.

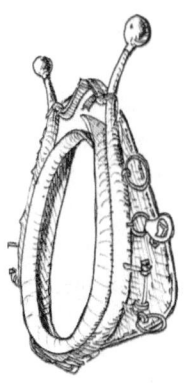

CHAPTER 9

Settling into Wilderness

O N THE FOURTH DAY, JERRY PLANNED TO RETURN TO THE OFFICE. After breakfast, I packed my personal things while Jerry did the dishes. He caught the horses and mules while I swept and mopped the cabin floor—men's work versus women's work demonstrated? I stacked the garbage, empty propane tank, and personal gear on the porch to be loaded onto the mules. After closing the windows, Jerry pushed the twelve-inch bolts through the half-log shutters from the outside. Inside, I screwed a large nut onto each bolt, securing the cabin from grizzlies.

As I looked back, more clouds were gathering, rain looked likely. The cabin nestled in the trees; *I would like this place for my summer home*. It would be lots of work to keep the cabin supplied with wood, light, and food, but I would like the solitude. It was a relatively short ride to Indian Meadows, which caused less saddle pain. At the station, I could exchange my saddle, which would make future trips more comfortable.

Jerry took a detour by Heart Lake to show me one of the heavy-use areas. I enjoyed the greenery once we left the fire. I smelled the clean fragrance of the wet earth and saw water drops clinging to the ends of pine needles like jewels hanging by invisible threads.

We crossed a tiny drainage. "Later, there will be spawning trout in this stream. To protect the fishery, we built this bridge." Jerry pointed. "If too much silt is in a stream during spawning, the eggs will suffocate." Further on, "This peninsula has been damaged by too many campers." Jerry dismounted, indicating an area to our right.

I gingerly stepped off Rambo, cursing the saddle; caught my breath; and followed Jerry.

"This area was bare soil. Year before last, the Wilderness Guard transplanted three hundred seedlings. Only one-fourth survived. She even carried buckets of water from the lake to water them. You will need to water them this summer." He pointed out tiny Ponderosa pines six to ten inches tall. "We keep the area closed to all traffic. Nail the special orders onto this post. Make sure there is always a sign here. People sometimes tear them off."

We returned to the tied animals. As it turned out, there were enough rainy days that I did not need to water the seedlings, but I did move some logs and branches to protect them.

We rode to a hitching post. I saw that there was only a small level area, so it was in constant use, and the earth was hard-packed and covered with campfire ashes. We tied the horses and mules to the rail and walked to the shore. We met two campers who were fishing.

"Hello. I'm Jerry Burns, and this is Cindy Peck, our Wilderness Guard."

Wow! It was the first time I had heard that. What a thrill! I was really the Wilderness Guard; I really had a job in a designated Wilderness. What an awesome responsibility. I knew how to record each trail I rode and each party I encountered. That data would be used to determine the usage in the Scapegoat Wilderness and the adverse effects on the plants, wild animals, and soil, which in turn would affect management decisions.

Arriving back in town, we put the animals in the village pasture. Jerry, who was also the law enforcement officer for the district, was called away. I unloaded the truck and put the tack away. I studied other saddles, saw one with red leather, which made me suspect it was made for looks, not use. I found another with a good sloped seat, low cantle, and good swells; it fit better. I moved my saddlebags and my wall tent, as Jerry teasingly called my rain duster, to the new saddle. What a relief it would be.

My tour of duty would be Thursday through Monday. I would be by myself with a horse and mule. The trail crew would also be working in the Wilderness, but their scheduled eight days on and four off would coincide with mine only occasionally. I expected to see them rarely.

I was looking forward to my day off. I needed to buy a warmer jacket and waterproof my chaps, boots, and hat. If the weather stayed wet, it would become a weekly chore. The next morning, I awoke to the sound of a truck door slamming. I looked out my window and saw Tim of the trail crew. I had thought he was supposed to be on the trail somewhere.

I opened the window and called, "Morning, Tim."

"Mornin'. Heard on the radio from Silver King there are eight inches of new snow this morning. Keith said there were four inches at Webb."

"It feels cold enough." It was June 20. It was supposed to be summer, with warm, sunny days.

"Got to get these supplies back to Indian Meadows; we ran short. See ya in a couple days."

"OK, bye."

I went to Garland's Town and Country Department Store for a warmer jacket. It had gotten even colder with snow in the Wilderness. I tried on the Filson wool jackets and chose the heavier-weight one. Filson has been making heavy wool coats, canvas pants, and heavy work clothing since the end of the 1800s. I also found silk scarves, bought one to wrap around my neck for added warmth, and bought a pair of deerskin gloves. Those purchases would bring my bankroll down to almost nothing, but I had to stay warm. Even though I had been raised in Wyoming, the last fifteen years in Arizona had spoiled me with warm weather. I was not as prepared for cold weather as I had thought. I was glad I was being fed while working; if I had had to buy my own food, my start-up funds would not have made it to payday.

My first trip alone was a day trip, and it took three attempts to be prepared. Each time I had to go back into the office, I had to go through the double-lock combination. I was the only one on duty that early. It was spooky to wander around the unfamiliar, dark, deserted office. I had to do

better, or I would be wasting time and energy.

I discovered that my radio was dead when I reported into dispatch. I went back through the double-locked doors into the office again to change batteries. I tried once again to radio Helena Fire Dispatch.

"Helena, Peck reporting on duty to Heart Lake," I said to report to work. When using the radio, we called first, followed by our last name.

"Peck, Helena. Copy," Helena answered.

"Peck, Sanders." Tim was calling me and wanted more bacon. He would meet me at Indian Meadows.

"Peck, Jones."

I wondered where he and Carol were. He said they needed more meat.

We needed to be a team, supporting one another, especially working in difficult circumstances of weather and location, and I was glad to help. I went back through the double locks to find the meat in a large freezer in the basement of the office. I stumbled around in the dark, trying to find light switches. I felt as though it would be noon before I was out of there. I rattled through my keys, trying to find the right one to the freezer. In fear of theft, the district had everything locked, which necessitated the use of many keys. The primary key only opened the Forest gates and the barn.

By feel, I found packages of beef and bacon. With freezing hands, I went back up the stairs, turned the lights off, and went through the locked doors. I checked to make sure everything was secure.

It took a few tries to line the truck up before I hitched it to the trailer and checked the safety chain, lights, and breakaway brakes. I was frustrated and stressed but finally ready to leave the station. I thought I had everything together.

I drove to the pasture to catch BJ, a young sorrel gelding that Jerry had assigned me. I followed the procedure Jerry had demonstrated. I honked the horn and yelled, "Come on, boys! Come 'n' get it!" I could tell they were unused to a female voice; they disobeyed. I walked out into the field, rattling the grain cakes in the bucket. That got their attention. They ran full speed; the ground trembled, with clods of earth flying from their hooves. I turned and ran for the corrals. I said a quick prayer: *Thank you, Creator, for making horses so they do not like to step on people.* Of course, that meant they might step on someone by accident.

Among the milling horses, I picked BJ, and I put the halter on him. I opened the gate to the pasture so the other horses could return to graze. I led BJ out the other gate and closed it behind me. BJ was a new horse. Though he was young, he seemed gentle. Jerry said he had good quarter- horse breeding.

BJ did not want to load into the trailer, so I used the dog whip gently behind his front knee. He lifted his foot, and he stepped. He was rewarded by the grain cakes I had put in the trailer manger. I fastened the back chain behind his butt and closed the door. Latching the chain was important because it prevented him from backing out unexpectedly and hurting me. He kicked and stomped the trailer floor as I drove. He really disliked trailering. I drove extra carefully in the hope he would calm down. He was quiet on the highway but restless again on the dirt road.

At Indian Meadows, Tim and Race were packing their supplies into mantis in preparation to load the mules.

"Hi," I said to them. "I thought you were up near Silver King."

"Hey yourself," Race responded.

"We got terribly cold and wet in our camp. Would've stuck it out, except the snow flattened our tents. That did it, so we came into the Indian Meadows cabin to get warm and dry out," Tim told me.

"I have your bacon. Do you know what Keith wants me to do with his meat?"

"I think Keith will come into Heart Lake and meet you there."

"That'll work."

Tim and Race headed toward the Silver King Trail. My task was to go to Heart Lake to give bear-safety, pack-it-in, and pack-it-out messages to folks and to pick up trash, clean fire circles, and bury feces.

I unloaded BJ. He had skinned his ankle fighting the trailer a little. I hoped he would not go lame. The bridle was big. I looked around the tack room for a leather punch. I found one in a cupboard with horse medicines and punched new holes in the bridle for a proper fit. Also, the saddle needed attention; I punched holes in the latigo for the cinch buckle. I hoped this saddle would be right for me; otherwise, luckily, I was only out for one day.

I must have been a sight. I had my old brown Stetson pulled to my ears and a silk scarf wrapped around my neck twice and tied in front. I was wearing the heavy Filson jacket under my long Australian duster, heavy shotgun chaps, and lace-up packer boots. I was so well clothed that I could hardly move, making it difficult to mount my horse.

My Montana wilderness work garb.

I led BJ into a dip so I had the advantage of higher ground to mount. BJ did not want to leave Indian Meadows. I had to use my spurs, voice, and reins aggressively to make him move. He tried to sidestep out from under me, tossed his head, and kicked up his heels. When I finally arrived at the gate, I had to dismount to open it, lead him through, close and lock the gate, and then struggle to remount. Two people walking on the trail frightened him. He clamped the bit in his teeth and tried to run. I kept him in control, but he pranced sideways, avoiding the people. Next, he shied at the trailhead sign and again at the bridge on the trail. He finally began to settle, but then he started to limp. We still had many miles to go to reach Heart Lake

Heart Lake was a two-hour ride from Indian Meadows, and rain was sheeting down. Who would have been out in that weather for fun? The saddle was a pleasure to sit on but hard on my ears. BJ's every step caused a rhythmic squeak like fingernails on a chalkboard. I needed to find a different saddle.

After I tied BJ to the hitching rail at Heart Lake, I looked around. "Now what?" Reading the Wilderness handbook or a list of general duties was different from facing a designated Wilderness of 103 miles of trail and innumerable campsites.

"Jones, Peck," I radioed. I still didn't know how Keith was going to retrieve his meat.

Soon came the answer. "Peck, Jones."

"I am at Heart Lake."

"Thanks. See you soon. Jones."

We never talked too much on the radio, because everyone could be listening. It was meant for business only.

I picked up garbage and cleaned fire rings in the campsites. I saw areas that needed naturalizing. To naturalize a campsite, I made it look as if no one had ever used the spot. That meant all the stones from the fire circle had to be removed. The ashes had to be shoveled and scattered where they would not be seen. If the area was badly trodden, I needed to re-create a natural look by scattering duff and sticks to cover the impacted area. Sometimes it was necessary to transplant vegetation.

People tended to camp where others had camped. Conversely, if an area looked as though it had not been used, people were less likely to camp there—another important reason to naturalize and disguise old campsites.

Time slipped by quickly. I grabbed my lunch from the saddlebag and sat against the trunk of a spreading Douglas fir. The sun came from behind the dark clouds for a few minutes. What beauty! Before me lay the crystal-clear lake. Sparkles danced over its surface, water gently slapped the shore, and lodgepole pines and Douglas firs rustled in the slight breeze, which also kissed my cheeks.

"Hi." Keith startled me as he rode up. He was also bundled in chaps and a duster.

"Hi." I jumped up to take the meat out of my saddlebag. The day was so cold the meat was still frozen solid.

"Thanks for bringing in the meat. Have a good ride out," he said.

"You're welcome. Anytime. Stay warm," I responded as Keith turned his big gray horse up the trail.

I explored the lake shore, looking for more campsites needing attention. I was appalled at the amount of toilet paper and feces deposited everywhere. A shovel was a necessity to remove and bury them. *Why can't people be more fastidious like cats and bury their messes?*

I was cleaning a fire circle, sitting on my haunches, and picking bits of aluminum foil and charred cans out of the ashes, when I heard a slight rustling noise beside me. I turned slowly to prevent frightening whomever. I saw low juniper bushes, a log rotting into the soil, and a clump of grass. A chipmunk appeared from behind the log. He eyed me as if to assess the danger. Then he stood on top of the log, trying desperately to reach the seeds of the grass stalk. He managed to pull one stalk over. Holding the seed head like corn on the cob, he munched the seeds. He chewed briefly, making his whiskers bob up and down. When he let the grass go, it sprang up, reaching for the sky. The chipmunk reached for the next grass stalk. He teetered on his hind legs, trying to bend the stalk, but the stalk was uncooperative. He scrambled off the log to the base of the stalk. He held it in both hands, nibbled through the grass, and felled it. He scrambled to the seed head and nibbled the seeds off. Finished, he scampered away. I felt honored the chipmunk had accepted my presence; it was a companionable moment.

It was time to leave. I went to the hitching rail, untied BJ, and mounted. I dismounted a few times to pick up an occasional candy wrapper and pieces of brightly colored plastic twine along the way. Later, I learned the packers used the twine to tie one pack animal behind the other. If one pack animal pulled back, the twine would break. The packer would leave the broken pieces on the ground and use a new piece to retie the pack string. The packers were leaving a trace of their passing, which was poor wildland ethics. BJ's limp worsened.

I had had to walk miles leading a limping horse before. Once, when I was riding in the Rincon Mountains of Arizona, my horse threw a shoe, taking a large chip of hoof with the shoe. I did not want him to damage his hoof any further with my additional weight, so I dismounted and walked in new, tight cowboy boots. By the time the corral was in sight, I was limping as badly as the horse. While backpacking, I had large, bloody blisters and kept walking. So, I did not have much sympathy for BJ.

I walked several miles, leading him. At least while I walked, my ears stopped ringing from the incessant saddle squeak.

The forest floor was covered with arnica; their heart-shaped leaves held raindrops as if in the palms of hands. Their yellow flowers curtsied in the wind and brightened the gray day. It was good to be in the woods again.

Back at the office, I put everything away and left a note telling Jerry about BJ's lameness. As I left Jerry's office, I saw the timber crew were ready to leave for the day.

"Come join us at the Wheel," a gal with a big smile and sparkling brown eyes said as she walked toward me. I remembered seeing her previously around the office.

As I walked into the Wheel, I saw a long bar along the east wall, a row of tables parallel to the bar, and a wood heating stove. Three gambling machines, which were legal in Montana, stood along the west wall. I was unaccustomed to visiting bars, especially walking in by myself; I felt uncomfortable. Everyone was engaged in conversation. It was like a house party where everyone knew everyone else. I saw the timber crew toward the back. A few sat on stools with their backs to the bar. Others sat at a nearby table, facing each other, talking.

The round and jolly Mo waved to me. "Come meet the rest of the crew. This is Dave. He's the fire management officer. Rob works recreation. This is Donna, Terry, and Nancy, who work on the timber crew with me."

"Hi. I'm Cindy. I'm the Wilderness Guard this year."

"Is there much snow out there?" Dave asked.

"It's really wet. Most of the snow has melted around Heart Lake and Webb cabin."

"Wet where we're marking timber too. Really muddy." "Where'd you come from?" Mo asked.

"Arizona. A small town of seven hundred people down twenty-five miles of dirt road, sixty miles from the nearest town," I answered.

"Then Lincoln seems big to you?"

"Definitely, and less isolated too."

"Do you have horses?"

"Yes, two. Bill, my husband, rides on the Forest Service land that borders our place. We also have a dog and three cats."

"You're a long way from home," Donna said. I felt their warm welcome. Lincoln wouldn't feel as lonely with my knowing them.

"Yes. Three days drive, but this is the job offer I received, so here I am. Do you all live in Lincoln?"

"I live in a nearby village that has a school, a bar, a post office, and several ranches," Mo answered. I wondered if the ranches I had seen as I drove by the log hay structures were near Mo's home.

Dave cut in. "I live at the station. My appointment is year-round."

"I teach at the village school in winter," Mo added. "We live in Helena. The timber department is zoned, so we are sent all over central Montana. We will be in and out of Lincoln all summer most likely," responded Terry for herself and Nancy.

"I live in the same village as Mo," Donna said. "But I live up on the hill, not at a ranch like Mo."

"I came from the east and married into an old ranch family. My life has been very different from what I anticipated as a child," Mo added with a giggle.

I was pleased to meet more employees and liked the crew, as they were down-to-earth and friendly. Maybe I had found others to talk to about the quirks of working for the Forest, such as supervisors who were uncommunicative. It was becoming late for me, so I ordered food. Fried chicken, fried zucchini, fried mushrooms, fried cheese, and fried potatoes were all they offered. I chose chicken and zucchini.

The following day, I had time at the station for a change; I was usually in such a hurry to gather things to leave. Time was short to find items I really needed, such as lag bolts, trash bags, concave nuts, nails, and a hammer. I found the needed signs, a staple gun to post-closure orders, an ax, and a one-man crosscut saw, all were necessary for my tasks.

After spending much time rummaging and searching through the station, barn, fire shed, and shop areas, I still could not find a vise grip or end wrench that fit the bolts. I substituted a pair of pliers. With my list of tools completed, I felt more prepared for my assigned tasks. I carried a three-inch folding knife on my belt for fixing leather, cleaning hooves, or cutting food. I washed it thoroughly between hooves and food. I needed to oil my boots, gloves, and chaps to waterproof them again before heading out the following day.

The bunkhouse was a nice facility, with two bedrooms on each side, a bathroom between, and a large common area in the middle. The bedrooms each had two built-in twin beds and a built-in closet with shelves. There were shelves along the wall above the heads of the beds. The rooms were furnished with mattresses and mattress covers only. Everything else the employee provided. The rooms were adequate for one person, but it would have been tight to share the space with another person for any length of time; my own things took up all the shelves and the small closet.

Will Has Our Backs

In mid-June, I had met all the people I would be working with in the Scapegoat except Will. Jerry had told me he was at the U.S. Army muleskinners' reunion in St. Louis. As I approached the office, I saw an elderly man with a tan felt hat sitting askew above a tanned, lined face full of character.

"Hello. I'm Cindy Peck," I said, introducing myself.

"Hi. Willis Vigen, usually called Will," he responded in a pleasant voice.

"I'm headed to Webb today," I said as I turned to walk beside him toward the barn.

"I'll be packing supplies into the Scapegoat for the trail crews," Will said. "We might as well load the horses and mules into the big trailer and save taking the two trucks up there."

"That sounds like a good idea."

I had chosen another saddle that fit my body, and I put it on the saddle rack in the trailer. I helped Will load saddle pads, pack saddles, halters, mantis, and bags of grain cake. We then went to catch the horses.

At Indian Meadows, with everything secured on the mules, we headed into the Scapegoat with the sun warming our backs. Will rode Paladin, a slender, gigantic Tennessee walker. Rambo, my horse, was a slow walker compared to Paladin but faster than BJ. The previous Wilderness Guard had given Rambo treats from her pocket and spoiled him. Now he butted me with his nose, trying to find treats; he nearly knocked me over. What a nuisance.

Leading three mules, we still made good time toward the cabin. The sky was clear and deep blue. I could finally see the pristine snow-covered peaks shining between the trees. *Incredible! This must be how the mountain men saw the snow-topped peaks and new country unspoiled by humans*, I thought. I saw why the mountain men had called the Rocky Mountains the Shining Mountains.

"I met a bunch of backpackers here." Will indicated a spot with heavy timber hemming in the trail. "A few of them stepped to the left, and others stepped to the right. The mules did not like it one bit. It looked like an ambush to them. The hikers did not understand that they should all stand on the same side of the trail. I finally led the mules through, but they were jumping around and shying. Lucky no one stepped on."

Arriving at Webb Cabin, we shared the work of unpacking, putting the stock up for the night, feeding them, and opening the cabin. I cooked dinner; he did the dishes. In the morning, he was up before the light, started the fire, and started the coffee. When he went outside, it was my cue to rise. He heated water to shave and did so by feel since there was no mirror. He cooked hot cereal, and I did the dishes. I was glad he did not eat eggs and bacon every morning. I feared I would gain too much weight if I ate like Jerry.

Will had bright blue eyes that twinkled under bushy eyebrows. His battered tan hat had sweat stains around the band and a ripple on the front brim where he grabbed it to take it off. He wore old shirts with a silk scarf tied haphazardly tied around his neck and a vest with innumerable pockets in which he carried everything: wallet, knife, and kerchief. His jacket was decorated with repair patches sewn on by hand. Jeans with sewn-in-creases up the front of the legs and roper boots made up his usual garb. He was a quiet man with a wry sense of humor who went about his work with a slow, methodical determination. I liked his stories about himself and the mules he worked with. I found it a pleasure to work with him.

He told me he had joined the army at the age of seventeen, lying about his age. Because he had been a ranch boy, the army had used his knowledge of animals and used him as a muleskinner. He had been at Pearl Harbor when it was bombed on December 7, 1941.

"When the bombing started, I was in the pasture catching mules. I ran for cover, dove under the fence, and hid in the bushes. The pasture was strafed. The mule herd parted as the bullets hit. None of the mules were hit. Can you believe that?" he said. "The army had all matching mules—big sorrel ones with a white blaze. They were sure a purdy sight, a pack train of nine matching mules. I packed ammunition and supplies to the soldiers up in the mountains."

The next morning, we awoke to rain as hard as I had yet seen. One day of sun at a time must have been the best the Scapegoat could give me. Rambo whinnied and came looking for breakfast and poking me for a treat. What a nice morning greeting! We put tack on wet, unhappy animals.

Even when we were not packing anything, we put the pack saddles on the mules and took them with us. Otherwise, they would have been distraught and maybe hurt themselves trying to follow if left behind. After all, a mule's mother is usually a mare; seldom is a stallion bred to a jenny. Perhaps that is why mules are attached to horses.

Of the three mules, Wally was shivering from the cold when we saddled him; he was still cold as we rode along the trail. I was worried about Wally. Bo and Skunk seemed to be doing all right, even though they were showing their discontent by being slow and trying to turn back.

Will's favorite mount was always Paladin. They had a special relationship. Will did not like anyone else to ride him. Paladin was a gigantic, slender salt-and-pepper-colored horse. His back was at most people's eye level. When he was saddled, the stirrup was waist-high. Will was often

seen teetering on an unlikely stump while trying to mount. Thoughtful of his rider, Paladin stood still when Will mounted (most of the time), ate only elk thistles along the trail, and whinnied his greeting in the morning as he looked for a handout.

The Mainline trail was deep in oatmeal-like mud. The horses and mules slipped; tried to walk on the side of the trail, bumping our knees and the packs on the encroaching tree trunks. They walked with heads hung low and shook raindrops off their faces periodically.

My Stetson leaked. I pushed the creases out of the crown to allow the rain free flow off. When I tilted my head, the puddled rain poured onto me, but at least it was not leaking. When we arrived at Heart Lake no one was there so we turned toward the Aulz cabin site to see how the trail crew was faring. We startled them as we came around the turn. They were riding with their heads hung low.

"A little wet?" Will said in greeting them.

"The tents were leaking. The wind finally blew the cook tent down; we quit. We spend all our time trying to keep the camp up; can't work in this shit," Race complained.

"The pack's slipping on Rosie," Tim said.

Cursing, Race stepped off his horse and tied Rosie to the nearest tree, but it was so big the lead rope could not go around. He waded through tall, wet grass and tied her to a smaller tree. Race was wet to the knees; boots squishing at every step. Tim sat on his horse and let Race hassle the wet ropes and stiff tarps as he muttered under his breath.

"Might as well hole up at Indian Meadows, dry out, and work a trail from there if this weather keeps up," Will said, showing his wise cowboy logic.

"Yeah, if we can get this outfit to Indian Meadows," said a discouraged Race.

"Well, we'd better get along," said Will. "Take care. Bye."

"Bye." It was an opportune time to leave. Language and tempers were sure to become worse. I looked at Wally. He was still shivering a little; he must have been getting warmer from the exercise.

The rain continued as we started up a side trail to the outfitter camp. Part of my job was to check the outfitter camps to make sure they were complying with the Bob Marshall Wilderness Management Plan and their outfitter-guide permit. If the camp was in non-compliance, I was to notify Jerry by radio so he could take appropriate action.

"Outfitter camps are always good places to stop and warm up with a cup of coffee," said Will.

I had never met someone as addicted to coffee as Will. Of course, he preferred it laced with Bailey's Irish Cream.

"They won't be setting up camp till late August," he added with disappointment in his voice. There would be no coffee in the camp that day.

The camp was in a little valley meadow with tall trees all around. The corrals were near the trail. The logs for the cook tent were leaning against a tree. It looked dreary.

"Do you want to stop for lunch?" Will asked. We had been riding for four hours and were wet, cold, and in poor humor.

"No. It's too wet to sit anywhere, and if I get off, my saddle will be wetter."

"The circle route I was going to show you will get us back to Webb in the dark. Do you still want to do that?"

"I don't see any benefit in going so far." Will had shown me more territory which would help me patrol in the months to come.

"Let's head back then," Will said.

My Stetson began to leak and soaked the back of my neck. I felt as if a wet, cold worm were wiggling down from my head, around my shoulders, and between my breasts and puddling in my belly button. My toes were numb. My leather gloves had been wet since morning. I had taken one off. I had my hand under the front of the saddle pad, taking advantage of the horse's warmth. The rain turned white— snow. If I had not been so miserable, I would have thought it was pretty. But I was feeling cranky.

"This is where Bo fell off the trail. Wally is a troublemaker. He pulled back, and Bo tried to get out of his way but slipped and rolled down the hill," said Will.

Bo looked askance at the canyon; she feared being pushed off the trail again. Riding closer, I investigated the canyon. It was steep, with a few aspen trees sprinkling the slope. I looked at Wally; he was no longer shivering. I was relieved he was doing well.

"Bo landed about twenty feet down, up against that aspen. She was on her back and couldn't get up. I slid down to untie the pack to free her. I roped her and dallied the rope on the saddle horn. Paladin pulled her to her feet. Every time she comes by here she's afraid, as if it's going to happen again," said Will.

If that happened when I was by myself, I would have been unable to help the fallen mule. It made me realize again how watchful, aware of my surroundings, and careful I needed to be to avoid an accident.

Webb cabin was a wonderful refuge seen through the freezing rain and fog. The corral was a quagmire. I dismounted and removed the saddle and bridle. The saddle had gained many pounds; it was saturated. We placed the wet saddles on their racks with unusual speed despite our stiff, cold hands. We put the stock in the back corral. We left the front corral gate open for Keith and Carol. We expected them to arrive from Windy Pass. We gave the animals extra feed to keep them warm and went into the cabin to start a good fire and coffee. I believed one should always take care of the animals first. Obviously, Will did too.

Standard procedure was to boil the water, throw in a measure of grounds, put the pot on a cooler spot on the range, and add a cup of cold water. The grounds settled, and we had good coffee. Even if it had been bitter, we would have been happy to drink anything warm.

Will added Bailey's Irish Cream to his coffee. "Do you want some?"

"Anything to warm me up," I said. Boy, did that taste good. Will made me a believer in Bailey's, a mix of whiskey and cream; that did not sour.

We hung our wet clothes, chaps, raincoats, hats, boots, socks, and gloves from large nails in the beams. I sat at the table, filling out the daily trail encounter and occupied camp forms. I studied the Scapegoat Wilderness information. I thought I had consistently held up my end of the work and I had not complained.

I told Will, "BJ was lame the other day when I took him to Heart Lake. He was especially tender when going downhill. I looked at his front foot. I saw what looked like a hole in his heel."

"Did you tell Jerry?"

"Yes, but he was involved with law enforcement stuff and didn't seem interested."

"I'll look next time I'm in."

We were enjoying the warmth of the wood range. Will reminisced. "Before the floor was fixed, we had a hard time keeping squirrels and mice out of the cabin. One Wilderness Guard would bury her head in the sleeping bag and let the mice run over her. She was a strange one. Wouldn't set traps for them. She fixed her own food, was a vegetarian, and wouldn't share a meal." I presumed that he meant he did not think I was as strange.

Keith and Carol came in as wet and cold as we had been. They put one bear box on the table, mud, and all, and the other one under the table. Bear boxes are really two-by-four-foot ammunition boxes made of steel, with eight latches to keep them closed. The trail crew used them to protect their food and grain pellets from grizzlies. Their wet clothing soon joined ours, hanging from the beams.

As I cooked, I ducked or was slapped in the face with wet clothing. I had to dodge puddles on the floor. I found a can of peaches and Bisquick mix. I baked a cobbler in the wood stove oven—no use in wasting heat. I hoped it would raise spirits by having something special; chicken fajitas and salad completed our dinner.

The cabin felt crowded with four of us, but there was still one empty bunk that was being used as a shelf for personal belongings. Will used the single bunk behind the door, where Jerry had slept. Carol rummaged around on her bunk above Keith's. I guess she was undressing for bed. It sounded as if Keith slept in his clothes. Because it was a coed sleeping arrangement, we were considerate of each other. I pulled my jeans off when I was under the sleeping bag, but kept my shirt on, only unhooking my bra.

After breakfast, we all agreed it was too wet to work on the trails. Instead, we would catch up on work around Webb.

"I want to check the spring. Don't want a beaver making his home there again," Will said. "Beaver makes for bad water."

All free-flowing water should be considered contaminated. Where there was wildlife, including beavers, there could be giardia, an organism that, when ingested, could attach itself to the intestines. It causes severe abdominal pain, nausea, and diarrhea. My son once contracted giardia from drinking stream water when working in Wyoming on a geological survey. When he came home, he looked like a survivor of Auschwitz. An older fellow in Pleasant Valley also became seriously sick, could not keep any food down, and was taken to the hospital. They nearly lost him before someone connected his outdoor work with the possibility of his drinking free-running water. He was treated for giardia and improved quickly. So Will's idea to check the Webb water supply was a good one.

There was other maintenance that needed addressing. "The tack shed could stand straightening. Also, the wood supply is getting low," said Carol. Of course it was up to us to keep firewood supplied and the tack room neat but I had been so involved with learning the territory I had not done so.

"I'll go to the spring with you," said Keith to Will.

Keith and Will headed toward the drainage surrounded by a thick stand of Douglas timber. I remembered the water supply to White Grass Ranch was from a spring up the mountainside. Dad had dug a large hole near the spring, in which he had built a five-by-six-foot cement box. Several screens filtered the water as it flowed through the spring box. The water then flowed out a lower pipe that serviced the ranch. After snowmelt, we would have to go to the spring and take all the plant material and silt out of the spring box so water could flow freely through the pipe. I expected Keith and Will to be cleaning out a similar spring box.

Carol and I pulled out the six-foot two-man crosscut. We took logs stacked behind the tack shed; placed them on the sawhorses; and began the lean-forward, pull-back motion of a sawyer, as I had done with Jerry on my first trip into the Scapegoat.

"You're pulling in an arc; that's why it's binding," Carol told me.

"Tell me when I'm pulling straight." I adjusted my pull.

"That's better."

Will said the spring looked good, had no beaver signs but dug it deeper. Keith got an ax to chop firewood. Will went into the tack shed to organize it.

The wet wood made hard work harder, much of the dry wood we moved into the cabin. Soon Keith took a turn on the saw. We began alternating, chopping awhile, sawing, and helping Will in the shed. We stacked the stove wood against the back wall, where it would dry for future use.

When we broke for lunch, the fire in the cabin felt good as we defrosted our fingers. I put water in a saucepan on the wood range and added diced potatoes, chopped onions, canned corn, and crisp bacon pieces—instant corn chowder, backcountry style. It warmed us from the inside as the fire warmed us on the outside.

"I'll drag more logs in. With this weather, we'll need lots of wood," Keith said as he headed for the corral to catch Spike. He saddled up and found a fallen tree. He put one end of his lariat around the log and dallied the other end around the saddle horn. He spurred Spike, who pulled it to the sawhorses.

Rain is a source of renewal, with the rain, the snow melts quickly. With the receding snow, up pops little spring flowers: buttercups, with their sunny yellow heads, and spring beauties bobbing their delicate lavender blossoms. New bright green tips appear on the fir tree branches.

But the dark, foreboding skies and sullen black surface of Webb Lake made me feel depressed. Everything was wet; days were dark and dreary. It was hard to work with cold, stiff hands and damp, binding clothes. I could not warm my feet and they had turned white and pruney from the constant wet.

The rain continued for the next few days. Keith and Carol went to work on the trails anyway. I patrolled past Parker Lake with Rambo and Charlie, my pack mule, as company. Approaching Parker Lake, I entered thick, dark timber; the lower branches swept the ground. The stock hesitated as if it were threatening. I, too, felt apprehensive in the dark, unnatural silence. People talk about the quietness of the woods, but there is a subtle sound. Usually, there is wind rustling leaves or sighing through pine trees to the accompaniment of bird-song; squirrels chatter and drop nuts that plop onto the forest floor. But this was an ominous silence—no wind or bird sounds, only the almost inaudible drops of rain falling from the laden boughs onto the needle-covered ground. It made me imagine a primeval time when man was the hunted, not the hunter; when shifting mists hung over the land and creepy things crawled out of the mud; when large animals preyed on the smaller ones. Back in the present, the mists were swirling along the edges of Parker Lake, which added to my apprehension.

I thought a grizzly might have been lurking, hidden by the heavy timber or wolves stalking. Perhaps a pack was waiting for a tasty morsel, maybe me; prickles ran down my back. I shook my head to throw off those morbid thoughts. I convinced myself it was only a dark, dreary, wet day and I had a job to do.

I checked the grizzly feeding area. It made Rambo, Charlie, and me nervous. The grizzly was still feeding there. New clods of earth had been thrown from the hole; new bones exposed. I did not see him, but I hastily made an unorganized retreat with Charlie leading the way. Pack mules were supposed to follow, but he wanted out of there fast. I was also glad to leave.

I made the loop past Twin Lakes. An eagle sat on top of a charred dead tree, watching the lake, hoping to find food. A deer and her fawn drank at the shore and bounded away. Frogs chirped in the puddles in the trail. They went silent as I approached and chirped again after I passed. The wind rustled the dead tree branches. One fell with a crash.

I had a saddle that finally fit and had no squeak. I tried to convince myself life was looking up. I was comfortable. I enjoyed the sounds around me. Despite the drizzle, it was not such a bad day: I'd had worse. No grizzly or wolf attacked. Rambo and Charlie were behaving better. I found my way around the trails without feeling lost. Webb cabin would be warm since Will would have banked the fire.

Flagging Reroute

It was still June when Jerry and Charley were going to flag a reroute for the Twin Lakes Trail. The plan was for it to contour the hills and pass the marsh to prevent damage horse traffic would cause on the fragile, wet area. I was joining them for part of the ride.

In preparation, I saddled Rambo and packed my gear onto Luke, who was a nice old mule with good manners. He led well, stood still when I packed him, and nuzzled me when I rubbed his head. He had big, long-suffering brown eyes. I loaded the shovel, ax, crosscut saw, nuts, bolts, pliers, my personal duffel, and two fifty-pound bags of grain pellets, one on each side for balance. Rambo still butted his nose into me, looking for treats. Some days, I thought he was getting better, only to have him become a nuisance again. He would not keep his mind on the trail or learn to stand still when saddled. His wiggling tangled the mule's lead rope when I tried to mount. If the lead rope slipped under his tail, we would have a rodeo, bucking and rearing. I could not trust him to warn me of danger, as a reliable horse would have. He was scatterbrained. I needed to be alert to avoid an accident.

Charley was riding a stout, high-headed sorrel named Oscar. High-headed horses tended to throw their heads and might slug you in the face, which could break your nose. Charley looked uncomfortable on a horse; as if he rode seldom.

Jerry was riding Ribbon, a lanky roan. They looked fine together, both long-legged and energetic. Unlike Jerry, who exuded confidence, Ribbon showed fear by the whites of his eyes showing. I wondered what had happened to him in his past to cause such fear.

When we all left Indian Meadows, Jerry led Skunk, the skittish white mule, loaded with a filled propane tank and their personal duffels. Charley and Jerry joked and laughed together as we rode along. I missed much of what was said because of the mule between us and the squishing sound of hooves on the muddy trail. It felt like they had a good companionship, which put me at ease. At the junction, I turned toward Heart Lake as they took the shorter route to Webb.

At Heart Lake, I saw three young men fishing from the shore. They glanced at me and then quickly turned away. I suspected something was amiss. I tied Rambo and Luke to the hitching rail and walked to the shore.

I greeted them with a smile, no reason to cause them to put their guard up. "Any luck?"

"Not yet," one replied.

I walked along the shoreline to the next fellow. He was putting a half-dead golden trout back in the water.

"I'm releasing him," he explained nervously as I approached.

"The limit is three trout or five graylings. It's dead. Might as well keep it," I said as I stretched with my shovel and dragged the fish back to shore. *No use in wasting perfectly good fresh fish*, I thought.

As I went farther along the lakeshore, I heard him call to his friends, "She saved my fish."

As I cleaned a few campsites and buried more feces, I thought, *They don't have fishing licenses. If I ask to see their licenses and they have none, I don't have the authority to give them a citation. I would look foolish. But I should do something.*

I returned to confront them. "To fish in the Scapegoat Wilderness, you must have a valid Montana state fishing license, you know?"

They were no longer fishing but standing by their campfire. "Oh. Yes," one of them answered. I left it at that. I thought they were going to stop fishing and avoid the chance of getting fined. My uniform was a sign of authority, but they did not know I could not cite them.

I mounted Rambo and crossed the bridge leaving Heart Lake. I passed an old campsite that needed to be inventoried and erased. I tied the animals, measured the impacted area, and took pictures. I heard the radio in my saddlebag.

"A large cell is developing over Pyramid Peak. It looks like it has strong winds, lightning, and lots of moisture," the radio squawked. It was John, the fire lookout at Silver King; he had manned the lookout for several years. As a radioman in Vietnam, he could detect subtle information by the intonation of one's voice.

Pyramid Peak was ten miles straight northwest of me. That was the direction from which all the storms had been coming. I figured I had time to finish the two campsite inventories. After taking the measurements and pictures, I cleaned the camp, threw rocks from the fire pit, and dug out and scattered the ashes. I found sticks and pine needles to cover the old fire area.

I was almost done, when I heard a loud boom— thunder. With so many trees in the canyon, I could see only a little sky. I could hear the storm approaching. Between me and the cabin was an exposed ridge. It came to mind that riding an exposed ridge in a thunderstorm was a good way to shorten your life. It was time to head for shelter fast before the storm was on top of me. Fast with a pack mule was still a walking pace.

When I reached the ridge, I turned my collar up and buttoned my duster against the wind. I saw dark, foreboding clouds boiling over the mountain. I saw flashes of lightning. I heard rumbles of thunder. The wind was strong enough that Rambo's mane and tail stood at a right angle from his body. He hung his head to protect it from the cold blast. I arrived at the cabin before the lightning threatened me and had a few minutes to unsaddle and unpack before the rain began.

"Why are you coming in early?" asked Jerry.

"I didn't want to get caught on that ridge in a lightning storm," I answered. I was embarrassed about coming in early but felt it was the safest thing to do.

"Safety first," Charley added, but he did not sound convincing.

After I had stowed my things, I went out onto the covered porch, where they sat looking over the lake enjoying the drama of the storm.

"Do you want a beer? There's one in the fridge," Jerry said.

With beer in hand, I joined them. Maybe I had misjudged them. They had invited me.

The storm gave us a lively show of pelting rain; wind set the big trees swaying. Thunder shook the ground and echoed in our little valley. Lightning cracked with a vengeance. We heard a tree fall nearby. Shortly, the rain turned to hail. The temperature dropped ten degrees. So much for thinking we would have a day without rain. There had been only one dry day in a month.

I was interested in the new trail route. I asked to go with them in the morning. As usual, I took care of my stock, saddling, and packing, while they took care of theirs. A misty rain fell as we left the cabin. We stopped twice to remove downed trees from the trail, all with the crosscut. I noticed Charley's saddle was slipping so I put it back in place, tightened the cinch for him, and held the horse while he mounted. We followed Meadow Creek to show Charley where the grizzly bear had been feeding on the horse carcass and then backtracked to Twin Lakes. The circling storm was turning darker.

When we reached the site, we tied our horses to charred black tree trunks and went on foot to flag the reroute. Jerry secured red plastic ribbon on the trees to mark the new route so when the trail crew came to build the trail, they would know the intended route. Jerry decided where the bridge would span the bog. The bridge was primarily for the protection of the bog and the wetland habitat; of secondary consideration were visitors to the designated Wilderness.

Snow began to fall as I scouted ahead to help Jerry and Charley determine the contour and flag the way. We waded through hip-deep, wet grass. My soaked leather chaps hung heavily from my hips but were keeping my legs relatively dry. My boots squished at every step. We continued to work as if it were a nice day. We headed back to the cabin as the snowstorm was turning into a blizzard. Snow drifted on my saddle, melted, and soaked my seat. It seeped along my legs making me uncomfortable with wet pants and wet, cold feet. To keep snow from drifting down my neck, I held my shoulders to my ears. They were cramping from the unusual position. At home in Arizona, June was one of our hottest months, but in Montana, I was riding in a blustery snowstorm.

Jerry and Charley told me about the Canyon Creek fire, which had left 2.8 million acres of the Scapegoat Wilderness charred. It had occurred the same year as the big Yellowstone Fire, in 1988. The Canyon Creek fire had started as a lightning strike on June 25, near the west boundary of the Scapegoat. The trail crew and Will were working in the Scapegoat and became used to the smoke. Then, on September 6, a rare, catastrophic wind event of fifty miles per hour tripled the fire size. Radio contact with the trail crew on the Middle Fork and with Will at Webb was lost because of the air turbulence. It was imperative to get everyone out of the Wilderness, as they were in the line of fire. Jerry saddled Spike and made a mad run into the Scapegoat at dusk.

"I made a quick stop here to warn Will. He didn't seem too impressed, but I convinced him to get out," Jerry said. "Sparks were falling all around; fire jumped the trail behind me."

When Jerry arrived at the trail camp, the crew saddled their horses as Jerry helped to quickly saddle the mules, and they headed for the mountain, where Jerry knew of a bare talus slope. In fear, two mules refused to lead, so Jerry cut their pack saddles off, and turned them loose to fend for themselves. But the crew, with four riding horses and Skunk, made it to the talus slope. By morning, the fire had died down enough for the radio to work, and called to be helicoptered out.

Weeks later, Jerry rode into the fire area and found the horses and Skunk had joined the recalcitrant mules along the Middle Fork river in a green area. Nearby Jerry found only the D rings and buckles from the packs he had cut off.

Forest fires can move fast and cannot be outrun, as has been demonstrated by experience. The book *Young Men and Fire* by Norman Maclean details one tragedy in which firefighters were overrun east of here near Great Falls.

As they related the Canyon Creek fire incident, I observed the respect Jerry and Charley showed for each other. They were two coworkers together, not so much boss and employee. I also realized that no matter how desperate the circumstances, Jerry would have my back. That quality in him seemed as much his nature as it may have been his military training and gave me a sense of security.

The next morning, I was up first, lit the fire, started the coffee pot, and went outside. The early morning light reflected on the lake, and the trees sparkled from the snow and frozen rain droplets on their branches. Jerry came out to feed the stock. I went back inside to fix breakfast, while Charley gathered his personal effects.

It was difficult to accomplish much work in such bad weather. With wet gloves, the wet tools would slip and slide in my hands. That evening, I had a discussion with Jerry.

"If the weather is bad in the morning, I would like to come into the station with you. I could really use the time with the management books and to enter the data from the trail encounter and occupied campsite forms into the computer. If it isn't raining, I would like to stay and get more campsite work done. OK?"

"That sounds alright to me. How do you like Rambo?" he asked.

"He's OK but a bit scatterbrained. He can't keep his mind on his business," I said.

"Do you want to ride Ribbon?"

Was the offer a challenge? Ribbon had a bad reputation. I did not know if he was a better choice. "I'll ride him if you like," I replied. I was going to accept the challenge. I had ridden difficult horses before.

After breakfast, Jerry caught and brushed the stock. I was left to clean the cabin. Charley helped me bolt the log shutters. We stacked everything on the front porch to ease the packing onto the mules. I saw that Jerry had saddled Ribbon for me. What a surprise. I had never expected he would saddle my horse.

Jerry walked by Ribbon with a manti in his hand; Ribbon shied and pulled back, the lead rope tightened. He lunged forward and settled down. I put my lunch, water bottle, radio, and paperwork in his saddlebags. He shied again and went over backward. All four hooves pointed to the clouds. It was a ridiculous sight, like a turtle on its back, but it was frightening too. I remember a friend of Dad's whose pelvis was broken by a horse going over like this with the rider underneath. Ribbon quickly rolled over and jumped up. He stood trembling from fear and snorting as if someone had harmed him. But it was his own fault. He had no reason to be frightened. With six inches of muck in the corral, mud was all over Ribbon and my saddle. I talked to him quietly and proceeded with the task at hand. I checked the saddle. The saddle tree was not broken, and no real damage had been done.

Jerry stepped onto Rambo, who immediately bucked and reared. Jerry jumped off, reprimanding him with harsh words and a jerk of the reins, and then mounted again. Rambo still crow-hopped but settled. Maybe the horses were complaining of the cold, wet, and mud. The constant wind was unnerving. We headed out, Charley led the way and Jerry brought up the rear, leading the three mules.

I had to hold on to my hat, or it would have blown away. The horses remained skittish. The trees were whipping back and forth. Large branches and leaning trees squeaked as they rubbed against each other. Branches broke off, crashing to the ground. Ribbon shied and spun. I was afraid he was going to go over backward, pinning me under him. I decided to bail. I tried to dismount on the uphill side, but by the time I freed myself, I was on the downhill side. I lost my footing and somersaulted; juniper bush stopped me from tumbling all the way down the canyon.

"You alright?" asked Charley. "Are you hurt?" asked Jerry.

"I'm fine," I said, as I climbed back to the trail. I was so well padded with foul-weather gear that I felt like a football player in protective gear.

"I think those big chaps blowing in the wind spooked him," Jerry said, and I agreed.

I tied my chaps more securely. Ribbon had settled and was standing between Charley and Jerry, both of whom remained mounted. I led him to a rock to make mounting easier and stepped back on. You can never let a horse know he has the best of you, or he will continue to misbehave.

After a while, Charley stopped suddenly. "G-g-grizzly!" He saw the unmistakable broad head with little, round ears.

I immediately thought of people's safety over the ridge, campers were tented at Heart Lake. But this was bear country; the trailhead had information about bear safety. I talked about bear safety every time I saw people. They were informed and warned of bears and other wildlife. They better take responsibility for themselves.

The grizzly was coming along the trail toward us. The wind was blowing so hard he could neither hear nor smell but suddenly he saw us. He bounded away much faster than one would have thought such a massive creature could move. I saw a glimpse of his distinguishing hump and roly- poly rear which shone like reddish-brown velvet. Checking his track, we discovered he was only a medium-sized grizzly, probably an adolescent looking for his own territory. The grizzly up Meadow Creek was considerably bigger, a full- sized adult.

Arriving at Indian Meadows, we followed the routine: we took care of the stock, loaded them into the trailer, and returned to Lincoln. It had been a short trip. I had learned more about Wilderness management by being involved with the reroute process.

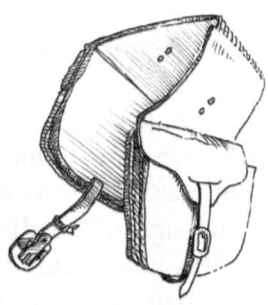

CHAPTER 10

Dogging It

"YOU MIGHT AS WELL USE BRANDY. HE'S ALREADY AT INDIAN Meadows," Will said. It looked as though we were going into Webb together. I had been on the job five weeks, and I had settled into a rhythm of work and tasks on my days off. On this tour of duty, I was starting at the same time as Will.

"Wasn't Race using Brandy?" I asked, concerned I was taking someone else's mount.

"Yes, but Race walked off, so he won't miss him," Will answered.

"What do you mean he walked off?"

"Well, he walked off when he and Tim were packing to go on duty," Will said hesitantly.

"Does that mean he quit?" "Maybe not. We'll see."

The weather, frustrations, wet tack, packs that would not stay balanced, and working with Tim must have gotten to him. I knew Tim was less capable of doing the continuous hard work the job demanded. Tim was older and looked to me to be unhealthy. Race carried the extra burden.

The constant rain had made the trails into elongated frog ponds. The frogs would sing loudly, stop as I rode by, and continue as soon as I had passed. I had become used to the woods being noisy with horse and mule hooves splashing and thumping and frogs singing.

At Indian Meadows, I saw the stock were in the enclosure, happily grazing on the luscious, tall grass. Will pointed to Brandy. He was a big red roan with clear, honest eyes. He looked as if he were half draft horse and half quarter horse, round and solid, and the type of horse I liked best. He was so fat his backbone formed a valley down his back. Riding him would be like riding a fifty-gallon barrel. My legs would be stretched, and the saddle could slip easily, but that was nothing I had not encountered before. He came to me to be caught. I took an immediate liking to him and was looking forward to riding him. Will chose Skunk and Bo for packing and Paladin, his favorite to ride.

What a beautiful day it was finally sunny and warm. It was only the second nice day since I had started work. *Hopefully the trails and corral at Webb would be drying out*, I thought. I led the way with Skunk; Will followed on Paladin and led Bo. We saw several cars at the trailhead. People were going into the Scapegoat to take advantage of the sunny day.

"Good morning. Where are you going?" Will asked one family who were preparing to leave with daypacks slung on their shoulders with fishing rods sticking out.

"Hi. Heart Lake for the day."

I watched a group of nine people on horses preparing to leave the trailhead. Dudes in sneakers, colorful pants, and assorted headgear more appropriate for a ball game were being led by a cowboy guide. He wore a well-used Stetson, scuffed packer boots, and stained leather chaps ;he looked like he could take care of them.

We also talked to a young outfitter and his ten-year-old daughter. He was taking three days to check his hunting campsite by Bugle Mountain. He was well supplied, by the looks of his tidily packed black mule and the stuffed saddlebags on each riding horse. They had serviceable cowboy hats, slickers, and sturdy boots. He said it was his first trip into the wilderness this season. Entry into the wilderness was increasing, as the fishing season was getting better, and weather improved.

About two miles along the trail, Will and I met a family of five with two dogs not on leashes. The man obligingly caught the growling, barking dogs. He sat beside the trail, holding their collars, as we passed. However, he let them go too soon. One of the dogs attacked Bo, jumping, and biting at her belly. Bo bucked and kicked it, knocking him to the ground. The dog sprang back to bite her again. She sidestepped and the dog leaped to bite Brandy; I kicked him in the mouth, and he cowered. The other dog went after Paladin and Will. I grabbed both mule lead ropes and moved away. Will had quite a rodeo with Paladin kicking and bucking. The dog under him was jumping and biting, trying to rip Paladin's belly the way wolves do when they go in for the kill; bright red blood was flowing down his chest.

Will tried to release his ever-present lariat to rope or whip the dog. He yelled at the owner repeatedly, "Catch those dogs!"

"Spot, come! Stop that!" the man screamed. His wife and crying children cowered and held on to one another in fear.

Their dogs were disobedient. Paladin and the dog kept going around and around. Paladin bucked, sidestepped, and kicked. The man danced around, trying to catch his dog. By a miracle, he finally reached under the swirling Paladin and caught his dog. A branch knocked Will's hat off. I saw his wallet bounce out of his vest pocket. Paladin had bloody wounds; the dog's mouth was bloody. Bo also had a few bites that had swelled but did not bleed.

I was less available to dog attack, since I had moved farther along the trail. I was lucky to be riding level- headed Brandy. I was angry at the stupid people. But it was unprofessional for a U.S. Forest Service employee to let anger show.

"Regulations state that dogs must be on a leash on the trails," I said with authority. "Get those dogs on a rope. There is another horse group coming this way." Someone with less experience than Will would surely have gotten badly hurt.

"We don't have a rope," the man said. "We'll take them back to the car. I'm really sorry this happened. The dogs have never seen horses before."

Will stepped off to retrieve his hat. It had been stepped on; he punched the crown out and slapped it onto his head. He checked Paladin for injuries. His belly and chest had a few small, bleeding bites. Will found his wallet. He had not known it had flown out of his pocket. He found a stump to climb back onto Paladin.

"Can you take the mules into Webb?" Will asked with concern showing on his face. "I am going to follow those people and collect names and an address for reference in case of further problems."

"Yes, I'll be fine. Take care of yourself and Paladin," I responded.

I rode ahead with Skunk tied to the back of Bo's packsaddle. Will, on a trembling Paladin, turned to go back to the trailhead.

Along the way, I saw the old phone wire that Jerry wanted removed. I tied Bo to a tree, with Skunk tied to him and Brandy to another tree. The wire was a remnant of an abandoned telephone line between the valley and Bugle Mountain Lookout. Years ago, this line, strung from tree to tree, was used by the fire lookouts communicating with the fire base. If the phone went dead, the lookout's job was to hike down the mountain with tree-climbing gear, extra wire, and tools to repair the line. Then the lookout went back to the tower to watch for lightning strikes or smoke. Radios were not extensively used until after World War II.

I pulled and tugged to untangle the wire from the brush. I did not have wire cutters with me. It was another item to put on my needs-list. I realized I was purposely lagging because I was concerned for Will. I lagged to avoid becoming too far ahead in case Will needed me.

"Vigen, Jones," the radio crackled.

Will didn't have a radio with him. I did, so I answered. "Jones, Peck for Vigen."

"What is your location?"

"A mile from the Wilderness Boundary. We had a dog- and-horse incident. Will has gone back to get information." Again, I was careful of too much information going over the airwaves.

"Are you alright? Do you need help?"

"I'm fine. Paladin and Bo were bitten, but it doesn't look bad. Thanks for the offer." Had Keith called Will because we were late? It was comforting to know he would come to help. How thoughtful. Keith and Carol were working eight miles from my location.

Will caught up with me and explained that the people were sorry. Bo had knocked all the dog's front teeth out, which had prevented Paladin from being hurt worse.

"Good thing Skunk didn't kick him. She would have killed any dog that attacked her. She has excellent aim. I'll go into Webb to doctor Paladin," Will said as he passed me.

"I'm glad Paladin is going to be alright. I'll see you at Webb later," I said. I thanked Spirit Guide; it could have been much worse.

I had two signs to nail into the Wilderness Boundary signpost. I also reset a signpost that had been pulled out at Heart Lake. I figured a horse must have been tied to the sign instead of at the nearby hitching rail and the horse pulled back, uprooting it.

Continuing around the lake, I took inventory, snapped pictures, measured, dispersed the fire circles, and threw ashes. Nothing was going to change, maybe people cannot learn. I carried the shovel around the shoreline and buried the ever-present feces and toilet paper. At the cabin, I would find a legal description of the camp locations from the map for documenting the issues. At the station, I would find the distance from the trailhead and figure the LAC rating. I wrote the information on the inventory forms. I would later put it into the computer for the annual Wilderness Report to Congress.

Shadows lengthened. It was time to be at Webb. I wondered how Paladin was doing.

Will came out of the cabin to greet me. "How's it with you?" I handed him the radio. I unsaddled Brandy and Bo and carried the panniers, tools, and tack into the shed.

"Jones, Vigen," The radio crackled, Will was calling Keith.

After a pause, there was a response. "Vigen, Jones. How're Paladin and Bo?"

"We're all right, not even stiff."

"Glad to hear it. Could you bring us a package of meat tomorrow?"

So that's why Keith radioed earlier! I thought.

"Sure. I was going to show Cindy Arrastra Pass. Your camp isn't far out of the way."

I felt as if the deer who stayed near Webb cabin was a friend. Since we fed the stock grain, undigested but nutritious matter remained, which the deer ate. Will thought the deer were lacking nutrition, possibly minerals, because their natural salt licks were far away in the populated valley, unavailable to them because of people and dogs. I wished I had had deer in Arizona that would eat manure. It would have saved time in cleaning the corrals. One mule deer had a floppy ear. Frostbite had probably damaged the cartilage. For a wild animal, she was friendly and big-bellied with fawns. I looked forward to seeing her little one.

Keith and Carol's camp was in the Canyon Creek burn. Tim was with them since Race was still away. Camp consisted of backpacking tents for each. A kitchen tarp stretched between three charred tree trunks and a canvas fly for the saddles. The corral was an electric fence with colored plastic ribbon with wires woven inside and D-cell battery unit for power. We put the meat and paper towels inside the bear box and clamped it closed again. The camp looked neat, but everything was soggy and uninviting.

Will and I headed toward Arrastra Pass. He told me, at the top of a pass, one could look down into the North Fork country. Keith and Will talked about that country with reverence. They each had spent much time working in the North Fork. We went by Meadow Creek, the skull was still in the hole, but a large piece of vertebra, a hip bone, and a leg bone had been carried out. No bear was in sight.

We continued northwest along Meadow Creek, with its beaver dams, willows, and small ponds, and past the Dry Creek Trail Junction; forded Meadow Creek again; and began to climb. A small detour brought us into another outfitter campsite. It was deserted with no coffee.

The outfitters were assigned a permanent campsite, from which they guided their hunting trips or pack trips. They paid for an out-fitter-guide permit. According to their permit agreement, they could leave the corrals and tent poles on the site. Everything else had to be packed out at the end of hunting season. It took many trips to pack all the tents, stoves, bunks, and other supplies in and out of the Wilderness.

Back on the main trail, we recrossed East Fork Creek. We were in a thick, old forest of Douglas firs and spruces. It was dark, wet, and dreary. We stopped to saw a downed tree out of the trail and then continued. It was getting late, and as we gained altitude, the tempera-ture dropped. The place felt lonely, as if it were an extraordinarily long distance from anywhere. Will stopped at a bad windfall. Fallen trees were criss crossing one another. The surrounding thick timber and its spreading branches prohibited our passage. I loved learning about a new country, and this trip had shown me an escape route if the Wilderness blew up in fire, which seemed unlikely with all the moisture we were getting, but one never knew.

"If we cut out all these trees, it will be dark before we get back to Webb," Will said. "Do you want to turn back or cut these trees out?"

"I think we should go back. You have shown me lots of new territory. I could find my way over the pass from here if I had to," I said. Will was easy-going; I did not feel I had to prove myself.

As we headed back, snow started to fall—lots of it. It was heavy, wet snow. The nice, sunny morning was long gone. I knew from living at White Grass that in the northern Rockies, it might snow every month of the year. It was nearly four o'clock, and we had a three-hour ride back to the cabin. Bless Brandy! His steady, good walk kept covering the miles. My knees ached, so I stepped off and walked for a while to ease them.

Chaps flapped about my legs and plowed through the mud. Will rode with his head down and his shoulders hunched for protection from the wind-blown snow ahead of me were Bo and Skunk; their heads hung low too. I thought of the nice, warm, dry cabin, which would be especially inviting with its fire and Irish cream coffee on a night like this.

I really liked Brandy, but Jerry encouraged me to use the less reliable stock. I felt I had not been hired to train stock. I needed reliable animals since I was working alone most of the time. Even with a radio, I could be out of contact, because there were many dead zones. BJ had something wrong with his foot. Ribbon had bad habits, and I thought he was dangerous. Rambo was scatterbrained and, thus, undependable.

I was not sure what was expected of me, since I still had a hard time understanding Jerry. I thought he had been hazing me on the first trip out. The days had been extra long, and he had not taken breaks for rest stops or even a lunch stop. Jerry was easier when Charley was with us. I was puzzled about why he had suggested I ride Ribbon; maybe it was another test. I was glad I was with them when I flew off Ribbon.

My feet were permanently pruney from being wet all the time. I worried about getting trench foot like World War I soldiers. I had seen only two sunny days in June. I lived in my cold-weather gear during what was supposed to be a summer job. Who would have expected it to snow each week and rain the rest of the time? Much of the rain was going down the Missouri to the Mississippi. Those low- lying areas were flooding. Bureau of Reclamation levies were breaking; towns were being washed downstream. I was at mercy of the headwaters.

I felt like going home to warm, dry Arizona. I missed Bill, the dogs, and home. I did not feel comfortable talking to anyone about my frustrations. *How did I get myself into this job anyway?* My long-term goal was to have a permanent job—a career. I had considered my skills with animals and my knowledge and experience with the outdoors unmarketable, so I had discounted their value. Now I thought *Here was a place that would appreciate those skills.* Feeling sorry for myself served no purpose but bogged my spirit down. I straightened my shoulders and pushed out my chest. I had to cowboy up and continue. *I signed up for this, and I am not a quitter.*

I forced myself to look on the positive. I had done what my family and society expected: I had finished high school and business school; gotten married, though too young, and definitely too naive; borne two children with great ease; and taken care of things as necessary and supported my husbands with their work.

Even though the Wilderness work was difficult, I could not let myself or anyone else call me a quitter. My parents had taught me to stick it out. As the western song says, *"If it is a fence, fix it. If it's work, get your back into it. If it hurts, hide it."*

That philosophy had worked well for me. I was determined to work through my frustrations. Monday evening, when I settled in the bunkhouse, I called home. Bill was always supportive and encouraging and wrote frequently.

He was planning to come up to visit in August. He wanted to see all I had been telling him about. It brought back memories of Bill and my first summer together. Our relationship was unconventional. We had married when he was in his fifties and I was in my thirties. He had had children grown and gone, and mine had been in elementary school. I had had no job opportunities and wondered what to do; now I had opportunities.

Rambo

The Fourth of July three-day weekend arrived. I expected many people in the wilderness. Since I had arrived in late May, much had happened, I had learned a lot, and I had worked with many new people. I was developing a feel for what I was supposed to do. I had the tools I needed, even a pair of much-valued vise-grip pliers for sign installation and wire cutters to remove old phone lines.

It was the second sunny day in a row; raising my spirits. At the office, I saw Terri, whose job in recreation was picking up garbage and cleaning privies, responsibilities similar to mine in the wilderness, but in campgrounds.

"You ride horses to work?" she asked. "I'm scared of horses."

"Yes, I'll be catching a horse and mule shortly and taking them to Indian Meadows. I'll be packing in for five days," I replied.

She was a tall gal in her late twenties, with big brown eyes and swept-back hair to match. She wore shorts regardless of the weather, showing her strong, tanned legs with hiking boots and two pairs of heavy socks. She went backpacking with her boyfriend every day she had off work but was terrified of hiking alone. She jabbered along, constantly asking questions.

"I have to check Copper Creek Campground, near Indian Meadows. Could I watch you pack up?" she asked.

"Sure, but I've got a few things to do here first."

"So do I. Call me when you're ready to get the stock."

I finished putting wilderness data into the computer, caught and loaded the stock, bought groceries, and packed two fifty-pound bags of grain cake. I then drove to Indian Meadows. Terri met me in time for lunch. We saw smoke coming out of the cabin chimney and decided to take advantage of the fire and shelter.

Since Race was back at work, I saddled Rambo and the mule Charlie. Terri held the panniers open for me to drop in the fifty-pound bags, one on each side. I added my personal gear; groceries; and, the ever-present ax, shovel, and crosscut saw. I buckled up the panniers and tied it all securely with a lash rope.

"How do you pull the mule along?" Terri asked.

"I lead him with this rope. I keep one hand on the lead rope and the other one on the reins to control the horse," I explained as I mounted.

"You wouldn't catch me dead up there."

As usual, I was all bundled up in my foul-weather gear. The morning sun had given way to clouds, and it looked like another five days of wet riding.

"I can't believe you go out alone."

"Ever since I was a child on my folks' ranch, I've always been out alone."

"Bye. See you in a few days." Little did I realize I would see Terri sooner.

I discovered she was right about one thing: Charlie did not lead. I pulled him along, wrenching my shoulder. Charlie was slowly tugging my saddle backward. I stopped to reset the saddle and tighten the cinch. I made a loop in the lead rope and dropped it over the saddle horn which, I knew, was dangerous because I could not release the mule fast in case of a problem. At least my arm would no longer be pulled out of my shoulder socket.

I sang, enjoying the soft patter of the rain and the fresh smell of wet earth. Jewels hung from the fir needles and sometimes fell through the air to vanish on the ground. *The Great Creator at work—what magic!*

Suddenly, Rambo jumped, spun, and ran toward the thick Douglas fir forest. I knew I would not fit through the thick timber, so I pulled with all my might on the right rein and held his nose to my knee. He kept going. Suddenly, we were wrapped around a tree. I felt excruciating pain; my leg was the bumper between the tree and Rambo's ribs. The pain took my breath away. Rambo was tangled in the tree. Charlie's lead was too tight for me to easily lift off the saddle horn and prevented Rambo from moving.

With difficulty, I disentangled myself from the tree, the rope, and stepped off. Standing on one leg, I talked soothingly to the trembling Rambo. Patient Charlie, who had been jerked and dragged along, only looked at me as if to say, "What's going on here?"

I untangled Rambo and Charlie and tied them to trees back beside the trail. I calmed my fright, and my heart slowed. I pulled the radio out of the saddlebag. "That's a fine place to keep it," I said aloud, reprimanding myself. "If separated from the horse, I would have no communication."

I retrieved my hat where it had flown off and Rambo stepped on it. I punched the crown out with my fist. I plopped it onto my head, sat on a nearby tree stump, and stretched my leg. It hurt too badly for me to remove the layers of boots, chaps, and jeans. I could bear weight, my knee bent without additional pain, and I could wiggle my foot. I did not think any bones were broken. It could have been much worse. Spirit Guide was with me. I would handle the pain and go on to work.

"Nobody really knows where I am," I said to Rambo and Charlie. But they acted disinterested.

"Silver King, Peck," I said into the radio. "Peck, Silver King," John answered.

"I am momentarily off my horse, sort of by accident. I will continue into Webb." I wanted to hear a voice for reassurance.

"What's your location?" asked John, picking up on the fact that something was amiss.

"On the Mainline Trail, just south of the Heart Lake junction."

"How's the weather?" He was responsible for reporting the weather within his view to the USFS fire desk in Helena, but I suspected he wanted to keep me on the air to hear how I was doing.

"A mist. All overcast."

"Thanks. Over."

Now someone knew where I was and where I should be, come evening.

I went by Heart Lake. I found one large camp of seven and another small camp. I would need to come back the next day to talk with them. Now I needed to be at the cabin, put my leg up, and put cold on it.

At Webb, as usual, I took care of the animals, carried the grain bags and saddles into the shed; opened the cabin; and brought groceries, gear, and water inside. I lit the fire and put coffee on. I could not ignore my leg any longer. *"Oh jeez!"* It was blue and red from my knee to my toes and swollen. Sitting, I put my leg on top of the table, with a wet-cold towel on top. It felt terrible, but I knew the cold should diminish the swelling.

I filled the Coleman lantern, kept my leg up as much as possible as I cooked and replenished wood in the fire. I went to bed with it wrapped in two Ace bandages and elevated it on an extra rolled-up sleeping bag.

By morning, the sharp leg pain was gone; an extreme throbbing still remained. But as I put my leg on the floor, the pain surged back and more swollen and colorful than the night before. After breakfast, I caught Rambo and Charlie. I moved slower than usual, limping, and dragging the heavy injured leg. It was lunchtime by the time I reached Heart Lake.

I sat under a spreading Douglas fir. The ground was covered with pine cones and a few sticks blown from the tree but mostly hard-packed mineral soil. I propped my bad leg across the good one elevating it to relieve the throbbing. I leaned against the trunk. The bark felt rough through my jacket, the ground was cool, and a faint scent of smoke wafted from a dying campfire. Soon an ant came to investigate. He wiggled his front feet and head, walking first one way and then the other in an indecisive way. He disappeared, but more ants arrived. He must have spread the word: *"Come to the picnic."* A brave one climbed my boot and ran along my chaps. What was a picnic without ants anyway? The rough tree against my back and the ants reminded me of the continuance and normalcy that existed even in times of adversity.

After lunch, I continued work. I saw five strong, healthy men, all heavily armed with knives, pistols, and rifles, by a campfire. They stood ramrod straight, had crew cuts, and were clean-shaven.

"Hello. I'm Cindy, the Wilderness Guard. Having a good day?" I asked.

"Yeah. How's the fishing been?" the tallest one, with deep brown eyes, asked.

"People have been catching lots of graylings. Others have better luck catching golden trout. You know that the limit is three trout or five graylings?" I expected them to know that graylings are identified by their large dorsal fin, whereas trout have a considerably smaller one.

"The Montana Fishing Orders weren't very clear about this area," one said.

"I talked to a Fish and Game officer from Helena. They made it clear," I said. I remembered the game warden at orientation. "We hope to get a few golden trout. Not interested in

graylings," said the blond one.

"What do you plan to do with the guns?" I asked. I had been raised with guns. I accepted them as tools that needed thoughtful use. But I wondered why folks carried such large sidearms; we were not at war with the Scapegoat.

"It's legal to carry guns in the Wilderness," he answered defensively.

"Absolutely. I was just interested."

"Well, if we have a bear in camp, we can protect ourselves."

"Grizzlies are harder to kill than you might realize. A wounded bear is ten times more dangerous than a hungry bear. It would be better to avoid the problem by hanging your food and garbage ten feet from the ground and five feet out from the tree trunk at night," I said.

"I heard about bear-resistant containers. Do you know anything about them?" he asked. It seemed he was becoming interested in information rather than being defensive.

"They resist two hundred pounds of pressure per square inch. There are ammunition boxes that work but are too heavy for backpacking. Heavy PVC pipe with caps on both ends works well. Also, there are recreational equipment suppliers that sell bear-resistant containers."

"Well, I feel good with my gun," he said decisively.

"The federal laws are very stringent regarding killing grizzlies; self-defense does not justify killing," I said.

"Maybe we will hang our food."

I dropped the issue. They had the information they needed. I hoped they would be careful.

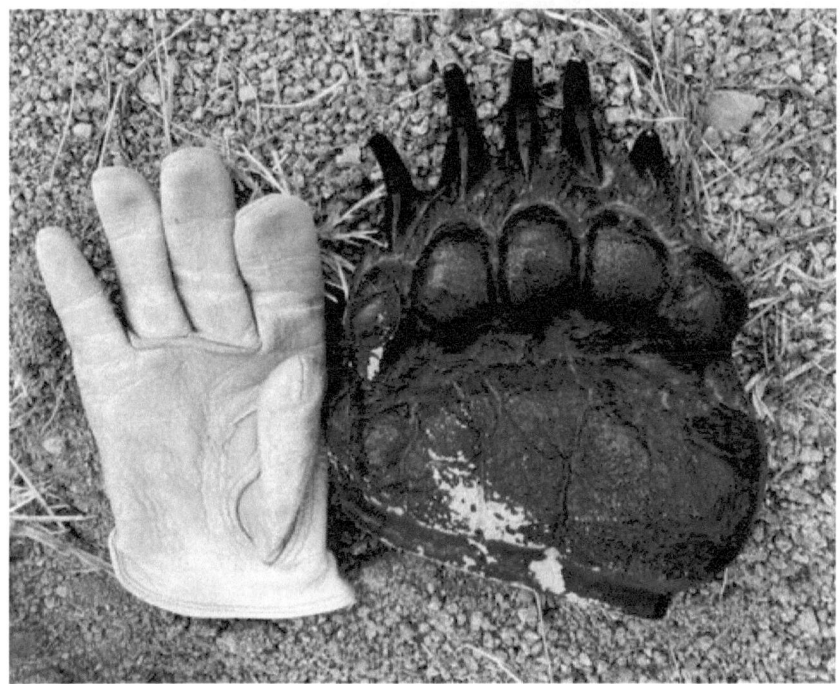

A casting of a grizzly bear print by the Craigheads;
compare the size to my work glove.

In 1959 the Craighead brothers, Frank and John began a 12-year study of grizzly bears in Yellowstone. Later their work continued in Montana, including the Scapegoat Wilderness. They hunted grizzlies in both winter and summer to tranquilize and put radio transmitters on them. In the process, they often surprised grizzlies. By appropriate response, neither the Craigheads nor their fellow researchers were ever mauled, nor did they ever have to shoot a grizzly. Being friends with my parents, I heard them tell the story of a fellow who was attacked by a grizzly while he was releasing it from the live trap. To protect himself from the enraged bear, he shot the grizzly five times. The sixth lucky shot severed the bear's spinal cord, dropped the grizzly, and saved his life. Grizzlies are not easy to kill.

Later, back at Webb, I took care of the stock and put the tack away, as usual.

"Silver King, Peck." I checked off duty on the radio.

"Peck, Silver King."

"Evening radio check." I reported

"How's the leg?"

"About twice its normal size."

"Take care. Have a good evening." He trusted me to ask for help if needed, a sign of respect; I was one of the guys.

"You too."

Ten minutes later, the radio crackled. "Peck, Burns." It was my supervisor.

"Burns, Peck," I answered with angst. Was I in trouble?

"Are you hurt?"

"I think maybe I am," I said as I poured myself a cup of coffee.

"Can you ride? Do you need a helicopter?"

"I can ride. No helicopter. I did my work Friday afternoon and today. There is a place at the top of the fibula that is slightly deformed—looks like pressure from the inside. It may be cracked."

"I want you to come out first thing in the morning." I was hurt and disappointed. I wanted to finish my assigned tour.

"All right." I checked off the radio.

Now they were going to take control. I hated others' taking control of me. I had everything I needed right there in the cabin. I could keep the leg elevated and keep it cool with wet towels, and I would be fine. But I also knew I should see a doctor, must obey, and ride out in the morning.

It was slow going, dragging my heavy, swollen leg, but I cleaned the cabin, as required. I made sure the cabin was supplied with wood and water. I bolted the doors and window.

"Nice morning," I said to a family who were walking the trail single file. The sun was shining. High, scattered cumulus clouds were flying past; a light breeze brought dry air, making for a pleasant morning.

"Why are you riding with your foot out of the stirrup?" asked the girl in the lead.

"I banged my leg pretty badly on Friday," I said.

"My mom is a nurse," she said as her mom approached us.

"It's awfully swollen." Her mom noticed the swelling even through the chaps. "Do you want me to look at it? Is your foot warm? Have you checked the pedal pulse?"

"I think it is warm. I haven't checked the pulse in my foot." I dismounted. The man held Rambo's and Charlie's leads as I unzipped my chaps, pulled my pant leg up, and unlaced my boot. She unwrapped the Ace bandages.

"Why are you riding with that leg?" she asked.

"How else would I get to the road?" I answered.

"I guess you are right. Your foot is warm, and the pulse good," she said. "You are going to see a doctor, aren't you?"

"Yes, I am sure my supervisor is sending me in to see one. Thanks."

She rewrapped my leg; the Ace felt good. I put my boot back on, but it was tighter. The chaps would not zip over my calf.

"Thank you," I said as I kicked Rambo into a walk.

"Good luck. Take care of that leg," they called as they continued to Heart Lake, and I went toward the road.

Jerry met me at the trailhead with Terri. Here goes, I thought. *"Do this! Go there!" Jerry will take control.*

"Terri will drive you to the emergency room in Helena. Here—I'll take care of the horses," he said as he took Rambo and Charlie's lead ropes.

I quickly grabbed my personal gear from Charlie's pack and Rambo's saddlebags before he led them away.

"Get into the truck and off the leg," he said.

I reluctantly obeyed. I knew he was right; I hated orders. Terri was full of questions, as always. "Does it hurt? Were you scared? Why didn't you come right in on Friday?" I did not feel like answering the barrage of questions. I hurt. I had lost control of my life.

"Please, let's go to the bunkhouse first. I'll be quick. I want my wallet. I want out of these boots," I pleaded.

"OK, but make it fast," said Terri.

Terri backtracked to the bunkhouse. I pulled my boots and work clothes off. I slipped into an old denim dress. The dress would make examination and x-rays easier since I could pull it up instead of undressing.

"Oh my!" said the emergency room doctor.

X-rays were taken. The diagnosis was a massive hematoma, with fear of compartment syndrome, which could mean surgery. He wanted the leg elevated and absolutely no weight bearing for four days. I could use crutches to go to the bathroom. I had to see the local doctor next week. If the swelling worsened, I knew it could cut off the blood supply to the muscle, and the muscle would die; my leg might never work right again. This was serious.

Terri drove me around Helena to find crutches and fill my prescription for Tylenol No. 3. I kept my foot elevated on the dashboard.

We stopped at a little café to eat; stir-fried vegetables as I missed fresh greens. I received strange looks with my leg raised on the bench, but so what? I had to do what I had to do.

Back at the bunkhouse, I called Bill. He was worried and gave me all kinds of advice, as had the emergency doctor. Bill was going to send an elastic surgical stocking to keep compression on the leg. I rolled up a big sleeping bag on which to prop my leg and settled in to read. I felt like a beached whale. *What a bore.* I was letting the district down.

I stayed flat on my back, looking at the ceiling, reading, or knitting. But knitting and reading were not exciting after working in the Wilderness with grizzly bears and wolves. I wondered where this turn in life would take me. Would the injury curtail my activity? Would it heal well? Could I continue working?

As I contemplated my work journey, I thought of Robert Frost's famous poem: *"Two roads diverged in a wood, and I took the one less traveled."*

The people at the office remembered me. Dave, the fire management officer, stopped to check on me. On Monday, Jerry and Charley came to see how I was doing, which I appreciated. Another day, Will came by after work. He made a pot of coffee for us and visited.

"We used the hoof tester on BJ, and pus squirted out. He has a deep abscess in his heel. I took him to the veterinarian in Great Falls. He will stay there for a while to be treated." I was glad Will had followed up on my comment about BJ.

"How long before he can be used again?" I asked.

"Well, maybe you and he will be healed about the same time," Will said with a grin. "You know how bad Ribbon has been? Keith and I decided to see how he would pack. We used him to pack the camp into the East Fork. He really objected to such lowly work. He snorted and carried on. But we finally convinced him it was in his interest to cooperate. Worse things could happen."

Will always threatened the animals with *"I'll thump on you"* if they did not behave. But his stern voice and a firm touch from his gnarled hands were all he ever used. I knew he would never hurt an animal.

"He went along pretty good for a while," Will said. "Then he pulled back and rolled himself down a steep hill. Keith hoped he was a goner, but no such luck." He chuckled. "He got himself together and joined the string on the trail. He tried that several times. I don't think he will ever change. I told Jerry the best thing is to sell him before he kills someone."

"Do you think Jerry will get rid of him?" I asked.

"Yes, probably, come winter," said Will.

I thought selling Ribbon was a good idea, as they had tried to use him in different ways but failed to find a use for him. I still thought he was dangerous, and worse, often inexperienced riders were using the Forest Service horses.

The doctor told me I should not drive, so I asked Will, "Would you mind taking me to the post office? I expect a letter from Bill. I was going to fix myself pancakes and sausage for dinner. I can make enough for two if that appeals to you."

"That sounds pretty good."

It had been a week since Rambo rammed me into the tree. The surgical stocking had arrived. It came all the way to my hip. I had to wear a skirt, as my jeans would not go over the swollen leg. Mornings were particularly difficult. I moved gingerly. The doctor finally agreed I could go to work on Monday with light duty.

"Oh my God! What happened to you?" said a lady with her young girl and dog as they came into the bunkhouse.

"I saved a horse from broken ribs; my leg was the bumper between the horse and a tree."

"I'm Rosanna. This is my daughter, Tina, and our dog, Silky. I work for the timber department out of Helena but will be working here for a few days. I'll be filling in information missing in the database for habitat types in certain timber stands," she said as she set her bags down.

Since I was about to be released to light duty, I offered to help, and she was pleased.

I wore my denim skirt, with my white surgical stocking sticking out beneath and I propped my leg on an extra chair. Searching for habitat types was interesting. I used maps and corresponding aerial photographs with overlays. I matched those with file numbers from Rosanna corresponding to each timber stand. While in the office, I had contact with many people whom I had not met previously. That helped me to feel I was part of a team instead of an appendage. Eventually, Rosanna, Tina, and Silky went back to Helena. I would miss their company. I also helped Laura, Jerry's wife, put together a watershed notebook she needed urgently.

Will needed more lead ropes and ties. While sitting with my leg up, I braided ropes for him. It felt like the ranch, where I had back-braided many lead ropes.

Everyone was concerned and helpful. Even Karen was friendly when I went for reimbursement for the crutches and Tylenol No. 3. I filled out papers for workers' compensation. The four days I had been on my back had been holidays. I had missed only one full day of work. Then I worked a week of half-days and a week of full days in the office. Each time I wanted to do more, I had to go to the village doctor for a release. He seemed to let me do what I wanted but did not understand why I would not take advantage of the situation and simply relax.

Will came into the bunkhouse a few days later. "I have to go pick up BJ tomorrow. Would you like to come?"

"I would love to."

"I'll check with Jerry, but I am sure it'll be alright," he said. With Jerry's approval, I went with Will to Great Falls.

We went over Roger's Pass, where, at the summit, I saw the sign for the Continental Divide Trail, which went from Canada to Mexico. As we came down the pass, the grassy plain of eastern Montana undulated to the horizon.

"Those rocks standing in the plains are called the Cockscombs," Will said.

I saw two ridges of solid rock protruding from rolling grasslands. They did looked like a rooster's comb.

"Wolf Creek is a pretty valley that leads toward Helena." I looked south and saw where a valley ran between the Cockscombs and the Rocky Mountains' eastern slope.

The highway dipped to the grassy plain. We crossed a bridge with cottonwood trees and willows.

"This is the Dearborn River. It starts up on Lewis and Clark." Lewis and Clark National Forest had been named because Lewis and Clark's route came through it. "A legend has it that a local Indian tribe led the Lewis and Clark expedition up the headwaters of the Dearborn and over the pass to Alice Creek," Will said. "I grew up in Bynum, just north, near Chouteau."

As we approached Great Falls, I saw the Missouri River. Grassy parks with leafy trees lined the river. Many trees had their trunks underwater from flooding because of all the rain. We wound around city streets to a western store for horse medicine. I had become unused to traffic; felt bombarded by the noise.

The vet had stabled BJ in a clean cement-floored stall. He was shod with a plastic pad to avoid mud or dirt from hindering the healing abscess. He had much healing to do before he could be used. He stepped into the trailer like a gentleman.

"Are you hungry?" Will asked. "There's a place to eat at the junction."

"Yes, that would be nice."

As we approached, I saw a single building with a few cars in front. Two scraggly-looking cottonwood trees struggled to survive beside it. A road turned to the north, with a sign next to the bridge: Sun River.

"I used to work on a ranch on the Sun River, up near Gibson Dam. That was a long time ago. Few of the old ranches are still running," Will told me.

A couple of cowboys were leaning on the bar along one wall. We chose a table along the other wall. Typical of western eateries, they served fried steak, hamburgers, fried chicken, and beans. I had a bowl of beans, a side salad, and a Coke. Will preferred a chicken-fried steak and a cup of coffee.

Back on the road, the late-afternoon sun shone in our eyes. It had been a good day. Will was fun. He had pointed out lots of new country. I remembered reading Ivan Doig's book *English Creek* about that east-slope country at the turn of the century. I thought, *Someday I should come this way and explore Bynum, Chouteau, and Augusta.*

Cabin Sweet Cabin

With a day off and my leg much improved, I went mushroom hunting. The doctor had said that mild exercise would help prevent blood clots from developing. I suspected my mild and his were different but I lived in my body and thought I knew what it could do.

I walked the lodgepole pine woods but recognized only non-edible mushrooms. However, I saw lupines, with their spikes of blue blossoms standing straight, and sticky pink geraniums bobbed gently in the breeze. In wet areas were tiny white Twin Flowers and white-flowered Bunchberries. There were a few dark blue Western Day flowers. I considered flowers my friends. I made a point to know their names. I tried to identify unknown plants in the *Peterson Field Guide* and commit their names to memory.

I took a great inhalation of relaxing mountain air; still found solace and a renewal of my spirit in the wild. I felt as much at home in the forest as I did in my house.

Back at work, Jerry said, "I want you and the crew to finish the Indian Meadows cabin. The administrators from the regional office will be holding an inspection and meeting there soon."

My leg was better, but I thought it was too soon to ride. I was happy to help the crew at the cabin. The crew would be sanding and sealing the ceiling, the walls inside and out, and the floors. My task was the floors; I sat while sanding, scooting along with my leg stretched out on the floor in front of me. If I stood for long, my leg still tended to swell and throb.

Will and the crew erected a canvas wall tent behind the cabin, where the furniture from the cabin would be stored and to provide shelter for us from the daily wet rains. They stacked the furniture as high as they could but kept a dresser clear to use as a table on which the Coleman stove sat to make the all-important coffee. Arranged around it were benches. We sat cramped together, shoulder to shoulder and knee to knee, but enjoyed having a dry, warm place for breaks. Then the tent started to leak, Keith stuck duct tape over the holes.

Race was back to work and took over as ramrod, using his knowledge of the building trade. Race was a precise craftsman of compact, strong build, he sported a heavy, curly head of hair and a sandy-blond beard. He was the hardest worker of a conscientious and hardworking crew. He checked our work to make sure it was up to his standards before we continued to another task.

"Llamas can kick in all four directions at once," Keith told us during a break. "Don't they, Will?" We were crowded in the tent with cups of coffee nestled in our hands.

"It sure looked like it," Will answered.

"We were coming around the corner near where you and Will had the dog incident. We had five pack mules lined out," Keith said.

"Paladin has been wary of that spot ever since," Will added.

"There in front of us was a hiker with two llamas carrying brightly colored packs. Surprised, the llamas jumped straight into the air when they saw us; all four feet stuck out like a grasshopper. The hikers tried to settle the llamas; Paladin went berserk. Will dropped the lead rope and flew off Paladin, landing in the bushes. Paladin stepped away, turned, snorted, and showed the whites of his eyes. Bo shied

Webb Lake Cabin, showing corrals and tack shed to the left.

into the trees, but Skunk stared at the apparition, in preparation to attack with her hooves. The other three mules backed up to escape the craziness, bumping into each other and scrambling for footing. They could not go far all tied together. I was bringing up the rear of Spike, who froze.

"He did not want to get closer to the apparition either," Keith said with a chuckle.

"Good thing I wasn't hurt, just a bit stiff," said Will.

"The llamas were as afraid of the horses as the horses were of them. The hikers were really nice. As soon as they salvaged their scattered things, they took the llamas way off the trail to let us by."

It was fun to work with the crew, swapping stories and joking. Having worked the Wilderness alone since the beginning, I suddenly realized how much I missed good company.

I went with Will to Helena to pick up scaffolding so the tall sections of the cabin could be sanded. Will drove the three-quarter-ton flatbed truck. He took the opportunity to show me more territory.

"This pass was the old route to Helena before the highway over the 6,373-foot newer route was built. I still like this way better. There are old ranches along the way and it's not as steep," Will said.

We arrived at the Helena rental place, where the salesman was busy with other customers. Will decided we should load the pieces we needed. After finishing with the customer, the salesman came to count what we had loaded and filled out the paperwork with Will.

"Looks like lunchtime," said Will, looking at his watch. "How about getting something at the deli counter in the Country Market? We can eat in the truck."

That sounded good to me. I discovered the Country Market, besides the regular food-market fare, specialized in bulk foods. I bought a flat of fresh raspberries, another of blueberries, mason jars, and sugar to make jam for my family and to share with the crew. Will selected a box of hot wings and a tub of melon balls for us to share for lunch. I licked my fingers clean with satisfaction.

Back at Indian Meadows, the crew unloaded the scaffolding and we were back to the station by quitting time. Will helped me carry my supplies into the bunkhouse, and I had a busy evening making jam.

I wanted to do something special for the trail crew, Will, the office people, Jerry, and Charley, who had been so thoughtful during the time of recovery from my smashed leg. I invited them to the bunkhouse on a Friday evening for a Mexican dinner of fajitas, with tortillas, guacamole, Mexican rice, and salad. They were to bring their own beer if they wanted. It was a jolly evening full of camaraderie.

The following week, Race had set the scaffolding up to finish the outside. After all the inside logs were sanded, sealed and dry, we sanded the floor, using electricity from noisy generators brought from the station; the men taking turns running the floor sander. I scooted along the floor sanding the edge where the big sander didn't reach. With sanding finished, Carol and I vacuumed all the walls and floor. We could then seal the floor.

When all was dry, Carol and I had a good time arranging the furniture; washing the dishes, pots, and pans; and putting them in the cupboards. The cabin smelled fresh and looked nice and homey. It was a job we were all proud of, and I was part of their team.

Working on the Indian Meadows cabin reminded me of when Dad had built our log home on the ranch when I was seven. I had my own bedroom with my own back door and small porch. I could climb the attic stairs next to my room and imagine I had a hideaway all to myself.

George lived on the ranch in the winter repairing bridles, saddles, and harnesses in our basement. He taught me to braid leather, back-braid lead ropes, and repair bridles and saddles so I could be helpful.

George could make the most beautiful braided leather bridles, with beautiful intricate knots for attaching to a bit and adjusting the size. My first functional braided piece was a door pull for my grandparents' front door, which tended to stick. But I made many lead ropes and repaired bridles too.

Since those childhood experiences, I have loved making and building things, and I enjoy using my hands and tools. It is great satisfaction to see immediate results. Working with the crew to finish the Indian Meadows cabin gave me that same satisfaction of seeing a job well done. When the Indian Meadows cabin was finished and I was better, I went back to patrolling the Wilderness.

"The Mainline Trail is a mud hole made worse by outfitters taking mule strings into their hunting camps daily," Will told me.

I wanted to avoid the deep mud, so I went to Heart Lake via the Lone Mountain Trail through a back gate. I had yet to go that way, and it was a slightly longer route. I knew I would enjoy seeing new territory. It would also be my first ride since my wreck with Rambo.

"Charley and I have made a new rule for you," said Jerry as he came out of the office. "We don't want you to ride Rambo anymore. You like Brandy; use him, and you can use Luke, a quiet, well-behaved mule. They should work out well for you. By the way, your hat is showing its age."

"It keeps me dry." I defended my old brown Stetson, which had served me well for twenty years.

"Your tent should keep you dry too," he said, referring to my Australian duster. *Cowboys only tease people they like; maybe I had moved up in Jerry's estimation I thought.*

"Thanks," I said sarcastically. "Bye. See you Tuesday." I grabbed the radio from the shelf and headed to the truck.

"Peck, Jones." Keith was calling me on the radio.

"Could you bring us some twelve-inch spikes?" asked Keith.

"Where are they?"

"You'll have to buy some. We used all the ones from the barn."

I made arrangements with Karen and went to Ace Hardware.

It was August, and I was preparing for another trip into the Wilderness. I drove to the pasture west of town, honked, and called, as usual, but there was no response. I could not see the stock anywhere. I turned the truck and trailer around. I drove back along the side road and highway, looking more carefully for signs of the animals.

Still finding nothing, I drove around to a driveway that might give me a view of the back side of the pasture. That failed, but it did show me how big and deep the stream that entered the pasture was. I had difficulty turning the truck and trailer around on the narrow driveway. I felt useless, I could not even find the horses.

After parking back on the highway, I took two halters and the bucket of grain cakes, ducked through the barbed- wire fence, and went searching toward the willows that surrounded the stream, an area hidden from outside the pasture.

"Come on, boys! Come 'n' get it!" I called into the wind, and I shook the bucket of grain cakes. The rattling noise usually brought them running. I was feeling incompetent and foolish. I found a way over one part of the stream, where I could get deeper into the willows. I thought I heard movement and struggled through more willows. I could see them across the wide, deep stream in a nice, grassy green park.

"Come on, boys! Come 'n' get it!" I repeated for the umpteenth time. Rambo and Oscar lifted their heads to acknowledge me but continued grazing. I kept calling while I looked for a rock to throw at them, thinking if I could break their inertia, maybe they would come my way. I found a small stone and underhanded it toward them, and they milled around but would not come. They had been working hard for several months; perhaps they wanted more days off work. Although I could sympathize with them, that did not help me do my job.

I looked at the stream. I was not going to wade the hip-deep cold water. If I waded through the stream, my boots would be wet for five days. With no change of boots and would probably ruin the ones I wore, I knew I would have to call for help, even though that would be embarrassing.

I retraced my steps through the willows, crossed the small stream, crawled through the fence, and crossed the highway. I called on my radio for help, but there was no response. I was near tears in frustration when I turned the truck around and drove to the station to tell my tale of woe.

"Charley, come help Cindy catch the horses!" Jerry shouted down the hall.

I was sure everybody was thinking, *Cindy can't even catch a horse.*

"We'll follow you," Charley said as they headed for another truck.

I returned to the wide spot where I had parked before; they pulled in behind me. The slamming of their truck doors assaulted me like a reprimand: *Can't you do anything right?*

We ducked through the fence with halters and the grain bucket. I led Jerry and Charley to where I had last seen the horses and mules, over the side channel and through the willows.

"Come on, boys! Come on!" Jerry called with his familiar-to-them voice.

They pricked up their ears but did not come. Jerry and Charley obviously did not want to wade the deep stream either. I felt vindicated. Charley found a stone and tossed it at the nearest mule, who jumped, bumped into a horse, and stirred up the herd. He tossed another stone, hitting one of the horses. That set them in motion, and they came splashing across the stream at a run.

We waded the side stream and intercepted them by a stand of Douglas first. I caught Brandy, and Jerry nabbed Luke. Since it was the first tour, I had used Luke, Jerry felt obliged to give me directions. "Luke is an old mule. We don't use him hard," he said as he handed me the lead.

"We'll drive the rig around and meet you at the corrals," Charley said as they went for the trucks.

I had eighteen horses milling around me as I led Brandy and Luke. The corrals seemed a long way off. I walked as fast as I could, tried to run, to extricate us from the rest of the running herd, pulling the reluctant Luke and Brandy behind me. We finally made it to the corrals and loaded up. It was a relief to be out of sight of Charley's and Jerry's accusatory looks.

We were on the Lone Mountain trail, Brandy was being his normal well-behaved self again, and Luke led well. What a joy he was, especially after the stubborn mule Charlie. I found a tree had fallen across the trail, so I pulled the crosscut out of the pack. While Brandy and Luke stood waiting patiently, I made the two cuts and removed the log.

Lupines covered the ground, and Brandy thought they were candy. He looked funny when he grabbed a bite—a mottled red horse with a bouquet of blue flowers in his mouth.

We followed another swale filled with flowers: creamy marsh marigolds, yellow columbines, tall dark blue monkshoods, and white globe flowers were abundant. It was a scene worthy of Monet. We skirted the south slope of Lone Mountain. As we gained altitude, the vegetation changed to lodgepole pines interspersed with aspens.

I saw movement out of the corner of my eye. Brandy perked up his ears as a young black bear scampered along the trail and ducked into the timber. I noticed lots of bear signs: dead tree stumps were dug out at the base, and old logs had been rolled over as the bears looked for ants and other insects, good protein sources. I was enjoying being off the muddy Mainline trail.

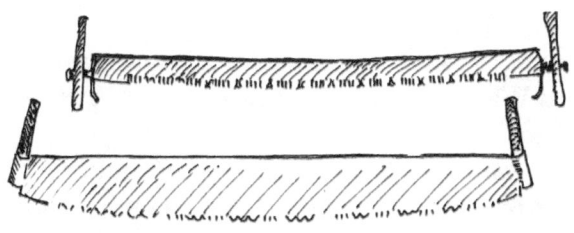

CHAPTER 11

Gros Ventre Trip with Dad

LISTENING TO THE CLIP-CLOP OF BRANDY AND LUKE'S STEPS AND enjoying the flowers and grass floor of the lodgepole pine forest took me back to a different kind of trip I had taken with Dad years ago, when I was nineteen.

White Grass had planned three dude trips going into the Gros Ventre country east of Jackson Hole. One pack trip had gone in for several days of riding and fishing in the high mountain lakes and streams and left the camp set up for the following trips. The weather turned cold and rainy; as a result, the second and third trips were canceled.

Since we were short-handed on the ranch, Dad called on me. He needed me to ride with him into the backcountry camp to help break camp and pack it up to bring to the ranch. We trailered our two riding horses and five pack horses with Little Man and Carlie, our dogs. We stopped at the end of the narrow dirt Gros Ventre Road. We had little to pack, since we were told the camp was already set up, and there was lots of canned food left there. Dad took a shortcut cross-country, which did not help us arrive at camp faster. Dad's shortcuts were always interesting but seldom faster. It was my pup Carlie's first pack trip. He followed Little Man, Dad's dog, who knew the routine.

At the camp, we unpacked, unsaddled the horses, and picketed the leaders; the others were turned loose in the same meadow; they would stay together. Horses are herd animals; when the leaders are tied, the others usually remain nearby, but there were a few individualists that could not be trusted, so it was essential to know each horse's characteristics. We would listen all night for the quiet that descended when no horses were stomping, munching, or intermittently nickering to each other. With the stock taken care of, we began to take care of ourselves.

"I'll get the water while you light the fire and organize dinner," Dad said as he picked up the pail and headed for the creek with Little Man and my puppy Carlie tagging along.

"Do you want a drink?" Dad asked as he returned from the creek. I was squatting over the fire, coaxing it to burn the damp wood.

"Yes, thanks. I'll be right there," I responded as I blew on the first embers, increasing it to flames and then turned to sit on the log.

Dad handed me a cup. It had been a long ride. I was tired and thirsty. I took a big swallow, only to find I had fire in my mouth; fumes went down my throat, burned out my nose. I could hardly breathe and tears stung my eyes. I tried to hide my misery so I would not hurt Dad's feelings. He thought he was treating me as an adult.

"I made martinis. I put them in my saddlebag to enjoy tonight," he said, sounding pleased with himself.

When he was not looking, I poured the warm martini out and filled my cup with the cool stream water that I had originally anticipated. He cured me, though. I have never again drunk a martini.

Dad talked about his plan to bring the camp out by a different route. He had spoken to the old-timers about a route from the Gros Ventre to Granite Creek. The directions were to follow a ridge above the treeline, stay left of Granite Peak, and pick up a game trail that went along the drainage of Granite Creek, and the ranch truck would meet us at Slim Bassett's place at the bottom of Granite Canyon. But plans do not always coincide with reality.

Before going to bed, we took down the extra tents and organized camp for easier packing in the morning. Shortly after dark, we doused the fire and burrowed into our sleeping bags. Carlie and Little Man curled between us. Dad talked excitedly about exploring new territory in the morning. Soon the faint night noises lulled me to sleep.

Morning was cool and damp; heavy dew coated everything. As soon as the sun came out, camp dried quickly, so we could pack. The horses were still grazing peacefully in the meadow and were easy to catch, and packing went well. We headed south.

The jagged peak that was our landmark looked a long way off as we climbed above timberline. I saw no more lush, stately lodgepole

CYNTHIA GALEY PECK 275

forest, only scruffy, wind-blown trees tucked into slight hollows or behind protective boulders. The exposed rocks were covered with green and gray lichens, and the meager grass struggled to grow in crevasses among the rocks. We wound our way to the southwest, toward the peak.

We stopped by a puny stream to eat our Spam and crackers; the only food left in camp—the pack group had been mistaken about the amount of food. The meager dinner the night before was the same menu. I hate Spam and could hardly eat it but knew I must. I did not know when the next meal might be.

Three peaks loomed to our right. Dad chose one and went to the left of it, as per the directions. We headed down the steep drainage. Dad was leading a packhorse; the others were loose and followed. They sat on their haunches and slid downhill. I rode drag, if they wandered, I was supposed to herd them back in line. There were pieces of game trails at narrow crossings but no real trail.

Near dusk, Dad decided the drainage was veering too far south; he thought we should have been going west, one drainage over. He turned west over a series of more steep hills, bogs, and downed trees. The pack horses barely fit between the close-growing trees. No game trails were visible. Dark descended. Dad kept whistling; I knew he was ahead. I tried to keep count of the five undulating, jumping white tarps representing the five pack horses weaving their way through trees and over logs. I could see two or three and occasionally four white tarps. Fortunately, I always heard Dad's whistling and knew that none of the horses would wander off by himself.

My pup Carlie was exhausted, so I lifted him in front of me onto the saddle. He was unhappy. Even Little Man lagged instead of romping up front, as he usually did. I would see his light coat following me occasionally. My legs were sore, and my back ached. If I had had a choice, I would have found a dry spot and camped, but Dad kept going. *Some shortcut!* There was no moon, but the stars were bright, indicating a clear sky and no bad weather approaching.

Finally, Dad called, "Lights below us! Must be Slim's." Dad's internal compass was right again.

I was so tired, hungry, thirsty, and sore I hardly cared, but I looked for the light. It shone like a small, lost fallen star way down the canyon. We still had a long way to go.

An eternity later, I heard a welcoming "Hello" from Slim, a gnarled, bowlegged, aging cowboy. "We've been watching for ya. Have any trouble?" He grinned.

Monty, Slim's grandson, brought the truck to pick us up. We all pitched in to take care of the horses. Afterward, we gladly accepted Slim's offer of dinner in his warm, cheerful little log cabin, and a mountain sheep roast in the wood range looked too good to believe. It was one o'clock in the morning, about twelve hours since the ghastly Spam and crackers. I am sure the roasted mountain sheep dinner would have been superb anytime, but it was especially welcome that night.

We did not linger and were soon driving the sixty miles of winding road back to the ranch. Monty brought his dog so we had the five horses and gear in the back of the stock truck and three dogs with the three of us in the cab. It was cozy and smelly, to say the least.

Hunting Season Approaches

By the time I was through reminiscing, Heart Lake was in sight. I had a job to do: more picking up trash, cleaning fire circles, burying feces, and trying to teach the campers Leave-no-Trace ethics.

I noticed the hitching rail was broken. I tied Brandy and Luke to nearby trees, grabbed the ax, and proceeded to fell a likely dead tree to replace the hitching rail. I scrutinized a way to fell the tree away from others. I made an undercut to direct its fall and then went to the opposite side to finish chopping it. The tree was taller than I had estimated, and it hung high in another tree, despite my planning. If I could not pull it loose by myself, I could use Brandy, but I tugged and pulled, and it crashed to the earth. I paced off the length I would need to fit between the tree posts and chopped off the excess. I dragged it, set the rail on my hip, and nailed it to the posts. I moved Brandy and Luke to the rail so they would not damage more tree roots. I then walked around the lake to inform people as usual.

"Hello. I'm Cindy, the Wilderness Guard. How are you on this fine day?"

"Great. Come by the fire, and warm up," said a man who stood ramrod tall with two boys over by a campfire.

"Thanks."

"I'm Harry, and these are my sons, Jim and Mark," he said. "We come from Malmstrom Air Force Base outside Great Falls."

I saw several people fishing farther along the shore. "What do you do?" Jim asked.

"Is that a mule?" Mark asked. "Is that your horse?"

The boys were full of questions. I answered and explained bear safety and low-impact camping.

"I know this is bear country, but I've never seen a bear here," Harry said. "I'm not going to worry. Besides, I have my gun."

"I saw a black bear just a little while ago near the lake. Also saw a grizzly over that ridge a few weeks ago," I said.

"You sure it was a grizzly?"

"He was coming down the trail toward me. I got a good look. Don't think I could be mistaken."

"What did it do?" Suddenly, there was more interest.

"He ran into the timber, and I didn't see him again. He was a young bear, probably establishing his own territory. Grizzlies are territorial. He will be using this area again, looking for food."

"Will he come into camp?" Mark asked.

"If he smells food and thinks he can get it, he might. It's good to keep your food hung in a tree ten feet up and five feet out from the trunk," I said as I pointed to a tall pine.

"That's not easy."

"True, but having a bear in camp is a lot worse. Someone could get hurt badly. Your carelessness could train the bear to feed in campsites and possibly cost the bear his life. You wouldn't want that, right?" I knew people had been killed by grizzlies north of Scapegoat in Glacier National Park.

"No."

"I see you've been catching some fish," I said as I approached their fire.

"Yes, we are about to put them on the fire for lunch." The boy held up a string of four pan-sized trout.

"Please break the air sac in the guts and throw them as far as possible into the lake. That way, they will not attract any bears," I said as the father took his knife out of his pocket.

"We hadn't thought of that," Harry said. "This area is so clean. I am glad people are taking care of it."

"Most campers are careful. However, this area is clean because I pick up garbage every week. The biggest problems are toilet paper with smelly deposits left behind trees and aluminum foil and cans left in the fire circles," I replied.

"What am I supposed to do?"

"In this area, the best method is to dig a cat hole four to six inches deep, deposit your feces and paper, and then cover it up. Place any vegetation back in its original position."

"I always thought you should burn the garbage."

"If there is a hot fire, some garbage will burn, but wind blows paper, which could start a blaze. Even putting the cans and aluminum foil in the fire to burn off smelly stuff is fine, but you need to go through the ashes and pack out any foil, cans, or other garbage that did not burn completely."

"I saw a can dump up on that ridge," Jim said. "Do you want me to show it to you?"

"Thanks. I will need to pack all that out."

We went up the ridge, under a large Douglas fir and behind a fallen log, there was a large trash heap. There was a new blue plastic tarp, ladies' casual shoes, and cans. Another layer exposed two small Dutch ovens, an air mattress, and a foot pump. Under that were several layers of cans, including a few dating back to real tin cans with lead on their bottoms. We spread the tarp, piled everything onto it, and dragged it back to the hitching rail, where Brandy and Luke were waiting. Luke shied from the crunchy-sounding tarp, but he let me load everything onto him, the panniers were full.

Twin Lakes Reroute

Will had been preparing for the construction of the reroute by Twin Lakes that Jerry, Charley, and I had flagged earlier.

He borrowed two mules, Muffin and Stanley, from another district to help pack the two-by-six-inch and four-foot-long decking to the bridge site. Will loved Muffin, a small mule. She seemed to be compatible with him better than anyone else on the crew, it seemed the feeling was mutual. She was sensitive about her hind end. He chuckled when she kicked at him when he put the breeching in place. He admired her spirit and her strength.

Each mule was packed with two manti bundles of decking, one on each side. Will led the first mule. Each successive mule's lead rope was tied to a loop in the back of the front mule's packsaddle. He tied the balky Charlie behind Muffin. When Muffin was tired of pulling Charlie along, she would kick him. He would keep up for a while. Again, he would lag and pull back. He would be kicked again and keep up for a while. Soon he learned that when Muffin put her ears back as a warning, he should pick up his pace, or she would kick him. I was tickled that Muffin could put Charlie in his place. I was glad I did not have to deal with that stubborn mule anymore. I liked Stanley. He was easy to pack and he led well.

"I want you to patrol the Landers Fork Trail. Clear any downed trees, and see if the outfitter camp is occupied up Baking Powder Creek," Jerry told me in one of his rare directives. "The trail to the Baking Powder Creek camp is to the right, a little past the Landers Fork Crossing."

I planned to take Brandy and Stanley with me on this trip. The stock had been moved to the Indian Meadows pasture. I did not have to chase them through the willows and across the stream. I no longer had to trailer them to Indian Meadows.

The Landers Fork drainage was a tributary to the Blackfoot River, which was famous for its trout fishing. Fly-fishing had become an institution along with the Blackfoot as popular as football games on New Year's Day.

We went over a ridge of thin, tall lodgepole pines and descended to a ford of the Landers Fork River. The crossing looked to be twenty feet across. It had large rocks sticking out of the rushing white-capped water and boiling currents. As we crossed, the water was above Brandy's knees and higher on the short Stanley. They both slipped occasionally on the rocky bottom. I was precariously perched on top. It would have been a treacherous crossing if the water had been higher, but Brandy took his time picking his way carefully, and Stanley followed.

I found a leaner, a tree that was hung up high in another tree; also called widow-makers because of the danger of their falling. It is difficult to tell which way these trees will fall when cut. This one was across the trail, so I had to cut it out. I tied Brandy and Stanley to trees at a safe distance and unpacked the crosscut saw and ax. The place to cut it was shoulder high, which was difficult and dangerous.

If the ax slipped, it could easily slash me. The tree was a spruce with tough, hard wood. I chopped for a while but finished the job with the crosscut. The tree snapped sideways. I jumped out of the way. Luckily, it missed me. Since the top of the tree was still caught, I had to make another cut with the ax. When it fell, I rolled and pulled the heavy log from the trail. I was breathing hard and sweating as I packed the crosscut saw back on Stanley.

The trail continued along the side of the canyon; big, billowing white clouds scampered across the sky outlining Red Mountain and the dark stands of timber on its lower shoulders. Below me, the roaring creek wound its way through the canyon. The rushing water flowed against the bank, erosion, causing a exposed a wall of mineral soil that glistened in the sun.

I was enjoying the rare sunshine. I took pictures and enjoyed myself. Scattered under the mature lodgepole pines were bunches of Oregon grapes. The cold weather had turned their leaves bright red. Sunrays highlighted their dusty blue-purple berries. Some lupines still had their blue flower clusters, though most were only showing bunches of orange six-fingered leaves. It was beginning to look like fall. Under the thicker timber were low carpets of twinberries, with their shiny dark leaves forming large, tightly woven mats hugging the earth. Their flowers stood proudly two or three inches above their leaves. Their tiny light pink flowers bobbed in the breeze. Standing taller in the mats of twin berries were ethereal meadow rues. They had scattered fern- like leaves, yellow stamens hung from thread-like reddish stalks that swung with the slightest movement of air.

Brandy stopped and looked suspiciously at the small bridge ahead. Because he was a level-headed friend, I respected his judgment. If he was distrustful of the bridge, I figured I had better investigate. On inspection, I saw the supporting logs looked solid, but one of the deck logs was rotten. I knew that unless it was fixed, a horse's hoof could become stuck between the logs and be injured. I made a temporary repair by kicking out the rotten log and nesting another log I cut to size. I had no nails to secure it. When I led Brandy across with Stanley following, they accepted my repair job without balking.

The trail descended and crossed Lookout Creek, a tributary of Landers Fork. I saw bear tracks. The bear was following the trail in front of me. Brandy raised his head to look around and perked up his ears. The tracks were fresh. I began to talk aloud. *"How are you doing, Brandy? Do you smell the bear? You sure are a good horse. I see your pack is riding well, Stanley."* My voice would calm Brandy and let the bear know I was near. It gave him a chance to avoid me. Grizzlies want to avoid an encounter much like people want to avoid an encounter with them. Grizzlies were hunted through 1992, so they still had a healthy respect for humans.

Crossing Bighorn Creek, I saw fresh, distinct tracks. I measured a print with my hand: it was seven inches, with the claw marks measuring another four inches. That made the grizzly paw eleven inches long—a big one—and the bear was still following the trail in front of me.

Bears look for lots of highly nutritious food during the summer to put on weight for winter hibernation. Man is their only predator, yet they do not fear man, as they can tear a human apart with one swipe of their massive claws. They are opportunists and are smart. If they find food in a camp, they will return.

Before we had refrigeration at White Grass Ranch, food was stored in airtight metal containers immersed in the stream. A black bear could smell and get the food even in those containers, and grizzlies are much stronger. Grizzlies can easily bite through tin cans or dig up garbage, as I had seen with the buried horse on Meadow Creek.

I knew the Nader outfitter camp was nearby, and the tracks were heading that way. I decided to check whether they had had any grizzly trouble. As I came out of the timber and looked across the small meadow, I saw smoke rising from the chimney of the cook tent. Someone must be here.

"Hello?" I stopped Brandy by the corral's hitching rail a distance from the tents, it is Western etiquette to stop a distance from camp and call. I heard a radio, but no one was answering. The two horses in the corral were restless and nervous, pacing the length of the corral, snorting with nostrils expanded. Brandy and Stanley were stamping the ground, alert and looking anxiously around. No one liked being near a grizzly, and the horses sure smelled one.

Anyone home?" I called louder.

A young man came from the cook tent.

"Good morning. I'm Cindy, the Wilderness Guard. I noticed grizzly tracks coming this way."

"Name's Tim. Yeah, grizzly's been in the grain cake. Left dumps all over."

What did he mean by *dumps*? I asked myself as I dismounted and tied my animals to the hitching rail. I had known bears to bury food. When I was a child, a black bear had stolen a pig from the ranch pen. As Dad had tracked her, he had seen where she had made piles of leaves and dirt in several places; he had found where she had buried the pig carcass, and later, he had found the bear. She had been in poor condition and had twin cubs with her. She must have been desperate for food to chance coming right into the ranch in daylight to steal a pig. I wondered if the dumps, as Tim called them, were buried food.

Tim showed me several scat piles—that was what he had meant by *dumps*. The high-protein grain must have given him a stomachache to leave so much manure.

"Were you in camp when the grizzly was here?"

"No. We just came in last night. I figure he must have eaten sixty or seventy pounds of grain from the bags he pulled off the haystack."

"Was there any other damage?"

"He went through the cook tent, making his own doors. He'd not bothered anything in the tent, it must've been too full of grain," said Tim as we walked to the cook tent, which had great slashes on both sides, as if made by a sharp knife.

"This is Sally." Tim introduced me to the young gal in the tent.

"If the flaps and sides of the tent are pulled up, the grizzly will still go through but won't damage the tent," I told them.

"Oh? Didn't know that. The dogs have been real restless, barking and running around all the time. The horses are restless too," Sally said as she carried the dishpan outside to throw the water out.

I noticed many particles of food on the ground where she had been throwing the dishwater. "Those food particles may also attract grizzlies into camp," I said. "You should scrape the dishes well or strain the water through cheesecloth to catch the small food particles. That way, you can keep the garbage together and hang it ten feet up and five feet out from a tree trunk. It's best to hang the grain pellets too. The grizzly will probably return."

"The boss doesn't want to bother. Sally and I are scared. If the grizzly comes back, we're outta here."

I had done what I could by explaining actions for grizzly safety, so I mounted Brandy, grabed Stanley's lead and went on my way. Their decision and the camp were not my responsibility but, for safety, I sure hoped they followed my directives.

As the hunting season progressed, there would be more problems with grizzlies in hunting camps because food was not stored properly. Previously, a hunter had killed a grizzly in camp. The wildlife officer had ridden into the Wilderness to inspect the incident and given the hunter a citation. Another problem grizzly had continued to kill sheep along Alice Creek. The state wildlife officer finally had to kill it. Maybe the grizzlies from farther north, who were known for killing hikers, were wandering into the Scapegoat Wilderness. Encounters usually ended with a dead grizzly, though it was seldom at fault. The trail crew had been living in the wild with grizzlies all summer and had not had an incident. Taking proper care of the camp made a difference.

Bears are not the only animals that can hurt you in the backcountry. As a preteen in Wyoming, I was sent into Wister Draw to look for missing horses. Wister Draw was a dark, heavily wooded old forest that brought to mind werewolf stories in Transylvania. It was scary, with big, gnarled, rotting stumps and formidable tree trunks. I hated going there, but I hid my fear. If the wranglers knew Wister Draw frightened me, they would tease me unmercifully, calling me a sissy, scaredy-cat, and such.

Riding bareback on Shane, I weaved my way through the darkest part of the thick Douglas fir forest, trying to be brave. Every stump looked like a black bear ready to attack. Shane was skittish, afraid of something he smelled. I stopped and listened for the horse bells, as I was looking for horses. It was unnaturally quiet. I was relieved to be near the end of a little-used trail. I heard a high-pitched screech pierce the air. I nearly jumped out of my skin when the osprey hit me. Frightened, Shane started to run as fast as he could through the heavy timber, jumping over many downed logs. With no saddle obstructing me, I lay flat on his back with my arms around his neck. I urged him on. The two ospreys took turns dive-bombing me, with one coming from the left and the other from the right, trying to drive us from their nesting area. It was a successful tactic, as Shane and I were leaving as fast as we could. The thick trees did not seem to hamper the ospreys' efforts to attack, as they hit me several times.

Finally, the thin trail dipped, and the ospreys fell back. We slowed. I rubbed my back. My hand had blood on it. My shirt was torn and I failed to find the lost horses. It was a bad day.

284 WYOMING RANCH GIRL

Although the ospreys had hurt me, I did not hold it against them. They were parents protecting their home and children. It was an instinct needed to continue the species. The thick timber protected their nest. The Snake River, where they caught most of their food, was about a mile away, an easy distance for ospreys. I was afraid of Wister Draw for some time and made excuses to avoid going there.

As I left Heart Lake, the big, billowy white clouds turned black and threatening. The wind picked up. I expected it would be raining again before I arrived at the Webb Guard Station.

Snug in Webb cabin, with dishes washed and put away, I enjoyed the fire crackling in the range, which gave a faint sweet odor of wood smoke mixed with pleasant dinner smells. I thought of the campers and hoped they would hang their food to stay safe from the grizzly. The rain was splashing from the eaves. The dreary weather reminded me of the dark, forbidding feeling of Wister Draw.

I had another evening of solitude as I sat at the table, working on my algebra. I had been taking college classes from the extension service of Eastern Arizona College, working toward a degree in the hope of making a better living. Since I would not be home at the start of the fall semester, I had arranged for the books and assignment schedule to be mailed. With their arrival, I had six weeks of college algebra to do by myself. I carried the algebra book with me everywhere: to the Laundromat, to Webb cabin, and on my day-off excursions. At the bunkhouse, I would rise at five thirty and study for an hour or more. At Webb cabin, when I burned out on working on equations, I would read my flower-identification book by the flickering light of the hissing lantern. It felt nostalgic. I imagined the smell of Dad's aromatic pipe from my childhood at the ranch kitchen in winter, where we sat around the table with a hissing and flickering propane lantern. It was a warm family remembrance.

I looked at my watch; it was bedtime. I had another long day of work ahead.

Riding the Top of the Rockies

"Cindy, I want you to go with Keith and Carol on the Continental Divide Trail," said Jerry. "Take tools for sign repairs."

Keith and Carol's tasks included trail maintenance and downed-tree removal. My tasks would be installation of signs, patrol and inventory campsites along the remote Continental Divide Trail. Carol told me it should take five days to traverse the route from Alice Creek Trailhead to Webb cabin.

Will drove, with Keith and me, pulling the big trailer with the four horses and three mules to the Alice Creek Trailhead. Will and I unloaded the stock trailer and started brushing the stock in preparation to saddle. Keith unloaded the truck and mantied our supplies and personal duffels in preparation to pack them on the mules.

Race and Carol had gone to the market and were bringing her dog, Smoky, and Keith's dog, Shoe String. Dogs were not allowed in the Forest Service trucks but could come on the trail. While we waited for Race and Carol, I talked to a man who was leaning against his pickup attached to an empty two-horse trailer.

"Hi. I see you have a horse trailer, but where are your horses?" I greeted him with a smile.

"My wife and her friend are riding," he said.

"We'll be riding up the Continental Divide Trail for several days. Did your wife go that way?"

"No, she went up Lewis and Clark Pass," the man said. He was referring to the shortcut Lewis had taken from Great Falls on the Missouri. Meanwhile, Clark had gone back to the Jefferson River to retrieve their cache. Lewis had planned to meet Clark above the Marias River.

Will ambled over, always glad for conversation. "Indians told him about the shortcut," Will said. "It was much shorter and easier than Clark's route."

"They must have come up the Clark's Fork and the Blackfoot River then?" I asked as we stood and looked up the trail. Montana's eastern front of the Rocky Mountains has few passes. I hoped to walk to the top of that pass before I returned to Arizona. I thought it would be a nice outing on a day off.

"Must have," Will responded as we heard a truck coming up the road behind us. We said goodbye and went to pack the mules.

Race and Carol had arrived with the supplies. The dogs jumped out of Keith's truck to run around with tails wagging, yipping in excitement, happy to be going on the trail. Carol had brought maple-iced doughnuts and hot coffee for us all. It was a nice surprise. A car cannot run without gas, and the trail crew could not work without coffee.

The bear boxes, which were really ammunition boxes, were packed with all the kitchen items, plus fifty-pound bags of grain cake and our food. When loaded, each box weighed ninety to ninety-five pounds. It was a load for Comet. The personal-duffel manti was a load of 180 pounds on Skunk. Cam carried the loose items, such as tools, trail signs, electric fencing, a Coleman stove, a lantern, tents, and extra gas. He had the easiest job, with a 150-pound load. Extra rubber boots were also stuffed within easy reach into the corners of the panniers. A good mule should not have a problem carrying two hundred pounds if the load is balanced properly which is too much for a horse, thus, many packers prefer mules.

With everything loaded and tied properly, we were on the trail by eleven o'clock. Will surprised me with a friendly goodbye hug before I mounted.

"Remember, we have a fence to build when you get back," he called to Keith.

"Right," said Keith as we pulled out. Race waved.

The trail followed the Alice Creek drainage which curved west straight up to the Divide in three miles of several steep switchbacks. It was a long, hard pull for the stock but did not bother Smoky and Shoe, who were trying to run ahead; their proper place was behind the last animal. At the junction of the Alice Creek Trail and the Continental Divide Trail, the sign was missing. I cut the branches off a wind-blown tree with an ax to flatten a place to nail the sign.

Keith and Carol stayed mounted but encouraged me. "You need to get that higher branch."

"Push the sign a little higher."

"The right side should go up more. Too much. Down a little. OK, nail it."

I found their directions good fun.

We watched the storm clouds as we followed the treeless, wind-swept ridge at 8,137 feet of elevation; thunderstorms threatened us from all sides. As far as the eye could see, white-capped mountains spread like waves on an ocean—tidal waves with combers all the way to the Canadian border, scattered whitecaps as far as the Flathead Lake Valley, and large swells. Only to the east could I see the mountains tapering to the rolling hills and grasslands of eastern Montana. The trail stretched miles in front of us as it undulated with the ridges of the Continental Divide. A few wind-blown, misshapen dwarf trees clung to the edges of the ridges. We held on to our hats and tipped our heads against the wind. The horses' tails flew leeward. As evening shadows lengthened, we rode off the ridge to the small cirque called Valley of the Moon, which would be our camp for the next two nights.

Keith enclosed a grassy area, with the portable electric fence for the animals. The fence consisted of fiberglass stakes pounded into the ground with special plastic fasteners attached. Plastic-woven ribbon with fine wires inside was threaded through the fasteners. The gate was a clamp with a plastic handle that connected to the D- battery charger, forming a rough circle. It was all compact and easy to put up, take down, and pack.

At dark, two horses were tied to a highline as a precaution. If the other horses broke out of the fence, we would have the tied horses to round them up. A highline is a rope strung seven feet off the ground between two trees. The horses were tied near the middle of the line about five feet apart to keep them from tangling and far enough from the tree trunks to prevent root damage.

We always cared for the animals first, like Dad had taught me. After the horses were unpacked and put out to graze, we put up the tents and kitchen tarp. Carol and I tied the kitchen tarp between three trees, with a makeshift pole at the fourth corner. Keith arranged the bear boxes under the kitchen fly to complete the kitchen.

As we secured camp and put gear undercover, a hard wind accompanying a thunderstorm came over the ridge. The ground quickly turned white with hail and snow. We pulled the tack under the kitchen fly to keep it dry. Keith squatted against an upturned saddle with his collar turned up, his silk scarf tied around his neck, and his chin tucked in like a turtle. The wet Shoe String climbed into Keith's lap. Scurrying around the crowded kitchen on her knees, Carol fixed dinner: hash browns and boneless pork chops. I lit the Coleman lantern. We ate in a hurry so we could crawl into the tents out of the wind. Keith decided to put the saddles in their tent.

As I went to my two-man North Face tent, I found it had collapsed under the weight of the snow. What am I going to do? I thought as I looked at the forlorn, faded lavender tent that had served me well for many years.

"Why don't you join us in the dome tent?" Carol said to me. "There's enough room."

"I'll hang the lantern in the tent. It'll warm up," Keith said.

"I would like that, if it won't be too crowded." I thought of the three of us and the two dogs all curled up with the saddles sandwiching us. It would be togetherness for sure. I transferred my duffel, sleeping bag, and Therm-a-Rest pad into the dome tent.

Keith and Carol were using the horse blankets for mattresses. It was smelly, but it kept the pads from getting soaked and the cold from seeping into their bones during the night. The propane lantern provided good light and a little warmth. Keith slept on the left side of the tent with his dog between him and the wall. Carol slept on the right side with her dog between her and the other wall. I was in the middle with my duffel under my head. When one of us turned over, we all had to adjust positions.

The crowding reminded me of my first backpack trip with Bill. We went to the Green River Lakes north of Pinedale, Wyoming, on a nice summer day. Our dogs ran ahead, scouting the trail, and we followed at a leisurely pace. When the sun started dipping in the west, we found a camping place. As the weather changed quickly in the mountains, it started to rain. We set the pup tent up in a hurry, threw our backpacks inside, and followed, as did the dogs. We scrambled to find space for everyone. We ate a cold dinner and slid into our bags early, hoping for clear weather in the morning. My head was on my lumpy backpack, the dogs trampled us, taking a long time to settle. My dog curled up in the crook of my stomach as I lay on my side. Bill was on his side, curled against me, with his dog curled in the crook of his knees. His feet were on his backpack. If anyone moved, everyone had to shift. Bill and I awoke stiff and sore from the cramped and restless night. It was still raining, so we packed up and headed home. In comparison, the night with Keith and Carol was uptown comfortable.

At the Valley of the Moon camp, we woke to over an inch of snow. Carol started the coffee and water for oatmeal. Keith and I made lunches to eat on the trail: compressed turkey sandwiches, fruit leather, jerky, and Twix candy bars. We sat on the ground under the fly to eat. Shoe climbed back onto Keith's lap. The shivering Smoky stayed close to Carol by the propane camp stove.

We backtracked and built several rock cairns along the open ridge where the trail and the Divide coincided. Cairns are carefully constructed, small rock towers that help mark the way. Large areas looked as if a demented rototiller had been at work but it was grizzly bears digging biscuit root, a favorite food. Biscuit root has an elongated root that the Indians roasted and ground to make a meal like cornmeal. It was especially sweet in the springtime, when Indian children liked to chew it as did the grizzlies. The wind whipped our dusters about our legs and pelted us with rain as we collected rocks to build the cairns.

Back toward camp, on the forested slopes, we cut the dangerous hangers from over the trail. Behind our camp, I found campsites to inventory and naturalize. While I worked, they took care of the camp and the animals. I took my forlorn little lavender tent down and rolled it up. As I was welcome in the dome tent, it was a much better accommodation.

As we prepared to eat dinner, the bugs came out. We heard three pitches of buzzing; the lowest represented the horseflies, whose bites left bloody holes. The middle pitch came from the bees vying for our food. It was hard to brush them away long enough to eat without eating bugs too. Then there were mosquitoes so thick I could not avoid inhaling them. There were tiny flies also, which made no discernible sound but were vicious biters. We had expected to eat dinner, not be eaten for dinner. We escaped them by going to bed early.

The morning arrived cool and clear. The insects must have frozen as they were gone. I helped Carol fix a mixture of scrambled eggs,

1992, Cynthia with brandy and mules, Skunk, Cam, and Comet on the Continental Divide Trail, Scapegoat Wilderness, Montana

fried potatoes, and bacon; food to warm us. We needed a good start for the day. We all worked together to break camp. When everything was organized and ready to go on the pack mules, I finished the campsite inventory and naturalized while they loaded the mules.

We followed a steep hogback ridge from the edge of the cirque to the top of the ridge. We were back in the unharnessed, cold wind. The horses' tails flew. I looked back at the Divide and the Valley of

Carol with Smokey and Cynthia along the Continental
Divide Trail, Scapegoat Wilderness, Montana.

Keith with Smokey and Shoe String taking a break along the Continental Divide Trail

the Moon, where we had camped; with the sun on it, the stream looked like a twinkling beaded necklace dropped onto a green carpet—beautiful.

As the sun tipped to the west, we slid off the steep, bare ridge. It was our first view of Bighorn Lake, a turquoise jewel, way below. Dark subalpine firs bordered the lake on one side, cliffs rose from another, and the burned trees from the 1988 fire were along the north shore.

I saw many campsites that needed lots of work. We tied the horses, Skunk, Cam, and Comet to burned aspens. We built a fire with charred sticks left from the 1988 fire to warm ourselves and heated water for hot chocolate. It was a relief to be out of the buffeting wind on the ridges.

Keith and Carol helped me clean up the near-by campsites. One site had flagstone set in walkways, three obvious tent sites, and a fire circle. All was paved with stone. Around the fire pit were two-feet-high stone seats. I could see the rock had come from the nearby cliff face. On a stump was a carving of a craggy face. Someone must have camped there for a long time to build so much. It would hardly have been a back-country experience to come to that camp. We removed all the rocks and flagstone. Keith cut the small stump close to the ground. There was little organic material to scatter to obliterate the site, but we did the best we could, kicking clumps of soil over the tracks so it looked natural.

"I'll go catch a few fish and work on the trail," said Keith, "if you don't mind finishing the other campsites."

I knew Keith disliked cleaning camps. We agreed fresh fish would make a lovely dinner. Carol and I walked along the shore, measuring campsites for inventory purposes, cleaning up trash, and naturalizing. I was glad Carol went with me; she was fun and a good worker. There were six more sites around the lake. We hurried, as we had a long ride before camp that night. As we looked across the crystal-clear water, we could see Keith on the other side, casting for our fish dinner. I felt as if he were playing while we worked but the prospect of a fresh fish dinner was delightful.

Keith caught three good-sized trout. We ate a quick lunch of the usual bread with compressed meat, jerky, and Twix bars next to the remaining embers of our hot- chocolate fire. Before we left, we cleaned our fire area.

Leaving the lake, we climbed back up to the Continental Divide. It was slow, steep, and tiring. The mules, with their heavy loads, went slowly and breathed hard. Their sides contracted and expanded rapidly as puffy clouds of moisture came from their distended nostrils. Once we were on top, the Divide continued to be a windswept ridge with fantastic views in all directions. I could see the distinct brown-and-black areas of fat fingers spreading up the slopes of mountains to the west and north from the Canyon Creek fire; many of the narrow drainages remained green. Patches of ground were overturned; again, Grizzlies had been digging biscuit roots. Grasses had overgrown the ridge trail and the edge of the ridge was dense with scrub fir. Although there was only one sensible way to go, we stopped to build several cairns so users would know their way.

I looked past where Keith had stopped. What was ahead of us made me anxious; the slope was cliff-steep, with scattered trees and an earth-slide trail weaving among them.

"This hill is the reason we always start at Alice Creek," said Keith. "It is too difficult for the stock to climb." As we started down the slope, I saw the mules with front legs jack-hammering, hind legs braced, sliding on their haunches.

I felt like the *Man from Snowy River*. I placed one hand on the reins and saddle horn while the other held on to my hat; the horses' tails flew parallel to the hillside. We slid down a mountain saddle that separated the Dearborn Headwaters, which flowed east to the Missouri River, the Mississippi, and the Gulf of Mexico, from the Landers Fork Headwaters, which flowed west into the Blackfoot and, eventually, the Columbia River. It amazed me that from where I sat, the rain falling onto Brandy's butt would flow to the Gulf of Mexico, and the drops that fell onto his shoulders would flow into the Pacific Ocean. I have lived near the Continental Divide for most of my life, and it still fascinates me. In 1993, the rains were causing the Missouri and the Mississippi to flood, wiping out bridges all the way to the Gulf of Mexico. Dams and dikes were washing out. Thousands of people were left homeless, as whole towns were gone. As much as I was complaining to myself, experiencing the rain upstream was better than experiencing flooding downstream. Shortly, we were in a canyon and out of the wind.

It was eight o'clock, a dreary dusk, when we approached our next campsite along Canyon Creek. The site Keith chose had been an outfitter camp. We ran the electric fence around a large grassy area surrounded next to standing burned skeletons of aspen and lodgepole pine trees. A small stream ran to one side of the meadow, where we watered the animals before putting them in the enclosure for the night; placing the electric fence across the stream, making it available to the horses, would have damaged the bank and polluted the water. Wild horses move constantly and eat a little all day long; when it becomes dark, they gather out of the wind and sleep standing. By contrast, our stock had only a short time each evening and morning to graze. It was important to give them as much time as possible to eat to keep them healthy. We had brought grain pellets to supplement the grass and give them the nutrition they needed.

Keith found a fallen log on which to put the saddles above the wet ground and covered them with a tarp. Carol and I set up the kitchen under a low-hanging tarp we slung between trees. Keith erected the dome tent. There was no woman's work or man's work, only work that needed done; we worked well as a team.

I chose to cook the trout, rice, and canned beans by the warm stove rather than set up the tent in the wet grass. My boots were squishy wet; my heavy leather chaps hung heavy; the waistband cut into my hips. I had visions of my toes being pruney for the rest of my life.

We ate by lantern light and shared the tasks of doing dishes and packing everything in the bear boxes for the night. We headed for the damp tent. Smokey and Shoe had turned in already and were snoring on the sleeping bags. After pushing them aside, we crawled in, knowing that the next day would be another long one, as we had twenty miles to ride to Webb's Guard Station.

The Continental Divide trail was my first long trip since I had hurt my leg. It began to throb. As the crew and the pack mules kept going, I slowed Brandy. I slid off to walk for a while with clumsy packer boots, chaps, and jacket. My duster flapped around my legs, nearly tripping me. I was in familiar territory that Jerry had shown me on that first day and I had been back to install a sign. When Carol hipped in her saddle to look back, she seemed surprised to see me walking.

"Are you alright?" she asked.

"My walking will help the circulation in my leg and maybe the pain," I said.

"Shall we slow down?"

"Oh no! I can keep up if there are no steep hills. I'll kick rocks and sticks off the trail and pick up bailing twine so you won't have to get off all the time." As tired as I was, I still wanted to be helpful. I was in my late fifties, and they were in their twenties. I did not want to be perceived as an old lady even though I was probably older than their parents.

The Middle Fork Trail contours along a side hill with many springs and small bridges. We stopped for a drink at Keith's favorite spring and refilled our water bottles. It was particularly refreshing with the slight taste of the nearby mint.

Near Mainline Trail, there was a dead-fall of several trees. Keith and Carol were on the crosscut this time. I enjoyed myself, picking and eating small low-bush huckleberries. After they finished with the logs, they picked their share of berries before we moved on. I had walked three miles and decided to ride on into Webb. We were looking forward to the warmth and protection of the cabin. Even the tired horses showed more will as they knew they were going home; pointing their ears and picking up their pace.

We saw smoke curling out of the Webb Lake cabin chimney. Will was there to greet us. It was six o'clock in the evening; we did not have to set up camp. Taking care of the stock and getting unpacked was not as daunting with the warm cabin beckoning us.

We had promised Will we would help build a fence for him on our days off. Will, being an old cowboy, owned several horses, mules, and cattle that he pastured in various rented or free fields and properties along the eastern slope. He could use such a pasture for a mare and foal, if he built a new fence around it. Race, Keith, and Carol offered to help. While I had a few urgent tasks— laundry and food buying—to do in the morning, I went to help during the afternoon.

While Race and Carol were stringing barbed wire along the north fence line, Will and Keith struggled with the old mesh fencing along the west.

"Hi. Where do you want me to help?" I asked.

"We're having hell stretching this hog wire," said Will. "Get that steel bar from my truck?" He wove the bar through the edge of the mesh wire and attached a chain.

"Can you back the truck up over there so the chain will reach?"

"Is this good?" I asked when the truck was in line.

"Back a little closer to the fence. OK, that's good."

He attached the chain to the trailer hitch. "OK, pull forward slowly." Will kept tension on the bar until the truck pulled the slack out of the chain. Keith was down the line, straightening and supporting the wire.

"Pull a little harder."

I could see the fence lift off the ground as it tightened. Keith was walking its length, setting it close to the posts.

"Hold it. That's good."

I set the brake.

"Bring the baling wire with you," Will called. "Here— let's tie these cross wires to the post while the truck holds the tension."

They tied the fence to the wood post with the baling wire. I was cautious. If something gave, the chain could snap like a bullwhip.

"I think that's got it. Back the truck, and see if it holds," said Will.

I backed slowly to see what would happen. It held, but neither Will nor Keith could pull the bar out.

"Well, I don't use it much anyway," Will said philosophically as he gave up. The bar stayed in the fence. "Let's tie it to the other posts."

The three of us, equipped with baling wire and pliers, walked the fence, tying the mesh to each metal T- post.

Race and Carol finished the north fence and joined us. We picked up the tools. Will lead the mare and foal into the pasture. We stood by to see how they accepted their new home. She was a small but well-built bay mare with the cutest little chestnut stud colt. They ran around the pasture with their tails in the air and then settled to eat. All was well.

"I'll take you all to the 7-Up Ranch for dinner," Will said. I remembered Carol had pointed to it when I first came.

It was a generous offer, as the 7-Up Ranch was the best restaurant for miles around, but pricey. We gathered there over steaks, baked potatoes, a fresh salad, and beer, telling stories of our experiences with horses and in the backcountry. It was a companionable way to end a good day of helping each other.

Men and Mule Power

It was mid-August and more than halfway through my summer in the Scapegoat. Each time I was back at the bunkhouse, Bill and I would talk on the phone. I was anxious to be home again with the sun, Bill, and our animals. I could do my tasks or contribute to theirs, they treated me as like another crew member, though I was much older; I was honored.

I was in the northern Rocky Mountains again; it had been nearly twenty years since I had been back for any length of time, and much felt familiar, but over the intervening period, I had grown and changed. But I still found a feeling of well-being and solace in the mountains and knew they were the Creator's masterpiece. I knew *His home was not only in the Tetons but everywhere.*

It was time to build the Twin Lakes trail reroute. Keith, Race, Carol, and Tim had been working on the bridge across the bog. Will oversaw the mules, who could pull the plow and grader. The horse-drawn equipment would save lots of handwork with a pick-mattock and Pulaski. I was familiar with the handwork that went into trail building from my time with Tommy, but I had not seen a horse drawn plow or grader and was excited to watch the process.

We were staging at Indian Meadows. I was to patrol the Landers Fork Trail. Everyone else was going to the Twin Lakes reroute site. Will and Keith had gotten all the parts of the horse-drawn plow and grader from the barn. The blades were wrapped in heavy canvas bags, and the handles of the tools were separated in piles on the ground in preparation to be loaded onto the mules. Special well-padded pack saddles were used to haul the heavy equipment.

"Hold still, or I'll thump on you," Will told the wiggling Comet.

Comet would carry the grader. Will and Keith attached the blade and handles of the grader to the packsaddle. The blade went on one side and was balanced with the handles and tools on the other side.

"Is this the way we hooked them last time?" Keith asked as he lifted the handles.

"If it doesn't work, it must be wrong," Will answered, demonstrating cowboy wisdom and stepping up to help Keith. "Pull the canvas over. Maybe the bar will fit," he added as he juggled the metal handles.

"Here's a rock. Hammer the bar over." Keith chuckled and handed Will a good-sized rock.

Constant mumbles emanated from Will and Keith, directing the mule. It took the two of them to lift and hang the blade on the pack.

"I'll pull on this side to balance the blade while you get the handles in place," said Will in an effort to balance the pack.

"Got the handles. Wait a sec, and I'll have the tools on too." Keith hung the handles and tools on the off side.

"Come on, Comet; let's see how you do with this," said Will as he led Comet to the hitching rail.

They repeated the same procedure to load the plow and its handles onto Cam. Charlie received the lighter load of personal gear and grain.

Keith led the mules, one tied behind the other, and Will followed watchfully. They had a fourteen-mile ride ahead of them to Twin Lakes, where Race, Tim, and Carol would help unload the equipment. They would spend the night at the nearby camp on the East Fork.

I hoped all went well with Cam's and Comet's packs. Brandy, Stanley, and I used the back gate to the Landers Fork Trail. I expected to cut several trees off the trail, do more campsite inventories, and meet Will at Webb by evening. The breeze was softly rustling in the trees. The trail was still wet. But the morning was so nice I had my duster tied behind the saddle—a rarity. I was glad I had taken the gamble and bought the duster before the job. I had had great doubts about spending $185 for a garment I would seldom use in the Arizona climate, but I had known it would be essential if I worked in Montana. The summer was one of the wettest Montana had known in decades.

"Peck, Vigen" I heard my radio crackle from my saddlebag, Will was calling.

"Vigen, Peck," I responded.

"What's your location?"

"I just passed Baking Powder Creek."

"Thanks." Will always ended the transmission with "Thanks."

I wondered what the call was about. Surely if there were problems with the packs or mules, I was not needed. Will was in his seventies; could he have been having health problems? But he sounded like his usual cheerful self. I guessed I could only continue with my patrol; I would know what was happening soon enough.

A downed lodgepole pine sixteen inches in diameter lay square across the trail. I tied Brandy and Stanley to nearby pines, pulled the crosscut out, put the radio against a stump so I could hear if Will tried to reach me again, and started sawing.

With several pauses to catch my breath and one to take off my uniform shirt—my tank top would be cooler—I finished the first cut. Luckily, the saw did not bind as the end of the log settled. After a drink of water, I started the second cut.

Stanley kept swinging around his tree, first in one direction and then in the other.

"Whoa," I called to him. "Quit that. I'll put hobbles on you if you don't quit." I tied him a little shorter and began to saw again. Stanley was still restless, so I tried to work faster for his sake but I discovered I could not. I decided his restlessness was his personal problem, and he was going to have to become used to being tied.

With several pauses, the second cut went through, and the log dropped onto the trail. I used the lash rope wound around the pommel for Brandy to pull it well off the trail.

I sat to cool off; it was finally a warm day. Stanley had settled and was standing quietly. I repacked Stanley. I wondered what the regulations concerning someone working with a tank top and uniform pants were. Working with the full uniform was sometimes uncomfortable. I guessed it did not matter, because no one came by. I ate my lunch of crackers with canned tuna and a Twix bar. I gathered and packed the radio and crosscut saw, put my uniform shirt on, mounted, and headed along the trail.

Soon the sunny morning had turned into a cloudy afternoon. It looked like rain again by evening. I pondered; were there problems in getting the plow and grader to Twin Lakes; I would be spending two nights at the East Fork camp as I needed to patrol Windy Pass and their camp was closer; I hoped to watch the trail construction and the use of a horse-drawn grader was rare, and I wanted to take pictures.

As I turned a corner, Brandy stopped. I quit my musing and looked up. There in the middle of the trail was Will with a big smile, sitting on the giant Paladin. Seeing him warmed my heart. It was a pleasure to work with him.

"Keith was doing so well with Cam and Comet that I decided to cut off at Heart Lake and see how you were doing," he said.

"I'm doing fine. I stopped to cut out the grandfather of a lodgepole. That took a while," I responded.

"Have you discovered the camps by Lookout Creek?"

"I was headed that way now," I said as he turned and we rode beside me into the camp. "There sure are lots of bottles and cans around those sites," I said

"I'll help if you like," Will said.

"Great. I know there are several sites bunched together."

"Hunters really like camping here," said Will.

"That explains all the empty whiskey bottles," I said as I began picking them up. "It's nice under these big green Douglas fir trees. It is out of the burn and near the stream for water too."

Will scouted the periphery of the sites, riding Paladin, while I dismantled fire pits and picked trash out of them. We were collecting a full load for Stanley.

"Remember those miniature Dutch ovens you found?" Will was referring to the large dump at Heart Lake. "Well, I pulled those out to save. They're really nice. I saved that tarp too. Nothing wrong with it," he said.

"It looked in good condition to me. I guess they were too lazy to carry it out." I remembered using it to wrap around the small pieces of trash, which made it easier to pack.

"Looks good here. Anything else you want to do?" Will asked as he stopped near me, sat askew on Paladin, and looked at the camp.

"Not today. Let's head for Webb," I said as I turned Brandy toward the trail.

I wished I could educate more people while they were in the camp, but catching hunters in camp was especially difficult and hunting season would begin after I was laid off. Then the law enforcement folks and Jerry would patrol for game violations.

The following day at Twin Lakes and I saw the crew's campfire and the nearby tarp tied between trees for shelter. Comet was in harness and wearing a light saddle. The grader and plow had been assembled, and the plow was hooked onto Comet's tugs. Carol rode him, giving him direction, and Keith walked behind, guiding the plow.

They followed Jerry's flagging. It quickly became apparent that cutting virgin ground was not like plowing fields as seen in movies about pioneers. The plow would catch on clumps of bear grass, causing Comet to come to a jerking stop and nearly throwing Carol over his head. The bear grass had tough roots that appeared to grow deep to China. Each time the plow caught on bear grass or tree roots; it came to a jarring halt. Then Keith jerked the plow around the obstacle and called for Comet to pull again. Will walked beside Comet to help keep him in line and moving slowly.

"Come on, Comet," Will would say. Carol kicked him and leaned forward.

Comet lunged to break through the bear grass. Keith hung on, trying to keep up, with his feet slipping on the wet, newly broken ground behind the plow.

"Whoa!" Comet went too fast.

"Oof." Carol had her breath knocked out of her by the abrupt halt as the plow caught.

I was running beside Comet with Carol's and Keith's and my cameras and video.

"Go, Comet."

"Easy."

"Damn!"

"Are you OK?" The bucking plow had thrown Keith to the ground.

"Yes, I'm OK," he said as he got up and brushed himself off.

"Back, Comet." Carol pulled back on the reins.

"Whoa." Keith wrestled the plow back into position.

"OK, I'm ready."

"Go, Comet. Come on."

The mule lunged ahead again. I could see that Comet loved to pull. He threw his considerable weight against the hames. He was becoming frustrated with the constant stopping, backing, and going. He wanted to set his shoulders into the harness and pull long furrows. Often, he could take only a few steps before he was stopped and then backed one step so Keith could adjust the plow to pull forward again.

"Come on, sweetheart." Will encouraged Comet with sweet talk.

Soon it was time for everyone to take a break. We had fresh boiled coffee with Irish cream and Twix bars. It was a drizzly day again, but if we did not work in the rain, nothing would be completed.

The second pass with the plow went easier, and the two passes with the grader were easier yet. I could see the satisfaction in Comet's demeanor as the pulling became consistent.

Two riders came by. "Hi! What are you doing? I've never seen anything like this," said one. I could imagine his surprise after riding fourteen miles of lonely quiet in the Wilderness to come upon all this noise and six people.

"We're making a new trail. It will be easier riding than the old one," said Will.

"Can I help?" The rider was watching Race dig out bear grass with a Pulaski.

"Sure, but be careful. If the Pulaski hits unevenly, it bounces back. Could cut your leg." Race demonstrated.

I was surprised Race was going to let him try. But our visitor had ridden far and looked fit, so perhaps that was enough reference.

The rider's partner, a woman, held their horses and watched with interest.

For the bridge, Race had chosen a three-foot- diameter fire-killed cottonwood tree for the mudsills. He cut it into several equal lengths with the crosscut saw. After much digging and figuring, they leveled and squared the sills. They felled several scorched lodgepoles for stringers and laid them on the mudsills. On top of the stringers, the crew nailed the decking planks that Will had packed to the site. Smaller lodgepole logs were spiked onto the decking edge, making a curb. We tested the bridge by riding the horses across. It was a fine-looking bridge, and the horses did not mind it after a little dirt had been thrown onto the new surface.

I enjoyed my time with the crew, watching the plowing and grading and taking pictures for everyone and videos for myself, but I had other work to do. I took the time to have lunch with the crew by the fire, sheltered under the manti. I had more coffee with cream; its warmth felt good in my stomach. Keith threw sticks for Smoky and Shoe to retrieve. After lunch, I mounted Brandy and took Luke to check more outfitter camps.

The rain fell harder and harder as the day wore on. Luke was easygoing and led well, which was a joy, unlike the balky Charlie. I checked on the grizzly feeding site. It always made my horse, mule, and me uneasy. I sang, whistled, and talked to Brandy and Luke until I could see the grizzly was not there. The rest of the horse carcass was now exposed. The skull had been thoroughly cleaned and dragged a distance from the hole. More bones were scattered about. There was little left to eat but lots of other food was now available, unlike in the spring, when the snow had first melted. I thought the crew would be closing the hole soon.

I went by Hoeffner's camp, thinking someone might be there, and I could find a cup of coffee, but no one was home. The tent sides were rolled up, so if a grizzly walked through, he would not slash new doors. I tied Brandy and Luke, covered my saddle with a manti, and went into the cook tent; a little fire still burned in the stove, with hot water on top. Someone must have left recently. I stood by the stove, warming my numb hands, and drank a little hot water with my Twix bar. I usually avoided eating candy, but with the cold, I was eating lots of it, and as a result, I was gaining weight despite the hard work.

As I have said, the rule of the Old West is a matter of respect: anyone is welcome to use a camp or cabin; however, you must leave it as you found it. However, many people using the backcountry do not know the old ethics. Uninformed or mean-spirited people make outfitters wary of strangers. With much thievery and vandalism, it is necessary for someone to stay in camp to protect it. Cattlemen often strip their line cabins to prevent thievery. Though understandable, the distrust is a shame, because there are no supplies for a backcountry traveler in an emergency.

Warmed a little, I was soon on my way. The manti kept my saddle dry to avoid my sitting in a puddle. So much water covered the trails that they had become elongated frog ponds. As Brandy splish-splashed along, the frogs jumped in front of him. Their croaking was a deafening, monotonous song. I heard another song: the unnerving howl of a wolf. There was no mistaking it. It was close. The hair on the back of my neck crawled. Brandy and Luke suddenly came out of their lethargy, perked up their ears, and looked around anxiously. We stood there on alert for a time; I was half hoping to see the wolf and half hoping not to. I did not see it, but it was a thrill to hear one in the wild. A sliver of sun low in the western sky peeked through the storm clouds. It was time to head back to the trail crew camp on the East Fork, where I would spend the night.

The camp on the East Fork was set up to accommodate a "show-me" trip planned for the Forest Service dignitaries into the Scapegoat Wilderness. To accommodate them, it was a bigger camp than the crew usually had. There was a cook tent with wood and Coleman stoves and a fly creating a porch, plus two dome tents. There was the usual large area enclosed by the electric fence, as well as a log saddle rack where the tack could be covered with a tarp. A log secured between two trees over a hole with a tarp surrounding it served as the privy. The water source was the East Fork river, which was filtered through a two-micron filter to protect everyone from giardia and other waterborne organisms. All garbage and grain cakes hung ten feet up and five feet out from a tree to discourage grizzlies. The food would be kept in the large ammunition boxes. If it had been sunny, it would have been an inviting camp, but we could not control the weather.

Will always brought a newspaper into camp, which he read before passing it on to the crew. Since they had all read it, I used it to make a fire in the small stove in the walled cook tent. I watched the tent fly fill, tip, then sluice rain water off; the Creator bringing water into camp, I grabbed buckets and dishpans, to collect enough water so no one would have to filter water from the stream and carry it to camp.

I wore new heavy wool socks, which were making my legs burn and itch fiercely. I took my boots and socks off and put my moccasins on. My legs were swollen and mottled red. I walked to the stream, kicked off the moccasins, and rolled my pant legs up. As an example of first aid in the backcountry, I stepped into the stream, where the cold water relieved the pain. However, my feet became numb quickly. I kept my pants rolled to keep them from touching the rash.

The crew came in, wet and cold from the trail construction.

"Nice fire. Thanks," said Will.

"How can we make clothes hangers?" asked Carol. She was taking off her wet outer clothes and trying to hang them. "Here are some sticks. I'll get some bailing wire,"Race said.

"That is quite a water-collection system," said Keith. "Won't have to filter water tonight." He was admiring the tarp water catchment and was pleased to have one less chore. I was glad I had been helpful.

"These sticks with the wire are working pretty good," said Race. "Anything else to hang?"

Soon walking around the tent was difficult with all the hanging gear: dusters, chaps, jackets, gloves, hats, and pants.

"What happened to your legs?" asked Will. "They look nasty."

"Thanks for the compliment," I answered, laughing. "Seriously, it must be an allergic rash, maybe from my wool socks."

"Have you got anything to help it?" asked Carol.

"I don't want to put anything on it. I just put my legs into the East Fork. The cold actually felt good. I could use some cotton socks tomorrow, if someone has a spare."

"Yes," said Keith as he rummaged in his duffel. "Here's a pair." They were a clean pearl-white pair. I was thankful for his generous nature.

We huddled near the cook stove, drinking coffee with Bailey's Irish cream. Carol and I prepared a dinner of pork chops, fried potatoes with onions, and canned beans. We had dried fruit and candy bars for dessert. We perched among tack, bear boxes, and hanging clothes.

The tent started to leak. We quickly rearranged saddles, equipment, and supplies stacking them in dry areas and left a flat spot for Keith, Will, and Race to sleep. Tim would sleep in one dome tent. He was a restless sleeper, so no one wanted to share with him. Carol and I slept in another dome tent. We took a Coleman lantern with us at bedtime to take the chill out of the tent. Everything felt damp. My sleeping bag took forever to warm up.

Morning broke with cloud cover but no rain. I cut onions and potatoes to mix with Carol's skillet of eggs and bacon on the Coleman stove as it was faster to use the Coleman stove than build a fire in the small cook stove.

We caught our respective horses, except Race and Tim decided they could walk to the construction site as fast. I headed along the East Fork Trail, wandering along the creek and through small meadows of short green grass with a scattering of lodgepole pines. I stopped and sat on a log for lunch. I let Brandy loose to graze close by. I held Luke's lead with my foot, allowing him to graze but preventing him from leaving. I heard the eerie sound of elk bugling. I remembered autumn on the ranch, when Dad and I had saddled up and gone to watch them bugle.

Blizzard

It was mid-September at Webb cabin. I had just completed the evening chores and was waiting for the coffee to boil and the cabin to warm. As was my custom, I turned on the battery-operated AM radio to hear what was happening in the outside world. After a few minutes of country-western music, the news came on.

"There is a storm watch over the mountains of northwestern Montana." That meant me. "This is the first major storm system of the season. People who are in the backcountry or driving in the mountains need to take extra precautions. This storm system is rated as potentially dangerous, with possibly up to ten inches of snow. This is a fast-moving system and should move out by tomorrow night."

I felt safe. I was not in danger. I had wood available, plenty of food, and enough hay and grain for the stock. My feeling safe in the Webb cabin was from my experience in making a home in unlikely places. If the storm was severe, I would hole up there at Webb. I had completed the tasks Jerry had assigned me for the summer, though I wanted to retrieve the wrecking bar the crew had left against a tree at Twin Lakes. That would wrap up all the projects I had been assigned.

I reflected on my time in Montana. The second half of the summer had gone quickly. I had worked as a team with much younger folks, who had treated me as an equal. I had learned new packing skills from Will and had enjoyed working with his level-headed cowboy ways. I had earned the respect of Jerry and Charley, and had learned to respect them also. I knew I would remember with fondness my Scapegoat Wilderness summer.

Midsummer, I had a wonderful break from work with Bill's visit. I showed him Indian Meadows and introduced him to the mules and horses, Will, and Charley and Jerry at the district office. We walked a little way into the Scapegoat where he could see the thick Douglas timber, like where I had had my accident. We stayed in the quaint motel I had stayed in on my first trip to the village. We had a special dinner at the 7-Up Ranch. Then he was gone again. It was a short visit.

Another break included several days' drive to Jackson, Wyoming, for a dear friend's ninetieth birthday gathering in Moose. Bessie acted temperamental. She stalled several times and would not start till I opened her hood, took off the air filter, and let her sit for a while then she would start again. The issue acted like fuel starvation, but why would she have felt starved after running for hours? She was a gas hog, so I kept the tank topped off. In fact, with towns so far apart, I filled her in at each town. I did not want to run out of gas far from a village. I would solve her problem eventually.

I was thrilled, as always, when I came over the Teton Pass and saw the stately Tetons. After growing up in those spectacular mountains, it took me years to recognize any other place as beautiful. Even now, I feel a need occasionally, to tuck myself into the Tetons to charge my batteries and renew my spirit. If I were an Indian, I would describe the Tetons as my place of power, a sacred place.

I arrived in Moose a little late. I parked by the Dornan's store and hurried into the camper to wash and dress. I put on my new black jeans, a dressy white shirt with a buckskin vest I had made, and my beaded Shoshone moccasins. That had been dress wear in Jackson Hole during all my years there, but was I in for a surprise. I joined the party at the Chuckwagon, looking for my friend Ellen. Most people were in dresses and city shoes! Only a few old-timers were dressed western, as I was. Jackson Hole had changed with an influx of city people. It was no longer a ranching community.

I had a good time visiting friends I had known since childhood. Ellen enjoyed her special day too. She had all her children, their spouses, and several grandchildren visiting. Many had come from afar to share her birthday. Several gave speeches about their special memories of growing-up years next to the Snake River with Ellen. I remembered that one of her children had fallen into the river as a young child and drowned. It had been such a tragedy, thankfully no one spoke of it. I had known Ellen since I was a child. When Bill had worked in Tucson, Ellen had been wintering there. She had become partially blind, so I had spent one day a week with her, driving, helping her shop, reading, and writing correspondence, and doing whatever else was needed. We had many pleasant days and luncheons together. I had gained a high respect for her gentle ways and admiration for her strong spirit.

At her birthday party, Ellen invited me to sleep on her porch, a special treat. I had expected to camp near Shadow Mountain, but I accepted Ellen's invite with grace.

I woke up to the sound of the Snake River rushing by and the sight of Buck Mountain shining before me. Buck Mountain was right behind White Grass Ranch. I had explored its slopes and knew which game trails to follow to the cirque that I saw near the top of the mountain. I knew the snowfields would have pink snow, colored from the organisms that lived in it. It was home.

The next day, I walked around White Grass, fighting tears. The ranch operation had ended with Dad's death, and the ranch buildings had deteriorated. There were broken windows and other signs of vandalism. What I saw was neglect, not a mission of preservation. History was being lost. It broke my heart.

I heard coffee boiling, bringing my thoughts back to Webb. I poured a cup and set the pot aside. Again, I spent the evening on algebra, having a progressively more difficult time. The problems were more complex, and I was confused most of the time. I needed an instructor.

In the morning, I discovered the radio forecast had been correct. Looking out the window, I saw a blizzard. I could not see the lake through the snow flakes. Snow was accumulating fast on the ground around the cabin. No going to Twin Lakes to retrieve the wrecking bar and pick up the pile of trash I had seen. The trail and the bar would be buried under the snow. I would feed the stock and have breakfast and then make a decision what to do.

I started a fire in the cook range, put on the coffee pot, and then bundled up to feed the stock and go to the outhouse. I gave Brandy and Luke extra pellets to help them combat the cold. Back in the cabin, I fixed hot cereal and continued to listen to the AM radio news.

1992, George Clover and Cynthia at Ellen Dorman's birthday celebration, Moose, Wyoming

"There is an accumulation of six to seven inches of snow on the mountain passes. There is a jackknifed truck on Stemple Pass. The pass is closed until further notice. Four-wheel drive or chains are recommended on all mountain roads."

The snow was building up faster than I had thought it would. I wondered if it would continue to pile up, signaling winter's arrival, or if it would melt before winter really closed in. Anxious, I turned on the USFS radio to see what was happening around the district. What if there was so much snow that I could not find my way out or that Brandy and Luke could not push through?

"Silver King, Lincoln."

"Lincoln, Silver King."

"Think we will bring you down for a few days off. When can we pick you up?"

"I can't tell you until Cindy checks in. She's at Webb."

"Anyone else in the backcountry?"

"No. The crew is in town." I broke in. "I am copying."

"Cindy is copying. I can get down to the road at about ten."

"Copy that. Ten o'clock on the road."

"Silver King."

John would walk down the mountain from the tower to Alice Creek Road, where the fire folks would pick him up, as usual. With Silver King down, I would have no contact. I was not supposed to be in the Wilderness without radio contact.

"Peck, Burns."

"Burns, Peck."

"I want you to come out."

"OK, no problem," I responded. "Silver King, Peck."

"Peck, Silver King."

"Morning, John. I'll be heading out also."

"Morning. Copy. You'll be heading out."

The summer was ending so abruptly. I was beginning to gather my things, when the radio came to life again: "Peck, Lincoln. What time do you expect to get out?"

"I can make it by one o'clock."

"Do you need someone to pick you up?"

"No, I have a truck at Indian Meadows. It has four-wheel drive, so I should have no problem." The stock was at Indian Meadows, so I didn't need to trailer Brandy and Luke, which made horse care easier.

"Copy; will be out about one o'clock and have a truck at Indian Meadows."

"Right. Peck."

How considerate that the fire management officer, whom I had met briefly at the Wheel and who was not directly responsible for me, was watching out for my safety and had visited me when my leg was hurt. I appreciated it. Before I left Webb, I made sure the lanterns were filled, the water bucket was full, and lots of wood was in the box, and I swept and mopped the floor. All my gear was packed and staged on the porch, where it would stay dry. I went to catch and saddle the animals. It would most likely be my last time in the Scapegoat, but I knew Jerry patrolled throughout the fall hunting season.

The corral is six inches of mud with several inches of snow on top. I was glad Will had suggested my getting galoshes with felt liners for footwear. Nothing else would have kept my feet so warm and dry. I saddled Brandy first, put a manti tarp over my saddle to keep it dry, and put the packsaddle on Luke. Bless their hearts, they stood still in the impossible weather like good boys while I placed the wet tack on them. I led Luke to the porch and packed my gear and the garbage onto him. I bolted the shutters and locked the door. I mounted Brandy, and we headed out into the blizzard, anticipating another challenge.

The trail was slippery and covered with snow. Brandy was a bit snorty in protest as we started. Everything looked different being covered with snow; small plants were buried, fallen trees were more distinct, and ladened treetops bent to kiss the ground, and hid rocks and dips. Great balls of snow fell on us as we brushed our way through bushes. I could not distinguish the landmarks I was familiar with. The trail looked like a fluffy white ribbon. I was exhilarated by the beauty of the Wilderness under its blanket of snow. No drug high could have been as exquisite as the clean, fresh feeling as the giant snowflakes drifted peacefully to the ground. However, the snow was accumulating so fast that I wondered if I could continue to follow the trail.

My deerskin gloves soaked through. I still had a three-hour ride. There were snowballs building in Brandy's shoes, making him teeter like a teenager wearing her first high-heeled shoes. The snowball would break, suddenly making him limp. It made for an unstable feeling sitting on him.

A great big clump of snow fell onto Luke's forehead and stuck. It had a pine needle sticking out of it; it looked like a miniature unicorn. Luke was barefoot, so instead of gathering balls of snow in his hooves, he had to contend with slipping and sliding. He had a particularly hard time going downhill. Without traction, he set his feet and skated. He kept following with the only complaint of his low-hanging head and long-suffering face. I felt sorry for Brandy and Luke.

The willow bushes at the Ringeye Stream crossing were bent so far over the trail that it was invisible. Brandy questioned my judgment as I kicked him forward brushing the snowy bushes when he could not see the way, but he trusted me. It still looked beautiful, but I was getting cold and discouraged.

The latigo was completely wet and had stretched so that the cinch was dangling under Brandy's belly; only my balance was keeping the saddle in place. I stayed mounted and worked the stiff, wet leather with my cold hands with little success. I could keep the saddle on by balance. If I leaned to one side or the other to avoid a snow-laden branch from dumping its load onto me, the saddle would slip. I would then stand on the other stirrup to slide it back into place. It was only another hour's ride to Indian Meadows. I could make it if nothing unexpected happened, though of course, when working around stock and in the backcountry I had learned to expect the unexpected.

As I wound through the trees, black images appeared to be coming toward me. Eventually, they took form becoming an outfitter with five hunters. The guide looked prepared for the weather. The hunters looked frozen and miserable, wearing light jackets with short plastic raincoats or plastic ponchos with baseball caps and cotton gloves. Their hiking shoes were inappropriate for the weather. They were already wet, and they were only beginning their trip to camp.

I must have looked like an apparition, quietly appearing through the fog of falling snow, several inches of snow on my brown Stetson, hunched into my Australian duster, with snow covering my shoulders. Brandy's mottled coat was covered with snow, and Luke's white pack and body also were covered with snow, making us appear like ghosts. I pulled to the side of the trail to let them by. I was thankful I had dry feet in the galoshes. I had dry legs due to the chaps. I doubted they could see my face until I sat straight and spoke to them.

"Hello. Quite a snowstorm," I said cheerfully.

The guide nodded, but no one spoke. That was unusual since most people spoke when they met me on the trail. *Oh well.* They were unhappy. They had a guide who had the responsibility; he knew the Scapegoat and the backcountry ethics. I did not need to talk with them.

"Have a good hunt," I said as they rode away. My hands were cold, especially the right one, which was holding the lead rope. The left one, holding the reins, was tucked under the edge of the saddle blanket, taking advantage of Brandy's warmth. I was doing much better than the hunters were. I felt sorry for them.

At Indian Meadows, I slid off to unlock the gate without using the stirrups, to prevent the loose saddle from slipping. After closing it, I walked the quarter mile to the tack shed, to get the circulation back in my cold, stiff body. I had been riding as still as I could so no meltwater would run into my clothing. I had a hard time tying the frozen lead ropes with numb hands and difficulty working the key into the frozen truck lock. I started the truck and turned the heater on. I shook myself like a dog shaking water from his coat. While I unsaddled and unpacked, fighting the wet leather and frozen ropes, the other horses were milling around, looking for a handout. The snow was deep enough that they were having difficulty digging to graze. I turned Brandy and Luke into the pasture. They ran to greet their friends. I threw flakes of hay, sufficient for them all, from the covered and fenced haystack behind the tack shed, unsure when someone would come to feed.

I drove slowly to avoid sliding off the hill. I felt let down that my last tour had been cut short. The season was coming to an end but I would be glad to head home to Bill and my animals.

"Peck, Lincoln." I recognized Terri's voice. "What's your location?"

"Just leaving Indian Meadows."

"Do you need any help? Are you alright?"

"I'm fine. Just got the stock taken care of and am headed to the station."

"See you soon."

I used four-wheel drive all the way to the pavement. There were no tracks coming from the campgrounds. If anyone had been camping, they had probably pulled out before the snow. I was driving a ribbon of fluffy cotton. The highway was slick, but I took it slowly. I pulled into the station without any trouble. The station driveway had a few tracks. It was Sunday, and only Terri and I were on duty. John and his driver would have been off duty as soon as they arrived at the station hours ago.

"I started at Copper Creek campground," said Terri, "but there was so much snow and mud I was afraid of getting stuck, so I came back."

"The roads are slippery," I said.

"I've been organizing slides for a talk I'll be giving at the school."

"That should be interesting."

"I like giving slide shows, especially to children," she said as she continued to sort slides, but I cut her off, as I was anxious to go to the bunkhouse.

Later, while I was again fighting my war with algebra, I heard a knock on the bunkhouse door. It was Dave, making sure I had arrived safely.

I appreciated the folks' concern and follow-up. I could take care of myself, but it was comforting to know that if I did not show, someone would start looking.

The next day, in the office, Jerry said, "You need to work on the annual Wilderness Report to Congress for the next two weeks."

I had never done any reports. How was I going to do it? What did it need to say? "I will need direction and explanation on how to do it."

"You have last year's report, don't you? I gave it to you in the spring."

"Yes." I said, but I had forgotten.

"Just follow that. I also need a special report on the Heart Lake Rehabilitation site."

All the information needed to be entered into the computer. Knowing the computer folks from working with Joanna's timber project was helpful. They showed me how to get in and work the appropriate program. On the computer were questions about range allotments, the number of outfitter permits, LAC inventory figures, trail encounters, and occupied campsite information. I would need to compile my tasks. I started with Linda, who found the original Heart Lake Rehabilitation plan on the computer. She also found the number of outfitters. There were no existing allotments, mining claims, or other special considerations in the Scapegoat Wilderness.

Over the summer, I had picked up the battery pieces, monitored and protected the habitation area, repaired hitching rails, and rehabilitated innumerable camp areas. I had to figure out the percentage of change of occupied campsites. I took the initiative to map the campsites on a contour map to show any changes in site density.

During the summer, I had accomplished all the tasks Jerry had asked of me.

I turned the report in to Jerry and then thought about the job. It had been hard at the beginning, yet I had learned what was expected of me as time went on. They had given me lots of leeway for initiative; on the other hand, a little more guidance, especially in the beginning, would have been helpful. I decided to make a list of things to carry into the Wilderness and things to do for whoever came next to the job. It was a seasonal summer job, I doubted that I would return. I was still hoping that my successful work would provide references to help me have work closer to home with the Forest Service.

That evening, Bill's daughter Sue called from Missoula. I had visited her a few times on my days off. She had an energetic pup that was not fitting into town life. "Can Aca go to Arizona with you? I can't keep her here. She barks at every passing kid—you know, the school is on my corner— and I must keep her chained. She would love the ranch and freedom."

"I'll have to talk to your dad. We already have enough animals," I answered. We had two horses, four cats, and another dog at home. Aca was a sweet young Australian shepherd, eager to please. She had been to obedience school; sat and heeled well but had much still to learn about living with a family. I called Bill, and he was fine with my bringing Aca home if I agreed. I called Sue back; she could bring Aca to me. I would have Aca in the bunkhouse for a few days. It was forbidden, but I figured a few days at the end of the season with no one else in the bunkhouse would be overlooked. It had been overlooked for Silky when Rosanna and Tina stayed in the bunkhouse.

I decided to spend the slack time to good advantage by working on my algebra. I went into the office basement with it. Mo and Donna were mapping timber data on the computer and allowed me to use one of their free tables.

"What are you doing?" asked Mo.

"I have been trying to keep up with a college algebra class back home. I have been fighting it for five weeks. I am lost but can't give up."

"I teach algebra at Helmville," said Mo. "Maybe I can help you."

"Oh, that would be wonderful!"

Mo helped me, and I kept moving forward. If I ran into a snag, she gave me a few minutes, and then she continued her work. I did not keep Mo from her work, since she would put data into the computer, ask it to print, and then have a long wait while it did its job. Then she could input more data. I would never choose to do classwork away from the teacher again; it was hell.

Mo and her husband invited me to join them for a barbecue at their ranch. Afterward, we went to their kids' football game in a nearby town. They showed me the way to the Blackfoot River, which was next to their ranch. I enjoyed the time with their family. It had been a long time since I had spent time with young children.

A few days after I handed Jerry the year-end annual report. "This annual report looks good," Jerry said. "I especially like the map you made to go with it."

The praise felt good. I prefer to wait for meaningful kudos rather than receive frequent shallow ones. I had worked for him for four months while waiting to hear it, but it was worth the wait. More than that, deeper than that, was the confidence I had gained from spending those months in the wild. I recognized the rhythm of death and regrowth, a continuance of the earth's processes. Extended time in the backcountry had helped me to see a bigger picture. I am less than an ant in the complexity of the ecosystem. Though so small, I like the feeling of being part of something so vast yet intricate. I care not so much for things money can buy but for intangible moments, such as the sparkling ripple of sunlight pushed by an unseen breeze, or a wafted scent of a wild animal, or fragrant plant, or reclining on the sun-warmed earth meditating to renew my vitality and hope. These things cannot be bought or held in my hands, but they are treasures that bring peace to my soul.

I was looking forward to heading home to Bill and sunny days. I packed my belongings into Bessie and cleaned my bunkhouse room. I asked Jerry when he was going to inspect it.

"Don't need to inspect. You always kept it clean," he said. He must have made periodic inspections during the summer. It was a compliment that he trusted me.

Everyone was invited to the end-of-season barbecue. I went to the celebration, where there was good food, good people, and laughter. They wished me a safe journey. Jerry, Charley, Will, and the crew made me feel respected. I had enjoyed working with them all, but I needed to head south. I started to leave the party early when Will seeked me out.

"Past the bridge over the Blackfoot river, there is a ranch with a large barnyard right beside the road," said Will. "They are friends of mine. You can park there for the night no problem."

I found the ranch, as per Will's directions, and parked there. I felt uneasy staying there without talking to someone but I arrived in the dark after all their lights were out; being a natural early riser, I left before anyone came to the barn.

Bessie ran well the first day through Montana and into northern Idaho but began stalling again. I would stop to let her rest. I took advantage of the rest time to walk Aca. She was good on her leash, but I learned, needed training off leash. With the rest, Bessie would start. At Nephi, Utah, Bessie quit again. Luckily, I found a mechanic. He changed the fuel filter, and all was well thereafter. What a simple fix. Why had no one else discovered it the times I talked to mechanics in Lincoln? Oh well. Life goes on.

Bill greeted me with big hugs and Aca with a sincere scratch behind her ears. It was great to be home. My own bed felt different, but soon was feeling natural again. I felt as if I were living with a stranger. I had changed, and Bill had changed. We had had four months on our own with experiences the other did not know and had developed a means to live without each other. We sat at the table for dinner, as was our habit, which gave us an opportunity to share what had happened in the months apart, but it was hard to know where to start. After sharing our experiences, we fell into our comfortable routine.

While Bill was working in Mesa or Phoenix and I in Montana, Bill hired someone to care for the animals. Now I was back doing the chores, caring for our horses, dogs, and cats. Bill had had a small propane furnace installed, but to be comfortable, we still mostly used the wood heating stove. Although we had a propane cook range, I liked to use the wood range, particularly when I made bread. I liked putting the loaves on the open warming-oven doors to rise. Also, in preparation for winter, I chopped a lot of wood for both heat and cooking.

CHAPTER 12

Working a Man's Job

I KNOCKED ON DARIEN'S OFFICE DOOR. IT WAS APRIL 1994 WARM enough that Bill and I had stopped using the wood heating stove, it was beginning to feel like spring, a time of renewal, and growth.

I received a call from Darien, "Hi, Cindy. Could you come into the office?"

I knew that in the spring, the Forest Service planned their summer projects. I knew Darien, the range staff, from my volunteer years with the Pleasant Valley Ranger District. He was manager of the grazing allotments. I wondered what he had in mind.

"Come in. Would you like some coffee or water?" He offered me a chair.

"Water would be fine," I answered as I sat on the metal folding chair, and he handed me a bottle of water.

"I need four grazing allotment studies completed this summer. I am thinking of hiring Sam Strong, who recently graduated from the University of Arizona with a major in range management," Darien said.

"I would like you to work with Sam on this project. You would be finding and reading existing Parker study sites, which are scattered on ridges and hillsides. It is a seasonal position—no benefits. I have funding for the two employees for four months." He continued to explain his program for the summer. "You must apply for the job online. When I am ready to hire, I'll look for your application." He was offering me another seasonal job, like the one the previous summer in Montana, and I was glad he had thought of me. He knew my sincerity in working was demonstrated by going to Montana to work

Working for the Forest Service in Montana had given me rehire rights. My strategy was working; volunteering had helped me move on to a seasonal job, which in turn had prepared me for further jobs. I still hoped seasonal jobs would move me to a permanent one.

"I would like that. I am unfamiliar with grasses but know many native perennials and forbs." I remembered the times with Betty and John Huebner, dudes of many years at White Grass and dear friends. Betty was a plant specialist. She had taught me many of the wild plants scattered over the Teton foothills. I had noticed that many familiar plants grew along the Mogollon Rim. Who could have guessed Betty's teaching would prepare me for a job?

"Sam knows the grass. If you know the forbs and other perennials, you should make a good team."

Sam, a twenty-one-year-old, partnered with me, a fifty- two-year-old. Darien took us to a study site. The Parker sites were clusters of three lines of one hundred feet each; a rebar stake marked each end. Years ago, they had been placed in a straight line, parallel, or in a star shape or other layout, depending on the lay of the land. We stretched a hundred-foot measuring tape from the first rebar to the last. At each one-inch mark, I held a pencil-sized bar with a one-inch circle welded at a right angle to its end. Looking through the inch circle, I identified which plants were there or whether it was a crown, an edge of a plant, or bare soil. Each site represented three hundred identifications tallied on a form with the abbreviated name of tribe and genus. We had to memorize many plant names and abbreviations. For example, few common grass abbreviations follow:

Bouteloua curtipendula, or side oats grama, marked with the abbreviation *bocu.*

Sitanion hystrix, or squirreltail, marked with the abbreviation *sifi.*

Aristida longiseta, or red three-awn, marked with the abbreviation *arlo.*

Panicae obtusum, or vine mesquite, marked with the abbreviation *paob.*

We walked many miles cross-country, up and down mountainsides with no trails. Sam walked faster, but I tended to find the sites, our strengths complementing each other. Sometimes we loaded horses into the trailer, drove as close as possible, and rode to outlying allotments. The directions to the Parker sites were handwritten descriptions of locations. They were dated from the 1930s into the 1960s. No GPS in those days!

For one site, we rode up a mesa from the patented Brewer Place on Crouch Creek. At Pine Springs, it was easy to find the Parker study site, but getting back, not so much. The top of the mesa was overgrown with bushy juniper trees fifteen to twenty feet tall. I could not see any distance for landmarks. Also, it was a cloudy gray day with no sun thus no shadows, which made finding the way more difficult. I was sure I was going the right direction but nothing looked familiar. *Could I be lost?* Finally, my brain clicked; I remembered that Visser, the mule I was riding, would know the way back to the trailer. I loosened his reins, he turned to the right, and soon I saw that he was following our previous tracks. I knew to trust my mount to find the way back. It worked again. We came down the hill, riding beside the creek; Visser shied. I was puzzled, as he was a calm, level-headed guy. Then I heard a rattle and saw the six-foot rattlesnake. Visser was avoiding the rattler. *Good mule.*

Though Darien's goal was to have four cattle allotments read, Sam and I read Parkers on seven allotments by the end of the summer. Darien was happy.

My dream of more seasonal work came at the end of summer, when Bill and I were having dinner at Kathy and Merle's Valley Bar with the District Ranger, Jordy.

"Do you want to work longer into the fall and winter?" asked Ranger Jordy.

"Yes. What would I be doing?"

"The Payson District timber-marking crew need another member for efficiency," he said.

Since I already had been hired for range, I could be used in other departments as funding allowed. The work would start in two weeks with a crew of six and continue until it snowed, it involved scrambling up steep slopes along the Mogollon Rim, carrying a day pack with water anf lunch, five liters of paint hanging from my belt, and a manual spray gun, a load of about thirty pounds. We were told which trees to mark, a prescription, such as "Trees more than nine inches in DBH with small-leaf mistletoe invasion." I was taught about DBH (diameter at breast height), seen defects, and how to measure tree height using triangulation. I saw lots of beautiful backcountry and working with a crew was fun.

I had the over-cab camper on Bessie parked near Payson to sleep for work nights but drove home for weekends. The Coleman lantern warmed the camper a little while I was awake, but with the lantern off, it was cold. One frosty morning, I stepped out of the camper, slipped on the icy step, and landed on my tailbone. I was crippled for a week, but was given the job of inputting the data we had collected. Then I was back in the field.

Achieving Benefits

"Cindy, the ranger wants to talk to you," Cheryl, one of the marking crew, said as she walked into the workshop.

Winter had arrived with snow; the tree marking project had been suspended till spring. We were cleaning all the paint sprayers, putting tools away, and entering the data into the complicated bean-counting computer programs. Why was I being called to the office? What could the ranger want?

With trepidation, I walked into her office and sat in front of her desk.

"I am offering you the thirteen-thirteen Wilderness position for Ranger Jordy in the Pleasant Valley District," said the ranger; I accepted.

Unbelievably, I was being offered a permanent job after only three years of seasonal work. I was ecstatic. After a trial period of six months, I would have medical insurance and a retirement plan. I was close to supporting myself. Maybe, in my mid-fifties, I was even starting a career. The Forest Service *thirteen-thirteen* job designation meant my employer guaranteed me thirteen weeks of employment each year; I would be laid off for the other thirteen weeks but guaranteed work each successive season. However, if another district or department had funding, I could work for them after the first thirteen weeks, extending my earnings. The system required me to only take two weeks off between seasons, a benefit to me. It was easier for the managers to use an experienced part-time permanent employee than hire a new one, plus they knew the quality of the employee's work.

My tasks would be like my seasonal job in Montana and the times I had been with Tommy. But now I was responsible, not only following. The job required much more inventory of trails, campsites, and signs. Also, I would be supervising the trail crew, as Tommy had before me.

The Wilderness job involved a teaching component, Leave No Trace, a land ethics program for the crews and visitors in the backcountry. I would be trained as a level-two law enforcement officer able to write tickets on violations of 36 CFR 261 regulations.

Unlike my five-day tour of duty in the Lincoln Ranger District, the Pleasant Valley Ranger District tour of duty involved four ten-hour days back-to-back. That meant eight days on duty with four days off. I had three designated Wilderness areas to patrol: the Sierra Ancha, Salome, and Hell's Gate. I customarily trailered two and sometimes four horses to a location where I would set up a camp for myself and the crew. I had to build a corral, set up a water trough for the stock, and erect the communal canvas tent. Often, I had the trail crew in camp. When we camped together, we would usually combine ingredients for meals. We were responsible for purchasing our own food; the Pleasant Valley Ranger District did not supply the crews' food as the Lincoln District had.

Aca loved to come with me on the trail; as I mounted, she would jump up and down, yipping exuberantly. She would not be quiet until I was on the move then she followed obediently.

One day, while patrolling the Rim Trail in the Sierra Ancha Wilderness, I saw many tracks in a muddy depression. I dismounted to see what I could read. I saw deer, coyote, and cougar tracks. The deer tracks were under all the others. The coyote tracks were on top of all. I tracked into timber. I found a deer carcass. The coyote tracks left the trail and ended at the carcass. The cougar must have taken the deer and carried it into the timber, and afterward, the coyote had come to eat.

Another time, I was riding Joe, a quarter horse/thoroughbred mixed gelding, and leading the mule, Walz. Aca was following behind Walz as she should. It had been a long day around the Rim Trail. I was on my way to camp, when I heard a scream. The horse and mule, startled, stopped with ears erect and countenance alert.

"Aca, heel," I said.

She looked puzzled, as if to say, "Why are you ordering me again?"

I was disconcerted by the scream. I had never heard such a sound; as if a woman were being tortured. I stopped and looked around. I saw a small fawn cowering under a New Mexican locust bush. It let out another scream. It is common for deer to hide their young. This fawn's mother had left it there for safety, but we had come too close and scared it. I knew the mother would soon come to the fawn's call. I left in a hurry not wanting to cause further alarm.

It was another sunny day without a cloud in the sky. My task was to find a trail route from the head of Workman Creek over a low pass into the Reynolds Creek drainage. At lunchtime, I stopped in a meadow to let Joe graze. I sat against an aspen tree to eat another squished sandwich and drink warm, stale water. After eating, I had an urge to roll over onto my stomach. As I lay prone on the ground, I felt an electrical charge emanating from the earth into me and returning to the ground, giving me a sense of euphoria. I felt it was a Spirit Guide encouraging me.

Another time, I was working with the crew to ensure the quality of work met the Forest Service standards. I dug into the hillside with a pick mattock to widen the trail. It was late August. The crew were disgruntled. They were working slower and complaining. Even though the work was in beautiful country, it was tedious: trimming brush, digging out roots, and swinging a pick mattock to move soil and rock.

"What is the problem?" I asked the crew in frustration.

"We want to go for a ride," one whined. "We're tired of just maintaining the trail."

I was scheduled to patrol and access the condition of the Coon Creek Trail, named for all the racoons that inhabited the area. I decided to take them with me. The route was many miles long with several switchbacks descending a thousand feet to hot scrub-oak hillsides, across Deep Creek, and up Moody Point Trail back to Aztec and camp, an extreme route. On the ride, one crew member lost his boot heel, the horses were tired, Aca was sore-footed, and the crew were exhausted. I was exhausted too but would not let them know. I had used one of Tommy's strategies to focus the crew. Afterward, they did not want to go with me on a patrol again but were content with trail maintenance.

On my days off, Bill and I often visited the retired Tommy and his wife, Lavern. Tommy was doing poorly but enjoyed the visits. He always asked about one trail or another and about the horses. He sold his horse, Duke, to a rancher. The rancher had problems with Duke and shot him. Tommy was sad; I was appalled. Duke was an excellent horse and no horse deserves mistreatment.

Much of the trail maintenance in Pleasant Valley R.D. was accomplished by volunteer groups. We hosted the American Hiking Club many times. The volunteers usually flew into Phoenix. We would meet them in a government van and go to the camp below Aztec Peak. They would take advantage of the tents I had set up.

I would serve meals such as chicken fajitas, hamburgers, fried chicken, with salads, and dessert of sopaipillas, brownies, or fruit. When I purchased the food, I had to remember everything since there was no resupply. The ten-by-twelve-foot canvas wall tent was the kitchen. I used the district's two-burner camp stove, sauce pans, cast-iron skillets, and a two-gallon coffee pot. Two folding tables were my workspace. Large coolers contained perishables. The first night in camp, I held a short orientation. Volunteers were encouraged to sign up to help with food preparation, cleanup after meals, or set lunch items on a table. Each person could choose a combination of items set on the table for lunch. After breakfast, with lunches made and cleaning done, I hefted my pack. We all carried trail tools to the maintenance site. Cooking breakfast at the beginning and dinner at the end of each day made for dawn-to-dusk work for me. I was paid for ten hours a day, regardless of how many hours I worked. I enjoyed the volunteers and working with them. They always completed quality work.

1995, Me with my horse, Joe, and pack horse, Bud, in the Sierra Ancha mountains of Arizona.

1996, Cynthia packing a trail crew camp into the Peak
Fire area, Four Peaks Wilderness, Arizona

Each day, I lifted the forty-pound saddle onto my horse and the eighty-pound bales of hay to feed him. My body grew stronger, I stopped using the lighter Pulaski, and used the heavier pick mattock which was more efficient in removing rock and soil. As I strengthened, my mind became more alert. I was more aware of the slant of light and the shadows telling me the time of day; of slight sounds alerting me to nearby wild animals; and of the smell of wood smoke, which signaled either campers or forest fire. With added awareness, I felt safer in my surroundings.

I enjoyed working the one-man crosscut saw, stretching back and forward in rhythm, to remove logs from the trails. I liked swinging an eight-pound pick mattock to widen the trails or nipping branches from the trail. Yes, it was hard work, but I gained strength and thrived using my obsolete skills and living outside. I worked with horses and mules as partners. I was helping Earth by preventing erosion and avoiding sensitive ecological areas. I often had an aching body, but my spirit soared. I liked the mountain breeze blowing my braid. Large Ponderosa trees surrounded me like a hug. I felt I was communing with ancient ancestors who tread this way previously. I respected this place and its four-leggeds and feathered inhabitants. I had found my niche.

Living in Ashes

The sixty-three-thousand-acre forest fire in the Four Peaks Wilderness started in early summer 1995. By July, with the help of rain, the fire was out. The Mesa Ranger District requested I come from Pleasant Valley District to support a restoration trail crew in the fire area. I would use El Oso Road, a steep, narrow, winding road near Roosevelt Lake, which started at an elevation of 2,000 feet and climbed to Lone Pine Saddle at 5,700 feet. I would camp with the stock on the saddle. The crew's spike camp would be several miles inside the Wilderness boundary.

The first day of each tour of duty, I would load the mules, my horse, and tack into the trailer. While the crew had a shorter drive with no animals to handle and no stops along the way. I had to stop in Payson to buy the food necessary for the crew for five days, no resupply. I packed the meat in a cooler with dry ice; the perishables went into another cooler. I met the crew at noon at Lone Pine Saddle. I loaded the coolers, the crew's duffels, camp tents, Coleman stove, and water onto the mules to take to spike camp. After unloading at their camp, I rode back to Lone Pine Saddle. I would still have to unsaddle, feed stock, make my lonely camp, and feed myself.

On the second day of each tour of duty, I filled five-gallon containers, each weighing forty pounds, from the water buffalo, a water trailer with dual wheels. I lifted two containers into each pannier and, with the three mules, I would pack twelve containers to spike camp.

On the third day, I drove the truck, pulling the buffalo, to the Roosevelt Ranger District workstation. After cleaning the water trailer with a chlorine product and rinsing it thoroughly, I filled it with fresh water. I drove along El Oso Road, pulling the water. Because it was impossible to make one tight switchback with a trailer, a scary special- built narrow track around a small hill made it possible to approach the tight turn safely.

On the first trip with the water buffalo, the truck did not have enough power to pull the steepest hill. I had to back around a sharp turn, empty some of the water, and try again. I backed and emptied water three times before the trailer was light enough for the truck to make it. Then there was not enough water to supply the needs of both camps and stock, causing an extra trip to supply water. I was given a more powerful truck for the following tour of duty.

The Wilderness manager at the Supervisor's Office decided a pit toilet for the trail crew use was too much impact on the Wilderness. Thus, they used garbage bags for feces. On the fourth day, I went to spike camp to pack the trash and the double-bagged feces out on the mules. I transferred all bags to the truck and drove them to a disposal location in Roosevelt. I knew it was a dangerous biohazard for me to handle and pack feces out on mules, transfer it to the truck, and then handle it again to dispose of at Roosevelt. My greatest fear was having the feces bags break.

On the fifth day, I rode to spike camp with the mules and empty panniers to pack the camp out. When we all arrived at Lone Pine Saddle, I loaded the camp items and my gear into the truck and the stock into the four-horse trailer. I had a four-hour drive home to Pleasant Valley. The crew had a two-hour drive to the Goldfield administration site. At the station, I would still have to unload and put the horses up, and feed them; long days.

"What is this?" my supervisor, who had come to Lone Pine Saddle, asked about the brightly colored plastic baling twine on one of the pack saddles.

"The leather was dry and broke. I braided four pieces of twine to replace the carrier strap. The buckle fits nicely into the braid to adjust the breeching." I tried to explain the flat braid I had made to replace the broken strap that held the britching. Thanks to George at the ranch, I knew how.

"It's a better repair job than I could have done at the barn," he said.

It rained about once a week, causing ash to flow across the trail and fill the trail with wet, compacted ash, obliterating the work the trail crew had completed. No vegetation remained. But as the weeks went by, oak grew first, making scattered green bouquets under gnarled black trunks. The Four Peaks fire rehabilitation project lasted three months. I ate ash, slept in ash, and had ash ground into my skin. I thought my hands and legs would be permanently blotched gray. There was ash on the saddles and pads. At home, I bathed with a scrub brush before I could see pink skin. The Four Peaks fire trail rehab was by far the hardest project I was ever assigned.

Moonlighting

During off-season at Pleasant Valley District, the Globe or Mesa District would request me to work during the winters, which I was glad to do. When I started at Globe, which was too far from home to drive each day, I slept on the office floor for four nights, which was unsustainable. The second week, I moved our small camp trailer to Globe for my nights away from home or when not in a trail camp at a work site. The trailer's heater did not work. I later discovered the roof leaked, which meant that after work, I was on a ladder, painting the roof with a sealer. Another problem was that the water froze. I wrapped the pipe with heat tape and pipe insulation to prevent future freezing. When it was fixed, I did enjoy the shower and flush toilet the trailer provided. I never did find a way to fix the heater, but instead, used an electric one.

Globe assigned me my biggest project with the Forest Service which was to design a new non-motorized trail route off any two-track road for the Arizona Trail. The route started at Picketpost Trailhead, near Superior, and went south to the Bureau of Land Management boundary near the Gila River. The original route was a combination of old road beds that were too steep, eroded, or followed desert washes that flooded. I walked nine sections of the Upper Sonoran Desert ecosystem. I used contour maps to study drainages, cliffs, and valleys, flagged the route and supervised building the twelve-mile alignment designed to prevent erosion and avoid cultural and ecologically sensitive areas. It was a three-winter-season task to lay out the route and more to build it. Paying attention to trail grade and using wildlife crossings at washes, made a good trail for hikers and horsemen, but the mountain bikers doubted it would produce a good ride but once they rode it, they were pleased.

I was concerned about a section of forest road near Cottonwood camp that was used by trucks, ATVs, bicyclers, horses, and hikers. Surely, a motorized vehicle would collide with a hiker or rider, with the Forest held liable. Bringing my concern to my supervisor, she arranged another alignment planned for a non motorized trail which I designed and supervised the building. In all, I was responsible for approximately twenty miles of new alignment of the Arizona Trail. I camped with, cooked for, and supervised the volunteer groups, who did excellent, quality work. It was a pleasure to work with them, and

Exploring to find a route for the Arizona Trail through the
Upper Sonoran Desert ecosystem, Globe RD, Arizona

I met a wonderfully diverse group of people and enjoyed the time we spent together.

My Globe supervisor mentored me by sending me to many useful training sessions. I assisted the Globe recreation staff with special use permits, developed recreation site issues, and the Salt River Permit Program. I learned many of the Forest Service standards, handbooks, and CFRs.

The river rangers invited me to an overnight float on the Salt River from US 60 to the SR 288 bridge near Roosevelt Lake. Our expedition included two rafts and our purpose was Wilderness patrols. It was February, it snowed, and the raft wrapped on a mid river rock, causing me and the other passenger to fly into freezing water and swim. In near panic, I struggled to swim, fully clothed, to the steep round-rock shore cut-bank. I forgot the signal to indicate I was OK which brought angst to the boatman before I remembered and signaled. The other passenger, being more comfortable in water than I, swam downriver and, dangerously affected by the cold water, had to be pulled into the other downriver raft. Our river ranger agilely leaped onto the rock safely. Other rafters stopped and, with a complicated rope system, pulled our raft off the rock. We joined our other raft and beached in a backwater. I discovered river folks thought nothing of nakedness, which was a good thing, as we had to remove all wet clothing and replace it with dry clothing before we became dangerously hypothermic. The second day turned sunny, and I enjoyed the trip through the awesome canyon, despite the unexpected swim.

One day, I was driving to Globe for work, when I met a scruffy young man on the Young road. By his green pants and White fire boots, I recognized him as a Hot Shot, a firefighter. An old RV was parked at an angle by the road.

"May I help you?" I asked as I rolled my window down. It was protocol to stop to help on the isolated Young road.

"My RV stopped running. I may be out of gas," he Responded.

"I don't have any gas, but the rancher back aways would. I could give you a ride and introduce you," I said.

"Thanks."

I shucked my provisions into the backseat of the Tacoma, crowding Chewie, my dog. The Hot Shot put his gas cans in the bed and squeezed into the front seat.

Waiting for volunteers to arrive, Picketpost TH, Arizona Trail.

The rancher gave us gas, glad to help. I took the Hot Shot back to his RV. After he poured the gas into the RV, it still did not start.

"You don't need to wait for me. I have everything I need to spend the night. A buddy will come for me tomorrow," he said.

"Good luck," I called. Chewie jumped into the front seat, and the two of us continued toward Globe.

It was dusk by the time I was on the paved road, driving slowly, watching for javelinas and deer crossing. I saw a vehicle coming fast behind me. The road was curvy, so I pulled over to let the speeders by but the truck pulled in behind me.

"Why did you pull over?" the policeman asked.

"It seemed you were coming fast, so I was getting out of the way," I said.

"May I see your driver's license and ID?"

"My purse is buried. I picked up a Hot Shot and tossed everything back. I have a dog in the truck," I said as I slowly stepped out and began digging for my purse.

"OK," he said as he stepped back nervously.

I moved slowly, letting Chewie out so she would not growl. I found my license and ID. He relaxed, and his partner came closer and started petting Chewie.

"You picked up a Hot Shot?" he asked.

"Yes," I said, and I explained my encounter.

Trail building volunteers resting in camp after a day of constructing the Arizona Trail.

Constructing the Arizona Trail with volunteers.

"Do you usually pick people up alongside the road? That could be dangerous."

"No, but I work for the Forest Service and recognized him," I said.

"Have a good evening," he said as he handed my license and ID back. They drove past as I loaded Chewie. The officer probably thought no one could have invented such a story.

The Sierra Club were the volunteers for a trail maintenance project for Globe RD on the Montana Mountain Trail. We backpacked several miles to the base of the mountain, where there was a spring, and made camp for five days. The Sierra Club provided food for themselves, making my tasks easier. They prepared large quantities and invited me to eat with them. I dug a long pit toilet. Each person was to shovel dirt over his or her droppings to prevent flies. They practiced the Leave-no-Trace land ethics I always used in camp.

After dinner, Chewie, who usually stayed by my side, would leave me, and put herself to bed in my tent, snuggled on my sleeping bag. If it was a freezing night, I would let her curl inside the sleeping bag with me; we could keep each other warm. I enjoyed working with the Sierra Club group. In all, I spent five winters working for the Globe District.

The Mesa District requested me to guide a leadership team made up of Washington DC, Forest Service Regional, and Ranger District administrators on a show-me trip into the Superstition Wilderness Mountains; a two-night trip. I was the lead of professionals much more educated than I, but I was to teach them Wilderness ethics and concerns. We camped in Angel Basin to camp. The next day, rode to the abandoned Reavis Ranch site. On the way, one of the people needed to urinate and could not wait till we were on level ground. He handed his lead rope to Rick, a Montana horseman familiar with backcountry challenges. The lead rope went under his horse's tail, and the rodeo began. I jumped off my horse to help settle horses and people. Rick landed down the steep hillside, his ribs hitting a rock. I held the bushes back so he could catch his breath and eventually climb back onto the trail.

Meanwhile, the leadership people suggested a helicopter, but we had steep-brushy hillsides and no radio contact. They suggested that we move on to a level place where we could radio for the helicopter. I responded that there might be no radio farther up the trail; we would be farther from the trailhead; there was no motorized conveyance allowed in the Wilderness. I explained that what they were viewing was not an unusual scenario for Wilderness. I directed the Mesa

A diamond back rattle snake beside the Arizona Trail, Globe Ranger District, Arizona.

R.D. employee to go to the nearest trailhead with Rick leading their horses. Rick knew he could walk but not ride. About four hours later when Rick finally arrived at the hospital, he had several broken ribs and a punctured lung.

After I had moved to Black Mesa District in Heber, Arizona, a certificate of award caught up with me. It read, "For your professional, positive, calm, and decisive response to the Rick Potts horse incident, March 3, 2002. Your leadership and willingness to share your passion for Wilderness helped refocus the group and resulted in a positive experience for all trip participants. On behalf of Rick and the Arthur Carhart National Wilderness Training Center, I extend my sincerest thanks."

CHAPTER 13

Attacked by Cancer

O N A JUNE MORNING IN 1998, I WAS LAZING IN BED, WAITING TO
see the rising sun slant through the eastern window. I did my
periodic breast examination as Bill snored beside me. I felt a lump.
I checked again, and yes; the lump was really there.

"Bill," I said as I turned and shook him awake, "I have a breast
lump!"

Half asleep, he said, "We'll make an appointment for a scan," and
turned over. It was his automatic physician's response.

I called Tami. "But, Mom, you told me months ago!" she exclaimed.

"How could I forget?" I asked.

"Maybe Aunt Nati's medical problems, caring for Jammi, and
Bill overwhelmed you," Tami said. (Both Tami and David called my
mom Jammi.) Bill continued to have his annual winter respiratory
infections and periodic heart attacks. He would see a cardiologist
wherever he was working but it was inconsistent care which made
for poor medicine.

I had totally forgotten about my lump; had I discovered it first at
home or in camp; had told Bill about it? He must have forgotten too.

A scan confirmed my findings but my mammograms did not
show the breast tumor. Bill and I had put off our twentieth wedding
anniversary trip because Bill had a ureter blockage necessitating
emergency care. Wanting to go on the trip, we had reservations on
a small cruise ship to Alaska coming up soon. Now the trip was in

jeopardy because of me. Aunt Nati was doing better and so was Mom. If Bill and I took the trip, Tami planned to visit her frequently.

"How critical would my outcome be if I scheduled treatment later in July?" I asked the doctor.

"Not critical at all. We are several weeks out before we could schedule anyway," he said.

"Let's schedule the surgery in July," I said.

With the cancer hanging over us, we went on the cruise. The ship accommodated about eighty people. We stood on the Athabasca Glacier, the apex of the North American continent; from the glacier, ice melt flowed into each ocean surrounding the continent. Standing there felt like standing on a mountaintop, a feeling of high altitude with fresh cool air and a view but it was an expanse of dirty ice and snow. We watched grizzly bears fishing at Glacier Bay and enjoyed the history of Skagway. We explored the rustic town of Haines and visited an eagle rehabilitation facility, where the most common injuries were caused by power lines and automobiles.

Back in Arizona, Bill drove me to Phoenix for surgery. Three-quarters of my right breast was removed; thirteen lymph nodes were removed; few had cancer. I had two inches of stitches and a drain tube stitched under my arm. Bill left me with my friend in Mesa, who could help take care of the surgical wounds, and I would be closer to medical help. Bill went back to work. When the drain and stitches were removed, Bill came to take me home. I was about to take a rough ride, I knew I had to hang on and keep an eye on the future. Spirit Guide would be with me giving me courage.

Three weeks later, I received a call. "We didn't get clean margins," the doctor said.

"What does that mean?" I asked.

"We have to take more tissue to make sure we have all the cancer."

My wound was healed and now I faced more cutting. I needed to fight this cancer. All my efforts and prayers had to go to that end. So on a furnace-hot August day, I drove myself south toward Globe, heading to Phoenix for more surgery. I wore a skirt and sandals for comfort in the heat.

Pop! A tire blew out.

Why am I being challenged, not only with cancer but also tires? I removed the tire iron and tire and started to change the tire. My toes were burning from the fiery-hot sand pouring into my sandals.

I was light-headed from the sun cooking my hatless head. I felt like giving up. But if I did, I would dehydrate and be found later as a flattened mummy.

A savior came around the corner in the form of the UPS truck. The driver stopped and finished changing the tire. Spirit Guide was at work again.

After surgery, I spent a night with my friend and then drove home.

As soon as the second surgical wound healed, it was time for chemotherapy. No one knows the outcome of cancer. I reflected on the adventures of my life; much of it had been good, but I had had challenges too. What beautiful places I had had the privilege to see and enjoy with my children. Perhaps my next life would be another adventure.

How fleeting this life really is. I remembered a graphic at Arizona-Sonora Desert Museum outside Tucson. Coming out of the mine exhibit is a walkway with geologic periods marked at intervals. The Cretaceous Period is a length of two feet, representing 145 million years; the Jurassic is a length of less than a foot, representing 56 million years; and three feet represents the Triassic Period of 201.3 million years. At the top of the walkway is a sliver to represent the time of humans. What a short time we have been on Earth, and even shorter is our life span.

Facing the possible end of my fleeting life, I thought about the things that are important, not new furniture or pretty clothes, nor things money can buy, those things wear out. Whereas connections to other people and experiences form memories that grow more precious with time. How little we really need for survival: shelter, food, and water. I remembered my backpacking trips. How simple life could be when I was carrying everything I needed on my back. If I had a greater knowledge of edible plants, water sources, and the other resources nature offered, I could have carried even less. Others have lived off the land with no supplies from stores. But in contrast, how complicated we often make our lives.

By myself each week I went to a Phoenix oncologist, who came to Payson weekly to treat patients; Bill was anxious, as his previous wife had died of breast cancer. My cancer scared him, causing him to be remote, holding his thoughts in, and seldom talking to me, which made me feel terribly alone.

Since the medical technicians were better in Phoenix, with sharper needles and better skills, I chose to take my treatments there. The oncology office was only a few blocks from the Forest Service Supervisor's Office. I could stay with my friend and could work short days at the Forest Service office in Phoenix for the Wilderness staff officer.

I had worn my hair in one braid that fell halfway down my back but with the prospect of losing my hair, I cut it short, much like a boy's cut to avoid great chunks of hair falling out, causing a mess in the house and clogging the shower.

In January, Tami was moving to Corpus Christi for a new job. When she went to find housing, she invited me along as I was between chemotherapy and radiation treatments. On the way, we stopped at Carlsbad Caverns and walked into the cave mouth and out the elevator, the other entrance but my energy was so low I almost couldn't finish the hike. We stayed in a hotel in Corpus. I was taking four ibuprofen tablets every four hours and still suffering from an extremely painful shoulder. She found a nice little apartment. Afterwards we took a side trip to Padre Island and the Sabal Palm Sanctuary. In the wetlands of south Texas, we saw a variety of beautiful shore birds and many alligators. We had a good time despite my pain.

By February, I was taking another course of chemo and working at the Forest Supervisor's office. Each weekend, I drove myself from home to Young.

Spring arrived as did the time for the 1998 Wilderness Rendezvous held on the North Kaibab, I was scheduled to give a mule-packing demonstration and training. I was weak from the chemo and radiation. While teaching several employees from the National Forest Service, the Bureau of Land Management and various county deputies, I could only lift a half bale of hay to demonstrate the sling-pack method, used in the Scapegoat Wilderness. Midway through the week, I drove to Phoenix for my chemo treatment. When I returned several coworkers were supportive and cooked dinner for me. I was so exhausted that all I wanted to do was crawl into my sleeping bag, but I ate a little to please them. I was gaining respect; I had advocates and wonderful colleagues in my field. It felt good.

Cancer treatments continued for a year: first chemo treatments, then radiation, and then more chemo. I drove myself to all but two treatments. I coerced Bill into going with me twice, but I could tell he was not going to come again. It is against my nature to insist but if someone sees my need and offers, I welcome it. When I drove three hours to home after a treatment, I often had to stop along the highway. Sometimes I had to nap, but several times, I was also sick to my stomach. I carried water to clean myself. I lost lots of hair; what little was left was baby-thin.

After I was finished with treatments, one of my coworkers, who espoused the Native American lifestyle, invited me to a healing sweat. I was instructed to drink a gallon of water the day of the sweat. The lodge was made of bent and tied willow branches covered with tarps, torn quilts, and old blankets. It looked like a giant ragged turtle. Turtles represent family, a woman's womb, a place of rebirth and renewal. Sweating cleansed, a purification of mind and spirit.

We gathered at dusk in shorts and tank tops around the fire, heating the rocks to make steam in the lodge. After some grateful prayers to the Creator, acknowledging each direction, north, east, south, west and to the sky, we crawled clockwise into the lodge. One friend handed me a small green juniper bough; we sat in a circle, the hot rocks were placed in a central hole, the door flap was closed making it cave-dark. Water was sprinkled on the rocks; the smell of wet earth permeated the lodge. The odor emitted from the juniper twig helped me to survive the heat. Prayers to the ancestors, to the earth, and for my health followed. Chemo chemicals were sweated out. I felt a new beginning. I perceived a special connection with the community of earth and fellowship with these friends.

The medical system considers you a cancer survivor after five years. But my nurse friend kept looking at me, watching for signs of returning cancer. Now more than twenty years have passed, she no longer looks at me as if she is assessing my health.

Losing Mom, December 26, 1999

Aunt Nati, Mom's sister, had an acute kidney infection, so I took her to the hospital in Phoenix and stayed with her for several days. Mom had recently been diagnosed with stomach cancer, necessitating surgery and, later, an oral anticancer treatment. I was overwhelmed in taking care of three eighty-year-olds. I was still recovering from cancer treatments. About then, Bill complained that Mom and Aunt Nati were taking too much of my time. I responded, "Don't make me choose between you or Mom and Aunt Nati." He stopped complaining.

At Christmastime, Tami drove from Mesa to meet us at Mom and Aunt Nati's. Bill and I brought gifts from Young to celebrate. Aunt Nati greeted us at the door.

"Inge can't get up," she said.

Bill took one look at Mom and pulled me aside. "She is dying," he said. "Take me home."

I guessed that Bill, as a therapeutic radiologist who had treated cancer patients previously in Florida, many of whom had passed, did not want to watch another death. However, it was a three-hour round-trip drive home to Young and back to Mom in Payson, which complicated things for me. Tami stayed. I drove Bill home and packed an overnight bag. Back in Payson, Aunt Nati told me that when I had previously visited, Mom had forced herself to dress and sit at the table. When alone, Mom had been staying in bed. Thus, I was unaware of how fast she was declining.

I sat beside Mom. I felt I needed to say something as a goodbye. "Thanks for teaching me whatever is good in me. I love you," I said not knowing if Mom heard me, but she seemed to relax.

Our priest came to give final rites. Aunt Nati, Tami, and I stayed with Mom as she quietly passed. We washed her and dressed her in her favorite outfit. The mortuary arrived to take her for cremation.

The following summer, I took her ashes to White Grass. We had a simple graveside service with close friends and family. I was especially pleased Judy and Rachel were there. I later placed her headstone, which was engraved from a granite rock I had taken from the meadow at White Grass.

I cannot remember being close to Mom. She was stern. When I was a child, she was always busy doing the office work on the ranch or directing the help at the main kitchen or in the dude cabins. I was at the barn. When she home-schooled me, we had a particularly difficult time, which created further distance between us. I often felt I was being reprimanded and that made me think, *I cannot do anything right.*

Though Mom and Rachel took short outings to pick berries or mushrooms and drove around exploring, they invited me only once that I remember. I went and had a good time picking raspberries in the Gros Ventre. I did hunt mushrooms near the ranch with Mom and Oma, which I enjoyed, but more often picked mushrooms on my own. I loved her though I felt I was a disappointment to Mom, whereas Dad was my buddy and asked me to work with him and go with him. Since I was not close to Mom, I had tried to make it up by being dutiful.

My Forest on Fire, 2002

I had been working for Pleasant Valley District for six years when, at age sixty, I decided my time of swinging an eight-pound pick-mattock, moving soil, building trails, and lifting eighty-pound bales of hay onto pack animals was past. Sleeping on the ground had lost its appeal; my bones and muscles ached. At a Forest Service training, I met Kate, the Black Mesa Ranger. I mentioned that I needed to move into developed recreation, Wilderness work was becoming too difficult. My criterion was to have a job no longer than a two-hour drive from home. Kate's district was within that range.

"I want to see your application. We have an opening in developed recreation," she said.

I applied and emphasized the diverse tasks and training I had had in Montana and Arizona. My application was accepted. I started work in March 2002 at Black Mesa Ranger District, Sitgreaves National Forest, Heber Ranger District. Using Bessie, I pulled my twenty-foot camper trailer from Globe up the Salt River Canyon through Show Low to Heber-Overgaard. David, who was visiting, and Tami helped with the move. Bessie had a hard time pulling the hills but had served us well for thirty years. I had to tell Bill, who was at home, that Bessie was getting tired and should not do hard jobs anymore.

As a permanent employee, I could rent a trailer space on the district administration site for a year. After a year, I would have to find other housing. When I was working in the office, I had to tie Aca to the trailer. After work, I would take her for a walk, often ranging far and exploring new territory.

Soon after I arrived at Black Mesa, the Rodeo- Chediski fire, a huge forest fire, started. Everyone on the administration site and in the Heber-Overgaard area was evacuated. Many employees and I moved to the Chevelon administration site many miles west. We patrolled, looking for fire starts ahead of the primary fire. It was often smoky. We took turns answering the phones back at the deserted office in Overgaard. On the last day I manned the phones, I could see the flames through the office window. The dozer driver was grading between the flames and the buildings; sometimes he was driving in the flames.

The ranger declared, "We are leaving now. Get in the trucks outside. At the golf course, each of you drive a vehicle staged there so we can save them from the fire. Keys are in the ignitions."

The direct route to Chevelon had been closed, so we drove north on SR 377. Stopping on a ridge, we made sure everyone was together. I looked south; there was the glow of the fire, bright orange/red to the east; the north was all smoky, and all around us was orange. There was a silver-dollar-sized spot of blue sky over Holbrook; everything else seemed to be ablaze. My heart was beating double time, and my breathing fast. I was frightened—perhaps all the village and District buildings would burn.

We drove to Holbrook, to Winslow, and south to Chevelon work-station to avoid the fire. At Chevelon, it was a relief to be safe in my trailer. Once while I was patrolling, I had heart palpitations and trouble breathing. I stopped the truck. When my heart slowed, I drove to the fire camp for medical support. The paramedic checked me and sent me to Payson for more tests. The palpitations were a panic response from the angst caused by the fire.

Eventually, the rains came to help the Hot Shots put the fire out. The buildings were saved by the courageous dozer driver.

The summer after the fire, I was directed to reroute or reestablish the trails in the Rodeo-Chediski area. Many of the trails were in the Lakeside District, the neighboring district. I wondered if I was going to work in ash during all my time with the Forest Service. I had worked in the Canyon Creek fire area in Montana; the Four Peaks fire rehab; the Raccoon Creek fire area in the Sierra Ancha; in the Pinal Mountains; and now the Chediski fire area. I had watched the Dude fire from my home in Young. Prevalent fires are a reality in the western landscape. Over ninety percent are started by careless humans, as was the Chediski fire.

After work, I would walk the dry drainages in the fire area with my dog, Aca. As the rain began, I was amazed at how quickly plants sprang from the ashes. I was delighted to see a little green sprigs. As gifts, I made wooden shadow boxes with the treasures I found: shiny round little rocks, pretty moths, and colorful dried plants. On the back of the shadow boxes, I placed the poem I had written:

Reflections After the Rodeo-Chediski Fire

Throughout eternity is change.
Bad things happen, floods, fire, famine.
Crops fail, homes destroyed,
Death.
Fire incinerates forests and dwellings.
Created from the rubble is new life.
Grass and flowers emerge.
There is still beauty, colors, shapes, textures,
Contrasts in nature.
Here are little treasures of nature
I collected in my evening walks
Among the blackened skeletal tree trunks
And flood-arranged creek beds
Of the Rodeo-Chediski fire.
Nothing remains the same.
However, regard the seemingly insignificant.
Observe the spirit of life.
Grasp and retain hope.

As I settled into the job at Black Mesa Ranger District, I read my job description: "to execute the Recreation Operations and Management Plan."

I asked my supervisor, "Where is the recreation management plan?" I remembered all the documents I had been handed to read as a seasonal in Montana. Surely, they had something similar here.

"Why don't you write it?" my supervisor said.

I did. For the Management Plan, I listed all the recreation sites, mapped them, and created a maintenance schedule. My goal was to create a document that would contribute to consistency in management. I also wrote camp host guidelines and made maps of the trails for the hiker information.

I often coordinated volunteer groups to maintain and build trails. Mostly, I supervised trail crews and recreation facility maintenance crews. As a supervisor, I believed my job was to facilitate my crews, ordering necessary supplies and helping to solve problems; often, I worked beside them. I I assisted the migration of Meaningful Measures, a complicated, detailed inventory system of Forest recreation facilities, into Infra, both complicated computer database programs. As a Forest Protection Officer, I spent much time patrolling, contacting the visiting public. I informed them of the pertinent Forest regulations, a traveling information center. Hopefully, it kept them safe and protected the natural resources. I seldom entered camps when I saw alcohol and guns as it was too volatile and perhaps dangerous. I continued to work for the Globe District during the winters, mostly on trails, rerouting and maintenance, planning, and supervising crews.

I was determined that my work would pay for the work- related expenses. For instance, I bought my vehicle, bought the camp trailer, and paid their costs. Bill took care of our property and house in Young.

My year of living at the Black Mesa administration site came to an end. I needed to find other housing. When I accepted the job at Black Mesa, I expected to work for five or six years. Buying a house seemed a better value than renting. I went to a loan officer and explained my circumstances and income to find out how much I could spend on a house. I did not tell the officer I had a little savings; that was for my security. I bought a nice modular home in Overgaard, spending less than the officer thought I could afford. The modular became my primary residence.

I was Bill's third family; he was twenty years older than I. He had paid for several college educations and had no savings or life insurance. I knew I would have the property in Young, two vehicles, and his Social Security to live on. The Young house needed many repairs, which he refused to do; work was not for my entertainment but essential for my survival.

Bessie pulled the trailer to Young, but I decided she needed to retire. I listed my permanent residence in Young, where there were twelve acres and a big home with a barn. Bill's heart and breathing got worse. He wanted to stay in Young but finally relented and came to Overgaard, as he saw the need. His being in Overgaard made life easier on me. I had only one house to take care of and no weekly commute.

Bill's Passing, 2006

Bill had been in hospice for a year; his final episode was an internal bleed. I called all the children. Sue Ann, Jane, and Fred arrived before his passing on June 1, 2006. I had been with Bill for more than thirty years.

I thought I was tough. I took only a week off and went back to work. A month later, I broke down; I had to find a quiet place to grieve; a place with no responsibilities; a place of no distractions. What was I going to do? I had previously experienced the losses of Dad, Mother, and Aunt Nati, but losing Bill was a whole new level of loss.

I called Carolea and Ben, dear friends who lived on McFadden Creek, south of Young on an isolated patented ranch. They had a simple one-room homestead cabin. I asked if I could stay in the cabin. They assured me I could. It had wood heat, an add-on bathroom, and a wonderful view of the woods.

Emotionally exhausted, I went to sleep before the sun went down but I was awake with it rising. I walked their driveway with a pick mattock. Swinging the pick mattock, I built drainage ditches to prevent water from eroding their driveway. It was familiar work, like building trails. It was rhythmic, meditative, and a healing activity. After several hours, I would take a break and walk to the big house. Ben would be up and have coffee percolating in a white enamel pot on the wood stove.

"Morning," he would say, greeting me. "Help yourself to coffee."

One morning, I was sniffling, sorely feeling my loss, and feeling sorry for myself.

"Get over it!" Carolea said sternly.

The comment was sharp; it shook me. It made me stop wallowing in self-pity. After a week, I went back to work at Overgaard. I still grieved; felt the void in my life. But I was at least able to go back to work. I felt loss, anger, and sadness. But I put one foot in front of the other and slowly forced myself to move forward. Life goes on; Spirit Guide would lead me.

As the summer ended and my vacation time approached, I realized I could not face the holidays. My only commitment was to go to work at Globe starting in January. Meanwhile, what was I going to do? I wanted to avoid anything about holidays—people, their happiness, giving or receiving presents, or even my daughter, whom I love and enjoy; I would run away. I wanted to be away from home with its many memories, nor did I want to interact with people, so I planned a road trip with Chewie.

Under the shell on the Tacoma, I built a bed high enough for a kitchen and a toolbox to slide underneath. I crisscrossed boards into a boat-type dresser for clothes. The bed was short for my frame, so I slept diagonally, with Chewie curled against my back. Sadly, Aca had passed, so only Chewie joined me. We crossed New Mexico to Texas. My first night in Texas but third of the trip, was a hard freeze. It was difficult to rise in such cold weather. I decided that instead of standing and shivering by the tailgate to cook breakfast. I drove to the next town and bought breakfast. It was rare for me to eat at a café since I needed to save money.

Chewie and I especially loved Big Bend National Park, where we hiked and explored for a week. I drove across Louisiana, Mississippi, and Alabama. The farther east we drove, the less dog friendly the territory became. There were no open areas; land was all privately owned, with No Trespassing signs posted. Arriving in Florida, I had a good visit with Bill's daughter in Tallahassee. I drove north across Georgia and South Carolina and visited Rachel in Pinehurst, North Carolina. I had a simple Christmas with her. She sent me to her hairdresser, who cut my long hair off. I donated it to a company who made wigs for cancer patients. I used my carpentry tools to repair the wiggly legs on her dining room table; drilling holes, gluing dowels into the holes, and replacing the screws, making it solid again.

I headed back to Arizona. A blizzard approached as I crossed into New Mexico, and the radio said both I-25 and I-40 were closed. I followed the detour signs, but after driving for a couple of hours, I found myself at an entrance to I-25. There were no tracks on the interstate, no vehicles had been on it. Four or five inches of snow had accumulated on the pavement. I turned onto the interstate anyway. I reasoned, I had four-wheel drive, and the Tacoma could handle it. If I had stayed on US 60, I knew, the steep, lonely pass to Magdalena was ahead, and it would have deeper snow. The interstate was a better option.

The Tacoma traveled along at about forty miles an hour with no skidding. Chewie and I were fine. As I descended into Albuquerque, I saw the eastbound lane was at a standstill. Semis had lost traction; smaller vehicles could not go around. There were miles of marooned vehicles. I stopped at the first convenience store. The driveway was inches-deep in freezing slush.

"Where did you come from? And where do you think you are going?" the cashier in the convenience store asked.

"I came from Texas and headed home to Arizona," I answered.

"Good luck with that. The highway patrol has all traffic in and out of Albuquerque blockaded."

I drove across town, praying the familiar motel on the west side would have a vacancy. They did, a smoking room, but it was warm; it had a real bed. I walked across the driveway to another convenience store for dinner as it was the only option. Afterwards, I walked Chewie up the hill where she dove into the snow, snow plowed. She would pop up, grinning and shaking. She found rabbits burrowed under the sagebrush. What fun she was having. I took my meager dinner into the motel breakfast area. The well-behaved Chewie was welcomed. The TV was showing the news.

"Where did you come from?" one of the over-the-road truck drivers asked. "This storm has had us marooned for three days."

As I told him my story, others turned to listen.

"Hope we can go west tomorrow. Looks like a possibility," someone said after listening to the news broadcast.

In the morning, I dug the Tacoma out of two feet of new snow, using the shovel I had secured to its side. The shovel had instigated many laughs along the way but I found it handy.

"Four-wheel-drive vehicles are allowed to go west on I-40," announced one of the truck drivers staying at the motel.

I managed to drive out of the parking area, which was not plowed, and onto I-40 with much slipping and sliding on the six inches of slush. It was much more difficult than my way into Albuquerque had been. But the snow plows were working. I went at a slow, consistent speed. Soon we were on the mesa, which was blown free of snow. Only a few low places had drifts across the roadway. The sun came out. It felt good to be heading home. I had worked through much of my initial grief. I knew more was to come, but for now, I was feeling better and looking forward to working in Globe.

"Don't make any life changes until a year after your loss," friends at work cautioned.

I had told my boss when I was hired at Black Mesa that I would work for five or six years or until my husband died. It was my sixth year. Taking their advice, I continued to work another year after Bill's passing and retired in October 2007. I listed the Overgaard house for sale, and I moved back to Young.

Moving into the old Young house, I realized how many repairs were needed. Rotting logs sat on the block foundation, rotted holes in the library floor exposing soil underneath. Bill and I had built an addition the second year we owned the property, twenty-eight years past. The plywood countertops needed to be replaced with appropriate material. The old cast-iron enamel sink needed to be replaced. I also fixed the leaky roof and bought new appliances. I donated the old wood range to the museum; its removal created more space. I was pleased with the repairs, but they depleted the small cash inheritance from Bill.

I went back to work as a seasonal employee, first to Globe; then, in 2011, as YCC coordinator at Pleasant Valley Ranger District; and then again, in 2012 and 2013, at Pleasant Valley, as lead for the Wilderness Stewardship Challenge and developed recreation in the Black Mesa District.

For the Wilderness Stewardship Challenge, I was assigned a four-wheel-drive truck. I drove to all the trailheads with trails that entered a designated Wilderness in the Pleasant Valley, Payson, Globe, and Mesa districts. I drove back roads and saw wildlife and beautiful territory. On the west slope of Four Peaks, I saw a bobcat; it was special. At the trailheads, I measured barren areas, took pictures, and inventoried signs. I had a lot of fun exploring new territory for the project.

The Forest Service was an excellent work home for me; diverse tasks in several districts, interesting projects at the Supervisor's Office and the opportunity to learn about archeology, timber, range, and wildlife management as they related to the recreation projects.

When I was laid off, I had twelve acres to care for. I completed more small repairs to the house. Outside, I cleared brush to mitigate the fire hazard. One day I was burning a large pile of dead branches and logs from the blackberry jungle west of the barn. There was no wind when I started the fire, but shortly, there was a blast of wind. It sent sparks flying; a dead oak tree thirty-five feet from the fire started to smoke. The wind was blowing the fire toward more dead timber. By the time I reached Hal, a young man who did odd jobs for me, flames were coming out of the tree. I called the fire department. Hal felled the trees, and the Pleasant Valley Fire Department sprayed water onto the fire and extinguished it. With the wind picking up, the fire needed water to extinguish it. All was well, except I had another fence to repair, two humongous downed trees to move, and more brush to burn. The local deputies arrived and threatened me with willful endangerment if I set a big fire again!

I rattled around in the old house. I loved the expansion of the dining room, with the new juniper rafter. The oak flooring I had installed looked good. The kitchen was cheerful, with new countertops and a new stainless-steel sink and appliances. But still, I was miserable inside. I felt grief, yes, but it was something more as if I had a sickness in my soul and in my body.

In October, I went to the urgent care in Payson. Over the next months, I went to other doctors, but still, I was sick. I had a runny nose and was coughing, tired, irritable, and achy. Spirit Guide was telling me to move out of the house to forge forward. The house that had been so wonderful for us as a family. Almost as soon as I made the decision to move, I felt better.

But how could I? I knew I could hardly take care of the yard nor did I need twelve acres. The property had been paid off years ago. I had already decided to stay in Young.

I placed a lawn chair under the tall standard-sized apple trees in the middle of the property. I sat, prayed, and pondered. If I divided the acreage, I could keep the middle piece with the apple trees and enormous sycamore trees and sell the old house and the southern meadow acres. The sale would provide funds to build a smaller cabin.

The lots sold quickly. I moved to the middle three-and-a-half-acre parcel, which was an open field with riparian vegetation along the nearby creek and the hill to the east. I had no building so I bought a Weather King shed, built in windows, and had it wired. I insulated and installed quarter-inch plywood as paneling presuming it would be a workshop in the future. I repurpose the bathroom sink and kitchen stove from the decrepit camper that had been on Bessie when I went to Montana to work. I had a wood stove installed. I had a temporary home of about 850 square feet.

Mother's furniture that had come from Germany with her parents was stored in the old barn for a month, thanks to the new owner's permission. I had many more belongings scattered across the meadow of my property. Living in a shed sounded so poor that I named it Casita. Tami came to my rescue by purchasing a metal shipping container; named Evergreen, from the lettering on its side. David was visiting at the time, so he helped fill Evergreen with the items scattered in the meadow. Before winter, thankfully, everything was under cover, the Evergreen packed and the inside of the Casita crowded with my belongings.

I looked at mountains of floor plans. None fit my idea of a functional home, so I drew my own. I sent them to a log company to be engineered for stresses and ordered the required logs.

In April, building started. The Montana log company shipped the logs. I hired a contractor. I wanted the house dried-in, not necessarily finished. It had to be a pay-as- you-go agreement. I was sure I did not have the money to complete the building. I remembered all the foreclosures a few years back, with people's homes taken from them. If I owed no one and had no mortgage, no one could take my home away. *Mort* meant "death," so I did not even like the sound of *mortgage*.

By November, I stopped construction. I was out of funds. The cabin was dried-in, meaning I had doors and windows, the outside trim was done, the roof was on, and a wood stove was installed. I still had hope; somehow, I knew the house would be finished but it was up to me to finish building. I sanded and chinked all the inside walls, sanded the plywood subfloors with a five-inch orbital sander, brushed the floor and logs with an exterior oil stain to seal them. I bought mismatched cabinets from the Habitat for Humanity Restore; installed new gliders in the drawers and painted them dark red for the kitchen. I used leftover plywood for countertops. I had the kitchen sink installed. Later, I laminated juniper, sycamore, and black walnut planks that had been cut on my property together to upgrade the plywood counters. Christmas came with a deep cold spell. I could not keep the Casita warm. After a year and a half, I bailed and moved into the house, where I had better insulation and a big wood heating stove but still had open stud walls and little plumbing.

I made shelves and a tall cabinet for the kitchen; put up the tongue and groove walls, installed the downstairs sheetrock but had help with hanging the sheetrock upstairs. I taped, textured, and then painted. I made an LED light from a half juniper log. I hung it over the kitchen counter, using the chain from the White Grass cemetery and an antique black-smithed meat hook to hang it. When the Grand Teton Park took over the ranch, they wanted the cemetery chain removed, so I brought it to Arizona now I had a use for part of it. I

2015, Cynthia's new log cabin

love my house, even if it still needs some finishing work. It is smaller than Granny Jones's house and easier for me to manage.

I have a small lawn and have planted a macintosh apple and a peach tree. Because I had elk and javelinas eating my plantings, I built a ten-foot fence, four-foot weld-wire fence with six-foot-tall barbed wire above it to enclose an acre. Elk do not jump over the ten-foot fence, and javelinas cannot push through the weld-wire.

CHAPTER 14

Finding Family

LOVING, CARING SURROGATE PARENTS MAY EMBRACE A CHILD AND take him or her in as their own. But for me, there was always a feeling of something missing, a hole in the center of my soul that I could not explain.

Many people visualize family as a tree with many branches, but I see family as an aspen grove. An aspen is not a single tree like a great, long-lived oak or a tall, straight, short-lived lodgepole pine. Each white-barked, quaking-leaved tree is part of a live network whose root system spreads, connecting them, benefiting each tree by shared nutrients from far-reaching areas. I think a family, like an aspen grove, has the ability for deep-rooted sharing, a relationship that surpasses understanding.

After I married Jim, with Tami and David in school, Mom told me about her first marriage to Max Wood and my first adoption, which was new information to me as previously she only told me of Frank Galey. Mom told me again about her miscarriage and about the baby the doctor brought to her after its mother died in childbirth. I was interested but past being surprised at Mom's revelations. I had never seen my birth certificate, and I did not ask; instead, I listened with interest as Her story was part of my history. Later, I learned that at adoption, the new birth certificate named only the adoptive parents.

Unfortunately, it was discovered that Max had a tumor that put pressure on his brain, which caused him to have spells. As a result, one time, he threw our puppy through a large window. For Mom's and my safety, Max's parents assisted with an annulment, and Mom and I went to live with Nana, Opa's sister, in Oregon. While staying with Nana, Mom met the cavalier cadet Frank Galey on a weekend with her friends at Cannon Beach. In time, she followed him to Carlsbad, New Mexico, where he was stationed, and they went to Bisbee, Arizona, to be married. Frank, whom I called Dad, adopted me, which changed my birth certificate to show only his and Mom's names. I often wondered about my birth mother. What had she been like? What had been her interests?

"Mom, don't you want to find your birth mother?" Tami asked. We were together celebrating my seventy-third birthday.

"Yes, but Mom said that Oregon is a lock-box state, and it would be impossible to find her," I responded.

"I will do some research if you want," Tami responded.

Sometime later, Tami brought me an application for my original biological birth certificate. I filled it out; enclosed five dollars; and sent it to Salem, Oregon. Shortly, I received the certificate. My mother was Marjorie Schrepel, and my father was Ethan Armstrong Folks. I finally had the names of my biological parents. Maybe I was on the track to find my birth family, the aspen grove from whom I had been removed.

By then, in my lifelong quest of self-discovery, I had come to believe my emotional, steadfast roots were not in my adoptive parents but grew into the mountain's rocky soil, the mastermind of the Creator. Thus, I stood like a short-lived lodgepole pine tree, alone, instead of an aspen tree with deep roots interlacing with the roots of all the other aspens in the grove. Weeks later, I was sitting with the Bible study ladies for lunch. In reference to the Bible lesson, one asked, "What do you want?"

"I need a new couch," said Mary.

"I want to lose weight," said another.

When the question came to me, I said, "I want to find my birth mother."

Everyone looked surprised, each turned toward me. Lauren said her sister was proficient in using *ancestry.com*. I gave Lauren a copy of my biological birth certificate with Marjorie's and Ethan's names on it. She passed it on to her sister, who, with further investigation, found four names that might have been my family members. I wrote and mailed a letter to each.

11/3/2010

Dear Mrs. Burnham,

I am Cynthia Peck. I happily live on a small farm in the mountains of Arizona with my two dogs and two cats. My daughter lives and works in Phoenix, and my son lives in Bend, Oregon.

I am looking for my birth mother, Marjorie Schrepel Burnham. In January 1942, my adopted mother was glad to get me after many miscarriages that threatened her life. I was raised on the White Grass Ranch in Jackson Hole, Wyoming. My best companions were the horses I loved.

If you are my birth mother or know her, I would love to hear from her.

Sincerely,

Cynthia Peck

Shortly, I received a phone call from a nice-sounding gentleman.

"My wife is Marjorie Burnham because she married me. I liked your letter. I wish we were related, but we are not," he said.

"Thanks for responding," I replied.

Four years passed. On a dreary February morning in 2014, the phone rang.

"Hello?" I answered.

"I am Marilyn. My mother was Marjorie Schrepel Burham and I found your letter on my mother's desk, even though it was years old. She may have been unable to answer, because she was having small strokes about the time your letter arrived. My sister thinks you are interested in Mom's medical history," the shy voice said.

I recognized the Schrepel name from my biological birth certificate. *This must be my sister.* With a burst of excitement, I said, "Oh! Do you like to knit, sew, and garden? What are your interests? Is your mom still alive?"

"No, she died in January, only a month ago."

We continued to share a few stories of our lives. Hhe had a twin sister, Carolyn; an older sister, Shirley; and a younger brother, Dick. I wondered if the connection we had begun would grow.

A few months later, I received a call from Dick.

"Hello. I am Dick . My wife, Robin, and I are coming to Mormon Lake, south of Flagstaff, for a campout. We would like to meet you. Could you come to our camp and have lunch with us?" Dick introduced himself as my half-brother on our mother's side.

I was so excited I almost cried. "I'd love to come," I responded.

Excited, I called Tami and told her about the invitation. She wanted to go too. Tami and I met in Payson and drove together to Mormon Lake. We spent two hours sharing the White Grass album Mom had made and an album Robin had kindly made of the family for me. It was a revelation— I saw their resemblance to me.

In September, Robin called to offer flight tickets for me to come to Portland to visit them and meet my sister Marilyn and her husband, Steve. My son, whose home is in Bend, Oregon, met me at the Portland airport and drove to Dick and Robin's. We visited the famous Portland Rose Garden; it smelled so good, was beautiful, and had a great view of downtown Portland. I had been born in that beautiful city but knew little about it. We toured downtown Portland, including art museums and a trip to Powell's Bookstore. We had delicious lunches.

After a couple of fun days in Portland, David and I drove over the Columbia River to Washougal, Washington, to meet Marilyn and Steve.

One morning, as I came downstairs for coffee, I heard Steve say, "Good morning, Sis."

I was taken aback. *Who is Sis? Me? Oh, my goodness!* I was being enfolded into the family.

"Good morning to you too," I answered. I should have added, *brother* but was too surprised to think quickly.

Marilyn asked me, "Do you want to know about your conception?"

"Yes," I said.

"Mom told me she was walking home from school, when a neighbor boy stopped to give her a ride; he raped her."

I felt only compassion for our mother. Having barely escaped a rape, I was sorry she had had to endure one and deal with the resulting pregnancy by no fault of her own.My roots were connecting.

"How awful. How sad. She must have had such a hard time," I responded.

Marilyn seemed surprised at my reaction, so there was no more conversation about that.

Steve drove us to Mount Saint Helens to see the result of the volcanic eruption. What a special treat. My question about our connection growing was answered. It was.

After three days with the Brunes, David and I drove to Bend. I enjoyed my visit with David and his wife, Midda, in their home. We walked the river path to the gallery where he was a partner, where his paintings were well received. I especially liked his landscapes depicting many of the rivers he had boated. I respect him for following his heart in his life journey. Then it was time for me to fly home.

In the summer of 2016, I drove north, pulling my tent trailer with Chewie and Lady, my two dogs. I stopped in Jackson Hole to visit friends and White Grass. Roger, caretaker, and friend, met me as I wandered by the Main Cabin; the ranch was a buzz of activity. The Western Center for Historic Preservation which had been founded to make adaptive use of White Grass Ranch as a training center for teaching historical preservation practices and techniques, had completed the ten-year project of rehabilitating the ranch from near ruin. Its formal opening as a training center coincided with the National Park Service's one hundredth anniversary.

I was invited to speak at the ranch grand opening ceremony. I spoke about the changes at White Grass. I shared that the Clovis people might have visited the ranch, as a Clovis point had been found in Jackson Hole. It had been an Indian meeting place, a working cattle ranch, a boy's ranch, and then a dude ranch, and now it was a training center. The large fir I had sat under to make and sell hat bands was gone, and there were fewer trees around the cabins. The iconic barn was gone; removed and rebuilt near Wilson. The Galey house, once my home; the Homestead cabin; and the Messler cabin had been burned. Not even ashes remained. Cabin number four had been moved off the ranch by old-time dudes, and it sat near the Snake River. I was sad for the loss of a western era and the loss of history, but at the same time, I was glad the ranch had new life. In summary, "Nothing remains the same; the only constant is change."

After the ceremony, I drove west across Idaho to visit David in Oregon. I left the dogs with David and Midda while I drove to Washougal where Marilyn and Steve greeted me warmly. They held a party for me to meet more family. They invited Dick and Robin; their sons and families; another sister, Shirley; and more cousins.

After a life with no siblings and most cousins far away on the East Coast, I had a mob of family.

Marilyn and Steve kindly drove me to Yakima to meet Beulah, my birth mother's only surviving sister. More cousins were there: Beulah's daughter and her husband, her son and his wife. A wonderful dinner was prepared for us all. I observed the unspoken communication they shared. There were so many new family members my head was spinning.

Beulah called me aside, and we sat near each other. "I want you to know the truth of your birth. I talked this over extensively with my sister Florence. She died earlier this year; you know. She and I agree. Your mother would not listen. She was in love with a neighbor boy, the romance went too far, and she became pregnant," Beulah said. Beulah was adamant that it had not been rape, as Marilyn had told me, but she understood why Marjorie might have explained the circumstance of her pregnancy to her daughter, to remove blame from herself. In 1941, it was the greatest possible embarrassment to be pregnant outside marriage.

"Why didn't her dad insist they get married?" I asked. "Oh no! No, that couldn't happen," she said adamantly.

"Marjorie must have been three months along at my wedding. Other neighbors and your dad were there, and no one was upset. Your father's family were friends with mine," she added.

I saw cousin Bob standing to the side, watching. I felt as if he were assessing me.

"We all knew you existed," Beulah said. "We only learned about you many years later and did not know how to find you. I am so glad to meet you. You look so much like your mother."

"Are you musical?" Marilyn asked.

"No. Matter of fact, Mom always said I was tone deaf and told me to stop singing or humming." I laughed.

"Marjorie sang and played the piano at gatherings. She was widowed when Dick was still in school. All three of us girls were gone and married by then. With the earnings, she put herself through school to become a teacher," Marilyn said.

"Marjorie was an explorer. She hiked up Mount Hood and went overseas to hike also," another added.

"She took Dick camping and hiking," Marilyn said. I obviously shared characteristics with my mother. It made me feel that my roots belonged with these people, my aspen grove, and the hole in my soul began to fill.

As the evening shadows darkened, Beulah was tiring, and we readied to go.

Bob came to me. "You must go back through Ogden to see our cousin Don Voit. He would love to meet you," he said. I realized I must have passed his test.

I rethought my trip plans. I had spent much time calculating a way to cross Nevada to assure my night there would be at a high elevation and cooler as my tent trailer didn't have cooling. I immediately chose the longer way through Ogden.

I phoned Don and Irene, as Bob suggested, and stopped by Ogden to meet them on my way home. As I left I-80 and found one road, the next turn eluded me. I stopped by a small park on River Road and phoned.

I let the dogs out to run across the green park among tall trees while I waited for Irene to come. The dogs were ecstatic to be out of the truck, and I followed them onto the expansive lawn. Soon I saw a small white car pull into the parking area, and an energetic lady stepped out and came my way.

"I would recognize you anywhere," Irene said, extending her arms.

I immediately thought, *And where have you seen me before?*

"You look just like your mother. I was quite close to her." She pulled me into her arms with a great hug as a greeting.

I whistled to the dogs, loaded up, and followed her to their home. I parked the trailer by their driveway. I met Don, her husband, and my cousin. They were glad to meet me and invited me back. My aspen grove was expanding.

Since then, Marilyn and Steve, Dick and Robin have come to Young. Cousins Bob, Dee, Ken, Ron, and Irene have come to visit me in Young. Ken and Ron invited me to follow them to Chaco Canyon. I had been longing to visit Chaco, so I quickly hooked my camp trailer to the truck and followed them. After Chaco, we went to Chinle. Ken drove us in the van to investigate the deep Canyon de Chelly, where besides beautiful scenery, I found a kitty. Ron and Ken let me take him in the van. I named him Tigger, and he is quite a character.

Ron and Dick invited me on an Alaskan cruise with more cousins. Each took the time to take me aside to tell me stories and more family history.

One of Dave's stories especially explained more about my mother. "Before your mother showed her pregnancy, she went to stay with her older sister Jessie and my father, Fred," said Dave, another cousin, who was on the cruise with his wife, Wendy. "My mother, Jessie, made Fred promise never to tell anyone about Marjorie's pregnancy. He said Marjorie hid in the closet when people came to visit, as she was so embarrassed. After Jessie passed, Fred felt compelled to tell me. I passed the information on to my brother, Don, and other family members. Thus, we finally knew of you and hoped to meet you one day."

I was finally putting the stories together. I had not been thrown away, but with the mores in 1942 and an extremely strict German father, Marjorie had had little option but to give me up for adoption. I was sorry she had gotten herself in such a pickle. My ranch childhood with animals had been better for my soul than anywhere else could have been. Spirit Guide had known where I needed to be.

I often went to camp in the Arizona desert during February when the spring flowers bloom. I have invited all the cousins to come camp with me in the desert; many have come. I had the opportunity to show each of them much of my Mogollon Rim country. I have become rooted in the family.

I had never thought of myself as alone; however, my perception of what was important in life differed from that of many, which had left me alone in many ways. Meeting my biological family changed me. They make me feel a part of them, a part of the never-ending grove, DNA recognizing biological connections.

Reflections, 2024

My mantra is "The only constant is change; nothing remains the same." Certainly, nothing in my life remained the same for long.

My childhood experiences made me independent, determined, and self-confident, though I have never felt confident in groups of people. My parents brought me to a place where my spirit was born, and my soul thrived. My teachers were good mentors, teaching me to love learning and reading.

I married Jim who gave me two great kids. I learned to raise them in tents, in cabins with no plumbing, and eventually in a conventional home. I learned to work as a team with my mate. I have often wondered if I would have married Jim if I had had Sage, my 1942 Plymouth, which would have afforded me the sense of freedom I sought. However, if I had not married Jim, I would not have Tami and David. But it takes two people working as partners to sustain a marriage.

I tried to teach my children that every action has consequences, so one must be aware of the repercussions that might follow. I wanted them to be kind and respectful of everyone and everything and be cognizant that a person is judged by the company he or she keeps. Tami and David are the greatest joys in my life. I am proud and respectful of them and their chosen life journeys.

Bill was a great provider, brought us to Young, and encouraged me to work for the Forest Service when that opportunity arose. However, he was not a support for me when Mom died or during cancer. No one is all bad or all good; we are all a mixture of both. We must choose the actions and attitudes we wish to espouse.

My working for the Forest Service gave me the satisfaction of accomplishment and earned respect from fellow workers and supervisors. It was a wonderful workplace, with the opportunity to

Working in my shop to produce charcuterie and cutting boards.

One of the cutting boards I made with an assortment of hardwoods.

live and work in the backcountry and to help Earth in a small way. It afforded me a living wage.

I may have made some poor decisions in my life, but have little regret. Those experiences made me the woman I have become. I am proud of my accomplishments. My river has come to a long scenic stretch with few whitecaps. It is a joy-filled ride. Difficult times may come again, but I am confident in the protection of Spirit Guide to help me through.

At the age of eighty, I keep myself occupied by working in my woodshop, making custom cutting boards, trays, and countertops by laminating various types of wood together. I brand them with an *H* and a *B* with a quarter circle between them, in remembrance of the White Grass Ranch. I go on the road with my dog in my truck and camper to events to sell my laminated cutting boards, charcuterie boards and trays in Arizona, Wyoming and Idaho where I also visit friends and family

I enjoy taking my pets camping. In summer, I grow some of my food. In winter, I knit my own socks and sweaters and make some of my clothes. It gives me pleasure to contribute to the village by volunteering with the Pleasant Valley Historical Society and to help local individuals in Young as I discover their need.

I enjoy sitting in my cabin, looking at the hill rising from my yard, where elk, javelina, and an occasional black bear wander by. I often see the nearby rancher's cattle grazing my hillside before they are rounded up and taken back to their range. The surrounding mountain landscape brings me solace and peace. My dog and cats are good company and keep me entertained. When it snows in Young, the snow does not last for seven months, as it does in northwest Wyoming. I appreciate Arizona's climate, though I will always love the Tetons. I look forward to more explorations with my extended family. I expect to meet new people and experience more adventures, though I am very content with my own company.

BIBLIOGRAPHY

Alderson, Nannie & Helena Huntington Smith, *A Bride Goes West,* Lincoln & London, University of Nebraska Press, 1942.

Back, Joe, *Horses Hitches and Rock Trails,* Chicago, The Swallow Press inc., 1959.

Burt, Nathaniel, *Jackson Hole Journal,* Norman, University of Oklahoma Press, 1913.

Conrad, Carol HRA Production Specialist Grand Teton National Park, Wyoming, *Cultural Landscape* Report White Grass Ranch.

Craighead, John J., Frank C. Craighead Jr., & Ray J. Davis, *A Field Guide to Rocky Mountain Wildflowers,* Boston, Houghton Mifflin Company, 1963.

Elser, Smoke and Bill Brown, *Packing in on Mules and Horses,* Missoula, Mountain Press Publishing Company, 1995.

Hanchett, Leland J. Jr., *Arizona's Graham-Tewksbury Feud*, Phoenix, Pine Rim Publishing, 1994.

Holscher, Patrick, *On This Day in Wyoming History,* Gloucestershire, The History Press, 2014.

Huyler, Jack, *And That's the Way It Was*, Jackson, Jackson Hole Historical Museum, 2000.

Gillette, Frank, Pleasant Valley, U.S.A., 1984.

Larsen, T.A., *History of Wyoming,* Lincoln & London, University of Nebraska Press, 1956.

Office of the Clerk & Recorder, Teton County, Jackson, Wyoming, *Warranty Deed 58707, Deed* book II, page 10, sale of White Grass Ranch.

Saylor, David J., *Jackson Hole Wyoming in the Shadow of the Tetons,* Norman, University of Oklahoma Press, 1970.

U.S., 88th Congress, *Public Law 888-577 (16 USC 1131-1136),* The *Wilderness Act of 1964.*

U.S. Congress, *Public Law 37-64*, Forest Homestead Act of 1862.

U.S.D.A. Forest Service, *Bob Marshall, Great Bear, Scapegoat Wildernesses Recreation Management Direction,* 1987.

U.S.D.A Forest Service, *Wilderness Management Plan Sierra Ancha Wilderness,* Phoenix, Tonto National Forest, 1998.

Whitson, Tom D., editor, *Weeds of the West,* Jackson, University of Wyoming Press, 1992.

Zachariae, Barbra, *Pleasant Valley Days*, Apache Junction, Pleasant Valley Historical Society, 1991

ACKNOWLEDGMENTS

FRIENDS AND FAMILY MEMBERS HAVE CONTINUED TO SUPPORT AND encourage my writing journey by asking pertinent questions and making germane comments. I send thanks to those family and friends for their unwavering encouragement. Special thanks for your extraordinary assistance in completing this book:

     Barbra Richards
     Bernie Huebner
     Bill Peck
     David Kinker
     Judith Schmitt
     Karen King
     Kathy Hunt
     Kelly Burton
     Roger Butterbaugh
     Marilyn Freegard
     Tamara Densmore

I am grateful for the many other friends who encouraged me during this project, thanks to you all.

The painting of White Grass Ranch that is on the cover of this book is in remembrance of Oma, my maternal grandmother.

The Will James drawing of a pack train, seen on the first and last pages, was drawn for the White Grass's advertising brochures, a piece of history I wish to honor.

David Kinker, my thoughtful and talented son, drew the illustrations of my treasured items for each chapter heading.

I am thankful for you all,
Cindy